DATE DUE

AUG 3 0		
APR 0 2 1997		
AUG 1 3 2001		

HIGHSMITH #4

PHIL WEYERHAEUSER: Lumberman

Phil Weyerhaeuser
LUMBERMAN

Charles E. Twining

University of Washington Press
Seattle & London

Work on this book and its publication were supported by grants to the Forest History Society, a nonprofit, educational institution dedicated to the advancement of historical understanding of man's interaction with the North American forest environment. It was established in 1946.

Library of Congress Cataloging in Publication Data

Twining, Charles E.
  Phil Weyerhaeuser, lumberman.

  Bibliography: p.
  Includes index.
  1. Weyerhaeuser, John Philip, 1899–1956.
2. Weyerhaeuser Company—History. 3. Businessmen—United States—Biography. 4. Forest products industry—
United States—History. I. Title.
HD9760.W49T85
1985   338.7'63498'0924 [B]   84-40663
ISBN 0-295-96218-6

For Marilyn

Contents

Preface   xiii

1. Legacy in Lumber   3
2. An Idaho Education   36
3. Rough Waters on the Clearwater   56
4. A Merger of Sorts   77
5. The New Order   93
6. Life under the NRA   114
7. Never Business as Usual   132
8. Timber Is a Crop   159
9. The Great Depression Is a Long Depression   185
10. A Time for Tree Farming   214
11. "Wood Goes to War"   238
12. Postwar Planning   261
13. The Changing of the Guard   278
14. There's More to This Business Than Boards   293
15. The Wanigan   313
16. The Changing Scene   332
17. The Green and Growing Forest   355

Appendix. Four Generations of Weyerhaeusers   382

Bibliographic Essay   384

Index   387

Illustrations

MAPS

Idaho   45
Western Washington   221
Western Oregon   229

PHOTOGRAPHS   *following page 110*

The Frederick Weyerhaeuser family, ca. 1890
John Philip Weyerhaeuser, ca. 1925
Nellie Anderson Weyerhaeuser, ca. 1898
Frederick and Sarah Weyerhaeuser with grandchildren
    Elizabeth and Frederick
Phil Weyerhaeuser, age five
Phil, Elizabeth, and Fred
Phil, Elizabeth, and Fred playing dominoes
Phil and Fred K. fishing with their father at Lake
    Nebagamon
Swimming at Lake Nebagamon
Elizabeth, age thirteen
Fred K., age ten
Phil, age six
Anna Holbrook Weyerhaeuser with Phil and Fred K.

Frederick Weyerhaeuser

Phil, Fritz Jewett, Fred K., and Ed Davis aboard the *F. Weyerhaeuser*

Phil prepared to fight for the honor of the Hill School

Members of John Markham's cruising party, 1916

Lt. Phil Weyerhaeuser, 1918

Family gathering, ca. 1920

The second generation Weyerhaeusers, ca. 1920

John and son Phil, 1922

Phil fishing

Helen Hunt Walker, age eighteen

Father Phil and baby Ann, 1923

Phil and Helen, 1928

John and grandson George, ca. 1930

C. L. Billings and Phil by the Clearwater

following page 270

Phil and his associates, 1933

Helen, 1936

Helen, Flip, Phil, and George

Family group, 1944

Phil and Dave Winton visiting a Swedish mill, 1939

In front of the company plane

Minot Davis, Al Raught, and Phil touring Oregon timber

Wells Gilbert, Minot Davis, and Phil

Phil, Harry Morgan, Sr., Charlie Ingram, and Al Raught at dinner meeting

Ray Saberson, Laird Bell, Phil, and Charlie Ingram at a 1949 dinner

Lunching in the Oregon woods

Phil and Fred K., 1946

Phil, Owen R. Cheatham, and George S. Long, Jr., 1948

Gus Clapp and Laird Bell, ca. 1945

Clyde Martin inspects the leader on a young Douglas fir

At Coos Bay in 1950

Phil speaking at tenth anniversary ceremonies of the
Clemons Tree Farm

Chapin Collins, Mrs. C. H. Clemons, Phil, and Col.
William B. Greeley

Platform party at Clemons Tree Farm

Weyerhaeuser family meeting, 1954

Board of Directors, 1955

Phil and Helen

Phil and Helen aboard the *Wanigan*

Phil looking at model of the Everett facility

Preface

This is the story of a man, his family, and his work. John Philip Weyerhaeuser, Jr., would never have approved of its writing for a couple of reasons: he probably would not have believed that anyone would be much interested, and he would have been the last to claim that he had accomplished anything especially noteworthy. He would have been wrong in both cases, and in serious discussion even he might have admitted as much. More important perhaps, he placed such a premium on privacy that he would have viewed a book on his life as an intrusion of the largest order. Phil Weyerhaeuser was a living definition of unpretentiousness and had been raised, through the example of family members, to believe that nothing but problems and pain could result from public exposure. The kidnapping of a son in 1935 only served to underline the truth of that persuasion.

Although Phil Weyerhaeuser was by nature a very shy person, in no way was he a weak one. Among his greatest and most notable strengths was an ability to know and do what needed to be done. His manner of accomplishment was seldom dramatic; he worked quietly and patiently and, insofar as possible, behind the scenes.

In the process, he provided essential leadership to an evolution in the policies and practices not only of the Weyerhaeuser Timber Company but of the forest products industry. It was appropriate that he do so, yet at the same time there was nothing that ensured the assumption of such a role. Phil was well born; but advantages, comfort, and security do not automatically nullify ambition or commitment to excellence. Phil Weyerhaeuser would have considered himself a failure had he merely conserved his legacy. He was not a failure. His company and the industry at large were better and stronger as a result of his contributions. The manner in which this was managed constitutes much of this story.

Central to the effort was Phil's conviction that the best way for a forest products company to operate was for it to own its own timberlands. This was not necessarily true then, and it remains a question worthy of debate. But Phil had no doubts. He was far more willing to invest in timberlands than were most of his directors. He saw such holdings as necessary if the company was to engage in sustained-yield management. The resource base had to be broadened, and there was no other way to do it. Thus he bought that which complemented what was already owned, including the purchase of cutover lands. While of less basic importance, there was a significant public relations consideration to all of this, a consideration that Phil recognized and used to good purpose. When decisions were being made in government offices and legislative halls, the image of the company was often crucial. Weyerhaeuser was big when bigness was assumed to be an evil. Nothing could be done about its bigness, but the company could prove itself to be efficient, responsible, and generally in accord with long-range public interests. That, of course, was a challenge. Throughout, in terms of its organization, the company had not only to grow up to itself, it had to grow up to increasing demands for accountability.

The years in which Phil Weyerhaeuser served, beginning in the 1920s in the Inland Empire, and from 1933 to 1956 with the Weyerhaeuser Timber Company west of the Cascades, were years of large demands and change. Within his tenure the country experienced the Great Depression and World War II, the reluctant acceptance by business of New Deal and Fair Deal legislation and bureaucratic requirements, and the adjustments occasioned by the managerial revolution. In the case of the Timber Company, the period witnessed its transition from what had been primarily a dealer in timberlands to an integrated manufacturer of forest products, from a liquidator of forest resources to a manager of tree farms designed to be perpetual in their providence.

Stories do not really tell themselves, but they can and often do turn out differently from what was planned or imagined. I had presumed that this would be a fairly straightforward business biography. It became a far more personal account. For one thing, it was impossible to write about just one Weyerhaeuser. Weyerhaeusers were family first, and the family Weyerhaeuser had come to represent and personify the corporate Weyerhaeuser in terms of both commitment over time and consistency of purpose. For another, Phil's style was personal; and he led the Timber Company when its size permitted it to reflect not only his wishes and vision but his manner as well. To an extent no longer possible, Weyerhaeuser's president was also its heart and soul.

I hope that one of the things this story does is reveal a bit of what it was like to be Phil and to work with Phil. Business histories tend to describe what happened, particularly in terms of what is viewed as "progress." I am more interested in the how and why of happenings. As an example, early in 1933 when Phil left Potlatch and moved to Tacoma to head the Weyerhaeuser Timber Company, he immediately became involved in a merger effort in the Klamath Falls district of Oregon that went on for some two years. In the end nothing came of it. Some business histories might neglect this endeavor because it proved to be of no apparent consequence. Nonetheless, it took a great deal of Phil's time and attention and therefore is important, especially because in its failure we can observe him responding to circumstances not to his liking.

A word about sources (although further comment appears in the brief bibliographic essay at the end of the book). I have avoided, perhaps too assiduously, any direct dependence on secondary works. That approach was used both for reasons of freedom and for reasons of conviction. It does seem that historians can do enough misleading without removing themselves unnecessarily from the evidence. As Josephine Tey reminds us in *The Daughter of Time*, "Real history is written in forms not meant as history," and "Truth isn't in accounts but in account books." In this case, for the most part the account books are Phil Weyerhaeuser's office files. If forced to approve this undertaking, he would have insisted that it stick to the facts and that it not be treated as some example of a larger movement or truth. "If it must be written," he would probably have said, "please just make it my story, and keep it simple and short." In that connection, the choice of title may be of interest. It is intended to suggest not only the obvious—the nature of Phil's work—but also the manner in which he viewed himself. Had he lived in more recent years, he might have admitted to being the chief executive officer of Weyerhaeuser, but one has the feeling that he would have maintained a preference for referring to his occupation as "lumberman," just as he did on his August 10, 1955, passport application.

Regarding the use made of interviews or oral histories, I will admit to having a rather conservative view of such sources. A former professor of mine once admonished, "Never trust a memory, not even your own," a precept that received some unexpected support in the course of this research. Laird Bell was an important associate of Phil Weyerhaeuser's and served for many years as chairman of the Timber Company board. When he decided to step down from that responsibility, Phil invited him to prepare some reflective remarks for the next meeting of the directors. Approaching that assignment with typical seriousness, Bell consulted his own primary sources. He subsequently wrote to Phil, "I have been going through the files and the diary I kept at the time and I will swear that most of the things mentioned did not happen." He added: "It is a very enlightening experience."

It should be noted, however, that interviews have been of considerable assistance in the course of my research although I have tended to use them more for shading than for substance. If, on the one hand, a remembered "fact" deserves to be treated cautiously, and especially so when it stands alone, on the other hand, memories of feeling, of emotion, and occasionally of passion provide insights not otherwise available. I wish to thank those who have been so helpful along the way. I talked with many who knew and worked with Phil Weyerhaeuser, including John Wahl, Arch McKeever, Earl Hartley, Jim Fadling, Frances Conners, Mary Shiels, L. J. "Roy" Rogers, Don Dooley, Joe Nolan, Gladys Clapp, Erma Knef, Howard Morgan, Jr., Bernie Orell, John Aram, Don Watson, "Nappy" Wildhaber, Sam and Nathalie Brown, Norton Clapp, Dave Weyerhaeuser, Dr. Ralph H. Huff, Rick Billings, Bob Pauley, Bill Hagenstein, Harold Nelson, Bob Boyd, Dan Smith, Bill Robinson, Marion Baldwin, John Shethar, Howard Millan, and Al Raught, Jr. The mere listing of these names serves as a reminder of many pleasant occasions.

There are some who have been of assistance in very special ways. The late Art McCourt graciously introduced me to the Tacoma community and to many of those who would be especially supportive. One was George S. Long, Jr., who soon became a very close friend and who, for purposes of this research, willingly served as "the keyhole to Phil's office." Jack Connoy, Ed Heacox, and Scott Witt have happily shared not only their experiences but their good company and have taken a continuing interest in the work. To them I am deeply indebted. The same is true of Ed Hayes of Portland, whom I had met earlier while doing research on his grandfather, Orrin Ingram. Ed has been the source of so much information, an excellent teacher in his own right.

I wish also to thank the Forest History Society, my employer during the project, and most especially Harold K. Steen, its executive director, and Karen Potter, who was the sharp keeper of the accounts. Historians are ever in the debt of librarians and archivists; in this instance Laurie Cadigan, Donnie Crespo, and Linda Edgerly cheerfully tolerated what must have seemed the eternal presence of "Professor Twining" at the Weyerhaeuser Company Archives. Their assistance cannot adequately be acknowledged because it assumed so many forms. I only trust that they know they were and are appreciated. So too are Lisa Keely and Ann Bennett for their preparation of many drafts of the manuscript. I would like to acknowledge the assistance of the staffs at the Tacoma Public Library and the Idaho State Historical

Society, particularly their help in newspaper research. I wish also to thank Floyd McLean for his artful cartography. And to those at the University of Washington Press, most notably Lita Tarver, Bonnie Grover, and Leila Charbonneau, thanks so much for your consideration.

To Phil's four children—Ann Pascoe, John Philip (Phil) Weyerhaeuser III, George H. Weyerhaeuser, and Elizabeth (Wiz) Meadowcroft—and their families much credit belongs, not only for their willingness to contribute to an understanding of their father but for their friendly encouragement and, most of all, their patience. Books in process are seldom pretty, but I never sensed a hint of discouragement from any of the family. In addition, I wish to thank Lynn Day, daughter of Frederick K. Weyerhaeuser, Phil's brother, for her interest and participation throughout. And a very special note of appreciation is extended to Howarth Meadowcroft for his numberless considerations and for making so many things easier and more pleasant.

I would also like to mention the fact that my brother George has allowed me to use him on occasion. A lawyer now, but a forester by training and interest, he lives in Longview and has had long experience in the beautiful woods of western Washington. There would be more mistakes had he not commented along the way.

On the personal side I must thank Rick, Gary, Court, Roger, and other tribal members for proving, time and again, that there is life after dark in downtown Federal Way. Finally, the most important of all, my thanks to Marilyn for enduring my long absences from home and my absent-mindedness when home.

Charles E. Twining
Ashland, Wisconsin

PHIL WEYERHAEUSER: Lumberman

Chapter 1

Legacy in Lumber

On Christmas Day, 1925, an elderly timber cruiser wrote a letter to his friend and boss, George S. Long, general manager of the Weyerhaeuser Timber Company. The company had just completed a quarter-century of operation, and the woodsman, noting the anniversary, expressed the wish that they could roll back the clock and start over, "this time to renew the timber that has been destroyed since our association began." George Long well understood those sentiments. Few who had spent time in the Douglas-fir region of the Pacific Northwest failed to appreciate the beauty, serenity, and majesty of the forest.

Long dictated a thoughtful reply. His message was an often repeated one: lumbermen were forever justifying their work to those who somehow managed to separate a need for the products of the forest from an aversion to the processes involved. "To look at the waste around a logger gives you a weird, dreary feeling," Long acknowledged, but "to look at the homes and barns and shelters that the lumber makes . . . gives you a sense of satisfaction." For many lumbermen, however, the satisfaction was too far removed from the stump. No one looked forward to the day when forestry would become a part of the work in the forest more than George Long, but that day had not yet arrived west of the Cascades.

Less than four hundred miles to the east, in the rugged pine forests of Idaho, lumbermen were wrestling with other problems. Unlike western Washington, where the seasons blended together undramatically, this was a harsh region in terrain and temperature. The Weyerhaeuser Timber Company played no part in these Idaho efforts, but individual Weyerhaeusers certainly did. Young Phil Weyerhaeuser, a third-generation lumberman, had been placed in charge of the most ambitious of the western plants, the Clearwater Timber Company, with headquarters at Lewiston. The building phase was well under way, and the company was spending money at a worrisome rate. Second-generation Weyerhaeusers, far removed from the scene, hoped that Phil was equal to the task of shaping a successful operation. Like the Clearwater Company for which he was responsible, Phil seemed to hold great promise. But he was only twenty-six years old; and regardless of ability, he obviously had much to learn about the industry. The company's more than 200,000 acres encompassed many of the region's best stands of western white pine, but the land was rough, the logging difficult and expensive, and the markets distant. Taxes, fires, and insects added to the risks. Managing Clearwater would be a formidable job.

Phil Weyerhaeuser's initial advantage lay in the two generations of family experience behind him. Phil's grandfather, Frederick Weyerhaeuser, had come to America from Germany as a teenager. His search for a place to begin took him to the frontier community of Rock Island, Illinois, in the early spring of 1856. There, chance led the twenty-one-year-old immigrant to a job in a local lumberyard. In the wake of the panic of 1857, Frederick became owner of a little sawmill on the banks of the Mississippi River. Searching for a new source of logs, the young millowner turned his attention upstream to the pineries of Wisconsin—most notably to those of the valley of the Chippewa. Extending his business first northward and later westward, Frederick Weyerhaeuser demonstrated an incredible energy and an astute ability to bring men and opportunities together. These attributes proved to be the makings for a family empire.

There was another side to Frederick Weyerhaeuser: that of the family patriarch. And this role cannot be separated from the man's business career. Frederick met Sarah Elizabeth Bloedel in the course of his second spring in Rock Island, and they were married October 11, 1857. Sarah's origins were identical to Frederick's. Both had come from the little Rhine River community of Niedersaulheim. But Sarah's family had emigrated when she was an infant, and sheer chance brought her to Rock Island to help her sister, Anna, who was expecting a baby. Anna Catherine was the wife of Frederick Carl August Denkmann, a fortunate union for reasons of family and, as time proved, business as well.

Frederick and Sarah Weyerhaeuser soon welcomed children of their own. John Philip arrived November 4, 1858, and more babies followed with a regularity that the last born would later characterize as "quite appalling." Elise was born July 11, 1860; Margaret, July 18, 1862; Apollonia, February 16, 1864; Charles, April 2, 1866; and Rudolph, March 11, 1868. More than four years passed before Frederick

Edward's birth on November 4, 1872. With that, the second generation was complete.

It is not surprising that John, the oldest son by nearly eight years, began to feel the pressures of parental expectations at an early age. His formal education was limited to the Rock Island public schools and a single year, 1877–78, at the Jennings Academy in distant Aurora, Illinois. John was nearly twenty then, and perhaps both he and his father were eager to begin their business association. Indeed, the son already had enjoyed educational opportunities far in advance of his father's.

Frederick Weyerhaeuser and brother-in-law F. C. A. Denkmann, in concert with others, incorporated the Rock Island Lumber and Manufacturing Company in the spring of 1878, and it was this organization that would provide John with his initial experience in the lumber business. The pattern was set whereby sons would be placed in management responsibilities, leaving the father free to scour the landscape for new opportunities. Like the commander of a conquering army, Frederick would appoint a trusted lieutenant to be in charge of a position already secured while he went forth into new territories. Even the sons were awed and amazed at their father's daring and prowess.

On January 11, 1881, John was elected a director of the Rock Island Lumber and Manufacturing Company, and two years later he became its superintendent. On March 31, 1885, he replaced his father as vice-president. By and large, these were good days for business, and the affairs of the company rested easily upon those responsible for its management. Spurred by increasing demand occasioned by rapid population growth throughout the Midwest, both of the sawmills of the Rock Island Lumber and Manufacturing Company were operating at nearly full capacity of 40 million feet per year.

John celebrated his thirtieth birthday in 1888, and perhaps the family by then wondered if the shy young man would ever think of starting a family of his own. Just how he met Nellie Anderson, a teacher at the local high school, is unclear. They began to get to know one another during the summer of 1889. That fall they announced their engagement, and they were married March 26, 1890.

Frederick wanted the best for his son and new daughter-in-law and, of course, looked forward to helping them as much as he could. But to John, such help seemed to verge on interference; already overly sensitive and insecure, he often interpreted his father's motives in the worst possible way. Frederick, on the other hand, was not one to sit idly and watch things poorly done or poorly managed. He offered advice and, when advice seemed insufficient, issued orders. During prosperous periods, it was possible to overlook many things, but harder times occasioned less patience on the part of the father and deeper "blues" on the part of the son. Frederick was forever wishing John were different—a wish that, sadly enough, John probably shared.

In the spring of 1891, Frederick Weyerhaeuser led a group on a western excursion, in part for pleasure but also to look the country over with a view to future investment. Other lumbermen, including members of the Laird, Norton, Musser, and Carson families, joined in the investigations. Northern Pacific Railroad officials made overtures, but no agreements resulted. Current investments in the pine districts of northern Wisconsin and Minnesota seemed more promising, and accordingly Frederick, in partnership with Edward Rutledge, an old logger friend from Chippewa Falls, made a large purchase in the Lake Nebagamon area of northernmost Wisconsin, about midway between Ashland, Wisconsin, and Duluth, Minnesota.

Also in 1891, the senior Weyerhaeusers moved from Rock Island to St. Paul so that Frederick could be closer to the northern Wisconsin and Minnesota lands. By living in St. Paul, he could at least spend most of his Sundays at home. As a result, John and Nellie moved into the House on the Hill, the family home in Rock Island, and John inherited the whole of the Weyerhaeuser responsibility in that city. He wondered whether the distance between St. Paul and Rock Island might temper Frederick's concern with day-to-day matters in Rock Island, but it did not. Letters containing detailed instructions became ever more common. "Keep your logs in deep water," Frederick cautioned in the spring of 1891. "I had expected to go to Rock Island tonight, but cannot get away from here—I have too much to do." Surely the advice was unnecessary.

Nellie was pregnant and was receiving some advice of her own. Her child would be the first of a new generation of Weyerhaeusers, and her mother, Lucy Anderson, recognized something of the opportunities and responsibilities likely to devolve to this offspring. "I hope he will be a real good boy and show how he can appreciate his blessing," she wrote. "I fear he will feel so important, Rock Island will hardly hold him." Despite this and similar expectations from others, the baby was not a boy. Elizabeth was born in September 1892. Three years later on January 16, the anticipated son arrived. Congratulating the parents on the birth of Frederick King Weyerhaeuser, a proud grandfather wrote from Madison, Wisconsin: "That the good Lord will keep him so that he may be a blessing to his Father and Mother is our prayer."

The elder Weyerhaeuser was busier than ever. Although the sons tried to be of some assistance, in truth most of the father's burdens could not be delegated. Success attracted scores of people with schemes or needs to the Weyerhaeuser office. "They bother the life out of him when he is in this vicinity," Rudolph noted. Nevertheless, by the summer of 1895 the second-generation Weyerhaeusers had been established in various phases of the business. Charles was with the Pine Tree Lumber Company in Little Falls, Minnesota; Rudolph had been sent to Cloquet, Minnesota, to manage the new Northern Lumber Company; and John was in Rock Island. Fred was still in college, but would soon be his father's assistant in the St. Paul office. It would be John who would lack a permanent responsibility, for reasons doubtless clear to his father. The sisters were married by this time, Elise to the Reverend William Bancroft Hill, Margaret to Professor James Richard Jewett, and Apollonia to Samuel Sharpe Davis; and cousins to Elizabeth and Frederick King arrived in the summer of 1895 with the births of Edwin Davis and Fritz Jewett.

But if the family Weyerhaeuser seemed to be prospering, business was not. The depression following the panic of 1893 was severe and enduring. For John there was an even more basic concern. Rock Island was declining as a center for lumber manufacture because the sources of its logs were being used up. Although John may have overstated his difficulties, this was truly an awkward position for him. He was the manager of an operation that was clearly on its way out; his younger brothers—Charlie in Little Falls and Rudolph in Cloquet—were in the building stages of their responsibilities. A possible solution involved the Weyerhaeuser-Rutledge partnership at Lake Nebagamon. John's father outlined the options: "You can have work [in Rock Island] for one mill perhaps 5 years and after that keep a retail Lumber Yard which might pay you $5,000 a year"; or, if John agreed to go north, "we could build you a mill where you might Saw Lumber for 15 or 20 years."

Nevertheless, John postponed the decision as long as possible, and in the interim another baby was born in Rock Island on January 18, 1899. Congratulations came from all of the scattered family members. Aunt Margaret Jewett marveled at the baby's size: "to think of your boy weighing ten pounds, when mine only weighed twelve pounds when he was six months old." The baby was named John Philip, Jr.

John Sr. had been spending an increasing amount of time at the Lake Nebagamon site during the previous summer and fall. In accordance with his father's wishes, he would assume the management responsibilities in that beautiful but remote area, and his family would make it their home. It was an invigorating scene; one hundred men were hard at work on the new mill, and a community of two hundred were constructing houses for themselves. For his own family, John located a scenic spot among the pines on a hill overlooking the lake and sawmill. By mid-November, construction of the sawmill and the railroad had advanced, and there were three logging camps and 180 men prepared for the start of winter operations.

It was the fall of 1899 before John finally settled his family in their Lake Nebagamon home, the Pines. Life there was truly of a frontier variety, but those who worried about the loneliness that Nellie might suffer worried for the wrong reasons. In fact, the coming year would be one of real tragedy for the family. If he looked closely, John might have seen more than sadness in his wife's eyes and more than tiredness in her body. But his eyes looked inward.

Among the major news items of the New Year, St. Paul readers learned of the consummation of a timber transaction involving local residents and distant land. If the details as reported were not entirely accurate, they were close enough in general terms. One can imagine, however, that Frederick Weyerhaeuser winced a bit as he read in the January 3 edition of the *St. Paul Pioneer Press*: "After long-continued negotiations for the purchase of 1,000,000 acres of pine lands in Washington, the Weyerhaeuser syndicate yesterday paid over to the Northern Pacific $6,500,000." The article noted that this was "one of the largest deals in pine land" that had been made in the West, further observing that this same "syndicate . . . already had practical control" of all the timber in Wisconsin and Minnesota. But as Frederick had long since realized, one of the first penalties for doing business in a big way was the interest it attracted. Although the American public may have reveled in accounts of those who dealt in unimaginable money and power, all Frederick wanted was to be left alone to work.

In the meantime, Nellie's health continued to deteriorate, and on March 26, 1900, ten years to the day from her marriage to John, Nellie Weyerhaeuser died. The final complication may have been appendicitis. Thus Nellie's return to Rock Island came under the saddest of circumstances. The funeral was held at the House on the Hill and was strictly a family affair. No record is required to imagine the poignancy of that scene: the J. P. Weyerhaeuser family all in a line, seven-year-old Elizabeth, five-year-old Frederick, and baby Philip, barely a year old and held in his father's arms. Nebagamon must have seemed even more distant and desolate than before.

One of those offering condolences was Nellie's close friend, Anna Holbrook. Anna was of New England birth and upbringing but as a young woman had moved to Moline, where she and Nellie became acquainted. Their friendship continued after Anna went to work as an assistant manager of a Chicago publishing office. She now poured forth her own grief to John. "To me she will ever be the truest, noblest, sweetest Nell I ever knew," Anna wrote. "My heart aches deeply for you and I would that mortal had the power to comfort you."

John had little time to dwell on his loss. The children and the Lake Nebagamon sawmill demanded much, but in neither responsibility did he feel adequate. He had not far to look to find a wife and mother. By the spring of 1901, Anna Holbrook was his "busy little girl down in hot dusty Chicago." And despite the heat and dust and distance, John found reason to visit her often. They announced their engagement in mid-July and were married November 7 by John's brother-in-law, William Bancroft Hill, at Anna's home in Holbrook, Massachusetts. Following a brief honeymoon in California, the household was complete again. A nurse-teacher, Aimee E. Lyford, with whom they had been acquainted in Rock Island, was soon employed. Miss Lyford would prove to be far more than an employee. She became virtually a member of the family, a best friend to Anna and Elizabeth and a comrade to the children.

Elizabeth, Frederick King, and baby John (Phlippy, or Flippy, as he was called then) explored the world together. Living in a house that overlooked the sawmill, they grew up at home with lumbering. They hiked, swam, fished, boated, gardened, and tried to build everything under the sun. Most important, they were the best of chums. As with many rural children, their isolation increased their need for each other. But their friendship was genuine and it would also be lasting.

John's health was becoming a major concern. In the fall of 1904, he suffered what he would thereafter refer to as a nervous breakdown, and it was not until the following June that he could leave the St. Paul hotel room to which he had been confined. During John's illness, his brother Charlie made frequent visits to Lake Nebagamon, helping with the responsibility and sending John reassuring reports. In view of the limited opportunities for schooling in the northern country, Charlie suggested that John might move his family to Minneapolis in the spring and assume management of a recently acquired sawmill in the city. He assured that the mill crew was "well organized and the work there would not be much in addition to the Nebagamon plant." John was feeling better, but perhaps Charlie and others assumed that he would be stronger than before. That would not be the case. For John, even a Nebagamon responsibility seemed large. And as for educating the children, he and Anna and Miss Aimee were managing just fine. Lake Nebagamon was a good place to grow up.

For the most part, however, the family avoided the northern Wisconsin winters. So it was in 1905 when John and Anna went to California for the Christmas holidays and then decided to stay through the month of May at the San Ysidro Ranch in Santa Barbara. Elizabeth was now thirteen years old, Frederick King ten, and John Philip, Jr., six. All were old enough to be encouraged to correspond with family members, especially their grandfather. The senior Frederick feigned sadness for the snowless circumstances of his grandchildren that Christmas: "I cannot see how Santa Claus can drive his Team in a Country where they have no Snow & how he can cross a River without an Ice Bridge." Young Phil happily informed his grandfather that Santa Claus had made it through somehow in spite of the obstacles.

Soon after their return home, Anna became ill and was hospitalized in Chicago. She had known of her condition for some time but had kept it to herself for fear of causing John additional worry. But in that June of 1906, the problems could no longer be ignored. It was feared that a tumor was malignant, and surgery was recommended. The operation proved to be entirely successful, but the period of recovery seemed interminable.

Among the most appreciated letters Anna received during her convalescence in Chicago were those from the children at Nebagamon. In one, Phil told of sighting a flicker, of the rain that had interfered with garden work, and of the steam launch in which he had been riding. Three days later he wrote again, expressing sadness "that you are sick and hope you will soon be well." And he concluded with a report card of sorts: "Miss Aimee says we are good children and we do try."

During these years Frederick Sr. was increasingly involved in Idaho timberlands. Despite the promising resources of the region, disappointment was common there. The elder Weyerhaeuser, as Charlie indicated in a letter to John, had favored a larger initial capital investment than his associates, sons included, and Charlie was now willing to admit, "Had we taken his advice, I think our Potlatch Company would have at least a quarter of a Million Dollars more money." This would be just one in a long series of decisions that indicated their father had more distance to his vision than most of those around him—not an easy thing to acknowledge about a father.

For John's family the important event that fall was Elizabeth's start in high school, the first formal education for any of the children. They had moved to St. Paul in order to allow for this, and Anna would finally join them there. As soon as she arrived, John left for a tour of the Idaho properties.

That winter was spent not in a new home in St. Paul, but first in California and then in Daytona Beach, Florida. John stayed only until mid-February, although his departure was not readily accepted by Anna. "I have rarely felt worse at saying goodbye than yesterday," she would write, realizing that from the date of her hospitalization the previous summer they had spent very little time together. Alone, she sometimes felt vulnerable to the unwanted interest that others took in Weyerhaeusers. "Why can't the world let us go the even tenor of our ways!" Anna complained, referring to an item in the Daytona Beach weekly. Yet in the next sentence she admitted, "it was fun today to watch the ladies at the dancing school look at our boys, and incidentally at the rest of the family."

Fortunately the boys possessed an ability to lose themselves in the crowd, to become so involved in their own activities that the world around them seldom intruded. They "banked," ran errands, built cars out of crates, and constructed bridges "over what they call a bayou." And when Washington's birthday arrived, Phil borrowed a little hatchet and tried to cut down a sapling in the nearby woods. As Anna described the effort, "It was harder work than he thought, but he was plucky even if blisters did hurt."

The summer of 1907 was like previous summers at the Pines, except that the games were a bit more complicated and the studies a bit more serious. The start of Elizabeth's school brought the family back to St. Paul and their new home on Goodrich Avenue. For the boys, the move signified mainly different opportunities for play, a homemade "automobile" receiving most of their attention. Despite their obvious health and happiness, Anna worried. They seemed so determined to remain boys and so unconcerned about the responsibilities of manhood and the family Weyerhaeuser. She also worried that the location of their home, away from the fashionable neighborhood of Summit Avenue, might have detrimental effects:

The boys are as full of pranks as ever, just ready to fool *all* the time, but well—no colds—for weather is fine and they are out of doors as much of the time as possible. Frederick delighted us with a fine report, head of his class and next to the highest average in school. I'm sorry it doesn't mean more for it is far from a good school, and the boys are a tough bad lot. I hate to have him even in school with them. He has no use for them out of school, is perfectly contented to play with Philip. After awhile he will find some decent boys, tho' this district has a reputation of bad boys. I met a lady today who realizes the fact and rejoices that her boys are grown up.

That Fred's involvement with those who were different might be beneficial seems not to have occurred to Anna. Some of her observations, however, were beyond dispute. Certainly the boys were "full of pranks," and they would in fact never cease to be boys. Their wives would later complain as mother now did.

Fred was a most unusual older brother throughout his life. He seemed always eager to accept Phil, involving him, encouraging him, treating him as an equal and, in time, more as the older rather than younger brother. It was a happy relationship, and the only possible disadvantage was that their delight in each other's company may have served to protect them from the give and take of more demanding or less dependable associates.

In the meantime, John was closing down the Lake Nebagamon Lumber Company. The timber had been cut; all that remained was to find a buyer for the mill equipment, and he appeared to have a likely prospect in George Atwood. The involvement with Atwood was of more than passing importance. Frederick and John became partners in a new venture, each with a 30 percent share in the Atwood Lumber and Manufacturing Company. Located at Park Falls, Wisconsin, on the main line of the Wisconsin Central Railway, this operation utilized primarily hemlock and hardwoods, the pine having been cut previously. Frederick expected that John would take an active interest, although George Atwood would serve as the manager. Time would prove this to be one of the few mistakes Frederick made, and John was along for the ride, for the most part downhill.

The work of closing down at Nebagamon and starting up at Park Falls continued throughout the summer of 1908, but it had little effect on life at the Pines. Anna, Miss Aimee, and the children had returned to Lake Nebagamon in late July, glad to be home. In Anna's words, "I need not tell you we find it still the loveliest, dearest spot on earth." She seemed unusually contented as she watched the children partake of the "simple life" their Lake Nebagamon home afforded. She was writing to John from a table on the front porch, looking down at "the beautiful lake as smooth almost as glass." The quiet of the scene was broken only by the slaps and shouts of a tetherball game between Miss Aimee and Phil. Fred waited none too patiently for his mother to finish her letter so that he might challenge her at checkers. "It would do your heart good," she wrote, "to see how happy the boys are, perfect joy, swimming the first afternoon we came, rowing beautifully, fishing . . . already building their work shop and busy every minute."

The following year was much the same: school in St. Paul and summer vacation at Lake Nebagamon. Elizabeth was now seventeen, and the efforts to keep her a "simple" girl seemed threatened by college, although it was finally decided that she was not quite ready for such a jump. She was enrolled at the Walnut Hill School at Natick, Massachusetts. The following year, 1910, Frederick would join his sister in the East for school, attending the Hill School at Pottstown, Pennsylvania. For him, however, not all would be unfamiliar. A classmate was Cousin Eddie Davis.

Shortly after the start of classes, Fred heard from his grandfather, who expressed pleasure that he and Eddie were "getting along in your school." Then Frederick told of a recent wedding anniversary: "Your brother Philip was the only Grandchild present who helped us to celebrate. We all felt bad not having you, Edwin [Davis] and Fritzie [Jewett] with us. We think 53 years of married life is a great blessing. Very few People are blessed that way. Your Grandmother and I should be very thankful to the good Lord for the many years He has given us on Earth. . . . We all had a good time." And he closed his note in what had become his usual manner: "I feel you and Edwin will do your duty and be a credit to your Father & Mother and all your Friends including Grandfather and Grandmother."

And so a new chapter opened in the life of the J. P. Weyerhaeuser family and, indeed, among the third generation of Weyerhaeusers— children away at school, making new friends, meeting different people, and confronting problems never imagined.

With his brother and sister no longer at home, Phil's life changed significantly. He too sampled a bit of the larger world by entering public school, although Miss Aimee continued to watch over his work and progress. A vacationing Anna wrote to him from Boston that September of 1910, expressing her happiness "that school was more of a joy and that you were able to adjust yourself to the conditions." She worried a bit that he and Fred had become overly dependent on their cousins and expressed the hope that Phil would soon find "some companion for a chum—find a manly little fellow . . .[and] have him up for supper, or out to ride when you and Miss Aimee go." Phil must have missed his brother and sister: they understood that occasionally mothers could be too much of a good thing.

One important aspect of life in the family of J. P. Weyerhaeuser was that the children were not sheltered from parental problems. Thus sixteen-year-old Fred K. learned from his mother of his father's continuing difficulties and concerns. "I was sorry to hear that Father is feeling discouraged, about things in general," he wrote. "Tell him to cheer up, the worst is yet to come." Elizabeth viewed the situation more seriously, assuming from an absence of letters that her father was working too hard. "Please don't do that," she advised him, "because I'm sure we would all rather have you enjoy life and go without things ourselves than have you sick again."

September 1911 found Phil beginning the eighth grade at the Irving Public School in St. Paul, Frederick entering his final year at the Hill School, Elizabeth enrolling as a freshman at Vassar, and Anna visiting her mother following her leave-taking from Elizabeth. So once more Phil and his father were keeping the St. Paul home fires burning—with the help, of course, of Miss Aimee. In that 1911–12 school year, Phil received high scores in all subjects—his deportment average was 93 percent—and, perhaps more impressively, he was absent only a single day out of 190. In January 1913 he joined his brother and cousin Ed Davis at Hill.

Watching with great interest was Grandfather Weyerhaeuser. Pleased that the boys were "all doing well" in school, Frederick shared his usual expectations: "I hope you Boys will be good and useful Men, a help to your parents and a credit to Family and Name." To this he added, "We have lots of timber and you can all have sawmills." The sentence mixed in nearly equal parts the hope for the future and the luxury of the very old and the young to be uninvolved in the responsibility of the moment. The immediate purpose was to make Phil understand that there were more important things in life than his present failure on the baseball diamond.

The following summer the boys visited some of that timber. In company with their father, Fred K. and Phil toured the Idaho properties in what amounted to their introduction to the western lumber business. The trip had special significance because John was about to assume greater responsibility in that region. Indeed, he and Anna would move to Spokane in the fall of 1913. Nearly fifty-five years old, John had never had a real opportunity to stand alone. His father had always been there, and if that presence was not consciously resented, it had made the second-generation boys less independent—particularly John, the first-born. Now he was planning for the future, but it was a future that involved his sons and their cousins, not him and his brothers. That future lay in the West, without question, and John would make every effort to share western experiences with his sons.

John had never felt so enthusiastic, so alive. Anna, of course, was aware of her husband's improvement, and was greatly pleased. As to the reason for the change, she wrote to Phil, "Truth is he does not fret or worry much." Indeed, he was already working for his sons. Accordingly she urged Phil to learn all that he could, warning that inheritance alone would not be enough. "It will take clever hard-headed men to cope with business deals in the future," she wrote, "and you boys will need to be alert or other men will get ahead of you in your own affairs." Phil and Fred K. had other concerns of a more immediate nature. Fred, now a freshman at Yale, probably should have been studying but was caught up in the 1913 football season and the many social distractions. He assured Phil that the stories that "Yale has degenerated, and become very wicked, also that the spirit has died out" were untrue. He concluded his note with passing reference to studies. "You and I have been working pretty steady, especially you," he wrote. "I've worked some 50% harder than ever before, which I'll admit isn't saying much."

A family reunion in California had been planned for the 1914 spring vacation. Fred K. was unable to join in the Pasadena gathering, but he seemed not to mind very much; his own plans included a Smith College dance, which, as he told Phil, he would attend "even if it breaks me." Fred expressed passing envy over Phil's plans for the California vacation: "I'll bet you run the devil out of the Peerless." He offered "an elder's advice" not to exceed sixty-five miles per hour "with any ladies in the car." Fred ended with a common complaint: Brother Phil hadn't written to him.

Phil's Pasadena vacation was important in an unanticipated way, for it was his last opportunity to see his grandfather. Frederick had taken cold on March 25, and subsequently contracted pneumonia. By Saturday, March 28, news of his illness was reported in newspapers throughout the country. Phil had already returned to Pottstown and school before the final critical period. The old gentleman endured long unconscious and nearly comatose periods, but to the end he had his alert moments, and each of his children had a final time to be with him before his death on April 4, 1914. The *New York Times* announced Frederick's passing in bold headlines:

FREDERICK WEYERHAEUSER, LUMBER KING, DEAD
LEFT $30,000,000 EARNED IN CAREER THAT BEGAN IN POVERTY
IN AN ILLINOIS LUMBER YARD
100 PARTNERS IN DOMAIN
FOUNDED HIS FORTUNE IN THE GREAT PINE FORESTS
OF WISCONSIN
WORK HIS ONLY AMUSEMENT

The article that followed was the usual rags-to-riches account, carrying the interesting—and, to the family, upsetting—contention that Frederick had "frequently been called the wealthiest man in America, not excluding John D. Rockefeller."

The *Daily Ledger* of Tacoma offered a slightly more personal account, noting in its headlines, "Every Man in Woods is Sad." George S. Long was quoted at some length:

Mr. Weyerhaeuser was the biggest man I have ever come in contact with, yet so plain and simple in all of his life, that his career illustrates that the truly great are the simplest and most approachable of men.

Mr. Weyerhaeuser possessed to a remarkable degree that rare attribute, distinguished from smartness or knowledge, namely wisdom. His judgment of men and business, his sense of justice and fairness, his old-fashioned honesty and integrity which cannot be impeached, all this coupled with a boundless energy and a cheerfulness and buoyancy of spirits, which was contagious to all who came in contact with him, rounded out the character of the biggest man I ever knew, and he was just as kind and fair and considerate as he was big.

The funeral, held in Rock Island, was a notable event. All family members, grandchildren included, attended, and it was appropriate that they did. After all, it was the grandchildren Frederick thought of when he made the western investments. "This is not for us, nor for our children. It is for our grandchildren," he had reportedly told his partners in the Northern Pacific timberland purchase of 1900. His own children mourned his passing, but in the mourning came the realization that the burden of responsibility was now entirely theirs. Could they manage?

They could and did, although not with the confidence and exuberance of their father. Their management was largely one of conserving the heritage, and the real leadership would come from others while the grandchildren grew and prepared themselves. It almost seemed as if Frederick's progenitors accepted the statement "It is for our grandchildren" as an order. But for the record, John replaced Frederick as president of the Weyerhaeuser Timber Company, and he and Anna moved to Tacoma, where they made their home for the remainder of their lives.

The 1913–14 school year was completed with fair success, and summer passed much according to plan, with Fred and Phil accompanying their father as he visited the various western operations. Phil returned to Hill School in September 1914, pleased that summer study had resulted in his passing some examinations but sorry that the continuing preparation had interfered with attending the opening of football practice. Even with that disadvantage, Phil apparently contributed his bit on the gridiron. Fred expressed pride in his brother's success and hoped that he would make the first team the next year. There were, of course, more important concerns. John suffered a relapse sufficiently serious to require hospitalization in St. Paul. Christmas plans had to be canceled, and it was not until January that Anna was reassured about his condition. Recovery was much slower than anticipated, and March found him still convalescing in the hospital.

One of John's torments was his apparent failure to instill the firm Presbyterian devotion of the second-generation Weyerhaeusers in his children. Thus he was particularly pleased with a letter from Phil that discussed reasons for studying the Bible. Whether Phil was more interested in pleasing his father than benefiting himself, he had to appreciate that his letter would bring joy to his father. As a matter of fact, pleasing others was something that came readily to Phil. Somewhere along the way he acquired a security, hidden behind his shy manner, that permitted him to think of others when most were thinking of themselves.

In the spring of 1914 Elizabeth graduated from Vassar. The following summer went all too quickly for the boys—a little work, a little study, and mostly rest and relaxation. By mid-September, Phil was on his way back to Pottstown and the start of his senior year at Hill. One of the first letters he received was from his Uncle Charlie, who wrote to tell of having just enrolled his son Carl in the freshman class at the archrival Hotchkiss School at Lakeville, Connecticut.

It is interesting that the Weyerhaeusers, so completely western in most ways, continued to think only of an eastern education for their children. Child after child would take the long ride to eastern campuses. But almost without exception they returned to western homes and western opportunities. Charles's son Carl would be that exception by remaining in New England. At the moment, however, he was just one more in the line of Weyerhaeusers leaving home for eastern schools, and it was reasonable enough for Charles to hope that Phil would drop Carl a note just to "say hello to him."

Uncle Charlie also promised to attend that year's Hotchkiss-Hill football game if Phil was scheduled to play. As things turned out, the Hotchkiss game proved to be the crowning success of Phil's season, in part because he played before a crowd that included Uncles Charles and Rudolph as well as his brother Fred. Congratulations rained down in the aftermath of Phil's contributions to Hill's victory. His father tempered his well-wishing with the usual concerns. "I am happy because you are happy," John wrote, "and I am also happy that no one was hurt." Most of all John was looking forward to Phil's opportunity for schoolwork without the distraction of football.

Fred was not setting any records for studying either. He was now editor in chief of the literary *Yale Courant*, a position that at the very least provided him with an office, a headquarters for his many pursuits. From that desk he admitted to Phil that he was anxiously awaiting the end of school. "This college life is getting dull," he wrote. "I was not born for a student and I get in a rut here and don't seem to get out of it."

At the moment, Phil seemed the more settled of the two. Among other things, he was beginning to think about ("worry about" would be too strong a phrase) the war. Indeed, on the back of Fred's lengthy letter, Phil had scribbled some questions concerning the European battlefield. He noted some of what he knew about German strategy ("The main army of the Germans acted on a pivot") and also mentioned the use of motor vehicles in the advance through Belgium. He then listed a few thoughts on the employment of balloons and airplanes, wondering about defense against aerial warfare.

In the meantime, Anna worried about Elizabeth, refusing to admit that her daughter was in love. Francis Rodman Titcomb—Rod, as he was always known—was from Concord, Massachusetts, and Elizabeth had met him while she was at Vassar and he was a civil engineering student at Harvard. Anna expressed her disapproval in the only positive way possible, hoping that her Betsey would find someone else.

In the process she compared her daughter's "obstinance" with Phil's cooperativeness. To him she wrote, "I'm glad you are always ready to join in the good times as planned whether you particularly care to or not."

Much of the spring of 1915 was given over to a campaign for the purchase of a car, a coordinated effort by Fred and Phil. The car, as Fred described it, was "a regular Marmon, of regulation colors, dark blue with robin's egg trimmings, seven passenger." As Fred reviewed the effort, he admitted that "this biz has worked well: First by some strange freak of fortune we got Mother to agree, although probably if she had known [our] vacations didn't jibe she wouldn't have agreed. Then she converted Father. He agreed in toto and probably doesn't give a whoop about vacations anyway. Then Mother gets cold feet when she learns some of the particulars and wants to call it off, but—too late. The auto is purchased." Anna's defeat was not total. She continued to try to limit the use of the car to vacation periods, but Tacoma was a long way from Pottstown and New Haven.

Through all these carefree days, there was a discordant note, distant yet disturbing. The war in Europe continued, using up so many of that same generation from other lands. Although life on American campuses was largely unaffected, it began to show occasional evidence of pending changes. Cousin Fritz wrote to Phil on May 10 and told of shooting "a little on the range at Wakefield" with his Harvard regiment. He reported having "merely fair luck," but his real interest involved Phil's social life, in particular a recent dance and date. In Fritz' words, "Both O.K., we dare to say."

At the end of the school year, Fred and Phil drove the Marmon across the country with Anna and Elizabeth as passengers. The boys subsequently spent the expected month "at work." They were members of a timber-cruising party led by a young but already experienced cruiser named John Markham. The area under investigation was on the beautiful and wild Olympic Peninsula at the source of the East Fork of the Satsop River, several miles west of the town of Shelton. Inaccessibility dictated that the crew carry all their supplies, including tent, blankets, food, and cooking utensils. Still, the diet was not spartan, for the fishing was excellent. The boys already knew much about the woods, but not the work. Now they began to learn from the ground up, the only course that seemed reasonable to John. That Fred and Phil obviously enjoyed the experience must have brought much pleasure to their father.

The two boys joined forces that September at Yale. A letter from Anna arrived early on, wishing Phil the very best in "this first year in college," then adding the expected: "You know I shall be terribly disappointed if you don't make Phi Beta in your course." Somehow Anna

managed to survive such disappointments. As for herself, she was becoming increasingly busy with Red Cross activities in Tacoma, something that would occupy much of her time for several years to come.

In the fall of 1916 the war in Europe had already entered its third
year. The opposing armies, powerless to attain any real advantage,
much less victory, faced each other across a lifeless landscape appropriately designated "no man's land." The slaughter at Verdun and the
Somme was beyond comprehension, the combined casualties totaling
more than two million for these battles alone. The military euphe-
mism was "attrition," but more agreed with Siegfried Sassoon, who
wrote, while gazing at the insignificant River Somme, "my thoughts
are powerless against unhappiness so huge." There was one last hope,
and it involved young men untried and enthusiastic—young men
across the Atlantic at places like Yale. One of them, Stoddard King,
had written a song for a college show. "There's a Long, Long Trail A-
Winding" was a plaintive blend of words and music that would soon
echo along the endless columns of British infantry as they marched
into the lines. The war came to places like Yale slowly—in occasionally unusual ways—but surely.

With Phil and Fred involved in their studies, Anna convinced John
that they should spend another winter in southern California. She was
less certain that she could get him to relax. Elizabeth, however, had
decided not to accompany them. Rod Titcomb had come to Tacoma
to work for the Tacoma Smelting Company, and Elizabeth clearly preferred the winter rains with Rod to California sun without him. Anna
wondered, somewhat selfishly, in a letter to Phil, how she would manage John without Elizabeth's help: "I know father will not crave hotel
or social life, so I pray for sunny days and good roads." John seemed
depressed again. Having returned from the Idaho operations full of
fears of growing labor unrest, his worry about war with Germany
seemed "far less eminent to him than Civil War between Labor and
Capital." Anna hoped that he was "unduly alarmed."

In a subsequent letter to Fred, Anna inquired what students were
doing at Yale to prepare themselves for war. Fred replied with a question: "What good is there in a zealous attempt by 3,000 young fellows
to be soldiers when the Administration is so uncertain and unable to
take the lead in any definite way." Apparently he felt quite strongly:
"I just get sick all over and wish something terrible could happen to
this country to wake it up to some kind of patriotic sensible course."

Phil in turn expressed to his father his indecision about the many
military training options becoming available in college. In reply, John
noted that Pierce County, which included Tacoma, had just voted $2
million to be used to purchase 75,000 acres for a military post. Camp
(later Fort) Lewis would be the result. John suggested somewhat

naïvely that Phil might do his training close to home. Indeed, like so many others, John viewed military training as something of an organized picnic: "It would be nice to ride out in the summer time to see you and you will have an opportunity to go home now and then."

The war generated great excitement among most young men. Helping to make the world safe for democracy was not yet a tarnished ideal; it was an aspiration earnestly held and proudly expressed. It was in this spirit that Elizabeth shared her feelings with Phil: "Your letter came today about going into the army and I want you to know how noble I think it is of you to think this is your duty, but at the same time I do want you two boys to keep out of it as long as possible." Anna was also thinking of her boys, and the troubled world troubled her:

All this talk of possible War makes every mother sad as it does every citizen for it means wholesale licensed murder, tho' I'm patriotic enough to want to do my share for the honor of my country even to the sacrifice of lives I hold most precious.

Only God can avert a crisis now it seems, for we are not dealing with any single nation but the whole world seems topsey turvey and ready to fight. England is as much of a menace as Germany, or our South American cousins. Our own Congress has acted like a blundering baby, petulant and selfish. First they kick the President because he doesn't then because he does till I'm more convinced than ever that our strong intelligent capable businessmen need to take hold of politics and shape the destiny of the U.S. rather than the mediocre theorist and ambitious big head that too often represents us in Congress.

American involvement moved inexorably nearer. On March 16 the *City of Memphis*, the *Illinois*, and the *Vigilancia* were reported torpedoed by German submarines in the aftermath of the incredible Zimmermann message exposé. President Wilson called members of Congress back to Washington for a special session that revealed a curious mixture of sadness and exhilaration. Recognizing the magnitude of these events, Anna wrote to Phil: "How history has been made this past week. No wonder you boys are fired to join something."

Four days after the April 6 declaration of war, John addressed a letter to his distant sons. He told of a lack of rail cars for lumber shipments and worried over the growing social unrest. Anna was increasingly involved in Red Cross work, and Rod Titcomb had left Tacoma for a new job in Gardiner, Utah. But the real reason for writing had to do with decisions involving military service, with both boys showing enthusiasm for the air service. "How shall I answer?" John wondered. "When I read about the Aviators that came down in the war I fear boys that is not the thing to go into. You are not mechanical enough Philip, and Frederick's eyes are not as I would think for far and close seeing, still you must act for yourselves." And act for themselves they did.

As a senior at Yale, Fred's choices were much clearer. In many ways, Phil, though a freshman, was as mature as his brother. But while seniors were given opportunities to leave school for military training and were reasonably sure of receiving degree credit for that training, underclassmen were encouraged to remain in their classes. The curriculum would take a military cast, and it certainly would not be school as usual, but it was far short of marching off to war. Anna attempted to assuage Phil's obvious disappointment and hoped that he would do as advised, rather than leave college altogether. "As never before in your life," she wrote, "you will have to decide between right and wrong, and there is so much of your Grandfather Weyerhaeuser in your make up that I can count on you to make good always, not only for yourself, but for him too."

Despite his poor eyesight and parental wishes, Fred finally maneuvered himself into the air service. Phil remained at Yale, participating in the Reserve Officers Training Corps, which had been established in January 1917. He reported the decision to his relieved and thankful parents. Elizabeth informed him that she was much involved in plans for her July 11 wedding, but she also reflected on the personal decisions each had been making, and observed:

Your letter, dear, about not doing anything for your country and feeling so selfish about it has made me think a lot.

I know that had you gone to France in the Ambulance Corps with some of your friends, it would have literally nearly killed both Father and Mother. She cried terribly when you spoke of it even in your letter. It's not that they aren't proud as Lucifer of you & don't want you to be patriotic, but it seems *so* hard to give up what one loves the very most. Your letter about coming home this summer & giving up your training made me wonder if I was terribly selfish in marrying and leaving home, especially when Father & Mother are so cut up about the War. But their feeling is only what everyone's is—intense Americanism with a great sorrow that war is necessary.

Phil was the only one of the four cousins not to be involved in military training during the summer of 1917. Ed Davis was at a summer camp at Barre, Massachusetts, where some 1,300 were being taught by a group of French officers. Fritz Jewett was in naval training at Newport, Rhode Island, and Fred was at the Government Aviation School at Berkeley, California, enthusiastically caught up in the work. He was already looking forward to the completion of training, his squadron being only the fifth to graduate.

Things were not as dull at Yale as Phil had expected. Naturally he gave a good deal of thought to his brother, then en route to France, and to others who had joined the active ranks, but he noted that many of his friends had returned for the fall session, including Peavy Heffelfinger, his roommate. The nephew of Yale All-American Walter "Pudge" Heffelfinger, Peavey was more outgoing than Phil, and as a result Phil increased his circle of friends considerably and had few free moments. At Yale, traditional schoolwork had become less important than ROTC. If others smiled at the "rich boys' road to war," to those in college it was serious business.

In mid-October Phil indicated that he would soon be starting classes in equitation, noting the presence of "30 horses and four guns" on campus. The four French "75's" had been acquired during the summer of 1916 for a camp at Tobyhanna, Pennsylvania, for Yale upperclassmen. Years later Phil would recall his sophomore year primarily in terms of the military involvement:

Sophomore year was given over very largely to military training. I remember vividly morning setting-up exercises on the old campus, trotting at "double-time" all over the streets of New Haven, and, for disciplinary reasons, doing stable duty at the armory [Yale Field]. Peavey Heffelfinger invited his present wife to one of the Sheff house parties, but was assigned to stable duty. I remember taking her out to watch him shovel.

The men in charge of our training included United States, French, and Canadian officers. Among them, a Canadian Captain [Raymond] Massey taught equitation, whom I next saw twenty years later playing the lead in "Abraham Lincoln in Illinois" on Broadway.

Phil found time to write his Uncle Fred of younger Fred's safe arrival in France, a consideration for which F.E. was grateful. To loved ones at home and helpless, a safe Atlantic crossing was no small consideration. "Any news you receive from him," Uncle Fred had responded, "I hope you will send on to me, and if you wish I will gladly make copies and send to each member of the family." It was F.E. who was now assuming the responsibilities of family leader. Phil also found time for a weekend trip to Smith College to attend a dance. His date was Helen Walker of Seattle, whom his parents had met the previous summer at a dinner party. Neither the couple nor the parents could realize the importance of this visit to Northampton.

Christmas of 1917 was celebrated in a gala family way at the old Rock Island home, the House on the Hill. Nearly everyone was there, except Rod and Elizabeth and, of course, those in service. One of Phil's first responsibilities upon his return to school was to purchase items requested by Fred, then training with a bomber squadron in Italy. Phil noted in a letter to his father that he had mailed some "$30 of chocolate, smokes, etc." with the observation, "He is supplying the regiment, I take it." Phil also told of having received another good letter from Fred, this one predicting that the war would be over in the spring.

Fred and his fellow officers were feeling that they had endured quite enough training at the Foggia airfield. He could only assume that the government was saving them for "the war after next." Most of his time was spent playing cards, writing letters, or taking walks. He complained, "It's too damned soft," especially when "there's a big fight going on up in France," and "we feel pretty useless down here, believe me." In France, the Germans had launched the long-planned offensive known as Operation Michael. Designed to end the war, it brought only changes in command, slight changes in battle lines, and a great deal more suffering.

But Phil was having problems of his own. What had been a generally happy situation at Yale, largely due to Helen Walker, began to deteriorate in April. He had virtually won the track managership, he wrote to Anna, when "comes a bolt from the blue." The "bolt" had to do with a geology lab he had not been attending. There were also problems with French, where low performance was only "partially my fault." Phil had been placed on academic probation, which meant "that a series of letters goes home telling the boy's parents that he has been loafing and is liable to be dropped from college, etc."

Anna counseled that he should spend more time on his studies and less time with Helen. Phil attempted reassurance. "No danger of my getting sentimental at my age," he wrote, yet admitted, "I will say that I like her far better than any girl I ever met before." Phil had been a good deal more honest to Fred about his involvement with Helen, indicating that indeed he and Helen were contemplating marriage. Fred responded exactly a month later, sending congratulations along with a question: "Does *she* know about it yet?" The she, of course, was Anna. Fred also expressed the hope that nothing rash would be done "because I'd like to see your blushing bride hitched."

If Phil began to study with greater diligence, it was not because he had forgotten his military training. Summer training was being arranged, to be held at Camp Jackson, near Columbia, South Carolina. Scheduled to begin July 5, the training would permit only three weeks of vacation following final examinations. Informing his parents of his intention to participate, Phil tried to be reassuring. "I shall be no disgrace to you," he promised. He completed his sophomore year without further difficulty, visited briefly at home in Tacoma, and was back in New Haven at the appointed time. Years later he recalled that trip to the 1918 summer camp:

[It] . . . was made in a train composed of old New Haven Railroad day coaches. Gas lamps could not be used because of going through the Hudson

River tubes. So it was dark after nightfall. We slept three to a section. The two backs of the seats—which could be flipped back and forth depending upon the direction of travel—were balanced half way to form a sort of upper. The lower cushions were turned crosswise to form a lower. One patient slept below and two above. Come a jerk and the whole house of cards fell down! A galvanized-iron can on the platform of each car provided water for all purposes. We felt as though we were really roughing it. We stopped at Washington, D.C., long enough for everyone to take a shower, and frequently on sidings did some calisthenics. The trip took forty hours, and it was hot.

At the time, Camp Jackson was a field artillery replacement depot, and the day before the arrival of the Yale contingent most of the cadre personnel at the camp departed for new assignments. As a result, the ROTC cadets were split up and attached to the training batteries as temporary officers and noncommissioned officers. For Phil it was something of a heady experience, serving "with boots and spurs" as his battery's supply sergeant. Since the new draftees were largely from Chicago's south side, one suspects that the experience included an education in matters other than those strictly military for Phil and his classmates.

If John worried about his sons that summer, he also worried about what they would do after the war. The experienced and eminently capable George S. Long, who had been with the Weyerhaeuser Timber Company since its founding in 1900, was now superintending the company's operations, leaving the uncles free to concentrate their western efforts on the Idaho properties. Since John's location was most convenient to these, he was expected to assume a leading role. Attempting to balance the general interest with a personal interest in his sons' welfare would raise some sensitive issues, and John must have had difficulty separating the two. After all, increased responsibility was not something he cared for, and he could admit—in private moments at least—that the only reason he continued any serious involvement was to ensure future opportunities for his sons. That future was drawing nearer and demanded a more active and occasionally assertive role on John's part.

He would have preferred to work through his brothers, or at least to enlist their interest in his objectives. His efforts would focus specifically on the Clearwater development in Idaho, and even more specifically on an early start of operations there. In this connection, Charlie, after spending some time in the Inland Empire, expressed agreement "with the scheme of having all the land looked [over] carefully so that when the property is developed, the man doing it will have all of the information possible."

For Phil, the Camp Jackson tour concluded on a happy note. He and his fellow cadets received their commissions as second lieutenants and, following a brief furlough, were ordered to Camp Zachary Taylor at Louisville, Kentucky. Only recently opened, Camp Taylor was designed to provide uniform training to new artillery officers, and it was the first such special branch school. Walter Millis, famous military historian-to-be, was a classmate of Phil's and a comrade-at-arms throughout, serving at both Camp Jackson and Camp Taylor. Millis would write an essay on the war for the *History of the Class of 1920*, and it seems likely that no other American college class was quite so well served in this regard. Of that experience, Millis observed:

At the beginning of September [at Camp Jackson], the sudden announcement was made that most of the students would be commissioned, and finally the commissions were issued. After a week's leave to get used to the spurs, they were sent to Camp Taylor, and found themselves enlisted men again to all intents and purposes.

The Camp Taylor episode was merely the ordinary military lunacy which no one ever expects to be rationally explained. The majority of the Yale men composed the 39th Battery under Lieutenant Geffert, but for some unknown reason, forty of them, chosen apparently at random, were detached and moved up four weeks in the course. The 39th later caught up three of these weeks, and the forty graduated just enough ahead of the others to make them salute once. They didn't try to make them do it again. While the 39th was still at Taylor the armistice was signed, and the sixty-odd men knew that they would never add to Nineteen Twenty's war laurels.

As silly as the Camp Taylor experience might have appeared in retrospect, at the time it was welcomed, largely because it had settled the question of the immediate future. Anna, who had been traveling in the East on Red Cross business, arranged to meet Phil at Woods Hole during that week between assignments. She was delighted with the opportunity, and apparently he was too. "I never heard him talk so much," she wrote to John. "He was so full of his experiences at Camp Jackson. He looks fine, strong and sturdy, straight and tall, has a good military bearing and looks mighty fine with gilt bars on his shoulders." Phil was proud of his commission. More than twenty years later, when he heard of many undergraduates who were not enthusiastic about military service or training, he tried to recall his own reasoning: "I cannot arrive at any other conclusion than that I was led by a desire to do the popular thing. Patriotism called for no sacrifice on my part."

The news of the war's end was received with relief and joy throughout the family. John wrote to Aimee Lyford, now a midwestern school principal, bringing her up to date: "Anna has been so busy with the Red Cross . . . , Frederick is on the Italian front, running a bomb machine, Titcomb is somewhere in England or France and Philip is at Camp Taylor, Louisville, Kentucky." The most important thing was that the family was "all well and so delighted that the war is over."

John also tried mightily to put into words his feelings for his sons. He tried to write for the occasion, which he viewed as epic, rather than simply telling them of his love and hopes for their happiness. Thus he addressed a letter to Lieutenant F. K. Weyerhaeuser on November 21, telling of his pleasure with the Armistice and his thanks to God "for keeping His arms about you and so protecting you from sin and harm." He went on:

When I held you as a baby I would think with an indescribable pleasure and pride of the day when your school life would close and when you would assume responsibility and take your place in the business world. That day is coming soon and I know you will do your father and mother credit in living an honorable, clean, unselfish life and will take a stand for the higher and better things as taught by our Savior. One so doing has made his life a success already. To measure life by the dollar yard stick is a mistake, and when one is advanced in years, to his surprise he finds possessions do not give the pleasure expected, but to make a success of an honorable undertaking does give happiness, no matter what it may be, if it is to make life more enjoyable and men better.

We will have places in our business for you to step into on your return, your uncles and father will do all they can to help you to develop the best there is in you and as soon as we find out your ability and limitations, the questions that seem difficult to solve will pass away. I am expecting you to make a good, big, broadminded, forceful man, one with strong executive ability, one who can handle men and affairs, and I know you will not disappoint me.

He sent exactly the same letter to Lieutenant J. P. Weyerhaeuser, Jr.

Thanksgiving 1918 came and went with the J. P. Weyerhaeuser family still scattered. Fred K. had wired his greetings from France, promising to be "home sometime maybe." Rod Titcomb was already on his way, scheduled to arrive in New York on December 5. Phil was due for release before Christmas, and if there was time, he planned on a Tacoma visit before returning to Yale for the start of the second term.

Phil did manage to get home briefly at Christmas, but the greater reunion occurred a few days after Christmas at the House on the Hill in Rock Island. Uncle Charles had accompanied Fred K. from St. Paul to Rock Island, there to find Eddie Davis and Fritz Jewett. Phil was picked off a train in Chicago to join the celebration. It was a gala affair, with so many present that the four cousins were forced to "tent down" in the front yard. The stories rolled on endlessly, and none enjoyed them more than Charlie. "How proud I am of my good Nephews," he wrote to John and Anna on December 29.

Charlie subsequently wrote to John concerning Fred's future, noting that his nephew had "left you for the war a boy, but returned a man," and indicating that he was certain Fred would be "pleased to assume any responsibility that you may give him." But none of the second generation assumed that inheritance lessened the importance of knowledge and experience. Although opportunities were to be provided, there was a sequence to these—a sequence that ought to result in the acquisition of the required skills and understandings. In Fred's case, Charlie was willing to help. "I do not want to be selfish," he wrote John, "but I wish it would be possible for Frederick to spend a year here at Little Falls."

John appreciated his brother's interest, but there were several reasons why Little Falls seemed inappropriate. First, the future of the lumber business was clearly not in Minnesota. Fred could learn more of its problems and procedures in a district destined for major activity in future years. Most important, however, John wished to have a hand in the practical education of his sons. This would be more difficult than it seemed, but his only hope for happiness involved the accomplishments of Fred and Phil.

Thus Fred K. began his practical schooling in Idaho, working with the retail yard auditor of the Potlatch Lumber Company. Many of the lessons came quickly, or so it seemed. "The problem of retailing lbr.," he soon wrote his parents, "is largely one of settling down in a dumpy little town and knowing all the neighbors." But, of course, only a few months previously he had been flying a Caproni over enemy lines. One can understand the difficulty of adjustment for Fred K. and so many millions of others, dramatic actors one day and ordinary workers the next. Nightmares would bother some, but a return to tedium troubled many more.

In the meantime, Phil was plugging away at Yale. He tried to convince himself that this was a "privilege" but admitted that it often seemed "rather fruitless." Like Fred, he looked forward to an involvement that would excite or at least interest him. There was, however, a more immediate worry; his romance was on the rocks. Phil was trying to become interested in others, but without apparent success. Given the circumstances, he found himself with an overabundance of energy. He rowed with a vengeance that spring and he observed that "everything is full of pep." Thinking ahead to summer, he inquired of his father about the possibility of working "with or near Fred," although he allowed that he would be happy to go cruising with John Markham "if you want." He was also eager to see his new nephew. Edward

Rodman Titcomb—the first of the fourth generation—had arrived on March 4, 1919.

Phil went west at the end of classes and spent the summer as he had done previously, working in the woods with the cruising and surveying parties, this time in the company of Walter Barton and cousin Fritz Jewett. Their work involved the timberlands of the Clearwater Company in Idaho. John fretted a bit about the boys, in part because the season was unusually dry and there were many fires. As to the work itself, he asked only that they show an interest, "and the men will take pleasure in showing you why, etc." And in something of an unusual admission for him, he noted, "business at all points could not be better."

In recent days John had been threatening to resign as president of the Weyerhaeuser Timber Company. It was not that this was a burdensome responsibility. Indeed, John was increasingly preoccupied with the Idaho properties, and he realized better than anyone that George S. Long was in charge of the Timber Company affairs. And although Long welcomed his company and his advice, in truth there was little for John to do. Anna, however, was firmly opposed to his resignation. Following a brief visit with Fred in the East, she wrote John from Chicago: "Your next years are to be such happy ones, but soon he [Fred] will be able to discuss understandingly the perplexing business issues. I hope you will continue for another year as Pres. of the W.T. chiefly because by so doing you should be able to help any successor to familiarize himself with needed changes, and the Co. should not be left without such an Executive. . . . Don't be too eager to change it all. Your boys will soon be a wonderful help."

Phil too was learning the business, and at the same time enjoying his summer out of doors, far from the Yale classrooms. At the end of August, John received a letter from Earnest J. Brigham, manager of what was known as the Allied Weyerhaeuser Logging and Engineering Bureau, commenting on the work completed by the three boys. Since they had been employed at John's behest, John had insisted that he personally pay their salaries. The boys knew nothing of this, however, and given their record, Brigham thought the earlier arrangements inappropriate. He wrote as much to John:

When Philip Weyerhaeuser and George Jewett and Walter Barton worked on the Clearwater Survey this summer they all conscientiously and efficiently performed the work intrusted them as well as any others in the same line were doing, and received the same rate of pay. In short, they stood on their own feet and held their various jobs through merit. . . . The fact that Philip was promoted on performance of work meriting this promotion speaks for itself.

The boys did not go down there and act like summer tourists. They became a part of our party—worked and sweated and planned—and earned the money paid them, and you may unhesitatingly be proud of them.

John was proud and pleased, but did not change his mind about the responsibility for payment. The experience for the boys had been well worth the cost; Phil had learned more than he could imagine, and learned it under circumstances that would seldom be available to him again.

Phil arrived back in New Haven on the evening of September 21, two days before the start of classes. There was "big excitement" in the East, largely as a result of a widespread strike against the U.S. Steel Company and riots and disorder occasioned by a strike among Boston policemen. But things in New Haven were relatively quiet, and Phil found the time to thank his father "for a very fine and profitable summer." He and Peavey had acquired an additional roommate, Egbert Driscoll of St. Paul. Most of his other friends were back.

John and Anna seldom crossed paths that fall, Anna substituting the YWCA for her Red Cross involvement and John preoccupied more than usual with business concerns. In western lumber, these were days of tremendous emotion and occasionally great tragedy. Anna's letter of November 16 to Phil noted the existing tension. "All Washington state is deeply stirred over the recent Centralia tragedy," she wrote, commenting on the tragic confrontation between American Legionnaires and members of the Industrial Workers of the World. She noted that the proximity of Camp Lewis was reassuring, "and I have great hopes that Law and Order will prevail in guarding against riots till justice is sentenced the plotters." Change was occurring, and not easily.

Phil too was busy; the engagement with Helen was on again. He hurried the news home and received an immediate response from Anna, who seemed genuinely pleased. "While I only know Helen from your reports," she wrote, perhaps forgetting their earlier introduction, "I'm sure she must be one of the finest girls living or you would not care to spend the rest of your life with her." As might be expected, she did urge that they delay marriage until Phil was settled with a steady job, "though of course Helen and you must reason this out sanely and thoughtfully." Anna indicated that she would not share the news with John and that Phil should write him directly.

Phil complied. Acknowledging the news, John wished them good luck and, after giving his blessing, stodgily added, "as a Father I really should call your attention to some things that I have gathered in life that may or may not be of value to you." He then recalled that the only thing his father had said about selecting a wife was, "Remember whom you marry will be the mother of your children." Next came a lecture on heredity, John advising, "One should study the lives of the relations, etc.," which to Phil must have seemed more a matter of horse breeding than love. Finally, John indicated the importance of a religious background (but since Phil remained outside the church, it was somewhat difficult to pursue that line). Nonetheless, John concluded:

I will feel most happy when you join the *Church*, Loyal Legion, and the Masonic Order.

Now Philip, I have advised you, think it over carefully and do what you think best. I will do all I can to get you well started in life, and I will be most kind to the one you select as a life's partner. Do good school work and when you get out think of putting in a year at Harvard. I feel you are going to make a good first class business man and I want you to get well started.

A year at Harvard would only prolong financial dependence, and thus delay the wedding. Still, Phil must have been pleased with his parents' reaction to the engagement. Elizabeth and Rod had broken the trail in such matters, and whether they realized it or not, John and Anna were far more accepting than they had been previously.

Phil's senior year passed quickly enough, and he and the class of 1920 endured the trappings and traditions of commencement. If Phil took special note of the completion of college days, it was in the manner of his homeward journey. This proved to be unhurried in the extreme. Anna had suggested that he take time for visiting, "for work will keep you busy in the West," but the suggestion was unnecessary. A month passed and he was still in the East, trying to sell his Stutz, or so he explained. Having failed at that, he drove to St. Paul with two classmates. There they planned to stay with Peavey Heffelfinger, although Phil telegraphed that he hoped "to be home soon." That hope was lost among St. Paul pleasures; an August 4 wire reported the "deal on car practically closed," with a "Sorry to have worried you" attached.

Although it must have seemed to John that Phil was little interested, these were busy days for the Weyerhaeuser Timber Company. It was beginning to gain importance as a manufacturing organization, and responsibilities of a new sort began to devolve upon those associated with the firm. For John, these were mainly responsibilities concerning the Idaho properties, where problems too often appeared insurmountable. Plans for logging operations had to be developed with the greatest care, for mistakes would result in additional expenses of critical proportions. In addition, the Inland Empire had distribution and sales problems inherent in the location: all important markets were distant and obtainable only by rail. There were also organizational problems, and the second-generation Weyerhaeusers never quite managed either to take command or to give authority to on-the-site managers. Although the Weyerhaeuser Timber Company operations west of the Cascades were themselves autonomous, there was a single guiding hand, and a most able one at that. But in Idaho there was no George S. Long, and the organizational and management questions were particularly vexing in these early years.

John heard again from Phil by wire August 6 and by letter the following day. Aware that his father was losing patience, Phil made no mention of fishing trips into northern Minnesota with Peavey Heffelfinger but emphasized the time he was spending with family. "I am staying now until Sunday, not because I want to but Aunt Louise has been very good to me and one of the best ways of my repaying it is to take [his cousin] Peg around," he wrote, knowing full well that his father could hardly object to that sort of devotion. "I am ready now to go right to work," he added, "and would have been sooner if I had known that you were nervous." The following morning, August 8, Phil was at last headed west, wiring that if his father wanted him to get off the train in Spokane on August 11, he would do so. John wired back: "Will meet you in Spokane." Phil's business career was about to start in earnest; he was soon at work in the woods under the general tutelage of Minot Davis, a company expert in logging and timberland matters, with whom Phil would have a long and valued association.

If his parents had been disappointed at the extent of his final fling at boyhood, apparently Helen had been more so. The engagement was once again off. "I am sorry to know your relations [with Helen] in Seattle have been disturbed," John wrote. "I had hoped you were happy and everything was all right." As if attempting to ease the pain, he indicated that Phil's Stutz, left behind unsold in St. Paul, might possibly be transported to Tacoma. In a hastily written and nearly illegible note to Fred, then back in St. Paul with the Weyerhaeuser Sales Company, Phil simply said, "No condolences accepted." He reported that he was currently at work with a survey party, trying to figure "how to run a railroad into a big body of timber behind Kelso" in a spot "pretty close to Yacolt where we worked together once." No doubt he was enjoying the experience, although to his brother he allowed that it was "a damnably dirty life here."

John, of course, tried to keep the boys informed on family news. Phil must have smiled while reading his father's account of progress on a new house in Tacoma. "I fear we are going to get the [former] Whitworth College ground for a home," he wrote, adding with typical lack of enthusiasm, "do not like it but mother wants it and she has been good to you and a great help to me, and I owe her a good home." Undoubtedly what Anna would have preferred was some genuine sharing of joys and pleasures, but a new home seemed the more possible to obtain.

It was an unusually wet summer and early fall, and Phil probably spent some miserable days in the woods, but at least he was doing a job by which progress could daily be measured. In the meantime, Fred was trying to sell lumber in Iowa, for the most part doing more trying than selling. John appreciated the frustrations of working hard with little result, and he offered encouragement from a distance. "Do not get discouraged, even if you do not sell any lumber," he wrote. "No one is." He further advised that Fred keep at it, "with a smile," trying to remind himself that he was learning much, selling or not.

Phil left the woods and arrived in Tacoma October 15. Ten days later, following a trip with Uncle Charles, Eddie Davis, Minot Davis, and his father, Phil was still looking for the right opportunity. John and Anna had decided to spend some of the winter in the warmth of California again, John having suffered another of his irregular but inevitable relapses. Before heading south, he had attempted to arrange for Phil's next involvement in the lumber business through an exchange of letters with H. C. Hornby, president and general manager of the Cloquet Lumber Company. Hornby wrote that they were looking forward to Phil's arrival and that he intended to put him into the woods initially, "where we are experimenting with cleaning up cutover lands."

Phil, however, made what proved to be a crucial decision. Rather than return to Minnesota, he chose to accept a series of assignments under the direction of George S. Long. Just what the basis for his decision was is difficult to say. Perhaps he understood the limited future of lumbering operations in the Lake States, but it may have been simply that he was hoping to renew a friendship with a certain young lady in Seattle. In any event, Mr. Hornby wrote to him expressing his disappointment. Hornby reflected on the complexities of the lumber business: "It is too big a problem and constantly changing, but the only way to get any portion of knowledge of it is to go into it, and am glad to see you make the move." As an aside, he noted that Ed Davis had decided to come to Cloquet and "take up this wall board proposition," adding that it seemed to have a good future, provided they could take it from the laboratory and put it in the mill. Along with Balsam-Wool, an insulation material, wall board was a result of work by Dr. Howard F. Weiss of the Burgess Laboratories in Madison, Wisconsin, an effort financed under the direction of the so-called By-Products Committee of the Weyerhaeuser group. This soon culminated in the organization of the Wood Conversion Company, for which Ed Davis was manager, an early example of the application of science to the forest products industry, the purpose of which was greater utilization of the forest resource. Also in Cloquet, Uncle Rudolph too had been looking forward to Phil's arrival in northern Minnesota, but he understood his nephew's decision: "I am delighted to hear that you are going to stay on the job on the Pacific Coast and work with the big men. . . . I am sure you will get more out of it in the long run."

Phil had no regrets about his decision. In a sense he was back in school—what might be called the George S. Long school of practical forestry—and his classmates were his brother Fred, Edmund Hayes, and George S. Long, Jr. The elder Long was an excellent teacher, much interested in passing along the knowledge that he had acquired but also interested in learning more through the experiences of his protégés. Phil later recalled his mentor: "He must have been a very considerate man because . . . he had us youngsters just out of school yapping around, but never was too busy to instruct us." Occasionally, Phil added, he would send the boys "off on wild goose chases just for our own benefit." In the course of that experience from mid-February to mid-June 1921, there was little of the logging and sawmilling activity that escaped their attention, and it was not always physical labor that was expected. Now and then Long would demand an essay describing this operation or that problem. The business was in large measure cerebral, and he wanted that understood.

The boys did not always work together. Phil began with a week of scaling at the Everett sawmill, followed by two more weeks of scaling breakage at Snoqualmie, Clemons, and Aberdeen. He cruised timber for a week near Seattle, and then for another week and a half at Snoqualmie. He spent a week inspecting shingle mill operations at Seattle and Everett, and a week visiting sawmills at Chehalis and Raymond. Then followed two weeks of trips to Snoqualmie and Everett, another week at Snoqualmie, a week at Cherry Valley, and a week in Idaho. Despite the full schedule, the energies of youth had apparently not been exhausted. Phil had found time to see Helen. They had resolved their differences and were once again making plans to marry.

On June 29 John addressed letters to Huntington Taylor, manager at Coeur d'Alene, and to John Kendall of the Sales Company in Spokane, requesting both to consider Phil for employment. The requests were simple and direct. To Taylor he wrote: "I want Philip to learn the grades of Lumber, how to take care of lumber, and as much as is possible about a yard & mill plant. If you can give him something to do he and I will appreciate it very much. He will not expect any pay. All he wants is an opportunity to learn. He has had much woods experience but not much about mill, shipping, etc." By mid-July, Philip was on the job in Coeur d'Alene.

On July 28 Elizabeth gave birth to another boy, John Weyerhaeuser

Titcomb, the proud grandfather reporting, "All are well." Phil also learned that his parents had recently entertained Mr. and Mrs. George H. Walker and their daughter Helen. The dinner had included Aunt Elise and Uncle Bancroft, then visiting. John was quite taken with his son's future in-laws. "We are all much pleased with the Walker family," he wrote. "I think you have selected a good fine helpmate and we will do all we can to make your life and hers happy." Phil, of course, had the greatest responsibility in that regard, as his father was quick to remind: "Work hard, learn all you can and you will come out all right."

The engagement was announced formally, and the acknowledgments soon arrived from family and friends. Aunt Lonie Davis in Rock Island wrote of their delight in receiving the news, but as an indication of the long memory of the second-generation members, she also expressed her "regret" that "you did not bring her to the dinner we gave at the Taft Hotel." At the time, dinner at the Taft had doubtless seemed a tiresome prospect, but Phil now realized that he had made a mistake. The most carefully constructed letter of congratulations came from Uncle Charlie, who expressed pleasure that Phil was "setting the right kind of an example" for his brother and cousins: "Philip, I suppose you were too young to know how very fond your Grandfather was of you. So for Miss Walker, your Mother, and all of the family, we expect you to make good. You can not do very much in any one day, but Philip if you will put your mind on your work, concentrate and know the reason why, you will be surprised how soon you will know a whole lot about the Lumber business." It was not bad advice, and came close to describing what would become Phil's method of operation. His security and satisfaction would come from doing as much as he could every day; he worried less about what remained to do, and relied on his ability to "concentrate and know the reason why."

At the moment, Phil was concentrating on the sales department of the Edward Rutledge Timber Company. Anna learned that he had sold his first car of lumber and immediately wrote a note of congratulations. "I'm mighty proud of the way you are working," she began, "and know Helen feels all sorts of thrills." Phil also heard from cousin Ed Davis. "You certainly have got a man's job, Phil," Eddie wrote, noting that in and around Cloquet there were rumors of closing down the mills for lack of sales. As to his own responsibilities, Ed told of plans to get the Balsam-Wool plant started up in October.

Phil was not yet sales manager, but the person in charge, Lawrence McCoy, had gone east to negotiate some large contracts, leaving Phil to manage the day-to-day sales operations. He reported that they were succeeding pretty well, expecting "to ship about 110 cars this month as compared to 87 last month and 57 the month before." Even if they were falling below the daily cut by some 25,000 feet, the trends were encouraging. Perhaps that was why Phil deemed the moment appropriate to raise the question of a wedding date. He seemed confident he would find something to do at Coeur d'Alene, "which will be very profitable for a year or so at least," he wrote his father August 24. That being the case, he would just as soon "get it over with," and he was reasonably certain that Helen felt the same way.

The plans were delayed briefly because of the death of Helen's father, but they soon selected October 25 as the wedding date, "if this is agreeable to you," Phil wrote his father September 23. The wedding was a very private affair, held at the Seattle home of Helen's uncle and aunt, Mr. and Mrs. Lewis E. Eyman. It was not a grand occasion for reasons of personal preference and in recognition of Mr. Walker's recent passing. A brief reception followed the ceremony. Phil had arranged for a honeymoon of only two weeks, which Helen chided him about in a letter before the wedding. She also shared her feelings about the prospect of managing their home in Coeur d'Alene: "I can't imagine anything more humiliating than a poor dinner, or having a wife who is incompetent, and that's the only cloud on *my* horizon."

CHAPTER 2

An Idaho Education

Phil and Helen spent their first Christmas together in Tacoma. Fred K. and John had just returned from the Western Forestry and Conservation Association meetings in San Francisco, followed by a brief visit to Uncle Fred and his family in Pasadena. After the holidays Phil and Helen returned to Coeur d'Alene, and John and Fred K. prepared to travel to St. Paul to attend the annual meetings. Anna took special pleasure in seeing the boys involved in the business, an involvement she had hoped would rekindle her husband's enthusiasm. But as usual there would be something to worry about. In the course of the St. Paul meetings, that "something" seemed to be Uncle Charles. Anna counseled that John should not let "Charles' over-enthusiasm to make things go" disturb him. Part of John's impatience no doubt grew from the contrast between Charlie's view of things and reality. As John described the 1921 results for Phil's benefit, they were anything but encouraging: "Everyone is sad and disappointed because of poor showing and with that no dividends. Save your money. Six of our large plants lost $7,000,000.00. Only one saw mill made money [Southern Lumber Co.]. Not a line yard made a cent. Many think the outlook is not good for 1922. I hope they are mistaken." Perhaps because of the hard times, attendance at the meetings was good, John noting that "Mr. Long & Boner & Case & Humbird" had represented the West.

John also reported that Fred K. had two job offers, "one in Minneapolis and the other in Spokane." John admitted that he did not know which would be accepted; Fred was planning to go east for a bit "before settling down." Fred chose the Minneapolis opportunity at Thompson Yards, but the "settling down" was not immediately noticed. Charlie, in St. Paul, kept John fully informed on Fred's activities, assuring him that "all the men like Fred very much." But Charlie and John had other concerns that were mutual, some of which again threatened to divide. One of their disagreements was over the level of investment in the Northwest Paper Company of Cloquet. Charlie and Rudolph favored a substantial increase in support, while John opposed, probably because he was so conscious of the pending requirements of the Idaho operations.

As to Idaho, disagreements continued, only some of which had to do with policy decisions. In one instance, John felt that his brothers were questioning the extent of responsibility that he had assumed. Charlie tried to reassure him that such was not the case; he and Rudolph had only wished to do their part: "And John, when we all paid you the compliment of going to Spokane on Clearwater business at your request, no one had any thought other than to be *kind* to you. I think it was thought that Rudolph or I could see the R[ailroad] people & save you four nights on the Sleeper. But *Brother Dear*, we do not get anywhere by writing letters." John was apparently so upset by what he considered to be an insinuation of overinvolvement that he had threatened to disassociate himself altogether from the Idaho properties.

The Inland Empire was indeed a most fragile empire, and from considerations of investment alone, Cloquet paper companies or almost anything else would have been preferable, had more than money been at stake. Sons were a complication. But so were fathers. Had it not been for John, the other three brothers would probably have made a serious effort to dispose of the Clearwater property, although whether they would have been successful is unclear. In any event, F.E. wrote to John that while he was "not adverse to selling at a good price," he would inform Tom Humbird, president of the Humbird Lumber Company of Sandpoint, Idaho (a joint family venture, Humbirds, Weyerhaeusers, and Ed Rutledge, all associates from northern Wisconsin days), that John would "act for me, and for our family as well." He continued, "If you wish to operate I am perfectly agreeable," and then spoke directly to the point: "Your boys are preparing themselves to run our business, and with or without Clearwater they will have plenty to do."

Other family considerations were at stake in the Clearwater matters. The Timber Securities Company had been organized to manage money for the family Weyerhaeuser in a manner that would be more effective collectively than individually. The nature of Securities Company investments varied, ranging from strictly financial matters to good causes, to investments that just seemed to be in the tradition of things. It had recently been necessary to distribute a portion of Securities Company earnings, and as a result John had received a dividend check for $70,000. The money, he thought, might better have been put into the Clearwater effort. That had not been a factor in the declaration of the dividend, as F.E. tried to explain:

You know why we have divided the earnings of the Timber Securities Co. . . . We divided it because we had to. You certainly are joking when you propose to give Clearwater to Idaho. Get over the blues John. We don't owe anything to speak of, our lumber business, I mean, and everybody who carried an inventory last year lost a lot of money. And John, there are other things that are much closer to my heart just now than profits or losses. We still have aplenty, and certainly riches are no sure blessing. Let's cheerfully and happily do the best we can. You were happier, I believe, when you were poor than you are now so let's smile again.

There was a bit of good news amid the gloom. Phil and Helen were expecting their first child, and, as John wrote after paying a visit to Coeur d'Alene, "The news you gave me made me so happy as I know that will be a great joy in your lives." Cousin Ed Davis had also shared a recent development: his engagement to Kay Mills, with plans to marry in the fall. As to his own progress, Ed noted in a manner that would become customary, "I have got a tough nut to crack in this 'Balsam-Wool' business." Phil was learning firsthand about "tough nuts to crack."

Phil went east in mid-April to attend the family meeting in Wilmington and to visit the new Baltimore distribution facility. C. O. Graue, purchasing agent for the Rutledge Company, wrote to him during his absence from Coeur d'Alene, reporting that business was on the mend, so much so that they were starting a third shift in the planing mill. Phil's sales responsibility with the Rutledge Company often appeared to be a large one. In truth, it was not, but it required hard work and long hours. Others, including his father, were agonizing over the sales organization and its all too obvious management deficiencies. The Weyerhaeuser Sales Company had come under increasing attack, and John had determined that the matter should be dealt with directly. Thus he had sent out invitations for questions concerning those problems, "suggestions for improvement or criticism of the operations of the department."

Basic to the idea of a single sales organization for the allied producers was the assumption that it was inefficient for representatives of these producers to be in competition with each other. Competition was stiff enough with those outside the Weyerhaeuser interests. That assumption, however, failed to take into consideration the fact that associated or not, each sawmill had special advantages and disadvantages in terms of reputation, location, kind of product, and all the myriad considerations affecting policies and personnel. In short, the very idea of the Sales Company flew in the face of many factors, including tradition. H. C. Hornby summarized the problem, noting that "there can be no question that the theory of the Sales Company is perfectly sound," but that "until the interests of those operating through the Sales Company are made more nearly identical, and personal interests submerged in the general good, it will not be the unqualified success which was anticipated at the time of its organization."

In reviewing the matter, various proposals were forthcoming. For example, Tom Humbird, then president of the Sales Company while at the same time representing the Humbird Lumber Company, supported F. E. Weyerhaeuser's suggestion that a small committee be appointed "in whose hands associated efforts [would] be placed." Humbird suggested that "Mr. George S. Long, F. S. Bell, Wm. Carson and F. E. Weyerhaeuser" constitute that committee, "with full authority," adding, "I am perfectly willing to bow to the decision of this committee in all such matters and think others interested would be." Above all, he recommended that the "committee be active lumbermen whoever they may be."

F.E. was not at all certain that he should be involved, even if he were willing. "When you consider the amount of friction that developed over my attempt at running the Sales Company, you must agree that as to these cooperative efforts, I am a disturbing element . . . and I really feel that it will be better for me not to be at the Tacoma meetings," he wrote to John. But the problems were not personal, at least not in the important sense. Hornby, for example, was firmly convinced that sawmill owners "could do better without the Sales Company for the simple reason that we could sell more lumber and get a better price than the Sales Company is able to." Again admitting that the theory might be sound, he expressed "no faith that this theory can be worked out on a co-operative basis," and he proceeded to list his reasons for doubt.

In fact, Hornby and others were attempting to resolve the eternal problem that confronts all institutions: localism versus centralism. At which level were decisions best made? The subject at hand was the Sales Company, but it was only one of a series of questions similarly posed, albeit one of the more important and enduring.

Uncle Fred's response gave some indication of the seriousness of differences on the issue. Reporting that Tom Humbird had "urged me to attend the Tacoma meetings and also asked if I would serve on a general committee if I were 'drafted,'" F.E. informed John that he would have none of it. "I have had my turn at the bat," he wrote. "I have been out of the game for three years, and I have lost much if not all of my nerve." There was more than a hint of bitterness as he continued: "Except from a very few, I did not get much if any support, when I needed it, and I don't know that conditions have changed much." Then, as if realizing that he was sounding bitter, he asked that John not "quote what I write here for I don't want to appear a grouch, or a knocker."

He suggested that either John or George S. Long should take up "the executive committee idea." He recalled that there had previously been such a committee, but "its members were so far apart in their opinions that the committee could not function." F.E. remained a staunch defender of the Sales Company, insisting that it had done well, given the circumstances. It would "do better if it is supported, but there must be an end of questioning its very existence." In a postscript, he said he had worn himself out, "in more ways than one, with the cooperation game," and suggested that John, Charles, or Rudolph take it up instead.

The meeting at Tacoma came off as scheduled in late May, with results that were not unexpected. In short, despite the accumulation of frustrations and disappointments, the principle and the organization of the Sales Company remained intact. For better or worse, with many involved still shaking their heads in doubt, the Sales Company's future was assured—a future that would have an important effect upon brothers Fred K. and Phil.

Even through John's perspective there were reasons for optimism in the late spring of 1922. Many believed that the Sales Company meeting had been a great success, and believed John's leadership was largely to thank (or to blame, if one disagreed with the results). The single troubling note was a series of destructive fires in the West, John informing Phil that there were many fires, with "Smoke very heavy" in and around Tacoma. There were also fires burning in Idaho; John read in one account of some 4,000 acres of Rutledge timber burning. There were reputedly "500 men fighting the fire and the I.W.W.'s [Industrial Workers of the World] active in getting men to quit." Although there were problems of that sort, the Rutledge mill was operating two shifts, with plenty of logs on hand for a third and orders on the increase. Phil was busy, and John watched him approvingly.

In mid-June Charlie wrote to Anna informing her that "the C. Lamb & Co. people of Clinton, Iowa, recently offered our St. Paul office some 310 shares of Weyerhaeuser Timber Co. stock at $350.00 per share." At the time, ownership was limited to a very few, and such offers were rare. Charlie saw it as a chance "to interest my nephews— what I call the third generation boys, in our business." Fred K. had agreed to buy $6,000 worth, and Charlie indicated he was sending a copy of the letter to Phil in the hopes that he too would be in a position to purchase.

Charles also mentioned to Phil that some Rutledge Timber Company stock was available at 80 cents on the dollar, although he advised, "I consider the Weyerhaeuser Timber Co. stock at $350.00 the very best buy that our boys can make." Nevertheless, Phil decided to take forty-five shares of the Rutledge at $85.00 per share. It is understandable, and perhaps laudable, that Phil preferred to invest in "his own company," but the money could have been better placed. Investment wisdom never proved to be an area of strength in Phil's case, and one is left with the impression that such considerations bored him.

Despite the familial closeness, there were problems within the extended family of Weyerhaeuser, and occasionally what seemed like an opportunity for one would prove to be a disappointment for another. A case in point involved Fred K. and his Uncle Rudolph. They had taken a real liking to each other, and Rudolph invited his nephew to accompany him with his family and the Jewetts to Europe in late July. Fred jumped at the chance. He wrote Phil of his decision, jesting, "Have worked so hard I need a rest!!!" Others were not amused. Uncle Fred, in fact, shared his feelings with Charlie: "I am very sorry that Frederick is leaving his work at the Thompson Yards at this critical time. It is making a rather bad impression upon all of us, for there was no real point in Frederick's going to Europe . . . other than to make company for Rudolph."

Charlie visited Phil in the summer of 1922, and shared with Phil, for some reason, F.E.'s letter of disapproval. Charlie didn't agree with his brother on the matter. It seemed a good idea for Fred K. to go to Europe, he wrote Phil later, since he had not looked "too strong to me," and the rest might do him good. Fred's European tour lasted six weeks, and he was all too aware that some had viewed his absence as irresponsible. As he described the situation to Phil and Helen:

Perhaps you read in the Seattle Scandal Sheet about my recent triumphal tour in Europe from which you will know that I spent some six weeks away from the shores of Minnehaha and TY Inc. [Thompson Yards, Inc.] which caused criticisms to be made in certain quarters, also divers nasty looks. When I got back the other day, some clerk in the office came up politely and asked me what my business was. So am sort of expecting to get the hook some of these days unless TY Inc. blows up of its own accord this coming week. I understand that Dad, G. S. Long, and others arrive here tomorrow; also there are sundry rumblings here in the Executive Committee. . . .

His circumstances were not quite so tenuous as he pretended, but it was true that there was much going on—decisions in the offing with important implications. As a matter of fact, Fred K. had spent an evening with Uncle Fred discussing, among other things, Clearwater. Efforts had been made to interest others in the property, but these had not succeeded. Fred K. wrote to Phil:

You doubtless know that the Wintons and Shevlins turned down the option on the Clearwater Timber and now the general feeling among the three brothers here is that we will have to operate the works starting in this coming year. Uncle Fred suggested that I write you getting your ideas as to whether you'd care to make that your life work if the opportunity presents itself. The N.P. and the Union Pacific are more favorable than ever to building a railroad up there into the Clearwater and I really believe that it won't be long before the Family will be ready to go to it.

As if to prove that the concerns of business had not entirely replaced those of youth, Fred closed by noting, "Nearly bought a new car yesterday," but "without your urging, I'll probably never buy another."

John, in the company of Charles and Rudolph, spent several days in October in Idaho, particularly Lewiston, considering possible millsites for the Clearwater operation. The Rutledge Company, meanwhile, confronted problems of a different sort. John wrote Phil that he was "so sorry" about the timber damages from the recent fires, and observed, "It will take lots of rush and good management to come thru the fire without considerable loss." As to family matters, he expressed the sincere hope that "Helen is getting along nicely and that she will have a fine baby."

In early November, John wrote Phil of his plans to go to St. Paul for the family meeting Fred K. had mentioned. The pressing issue would be "what will the Clearwater Timber Co. Stockholders do about development of their property if the N.P. & the Southern Pacific Ry. will build a line into the Clearwater Timber." John noted that all Phil's "Aunts, Uncles and the same in the Denkmann family" would be present. He was looking forward to a "most interesting time."

Phil and Helen were experiencing their own "most interesting time." Baby Ann arrived November 3, 1922. John was delighted to be a grandfather once again, although he could not avoid using the occasion to express a worry. "I hope the Lord will spare me long enough to play with your little . . . Ann," he wrote. Adding a note about business, John expressed reason for optimism, reporting that the B Mill at Everett was running twenty-four hours a day, and that all the coastal sawmills had all that they could do. He also noted that they were "looking for a good manager for the Clearwater Timber Co.," although it seems that even he was not considering Phil a serious candidate—at least not yet.

Phil and Helen decided to spend Christmas in Coeur d'Alene, delaying their visit to Tacoma until the summer. John expressed initial disappointment, although he did look forward to welcoming them to "our new home" (a statement he immediately qualified as "mother's new home as I have given it to her"). For Phil, the most satisfying Christmas present was a letter from the Sales Company office announcing an increase in his salary to $250 a month, "effective December 1."

Phil worked hard at the Coeur d'Alene sales office, but he also played with a certain exuberance. A lot of the boy remained intact. Sometimes the socializing had a semiserious purpose. Thus it was with the "Opus Est" or Niscot Club in Coeur d'Alene. Composed of men between the ages of twenty-one and forty, the club avowed to serve "as a medium through which the ideals and aspirations of the younger generation . . . may find expression, with the abiding conviction that the performance of civic duty is the obligation of every citizen, and that fulfillment of such duty can best be accomplished through organized effort." Phil and his friend Dave Winton were members. None of their many Coeur d'Alene friends were closer to Phil and Helen than their next-door neighbors, Dave and Kay Winton. Dave was associated with the Winton Lumber Company, with offices in Minneapolis and plants in Manitoba and Saskatchewan as well as in Rose Lake and St. Joe, Idaho. Both Phil and Dave were members of the local chapter of the Gamma Eta Kappa Fraternity, an organization with more social than civic intent. In any event, there was no lack of opportunities to gather for card playing and general foolishness, Phil probably excelling more at the latter than the former. Helen must have occasionally frowned, but for the most part she was a good sport. She had to be.

Following New Year's, John took Elizabeth and her two boys to Santa Barbara, from whence he went on to Rock Island for the family meetings. As he rarely did, John seemed to find genuine pleasure in the gathering. In his own words, "We visited for four days, attended meetings and had a real good time." He reflected that "seven brothers and sisters, the oldest 64 years and the youngest 50 years, all alive and well" was an unusual blessing. "I do not know of a like case," he wrote to Phil, "all well settled in life, no black sheep." He was "sure that the Lord has been good to us." For Phil's benefit he continued: "The blessing from God-fearing people is passed along to the children of the second and third generation. How thankful we all should be. You also have a fine blessing, good health, a fine wife and baby, a good supply of worldly goods. Best of all a good inheritance by a good name handed down from your grandfather."

Anna had not accompanied her husband, finding more than enough to do with all the decisions concerning the new house, which she now referred to as "Haddaway." This would become Haddaway Hall through usage and eventually officially, the accepted explanation being that "Haddaway" was simply a formal corruption of "Had Her Way," John seemingly having taken some perverse pleasure in the designation.

But the big news occurred far from Haddaway. Anna happily informed Phil that his brother had been elected manager of the Clearwater and that he had already given notice at Thompson Yards. For this she was pleased on both counts—the new opportunity and the departure from the old responsibility. She and others were becoming impatient with the Thompson Yards involvement. Anna wrote, "I can't quite understand a policy that continues the services of a Manager who is losing so much to the Stockholders each year," and she took the occasion to lecture Phil. "Don't you even dare get that kind of a reputation," she warned. "Even if your profits are small, be dead sure there is a profit and not a deficit when you are working for other people." All of which was more easily said than done, as a series of Clearwater managers would demonstrate, year after year after year.

Things did not develop as the J. P. Weyerhaeusers had hoped. John's meetings with the railroad officials made little progress. To Phil he reported that Fred K. was ready to leave for Idaho "just as soon as we know what the railroad people . . . will build." But the railroads were not interested, at least not yet. As John informed Phil after his return to Tacoma, "The railroads have lost interest in the Clearwater extension, so that matter is dead." He did add, however, "Just what we will do next I will know when I hear if the N.P. is interested."

John's preoccupation with Clearwater, with an occasional Haddaway Hall distraction, was interrupted quite unexpectedly. Fred K., having remained in St. Paul after the nondecision concerning the Clearwater, made some decisions of his own. He announced his engagement to Vivian O'Gara on March 21, 1923, and they were married the next day. One can only imagine how the news was received by parents and family. Indeed, Phil may have been the only one to offer sincere best wishes without hesitation. For others, the lack of forewarning, consultation, and formalities, in the sense of seeking advice if not permission, was overwhelming. This, and the fact that the bride was Catholic, must have seemed unwise and inconsiderate in the extreme. In any event, John and Anna made a quick trip to Chicago to attend a small ceremony in the home of the bride's parents, Mr. and Mrs. Thomas J. O'Gara.

Fred and Vivian could not know it at the time, but the decision was to be an important one for the Weyerhaeuser family. After an extended honeymoon, on July 1 Fred was in Spokane, looking forward to be-

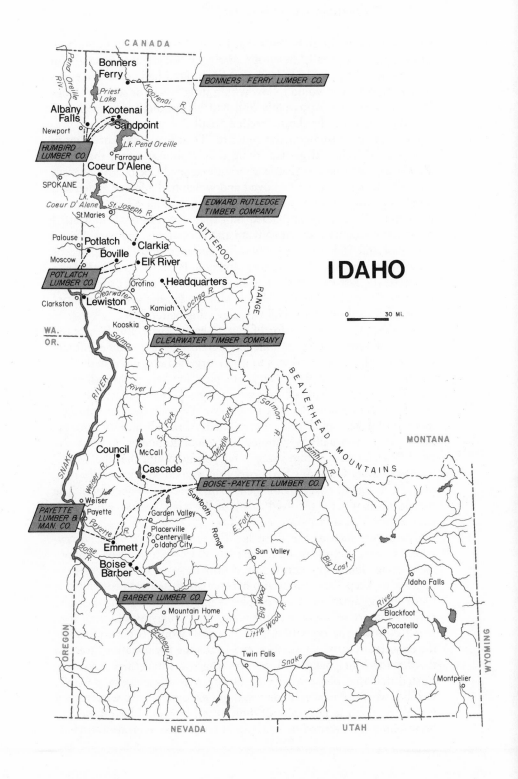

CANADA

Bonners
Ferry

Pend Oreille Riv.

Priest Lake

BONNERS FERRY LUMBER CO.

Kootenai R

Albany
Falls

Kootenai

Sandpoint

Newport

Lk. Pend Oreille

HUMBIRD LUMBER CO.

Farragut

Coeur D'Alene

SPOKANE

Lk. Coeur D'Alene

St. Joseph R.

EDWARD RUTLEDGE TIMBER COMPANY

St. Maries

BITTEROOT

Palouse

Potlatch

Clarkia

Boville

Moscow

Elk River

POTLATCH LUMBER CO.

Orofino

Headquarters

RANGE

IDAHO

Clarkston

Lewiston

Clearwater R.

Kamiah

Lochsa R.

0   30 Mi.

Kooskia

WA.
OR.

S. Fork

CLEARWATER TIMBER COMPANY

SALMON

RIVER

River

S. Fork

Middle Fork

Salmon R.

BEAVERHEAD

MONTANA

Council

McCall

Weiser R.

Cascade

MOUNTAINS

Lemhi R.

BOISE-PAYETTE LUMBER CO.

Weiser

SNAKE

Payette

Sawtooth

Garden Valley

PAYETTE LUMBER & MAN. CO.

Payette R.

Placerville
Centerville
Idaho City

E Fork

Range

Sun Valley

Big Lost R.

Idaho Falls

Boise R.

Emmett

Boise
Barber

BARBER LUMBER CO.

Mountain Home

Big Wood R.

Little Wood R.

River

Blackfoot
Pocatello

OREGON

Bruneau R.

Twin Falls

Snake

Montpelier

WYOMING

NEVADA

UTAH

ginning work at Potlatch. "Felt that I should get right out to Potlatch to start hitting the ball," he wrote, surely tempting Phil to remind him that the wedding had been back in March. Fred had come alone, expecting that Vivian would follow within three weeks or so after things were fairly settled. Apparently Phil had his brother's woods clothes stored away, which Fred now needed "badly."

Phil sent an unusually newsy letter to "Dear Dad" on September 7: "We are all well and getting along fine." He also noted that Mrs. Walker had returned to Seattle after an extended Coeur d'Alene visit, which he thought she had enjoyed and which had allowed Helen and him "to go away several weekends camping, and have had a wonderful summer." Fred K. had called him that very morning, indicating plans for a Tacoma visit with Vivian and her parents. Fred and Vivian paid Phil and Helen several visits that summer, and Phil allowed as how "it's mighty nice to have them living in Potlatch, so close." As to business, the last two weeks had been somewhat more promising in terms of demand for pine lumber, and although the sawmill was operating only a single shift, Phil was expecting better days.

The work was not easy for Phil at Coeur d'Alene. But he worked hard, tried various schemes aimed at increasing sales, and he learned. One of the things he tried was to get George S. Long interested in the possibility of selling Rutledge white pine lumber in Weyerhaeuser Timber Company distributing yards on the Atlantic Coast. "I think my idea was that if he paid the freight, we'd leave it there on consignment until it was sold," Phil later recalled. Although such an arrangement would eventually be adopted, Long had no interest in 1923. He liked Phil and wished him success, but left no doubt that the Weyerhaeuser Timber Company had better things to do with its money than invest it in freight costs for the benefit of some Idaho operation. The ownership may have involved many of the same people, but the organizations were as separate as could be.

Operations such as the Rutledge Timber Company were not expected to return much profit in the early years—the years of development. Large lumbering efforts hoped only to cover their expenses, or at least to keep such costs within reach of the investment outlays. Once the organization was completed in the sense of facilities and major routes of access—once the major improvements had been constructed—then the operation, it was hoped, would begin to provide the expected returns. In Idaho in the 1920s the organizations were in the development phase, and the Weyerhaeusers and their associates trusted that that phase was being managed as efficiently as possible. In other words, Phil was a participant in expansion, and was thereby forced to take a longer view of things than he would have if he had been selling on the road or working in an older organization such as the Everett branch of the Timber Company. But if it all seemed like a mad scramble up an endless hill, he and Helen were young and strong, much enamored with each other and enthralled by the beautiful world about them—a world of pine forests, rushing streams, and rugged terrain. They had found their element, and although they were not isolated from the larger world, they learned early that they had little need for that larger world in a personal sense. In the process, Phil and Helen became increasingly dependent upon each other, happiest when alone together in quiet circumstances.

That they were healthy and happy was apparent to everyone, even John. Still, he could worry that things might change, particularly concerning matters of health. Thus he wrote to Phil, "*In confidence,*" advising him to get "a good nurse to take care of Helen's baby, so she can sleep and get out in the air and so she can get strong, and January 1st I will pay you what you pay the nurse." This may have seemed a rather odd concern, but the explanation followed: "I like Helen, and I do not want you to make the mistake that I did with your mother."

Phil, Helen, baby Ann, and Mrs. Walker spent Christmas in Tacoma with John and Anna, and a pleasant time was had by all. Phil had tried to pay his father for their tickets, but his check was returned, John explaining that "as long as I am able I hope to pay your way at least one way." The big post-Christmas activity centered on a new radio, leading John to complain in a letter to Phil that he was finding it impossible to get "Rod or mother to go to bed until midnight on account of listening in." On New Year's Eve, John wrote again to tell how much they were all enjoying the wireless: "[Anna works] the machine and I listen, but the Ears & Drums in my old head do not work like they once did."

Phil had much of his father in him, although neither would have been able to recognize many similarities at the time. John had been ever the considerate son-in-law to Lucy Anderson, who was much in need throughout her long life. Although to some it might have seemed that he expected an unnecessary accounting of how the money had been spent, that was simply his nature with everyone, himself included. In truth, he gave because he wanted to make her comfortable and secure, and he expected nothing in return other than assurance that his objectives had been accomplished. Phil found himself in somewhat similar circumstances regarding Helen's mother, and his response was typical. Clara Walker wrote him a personal note on New Year's Day 1924: "I have done quite a lot of thinking since the other evening when you slipped the check into my hand and said those very very nice things to me. I know it is not easy for you to tell people of your innermost feelings and you know, I think, that it is far from easy for me to have any one give me money, so I appreciate enormously what you said to me and accept what you gave me in the spirit in which I want to and do feel it was given and that in that you gave it because you really love me more than from a sense of duty." Those who presume that children and parents or in-laws can share a home without difficulties are those who have missed the experience; but Phil, Helen, and her mother seemed to be managing pretty well.

Little by little Phil was assuming a larger responsibility at Rutledge, and not only in the sales office. He was, of course, able to use family connections as well as the Sales Company organization, and he seems to have been quite willing to work through both channels. In turn, the uncles expected to be kept informed, if not consulted, concerning questions that Phil and his generation came to understand in detail. Thus on January 11 Rudolph wrote Phil thanking him for information provided and assuring him that he would "come back at them [the Sales Company] again the first of February," indicating his unhappiness in having received "a very evasive answer" to earlier inquiries.

The Clearwater development hung heavily on the shoulders of John P. Weyerhaeuser. Not only were the directors uninterested in considering the future, they seemed uninterested in providing an opportunity for such consideration. The annual meetings of the various Weyerhaeuser organizations were scheduled to allow the directors to attend several of them almost simultaneously, since many were serving as directors on different boards. John complained about such scheduling in an April 9 letter to his fellow directors. Some might have shrugged their shoulders at this concern, but John's complaints were legitimate, as most who have served on boards would be quick to admit.

In early May, George S. Long invited Fred, who was back on the job in Potlatch, Idaho, and Phil to join the company directors on a tour of Klamath Falls, Oregon, there to look over millsites and timber owned by the Weyerhaeuser Timber Company. After describing the business at hand, Long wrote, "I know you will remember quite well that nice trip which we all had together down in Klamath County some years ago when we were all young and frisky, so that I want to tell you that . . . the invitation is extended most heartily to you and Philip." Phil responded promptly. Although he could imagine no trip "which I would enjoy taking more than that," he could not be absent for the period scheduled. He was not just pretending importance. He had recently been promoted to sales manager and his young assistant, Will Constans, was east for some six weeks. But in sending his regrets to George Long, Phil claimed to be sure of one thing, "that you will have no better time than we did on our trip before."

John had gotten his wish regarding a meeting of the Clearwater directors at which the future of the corporation was given serious consideration. And if everything did not go exactly as planned, at least he got matters off dead center, obtaining an apparent commitment to expand Clearwater's capital stock with a view to early development. It was not quite so easily managed, however, since holders of two-thirds of the stock had to vote in support of such an increase at a special meeting. Charles had informed his brother of these legal requirements, at the same time hinting of more subtle difficulties. "Please, John," he wrote, "do not let my letter or talks annoy you, because, in the last analysis, I want to do what you want done, and I fully appreciate that you have given much more time and thought to Clearwater matters than any of the rest of us have."

This proved to be the first in a series of complications facing Clearwater development. In June, Charlie was visited by a lawyer representing the Humbird family interests. The lawyer proposed that the Denkmanns and Weyerhaeusers organize a new company, in the process buying out the Humbird share at original cost plus 6 percent interest. This made Charlie, in his words, "hopping mad." F.E. again reportedly countered that if responsible parties could be found who would be willing to assume the Clearwater management, the Weyerhaeusers would be pleased to sell their stock at par, forgetting the interest. Charlie complained to John that such incidents made it appear as if "our partners take our family for a lot of 'chumps' and expect us to carry the burden while they are assured at least of getting their money back with interest." As for his own efforts, Charlie admitted: "I have changed my mind so often that it is hard for my brothers and partners to follow me." But he assured John that he was trying to help, as best he could.

A few days later Charlie talked with an assistant of Charles Donnelly, president of the Northern Pacific Railway. He reported the recent decision to increase the capital stock of the Clearwater Timber Company from 30,000 to 90,000 shares and move ahead with the development of a mill at Lewiston. Charlie then inquired whether the Union Pacific and the Northern Pacific were still willing to proceed in the matter. The N.P. official asked if there was any great urgency. Replying that there was none, Charlie pointed out that although "the Humbirds were in a frame of mind where they wanted to sell . . . I said that we Weyerhaeusers were more in favor of building the sawmill at Lewiston, and I also said that we had been rather waiting in the development of this property until such a time when labor and machinery were cheaper, and that we thought that time was rapidly approaching." Charlie's compass needle seemed to have settled at last, and he informed John, "I now am devoting my energies along the line of building the sawmill at Lewiston."

The next step in the proceedings was apparently up to John as president of the Clearwater Company. Initially, it was necessary for him to meet with Donnelly to determine the specific plans of the Union Pacific and Northern Pacific in the area. But John seemed in no hurry to do so. He had given his approval for a "small party" to go to Lewiston, ostensibly to review the situation and make recommendations; but since the group included likely candidates for the manager's position, the reviewers were also being reviewed. It had all been Charlie's idea and Charlie was in charge.

Phil was not involved in his uncle's "small party." He and Helen had taken Ann to Tacoma, where she was christened by Uncle Bancroft in a formal affair at Haddaway, much to the delight of John and Anna. Following his return to Coeur d'Alene, Phil took a trip in the company of Bill Billings through some of the Rutledge Company holdings, an experience he found "very interesting." Never one to overstate or exaggerate, Phil must have meant just that. No doubt largely responsible was Charles L. "Bill" Billings. Eleven years Phil's senior, he looked more like a college professor than an outdoorsman, and indeed much that interested him was bookish, including a fascination with the history of the American West. But his main dedication was to trees. After attending the University of Minnesota, he had gone west to Butte, Montana, to work for the U.S. Forest Service from 1910 to 1920. Following this he began his service with the Edward Rutledge Timber Company. As land agent for Rutledge, Billings was responsible for taxes, timber sales and trades, logging contracts, scaling, cruising, and fire protection. He was a thinking man's forester, forever reflecting on better ways to manage timber. How does one provide the means to maintain a growing forest while at the same time providing the resource to industries that had been established for the purpose of utilizing that very forest? The questions came more easily than the answers, but Billings was convinced that the answers, however incomplete or tentative, would first come in the management of private lands. One can only imagine the discussions that Phil and Bill had, with Phil asking more of the questions and doing most of the listening. In any event, the relationship became especially close and important— to both of them. Probably for the first time Phil began seriously to consider the issues that would occupy so much of his life: the practical introduction of forestry concepts into the management of timber resources.

It is unfortunate that individuals who work together don't take time to record at least a hint of their discussions and the contributions each would make in the consideration of problems. The fact is, of course, that one tends to record the unusual, and in this case nothing was more usual than to find Phil Weyerhaeuser and Bill Billings talking about forest management. Furthermore, it would have been out of character for either of them to compliment the other for a particular idea or effort. They were only doing their jobs. And if they stopped in the middle of a card game to mention something about logging methods or utilization, it was only because their jobs were all-consuming. Neither would have had it any other way.

In the Clearwater development, the Humbird interests continued to complicate matters. In August Charlie had received a new proposal from Paul Myers, brother-in-law of Tom Humbird and one of the trustees for the John A. Humbird estate. Myers's suggestion was to divide up the lands owned by the Clearwater, giving the Humbird family one-third of the timber in exchange for their stock in the company. The proposal was received without enthusiasm. As F.E. was quick to point out, this would mean "that our people would spend five or six million dollars developing the Clearwater property at our expense, which would benefit the Humbird holdings without their spending any money to improve their one-third of the timber land." Instead, he asked for a response to the earlier proposition, that "the Weyerhaeuser and Denkmann families go ahead and build the railroads and sawmills under a new corporation, which . . . would be the manufacturing company, and in which the Humbirds would own no stock, but which company would put all of the Clearwater Timber Company's timber under a timber cutting contract."

Despite the complications, by the end of September it was clear that plans would proceed with the Clearwater development, and Charlie, at least, was assuming that Fred K. would be general manager. Thus he sent his nephew the many accumulated papers and reports he had collected, acknowledging, "It may be an imposition to ask you to familiarize yourself with all of the above, but such information as you get sometimes may be of real assistance to your father when the time comes for developing the Clearwater property." Uncle Charles also suggested, "The sooner the man who develops the Clearwater property gets on the ground the better, because in my judgment it will take a man almost a year to thoroughly familiarize himself with all that a person should know." He offered in support Huntington Taylor's observation "that he was sorry that he did not have six months to study the Rutledge situation before he commenced building the sawmill and starting logging operations."

Although Charlie had been overly optimistic and enthusiastic on more than a few occasions, in this instance he seemed unusually subdued. He shared uncertainties with Fred K. on the questions outstanding. Nonetheless he wrote, "Somehow, I have always believed that before long one of my father's grandchildren would be running the Clearwater business." Then he made a curious and revealing observation. He noted that Fred would likely have an opportunity to manage one of the new Weyerhaeuser Timber Company operations being planned by George S. Long, and he came close to advising his nephew to "go west," because "I believe money can be made easier out of Douglas fir than out of Idaho pine." Charlie further observed, "possibly your main ability was to be a salesman and . . . possibly you ought to be in Mr. Case's organization." That, of course, was the Weyerhaeuser Sales Company, and if Uncle Charles was not prescient, he was at least discerning. After indicating his belief that "developing and starting of the Clearwater Timber Company would be about the hardest thing that was ever undertaken by any plan that we are connected with," he concluded with the hope that Fred and Phil were "giving a great deal of attention to the proper handling of White Pine lumber in Idaho." The reason was obvious: "Our family has a great deal of money invested in these White Pine trees, and you and Philip can be of real service to our family in learning the proper method of handling the lumber—the drying, handling, manufacturing, settling, etc."

Fred K. was invited to St. Paul in early November to discuss plans for Clearwater development. Apparently the question of manager had been resolved, but that resolution was soon brought back into question. John had earlier gone to St. Paul for meetings with his brothers, and after returning to Tacoma and learning that plans were proceeding to begin negotiations with the presidents of the Union Pacific and Northern Pacific, he wrote to F.E. expressing confusion. "At the meeting held in St. Paul, much emphasis was placed on first having a manager before anything was done, so that he could be in the meeting when the railroad contracts were being made," John recalled. "I do not think Charles has succeeded in getting a manager, etc." This was the sort of unnecessary complication that F.E. hoped to avoid, and his impatience with his older brother was evident in his reply.

"I thought the one thing that we did at our Saturday afternoon conference in St. Paul was to select your son Frederick as manager of the Clearwater Timber Company," he wrote. "I can't be mistaken in thinking that it was the unanimous opinion of all, who were present, including yourself. . . . [In any event] the management has been offered to him, and I suppose he will let us know in a few days whether he elects to accept it." Fred and Vivian, in fact, had gone on to Chicago, where they were talking the matter over before making a decision. It was also understood, F.E. continued, that Rudolph was "perfectly willing to turn the management of the Edward Rutledge Timber Company over to Phil, and that in case Frederick does not take the management of the Clearwater Timber Company, the second choice was to be Huntington Taylor [general manager at Rutledge] . . . but you state in your letter that you 'would much favor someone else' and so, of course, I shall not have any talk with Mr. Huntington Taylor, in the event Frederick does not take the management." Indeed, F.E. informed John, should Frederick decline the Clearwater office, "then the whole problem is back at your door," as far as he was concerned.

As things unfolded, "the whole problem" was returned to John. Fred K. elected to accept instead a position with the Weyerhaeuser Sales Company. F.E. expressed momentary disappointment, although he did allow that "in his own interest and his wife's, I think he is choosing wisely in going into the Sales Department." It is significant that Vivian's role in the decision was specifically noted. Such would hardly have been the case had Phil and Helen been the couple involved.

John seemed unusually relaxed in the midst of the Clearwater controversy. On November 28 he wrote to Phil, telling him of the beautiful weather they were enjoying, and how much they were all looking forward to Christmas. He did mention that the meeting with railroad officials had been postponed until December 15, which "means another trip to Chicago or St. Paul," and he added significantly, "I may ask you to go with me." He also invited Phil to Tacoma on November 30 in order that they might attend a white pine blister rust meeting in Seattle and forestry meetings in Vancouver, British Columbia.

But if John seemed relaxed to some, F.E. knew otherwise, and the youngest of the brothers tried to prepare the way by salving feelings. Thus he admitted he had noted "a bit of irritation on your part that Charles and I have busied ourselves about the Clearwater Timber Company matters," and assured him they had only been trying to help. He continued in a manner that would become habitual during times of internal controversy: "As you know, I have had very little practical experience in the milling end of the lumber business, and practically none in the logging end, and so it is almost absurd for me to think about trying to make a contract with the Northern Pacific and Union Pacific Railways covering our railway problems." It was imperative, therefore, that John attend the meeting on December 15.

Phil, along with Dave Winton, did attend the meetings in Seattle and Vancouver, much to the delight of his father. As John subsequently wrote, "I enjoyed the meeting . . . but enjoyed having you with me much more." Although father and son must have discussed the coming railroad negotiations, there is no indication that Phil and Helen gave much thought to the Clearwater possibilities. Rather it seems likely that they were taking increasing pleasure in their Coeur d'Alene situation. They had a cottage at nearby Hayden Lake, where they spent as much time on summer evenings and weekends as could be managed. By the summer's end, Helen was surely if not noticeably pregnant. She was not dependent on local society, although she did belong to the Tuesday Sewing Club and the Fortnightly Club, a small group that gathered every second Friday afternoon for literary or musical attentions, perhaps some bridge or mahjong, and the inevitable "eats." Phil also kept his social involvements at a minimum. Evenings with the boys he enjoyed, but no more so than evenings in the quiet of his home. He went through the motions of being a proud alumnus of Old Eli, but for the most part this consisted of football wagers with those less fortunate, such as Princetonian Dave Winton.

The December 15 meeting with the railroad officials went as well as could be expected. As Charlie later noted, he was somewhat disappointed by the railroad director's refusal to "accept our ten year proposition, still I think it is eminently fair that we pay for the 20 years." As he wrote to John, assuming that the railroad matter was settled and the financing arranged, "then you are now squarely up against the proposition of engaging a manager." Charlie continued, "I think you understand clearly that your three brothers favor hiring one of your sons to do this work, or, at least securing a man who is not in our organization, and, if that is impossible, then you decide upon whom you wholeheartedly will recommend to the Board of Directors." He could not avoid adding his own opinion: "In my judgment it is important that this man be a mature, all around good business man," qualifications that would seem to eliminate one such as Phil.

The New Year 1925 came and went with little discernible progress on Clearwater matters. In mid-January Charlie complained of his preoccupation, writing John, "I have done much if not anything else but consider men for the managership of the Clearwater Timber Company." After noting all of those who had been looked over, Charlie took John to task for his failure to become better acquainted with Huntington Taylor. "Now John," he admonished, "if you don't know Hunt Taylor, you are hardly doing your duty to the Timber Securities Company or to your son Philip." He continued that among all of those recently considered, "Hunt Taylor is the first man that I would take," although he quickly added, "in your son Philip and the three Cloquet boys [Ralph Macartney, Sherman Coy, and Fritz Wilhelmi], we have most excellent men, and as I look at it, the least need of going outside of our organization to get strong men." If nothing else, Charles was changeable. And in a second letter of the same day, Charles tried to remind John of previous agreements:

I want you to remember that the time before this last one when you were here in St. Paul, the day you went West, namely Saturday, October 25th, that in your presence your three brothers voted to make your son Frederick the General Manager of the Clearwater Timber Company, and if Frederick preferred not to accept this position, but accept a position with the Weyerhaeuser Sales Company, then we offered the general managership of the Clearwater Company to Mr. Huntington Taylor, with the understanding that your son Philip be made General Manager of the Edward Rutledge Company. John, I repeat this now, so that whatever may happen in the future, you must know that your three brothers tried to be loyal to you and your sons in connection with the development of the Clearwater Timber Company properties.

It was obviously a most sensitive issue. John had not been prepared for son Fred's decision to decline the opportunity—the most important single opportunity in the Inland Empire. To consent to that earlier decision involving Huntington Taylor would relegate Phil to Rutledge, a responsibility that even Charles had seen as requiring "a superman to pull it through without a tremendous loss to the stockholders." How could John, given his "natural modesty," dispose of Huntington Taylor and acquire the Clearwater position for son Philip, just about to celebrate his twenty-sixth birthday?

With this in mind, John went to St. Paul in January. In the discussions that occurred, there may have been only slight disagreement. Phil had been effective in the course of his short career, and he certainly gave an impression of experience beyond his years. Furthermore he was dependable, and inspired confidence through his slow-moving, unworried manner. Indeed, father John had recently attended an operatic performance of "Robin Hood," after which he shared an interesting observation with Phil: "I saw Little John, I thought of you."

In any event, Phil received a letter from his Uncle Fred, dated January 29—a letter that began with an amazingly casual tone: "As you seem to be elected to take up the development of the properties of the Clearwater Timber Company, I shall send you from time to time any bits of information that come to me that may be of interest." Phil, as everyone assumed, accepted, but it was an acceptance born of youthful energies, optimism, and faith. Uncle Charles had been correct in his belief that it would require a superman to make the Rutledge Timber Company a success. But the same would be true with the Clearwater development. Phil only promised to do his best.

CHAPTER 3

Rough Waters on the Clearwater

Many were surprised, and not all were pleased with the announcement that J. P. Weyerhaeuser, Jr., would be directing the development of the Clearwater Timber Company. Harry Shellworth, still in the employ of the Boise Payette Company, had been assisting at John's request in the effort to get the Idaho legislature to approve construction of a dam at Lewiston for power and log storage. Shellworth inquired about the possibility of employment in the Clearwater organization. In a response dated March 19, 1925, John assured him that "we would be glad to have you with us" but the management positions had already been determined, with J. P. Weyerhaeuser serving as president and treasurer; T. J. Humbird, vice-president; J. P. Weyerhaeuser, Jr., general manager; W. H. Farnham, secretary and assistant treasurer; and Theodore Fohl, woods manager, assisted by F. E. Rettig. Shellworth replied in some embarrassment that he had no idea "that the selection of the personnel had gone so far," so far in fact that "there is not much, if any, chance left there for me." He did ask that John keep him in mind for other possible opportunities, perhaps in connection with the Klamath Falls development.

John could hardly help feeling a little uncomfortable. He wrote to Shellworth on April 7 that it had never occurred to him that he was interested in leaving Boise Payette. On the more positive side, he noted that they were in the process of purchasing some forty-one pieces of property, and that Bill Billings or someone else would soon be blocking up the timber with a view to operations. John expressed his willingness to write to Phil, suggesting that perhaps Shellworth might be of some assistance in this effort. To Shellworth, who doubtless remembered Phil as a youngster for whom the woods was fun and games, this was a disappointment.

In the meantime, John Philip Weyerhaeuser III had arrived with rather less fanfare than had been the case with earlier generations. April 7, 1925, was the date, and more than a week passed before Uncle Rudolph made mention of "a new soldier boy in your family," but only after he had discussed at some length Phil's plans for building up an organization at Clearwater. Anna was properly enthusiastic. "I think *our* baby pretty fine," she wrote to Phil. She reported that John had gone with George S. Long and Minot Davis to look over the new Long-Bell Lumber Company operation. Anna presumed that Long-Bell would "be in the limelight just now," and that was all right with her: "What a chance it will give the W's to saw wood and keep in the background."

In Idaho, however, the Weyerhaeusers were hardly in the background. Rumors of plans for Clearwater development had long been about, but it was not until early April that Lewiston citizens began to receive definite information. On March 31 the Lewiston Commercial Club hosted a discussion of the dam and power project, and a Committee of Twenty-five was appointed to advance the cause. As reported April 1 on the pages of the *Lewiston Morning Tribune*, there was "no known opposition." Furthermore, "The people are not unmindful of the Weyerhaeuser written proposal to the city council to bring one of their largest mills to Lewiston in the event the city proceeds with the construction of the Clearwater dam and the construction of a power plant, which would of necessity create a pondage that could be used to advantage to the city for the storage of logs."

On April 4, more specific plans were revealed. Representatives of the Clearwater Timber Company and the Inland Power and Light Company presented a joint memorandum to Lewiston Mayor C. G. Braddock, indicating their intention to construct a 12,600-horse-power plant: "The Clearwater Timber Company, being thus furnished with adequate storage for its logs, will erect a new mill of a [yearly] capacity of approximately 200,000,000 feet." The cooperative arrangement with the private power company depended, of course, upon the city's willingness to withdraw its own application for a municipal power plant and upon the ability of the two companies to purchase the necessary land "at a reasonable price and generally upon the cooperation of the entire community which we desire and solicit." The memorandum also referred to the need for the Northern Pacific and Union Pacific railroads to construct lines into the timber. It was signed by J. P. Weyerhaeuser and Frank Silliman, Jr., for the power company.

It had taken a long time for things to come together. Phil later (in a 1953 interview) reflected on the problems and their resolution:

It was a question of building our mill and getting it built at the same time when we were inducing the Northern Pacific and the Union Pacific to build a railroad, and at the same time the Pacific Power and Light Company was building a dam. All of them had to be built contemporaneously, and some of the parties were reluctant to move as fast as we wanted to. So it was really quite an interesting game. In the first instance, the power company would not have anything to do with it until father got the city of Lewiston to say it would build a municipal dam. The city fathers were interested in having municipal power and getting the sawmill there. So they got themselves all heated up about building it. Then the power company became interested, and it was quite a difficult matter getting the city turned off and the power company set in their position. But it all came out about the same time. . . .

The Lewiston Committee of Twenty-five was increased to forty-nine in mid-April, and its chairman notified John Weyerhaeuser that "Lewiston is now combined and ready to proceed." John wired Chairman R. C. Beach immediately: "Will open an office in Lewiston at once and will look for much help from your committee." Two days later, April 17, John, Charles, Phil, Bill Billings, Fritz Jewett, and W. H. Farnham paid Lewiston an official visit, and Phil announced their intentions. "We are here to work and will at once institute activities in an effort to acquire property necessary for the milling and power development," he informed his listeners. He also expressed appreciation for "the fine spirit of the Lewiston people," and observed, "We feel that everybody wants to help and we will want lots of assistance." Phil's directness and sincerity left no doubt that the request was made in honesty and not for effect. It would be difficult to say no.

Negotiations with the railroads continued. Charlie informed John that a meeting with the railroad officials had been scheduled for May 8 in Omaha, and he hoped that John would attend, and possibly Phil and Fritz as well. Charlie was almost as relieved as his brother that the Clearwater decisions had finally been made. This was apparent in his letter of May 21:

John, the greatest tribute that we can pay father and mother's memory is for we four brothers to stick together and work in harmony in the future the same as in the past. I personally would rather our family lose all the money that we have in the Clearwater Company in preference to letting any hard feelings come between you and me on account of the Clearwater Company. I think I have told you repeatedly that I did not want to be the President of the Clearwater Company. I must believe that you think that you compliment me by writing that you expect me to be the President of the company, but as long as you are alive and in good health, I surely hope you will continue to be the President. . . .

As in all family corporations, there was a never-ending concern to balance the number of directors against the percentage of ownership, an exercise often lacking an exact solution.

Of immediate concern to Charles was the upcoming meeting of Clearwater directors, at which he wished to propose an increase in the number of directors from five to seven. The two new directors were to be Harold J. Richardson, a lawyer who had married a granddaughter of F. C. A. Denkmann, and Phil. At present the Humbirds were represented by two of the five—an overrepresentation, with the Weyerhaeusers also having two and the Denkmanns one. Now that the Weyerhaeusers, through the Timber Securities Company, had agreed to lend the Clearwater $2 million for twenty years, Charlie wrote John, "in my judgment no one could say that we were selfish if we had three Weyerhaeusers, namely, yourself, Brother Fred and your son Philip and our nephew Geo. Frederick Jewett as directors, but as the Denkmanns have always been so nice and kind to you, were I making the motion, I would nominate Harold Richardson to be the seventh director instead of Geo. Frederick Jewett." Charles noted that Fritz was young and had plenty of time for such things, but in the meantime John might wish to resign as treasurer, allowing Fritz to be appointed in that responsibility.

The meetings proceeded as Charles had hoped. Phil was elected vice-president (although this was of no great significance compared with the general managership), and cousin Fritz was elected treasurer. Phil left almost immediately for Lewiston; Helen and the children were to delay their move until a new home had been constructed there. For Phil the separation was difficult, but the new responsibilities left little time for melancholy. On April 21 he and others of the company again appeared before the Lewiston Commercial Club, and Phil, unaccustomed to the limelight, observed again, "We can have no feeling but kindness toward the people of Lewiston."

Anna visited Phil in Lewiston in June, finding him just beginning to get settled. She subsequently wrote, "How pleased I was with the new office, the new house, the new lot and the general new scheme of everything." Anna could still get enthusiastic about the beginning of a large effort, and her only concern was that John might not share her excitement. She urged Phil to express a greater interest in his father's involvement in Clearwater affairs. In early July, for example, she reported that John had been expecting "daily a call from you to go into the timber or a call for his advice of some sort." She acknowledged that this would mean listening "patiently over and over to his recital of the same thing and to his slow arrival at points but *if* you can only *listen* intelligently and not anticipate conclusions till he has arrived, you can make him happy—'tis not always easy I know, but it is such a joy to feel that he is *well* enough to take interest in business."

As a matter of fact, John did visit Lewiston often, usually unannounced. He would go directly to the office, arriving there a few minutes in advance of 8:00 A.M., to check on the arrival of the staff—including Phil. He would observe all that was going on, talking occasionally to the workmen, but keeping out of the way. He and Phil would discuss matters, but there was never a doubt that the general manager was giving the orders. How different it had been when John was the young lumberman in Rock Island. Phil understood what it meant to be in charge. He quietly yet firmly conveyed his resolve, but he also understood that there was much he had to learn.

One of Phil's advantages was his ability to be the unassuming leader, to recognize, without apology, his own inexperience. Thus he managed to solicit assistance with no loss of authority. A story of an early meeting between Phil and those who had contracted for the construction of the Clearwater sawmill described his effectively disarming manner. Phil said simply, "Look, as you all can see, I'm young and obviously not as experienced as those with whom you usually deal, and it's likely that you could take advantage of me." But he added, matter-of-factly, "I think you would do so only once."

This is not to say that all mistakes were avoided. Phil later talked about those days and about his relationship with his father, admitting that he had never really understood the degree to which his father and Mr. Long had worked together in conferring on matters of policy: "When I was manager of the Clearwater Timber Company at the time the mill was built . . . father was president of the company. He always leaned over backward—I would say now too much—to let me have my head. It probably cost us a heck of a lot of money. He did not tell me what to do. It may be the best way for someone to learn his way around, but it was an awfully expensive way to build a sawmill!"

If John was careful in not forcing himself or his advice on Phil, so too were the uncles. Once the decision was made regarding the general managership of the Clearwater, all pertinent materials and information were forwarded to Phil. Nothing was held back from him for any reason. One of the first major decisions involved a possible purchase of timber from Henry Turrish for $1.5 million. Uncle Fred indicated that they could probably afford to buy, but only if cruises assured the presence of 250 million feet or more of white pine. Phil soon recommended the purchase.

But as interested and as concerned as the St. Paul uncles were, they were helpless when it came to staying current on the particulars. This was apparent in a letter of October 15 from Charles to John:

Here in this office we realize that Phil has a real responsibility before him, and we have all said to our sisters, especially to Margaret, that if we could help Fritz and Phil and yourself with these big problems, that it would give us pleasure to do so. I presume Phil knows that in addition to the large sum of money that our family has agreed to raise for the Clearwater Timber Company over and above what will be called for our proportion of the capital stock subscription increase, that all of this Turrish money (if his timber is bought) comes from the St. Paul office, which makes a very big hole in our quick assets. We know you and Phil and Mr. Billings are looking after this timber estimating very carefully, but if Rudolph, Tom Humbird, Fred or I can help you and the boys, we want to do so.

In the midst of the day-to-day activities in Lewiston and in the Clearwater timber, there is evidence that some were beginning to look ahead. The week of April 27 to May 3 President Coolidge had proclaimed nationwide observance of American Forest Week, and the affiliated Weyerhaeuser companies had used the occasion to distribute a booklet advertising recent developments in forest management, *Only Natural Resource Renewable*. The booklet described efforts at fire protection, reforestation, and the manufacture of by-products, making particular mention of research work at Cloquet, Minnesota, where some $2 million had been spent that trees might be used "down to the last splinter." In truth, the efforts described were in their infancy; but those who would follow would benefit from this early concern and vision. George S. Long was largely responsible for the booklet, but Phil Weyerhaeuser would read it with interest and more than a little pride.

Phil and Bill Billings, in fact, were considering the feasibility of logging practices of a new sort. They had become interested in the work of Carl Stevens, a consulting forestry engineer in Portland, and Stevens subsequently began to correspond with F.E. in St. Paul. F.E. acknowledged that it "was not very clear to me"; his initial interest was, at best, lukewarm. "So far as I have observed," he wrote to Phil, "the question of forest management and of reforestation varies so widely, on account of physical conditions, that very few general rules can be laid down, and I see little prospect of any reforestation under private ownership, except where timber grows very rapidly and taxes are extremely light." Such an assessment, however, did not mean that the second-generation Weyerhaeusers favored policies aimed simply or strictly at an immediate return on investment. Indeed, the commitment to the long term, or to tradition, seems likely to have affected decisions in ways not always in line with those that might otherwise be judged most sensible.

Nonetheless, the annual reports were studied carefully. Charlie, who had been busy looking through the 1925 statements of the affiliated companies, was generally pleased with the results, expressing some surprise "to see how well the three Cloquet companies did, and also Potlatch." Bonners Ferry and Rutledge were different matters, although in the case of Rutledge he hoped for improvement now that they were "through with their fire killed logs and their Thompson Yards loss." Snoqualmie Falls and the Southern Lumber Company both did "remarkably well"; and as for the Weyerhaeuser Timber Company, its January receipts amounted to $2.9 million, which hardly seemed possible, Charlie observed. "I wish father and the rest of the men who started that company could see how well it has turned out."

Phil was not much concerned about annual reports as yet. Clearwater was more than a year away from the start of operations and his attention was on plans and preparations. These, however, were impressive. Even George Long expressed wonderment at the scope of the Clearwater development. Phil agreed, writing to Long that Long's characterization of the plant as colossal began to seem a "very conservative statement." But he immediately assured his former mentor, "So far I have not been spending sleepless nights."

Perhaps it was just as well that work on the new Lewiston house had gone so slowly and that Helen and the family remained in Coeur d'Alene. It simply was not a good time to set up a new household. Even with help, Helen was fully occupied with Ann and baby Flip, and she was pregnant again. George Hunt Weyerhaeuser arrived on July 8, 1926. The baby was fine, but Helen's recovery was slower than she would have liked.

While Phil was superintending the Clearwater development, brother Fred K., having chosen his future with the Sales Company, was working with Uncle Fred to accomplish a change in organization that both of them desired: the move of the Sales Company headquarters from Spokane to St. Paul. This, of course, could be justified without much difficulty, because St. Paul was much closer to the major markets. As the nephew indicated to his uncle, "the location of the head office in Spokane is analogous to the establishment of the management of the Potlatch Lumber Company in New York City." The justification was no doubt in part based on personal preferences of the two Freds for living in the East. As certainly they understood, a major problem for the Sales Company was the difficulty of coordinating with the sawmills. By removing the Sales Company headquarters, that problem would be aggravated.

Fred K. was now assistant sales manager for the Sales Company, much concerned with overall policies as well as day-to-day sales. Thus he recommended that the Sales Company board of trustees meet only twice a year instead of monthly and that an executive committee be formed to meet on a monthly basis. He further suggested that George S. Long be included on the committee. "While he might object to moving the head office to the Twin Cities," Fred observed, "I believe he would agree if the matter were put up to him in the proper light." As a matter of fact, privately Long continued to question the whole idea of the Sales Company but had long since decided it was one of those battles he would leave unfought.

In late August, Charlie wrote to John from his St. Paul office, telling of a "nice visit with Brother Fred, and he is much pleased with the progress of the work being accomplished at Lewiston." But they could not help worrying somewhat about the cost of it all, F.E. noting that "the boys have already spent over a million dollars, in addition to the money we have spent in purchasing timber, so it is very clear the capital stock of the company will have to be increased."

Phil, of course, heard directly from the uncles on many occasions, and not all their advice was particularly timely or helpful. Uncle Fred, the acknowledged head of the St. Paul office, was most often involved. He was the first to admit that his personal experience in the production end of the line was extremely limited. Still, he had been around, and had his own opinions on proper management. He worried that Phil and his "crew of youngsters" failed to understand the dangers of high-priced timber, and he also wondered, aloud, whether they appreciated the importance of how the timber was scaled, ensuring that only the best of the usable wood was considered.

All lumbermen understood the source of easiest profits and surest losses: it involved getting more or less value out of each sawlog. An analogy is available in the stockyard. If a steer was selling for a dollar a pound but it was the practice to add up only the marketable portions, not counting the bones, fat, and low-quality meat, a 1,000-pound steer might be worth only $400. That same general adjustment had been the practice for many years in the Lake States lumbering operations, and it was that experience that Uncle Fred now recalled: "For years we did practically all of our logging on the Cloquet and St. Louis Rivers at Cloquet. We had as scalers men who had been thoroughly experienced on the Chippewa River in scaling white pine logs on a straight and sound standard, with the result that we got a considerable overrun in the way of number four boards and poorer, lumber shorter than ten feet, and of course a considerable savings on account of the thinness of our saws."

F.E. did remember that subsequently a number of independent operators had come to the valley and the good old days soon ended. Led by William O'Brien of Stillwater, they began to insist that since number 4 boards were merchantable lumber, the logs should be scaled accordingly. But the lesson was clear enough. At best, profits were going to be difficult to obtain, and unless every advantage was pursued—and there seemed so few opportunities—profits would be impossible. There was no more certain method of obtaining them in the lumber business than to purchase timber cheaply and to scale conservatively. To a considerable extent, the game was one of overruns.

Although there was much truth in Uncle Fred's advice, it was advice largely unneeded, if not out of date. Phil and Bill Billings had a pretty fair idea about the relative worth of timberlands in the Inland Empire, and they were unlikely to pay more than the going rate. The days on the Chippewa of "straight and sound" scale were days gone by, although concerns for increased utilization and accounting procedures were not unrelated to that step between stump and sawmill. But the current problem for the Clearwater was the same one that George S. Long had been dealing with through the years for the Weyerhaeuser Timber Company west of the Cascades: the need to organize timberlands into efficient operating districts or units—a rearrangement of holdings that required buying, selling, and trading.

Phil was busily building and planning, attempting to estimate costs as closely as possible. On November 18 he addressed a letter to Uncle Fred in which he detailed the situation. The care evident in the accounting seemed, at least in part, to compensate for the large figures. In prompt reply, however, F.E. indicated that Phil's estimate of requirements for the development phase up to July 1, 1928, was very close to his own—approximately $15 million, including capital stock and loans. And Phil was duly thanked and complimented for providing "so complete a statement of what the costs probably will be." Fred was also encouraged by a recent conversation with a businessman passing through St. Paul who offered an account of his own dealings with the young general manager of the Clearwater. As F.E. happily observed, "I hope you were able to make as close a bargain as Mr. Dodge suggests you got from his company."

Much was happening during those hectic days of 1926 and 1927, and not just along the banks of the Clearwater River. The pace of expansion in the lumber industry seemed to reflect a belief in everlasting good times. In this instance, everlasting would prove of especially short duration, but for the moment most lumbermen worked with complete confidence, and not the least among them were Phil and his "crew of youngsters." Things were made considerably more pleasant by the completion of the home at 603 Ninth Street, a delightful residence with a wonderful view of the valley. Phil and Helen made the adjustment to life in Lewiston without difficulty, especially since some of their friends, notably the Billings, had also made the move from Coeur d'Alene. From the beginning, Phil would know almost everybody in Lewiston, and everyone wished to know his wife, who was beautiful, charming, and reserved. Phil was more than pleased to make the introductions, often in a manner whose purpose was momentary- embarrassment. "I'd like you to meet my wife, Helen; she was a Phi Beta Kappa," he would announce, and Helen would admonish, "Phil, you know how I hate that." With a look of genuine hurt, he would respond, "But you were."

Charlie, working very hard at his newly elected membership on the Boise Payette Company board and enthusiastic about "two big deals with the Long-Bell Lumber Company,"—a reference to plans for the construction of a mammoth Weyerhaeuser Timber Company facility at Longview—maintained that "as far as I know, the most interesting work at the present time is in connection with the Clearwater Company." Accordingly he requested that John write to him after his next visit to Lewiston. In particular he was wondering when construction of the last pier for the dam would commence, when the hauling of sawlogs would begin, and when the sawmill might start production.

If there seemed to be general agreement on most of the endeavors, disagreements about the Sales Company continued. F.E.'s preference was to make a greater effort in "promoting the sale of our own woods by relating our advertising more directly to our own products"—in short, to suggest that there was something special about the Weyerhaeuser stamp. As he well understood, however, such an approach was not favored by others. He observed a bit caustically, "Mr. Long, I presume, is so over-crowded with work that he is not able to give this publicity problem the attention it deserves."

In truth, Long, whose own experience in sales extended far back into the previous century, was simply convinced that quality and price were the only essential factors, and that lumber competitive in those respects would call attention to itself. Money expended in telling customers that lumber was consistently well manufactured was money expended unnecessarily; money expended trying to convince customers that poor lumber was good lumber was money wasted. Still, F.E. believed firmly in his own position. He planned to talk the subject over with F. S. Bell, in an effort "to acquaint Mr. Bell with our problems very fully, even though he may take no particular interest in helping us solve them."

Concerning other matters, F.E. told of having received some favorable reports on the developments at the Clearwater, although he was quick to note that "the success of the Clearwater Timber Company will depend very largely upon our ability to market the products at a fair price." Although not directly involved, George S. Long had apparently suggested that some consideration be given to the merging of the Inland Empire properties. F.E. found merit in the idea, and he asked John to give it some thought. "This at least would make it easier for us to carry on any definite sales program," he wrote, "as there would be less possibility of friction resulting from special efforts and perhaps unusual expense in selling certain products." It would also help to clear up the confusing and often conflicting ownership relations. But a merger possibility was premature. Harder times would reintroduce the subject, and as always it would prove to be a problem most difficult to resolve.

The Clearwater sawmill began operations in August 1927. F.E. sent a note of congratulations to Phil, saying he was "greatly pleased," especially since everything appeared to be working so well. This was unlikely to continue, he warned: "You must expect a lot of grief in the first few months' operation of a new plant." The smooth start-up was indeed misleading. The occasion bearing out Uncle Fred's predictions was particularly embarrassing. A special train of lumber dealers and guests, some seventy in all, "mostly ladies," went to Potlatch to visit the sawmill. They then proceeded by car to Moscow, where they were entertained by the Moscow Commercial Club, and went on by automobile to Lewiston. Things deteriorated quickly. "The dust on the road was most trying," John reported. The drive to Lewiston required two and a half hours, and "the temperature was then 96° in the shade." Needless to say, the ladies looked considerably worse for wear on arrival. And after all this, the Clearwater mill was not running well. John could only imagine that "many left with critical ideas of what we were doing." Aside from the need to get the operation in order, there was a lesson here: "Never send anybody to Lewiston during the latter part of July and all of August," he advised without qualification.

Of greater importance to Phil was a September 9 gathering in Spokane, involving the uncles, Tom Humbird, Will Farnham, Fred Denkmann, Harold Richardson, Fred K., and two attorneys. The purpose was to consider an increase in the Clearwater capital stock from $3 to $5 million. Phil would later kick himself for being too conservative in the matter of capitalization for Clearwater, but at the time it had to seem to the others, the ones paying the bills, that this was an extravagance. In particular, Phil recalled visits from Tom Humbird, who was accustomed to operating "on a modest basis." Whatever else, Clearwater was not modest. As Humbird walked around the plant at Lewiston, Phil would watch him shake his head as to this or that—water coolers in the sawmill, a cyclone fence around the property, and all manner of strange and unnecessary expenditures.

Inevitably there were disagreements about the decisions made at Clearwater, but more often than not they were the result of incomplete or erroneous information. Phil was proving adept at anticipating problems, and often the uncles found themselves having to apologize for concerns expressed before the facts were in. Through it all, Phil seemed unperturbed, doubtless realizing that the uncles, as Charles wrote, were "still doing all in our power to make matters easy for you." There was little gained by sharing every problem with distant family, no matter how interested they might be. Thus it was that Charlie ended one note, "Philip, I congratulate you on not writing too many letters." That part came easily.

On the home front, Helen was pregnant again. Things continued to happen in Lewiston society. Helen noted in a letter to Phil, who was in the East on business, that "The Green's dance was quite good, but gosh, it's terrible to be married and minus a husband at a dance." There were also "movies continually, a bridge luncheon today and two more in the near future." At yesterday's luncheon, Helen had made a grand slam, although she admitted that it had been "by mistake." Their local doctor was making arrangements in Spokane for the birth of their fourth child.

Frederick Weyerhaeuser was born in Spokane on October 22, 1927, but what had been an occasion for joy was shortly to be an occasion for grief. The baby died on the evening of February 7, 1928, the local paper indicating influenza as the cause of death, although Helen would later attribute it to spinal meningitis. It was a terrible shock. As Fred K. wrote to Uncle Charles and Aunt Maud, then touring the Mediterranean, "The news came to us by wire from Fritz without any warning although we did know the baby had a light case of flu or bad cold." Phil informed his brother that Helen was bearing up well, but he thought it would be good to take a trip somewhere.

Their trip, to California, was an important interlude for both of them. Their life together had brought a few disappointments but no real tragedy, and the loss of an infant son was an occasion for reflection. But neither Helen nor Phil was given to self-pity. Perspectives soon returned. In their mutual loss came the realization of what they had—and what remained to be done.

Spring found Phil back at work in Lewiston, overseeing improvements in production and trying to see past the accumulation of bills due. Following a visit to the Clearwater plant, Uncle Rudolph wrote a note of appreciation. He had been impressed with what he had seen: "I certainly want to congratulate you on the manner in which you are handling the Lewiston proposition, having it so well in hand." He added that the only thing lacking was "some orders, but I suppose this applied to all of the mills in various parts of the country."

Rudolph also wrote to John, cautioning him against pushing himself too hard, "especially trotting around Lewiston, up in the mountains and on the drives." He admonished John not to forget that he was "nigh on to 70 years of age," and suggested that he should avoid "strenuous work" in the future. What Rudolph may not have understood was that his oldest brother was enjoying himself more than he ever had. Contributing when he could, he was watching Phil with pride and without envy do the things that he had never been able to do: to lead—indeed, to inspire—those about him.

Years later, Phil recalled some of the Clearwater visits:

He would come to Lewiston often unannounced, stay at the hotel, and arrive at the office ahead of everyone else. Many times I would receive a curt message asking about my health occasioned by my arriving at the office later than he. This usually meant that I would follow him out to the plant and find him with some foreman, many of whom came to the company on his recommendation. He would spend all day, for several days, on the pond or at the plant, completely independent of me, often coming to my house in the later afternoon to play with the children and have supper with us.

On one of those visits, John attempted to cross the log pond via the logs, something he had undoubtedly done on many occasions back in Wisconsin. But he was younger then, and in 1931 in Lewiston, he mistook some floating bark for a log, and as Phil described, "was ducked."

Nevertheless, John had recently complained of his many involvements, and Charlie, arriving home from his world tour in May, immediately took up the question of his brother's continuing role and responsibilities. In fact, none of the brothers was willing to take John's place as president of the Weyerhaeuser Timber Company. But John had had enough, and no one could dissuade him. Apparently Ed Denkmann had hinted that there was too much opportunity for influence with John serving as president of both the Timber Company and Clearwater, the two major involvements. F.E. joined in expressing disappointment over John's decision to resign, doubting "very much whether Mr. [F. S.] Bell will be a more active president than you have been." In this, F.E. was soon proved wrong, and even at the time he acknowledged that it did seem "proper and desirable that Mr. Bell should become president of the corporation."

While his father and uncles had been jousting over matters involving the Weyerhaeuser Timber Company, Phil had been forcing himself to do one of those desk-bound tasks he found so wearisome. In a letter of June 6, he submitted a fairly formal general manager's report to the trustees of the Clearwater Timber Company. As a report, it could hardly be faulted, but its message was anything but encouraging. In short, given the expense of logging and the attendant small possibility for profit on each log sawed, Phil had to recommend that they manufacture as much as the mill could manage, operating a double shift. Uncle Fred agreed, but cautioned Phil to reduce expenses "as much as is reasonably possible." F.E. continued: "It is not necessary for me to make this comment, and possibly not advisable for me to, but, at the same time, I am sorry to see so great an overhead interest charge accumulate against the operation of your company." Uncle Fred's worries were well founded, but no alternative came quickly to mind.

Bill Billings and Phil well understood the essence of their difficulty. The expense of logging along the Clearwater dictated that only logs over a certain diameter could be utilized profitably. Smaller logs cost more than the lumber they produced would cover. In a sense, lumbermen had always realized that extreme care had to be exercised when deciding which logs to take. Their cutover accumulations of limbs, tops, and imperfect logs attested to that. But if they had been selective, it was a matter of taking some and leaving the rest behind, not a matter of taking some now and leaving the rest for later harvesting. It was the latter approach that was under consideration at the Clearwater Company.

In the spring of 1928, the Portland firm of Mason and Stevens had been employed for the purpose of surveying the holdings, reviewing the logging methods, and submitting a report recommending procedures aimed at economic utilization. At the same time, Billings studied the process from the sawmill end, working backwards. When the reports were put together, the company had figures available that would provide for a more intelligent approach to the entire operation. At the very least they knew the size and species of log required for a profitable operation, and they knew where to find the timber that would furnish such logs.

Future operations were guided by the results of these studies, and the term "selective logging" came to be associated with Clearwater. This association brought some favorable publicity but no great improvement in business. Phil described the efforts as simply "an attempt on our part to manage our business as intelligently as other industries are managed." And he added, "we thought we ought to prove out our methods, as least as far as we could, while our operation was still fairly new." Thus the loggers were directed to cut the bigger trees, almost exclusively the white pine, leaving the smaller trees to mature. It was rudimentary forestry, but perhaps the most important development was the willingness to seek answers by a more scientific means—by asking questions previously unasked.

In the meantime, more money was required before there would be any hope of a return on the investment. Phil inquired whether the Timber Securities Company would advance needed funds if the Clearwater stockholders refused to do so. F.E. responded affirmatively, subsequently indicating to John that the Securities Company would "keep on advancing money to the Clearwater Company as long as you, the President, wished us to do so." But he again noted the "enormous overhead that Philip will have to struggle under," admitting at the same time that he had no other answer in mind.

However difficult the problems at Clearwater, they were not the only ones in the Inland Empire. Particularly troublesome was a nasty management disagreement in the Rutledge Timber Company, the results of which found Fritz Jewett replacing Huntington Taylor as general manager. There was clearly a bit of uncertainty regarding Jewett's abilities, at least in terms of leadership. Still, the choice was not questioned, and certainly not within the family circle. Thus F.E. wrote to John in a post-Christmas letter: "Fritz has taken on a very great and serious responsibility. Whether or not he can make anything out of this unfortunate situation only time can tell, but, in any event, regardless of profits or losses, I think it is up to us to give our nephews an opportunity to show what they can do, for our most important problem is the developing of our own boys. Fritz has many fine qualities, and I am very hopeful that he will do as well as anyone could with the Rutledge property."

F.E. seemed generally pleased with the Mason and Stevens report, believing that it not only merited serious attention for the Clearwater operation but probably would apply, in principle, to Rutledge as well. While acknowledging that the Idaho operations had "suffered tremendously on account of the Panama Canal," he seemed optimistic about the long term. The Sales Company had increased its sale of white pine for the year by some 150 million feet, and the trends in price and volume were in the right direction.

Although Uncle Fred was also encouraging to Phil, he tried to indicate that there were limits even to the support for Clearwater through the family's Timber Securities Company. John Mahan, secretary for the company, had arranged to have $150,000 deposited to Clearwater's credit before Christmas, with another $100,000 available shortly after the first of the year. F.E. assured Phil that his capital requirements were not unusual, but he immediately expressed the hope that, with the advances now being arranged for, Phil would "get along without very much further assistance from this office." In other words, the Clearwater had better see the day when its earnings would cover the costs of operation, and soon.

The annual report of the Clearwater Timber Company for 1928 brought forth a good deal of comment. It was obvious that Phil provided more than enough information for critical appraisals, and critical appraisal is what he received. Uncle Fred was among the first to respond. After noting that there were many things in the report that he would like to talk about, he selected two subjects. He called attention to percentages of production by grade, noting that number 3 and poorer grades of lumber accounted for more than 63 percent. "Can it be possible," he inquired, "that this is what we should expect in the future?"

The second observation involved the production of some 17 million feet of red (Douglas) fir and tamarack (larch) lumber. F.E. found a disturbing statistic all too familiar to Phil: production had involved a net loss of "approximately $8.00 per thousand." F.E. could not help but recall a similar experience elsewhere: "It developed at the recent meeting of the Potlatch Lumber company, that Mr. [Allison] Laird was instructed by his board of Directors in 1922—seven years ago—to make a study and also to make experiments with selective cutting of his timber. He seems never to have given it very much thought since then. But seven years is a long time. However, if I remember correctly, the Potlatch Lumber Company did make some money in 1923, and perhaps the fact that a little profit resulted in one year has allowed us all to sleep for another six years." Phil got the message and had no plans to sleep for six months, much less six years.

Uncle Fred, whose own experience was largely limited to figuring things out from figures, soon learned from Phil that there were a great many other factors involved. As to the question of poor quality or, as Phil termed it, "a heavy degrade," initially this had to do with the placement of the logging camps. Phil reminded his uncle that they had gone into the second-growth timber near Pierce "in order not to have to wait too long for the completion of the railroad." As a result, nearly 80 million feet of the first logs came from that locality and averaged very poor. The problem had been further aggravated by "cup splitting in the planer," a tendency common in the milling of small timber. Phil was hopeful that the employment of a steam tank to treat the lumber would "make a material difference in the shipping degrade," and as he looked ahead to logging operations, it seemed likely that the timber would result in a much higher average quality.

The matter of mixed logs involved considerations of both logging and marketing. Many of those they shipped to could not accept carloads of nothing but white pine. Phil opposed dealing strictly in white pine, and he recalled a bit of history of his own. "You may remember," he wrote, "that we tried it at Rutledge after the fire," and soon discovered "how hard it was for the Sales Company to send Rutledge its proportion of orders, purely for the reason that they were offering almost 100% White Pine." In short, Clearwater was spending money in order to make money; "the mixed logs carry their share of the Camp costs, and camp improvement, landing chute depreciation, labor costs, drive costs and stampage." The inclusion of the mixed logs lessened the cost of the white pine logs, but just how that figure should be credited was difficult to say. Phil was ready to admit that they had manufactured and sold more fir and larch than they should have, "but I contend that it is necessary to have some. What the measure of it is, I do not know." He had not been impertinent in his response to his uncle, and he closed respectfully, requesting, "If you think we are wrong in this, I hope you will tell me." Whether F.E. was convinced was almost beside the point. Phil had explained enough for him to understand that the policy was clearly not a product of inertia, or sleeping for "six years."

F.E. did know that general managers disliked buying from each other to fill orders, even when the figures indicated that such purchases, on balance, made sense. And he continued to think that Clearwater might be better off to fill out its needs by purchasing dimension lumber. In the last analysis he felt that if the plant was operating at full production, every piece of mixed timber that passed through meant that a piece of white pine was not manufactured. Even allowing for the need for mixed lumber in filling shipments, he wondered whether Phil might not be able to negotiate "a sort of 'milling in transit' rate from the railroads," thus permitting the shipment to Lewiston of dimension from the coast, "and this at much less cost to the company than trying to manufacture mixed woods." As always, however, Uncle Fred wanted his nephew to understand that he was "merely trying to help solve this problem," and did not "claim to have any knowledge of logging conditions in the Inland Empire."

Perhaps because of his own inexperience, F.E. was more willing than most of his generation to consider forestry practices. Since his awareness was largely theoretical, he was not tightly bound by such strictures as "We've always done it this way." But even the most traditional of loggers would accept new methods once it was proved that such methods were better and did not add to operation costs. True, many would have to be convinced beyond doubt, but loggers were not inherently opposed to forestry practices. Despite the popular image of brawny men intent on acts of forest destruction, even the most hardened had to pause at the parklike beauty of the old-growth pine forest in the vicinity of Klamath Falls, Oregon, for example, and look upon the individual giants with respect. For most, the idea of reforestation was pleasing, in theory.

In following the changes in logging methods and philosophies in the Clearwater timberlands, what becomes apparent is that forestry visions could not exceed cost analyses to any significant extent. What was done had to be justified to those paying the bills. Thus in commenting on the Potlatch Lumber Company response to the Mason and Stevens report, F.E. wrote Phil that he was uncertain whether the effort had been "altogether fair to Mason & Stevens." At the same time, he thought it was probably about as far as Potlatch would go, "and so I am very glad to have them adopt any program which will tend to reduce losses we have been making through cutting heavy percentages of tamarack and red fir." Phil understood what his uncle was leading up to. He was arguing in behalf of the Mason and Stevens report as it applied to the Clearwater, suggesting that Phil ought to be able "to make a pretty close estimate" of the accuracy of the figures presented by Mason and Stevens. F.E. guessed that the report could have "materially modified our logging methods during the past ten years, had we had these figures before us, and had we appreciated their importance."

Whether or not F.E. understood, or could understand, all the considerations involved, there was no doubt that he was deeply interested. And he had the basics clearly in mind: "Of course, you have a magnificent opportunity to carry on a logging operation on a sustained yield basis, if the general scheme is practicable, sound and will prove profitable, but, as I see it, Mason & Stevens' report is merely a plan, or perhaps a method, by which you can determine, from time to time, what trees you ought to log. Changed market conditions or logging costs may make very important changes in detail but not in the general scheme." It was, of course, the qualifications to the general scheme that invariably made for the problems.

Needless to say, considerable time and effort was expended in attempting to justify the selective approach to logging. The timber to be cut was marked, and greater supervision was required to ensure that only marked trees were felled and that the falling was managed so as to protect the timber to be left. This required more than a simple change in official policy. Most important, it demanded cooperation from the crews. Changes in long-established practices involved much more than an announcement from the general manager's office. But company forester Ed Rettig reported "a considerable change in the foremen at the camps where we are practicing forestry." This, however, may have been largely wishful thinking in August 1929.

Still, there were some obvious advantages in the selective logging methods. Cutting all the timber from which a profit could then be realized left a growing stock, it was assumed, that would be ready for subsequent logging in twenty-five to thirty years. This second cutting would be considerably less expensive, since there would be no extensive areas of unproductive land to cross with the logging and railroad improvements. Furthermore, those mixed areas would contain, as a result of these cutting practices, the heaviest stands of timber at the time of second cutting, and it could be hoped that by that time the value of other species would have increased so that their harvesting would be profitable. There were other factors. A selectively logged area was safer in terms of fire protection, and tests indicated that white pine blister rust was not as likely to infect shaded areas as open ones. In a less tangible sense, the Clearwater Company had already received compliments on its logging procedures, and even the company's chief forester acknowledged, "it is certainly good for the eyes to see a nice green stand of timber around headquarters and not burned and barren hills."

The fall of 1929 was witness to many significant events, most notably the late October stock market crash. To lumbermen the country over, as to farmers, hard times were nothing new. To those less experienced, the lessons came swiftly and painfully. But the onset of the Depression did not stay other developments. On November 12, John W. Mahan died at the age of sixty-four. Initially the private secretary to Frederick Weyerhaeuser, he had served Weyerhaeuser family interests for more than thirty-five years, a man of unusual ability and unquestioned integrity.

The following month, T. J. Humbird resigned as president of the Sales Company after the death of Paul Myers and Will Farnham's illness. To replace Humbird, Frederick K. Weyerhaeuser was elected president of the Sales Company. "Congratulations," Uncle Charles wired from Cairo, in what would prove to be the last word Fred would receive from his warm and well-meaning relative. Uncle Fred also conveyed his congratulations, although he had some misgivings about his nephew "undertaking this strenuous job, for it seemed to have proven a knockout for everyone who has held it or been closely connected with the management, with the exception of Mr. Tate."

The first death in the second generation occurred on February 15, 1930, when Charles passed away following a brief shipboard illness. He had been fine when Maud and he had departed Cairo on February 8, "having such a good time, not seasick a bit." Within a week, Charlie had died. Maud, in her letter to F.E., observed, "It will be a long, lonely journey now." In many ways, life had been a long, lonely journey for Charlie. F.E. shared some of his own feelings with his nephew Fred: "It is still impossible for me to accept the fact that brother Charles has left us. I am as one in a dream. I suspect you never fully appreciated the bond of affection between us. Beginning at a time when I was not more than six or seven years of age, Charles has loved me with an affection that was more like a Mother's love, than that of a brother. It has been one of the great helpful influences of my life. But we shall not be separated for long, and love like his continues through eternity."

But life and its concerns went on. In the very next paragraph F.E. mentioned the Mason and Stevens report and the fact that he had become "very much interested." No one else, he allowed, "except possibly Phil seemed to give it a second thought but I still believe it is sound and worth careful study, although I scarcely know enough of the detail to express any very positive opinions."

If F.E. thought that the Mason and Stevens report was receiving scant interest, it was probably because he was expecting too much too quickly. The Clearwater operations were beginning to attract attention. In the March 15 issue of the occasional house journal, *4-Square News*, a featured article by H. A. Simons described the activities of the Clearwater Timber Company. Simons had been sent west from St. Paul to write about "the hottest logging story of years," involving a company "run by a pretty live crew of youngsters." The essence of the story was the introduction of selective logging operations: "They're farming timber, rotating their crops, harvesting what's ripe now, letting the young stuff mature." Simons's article would be reprinted, in its entirety, in the April 20 edition of the *Lewiston Morning Tribune*.

In the midst of deepening economic concerns for the associated companies and the industry as a whole, George S. Long died on August 2, 1930. Although retired as general manager of the Weyerhaeuser Timber Company for more than a year, he had continued to serve as chairman of its Executive Committee. Phil, of course, appreciated Long's qualities as a lumberman and especially as the one who had represented the Weyerhaeuser West Coast interests with such vision and integrity from the beginning and for three decades. Phil could not know that he would shortly be called upon to assume responsibility for the Long legacy. He did know that his friend George S. Long, Jr., was in need of comfort. Phil was not quite so innocent in such matters as he had been five years previously, on the occasion of the death of Mrs. Long, when he had written: "Since being old enough to realize what it meant, I have never been faced with a grief such as yours in the loss of your mother. I can't know just what it does mean, but do want to extend [to] you and your family my heartfelt sympathy, and make it brief for failure to know what more to say."

That was vintage Phil, and if five years later he felt inadequate in the manner of his expression, his concern was no less appreciated. Thus George, Jr., responded on July 8, 1930, "Before this, like you, I had never known what it is to have a deep grief so close to you," and he added, "One thing it has taught me is the comfort one gets from the sympathy extended by your friends."

Perhaps appropriately, Phil was embarking on an effort that would consume most of his energies over the next few years, that of trying to arrange a logical consolidation of the Weyerhaeuser interests in Idaho. George S. Long would have approved.

CHAPTER 4

A Merger of Sorts

The various lumbering operations of the Inland Empire had much in common in the problems they encountered. Usually the logging was difficult because the terrain was rugged, and difficult logging made for expensive logs. The lumber also had to endure the higher costs of rail transportation to markets, and compete with lumber moved by water from the South, the Lake States, and increasingly from the Pacific Northwest.

The idea of an Idaho merger was not new. What was new was getting the idea into motion, and as the years passed and conditions failed to improve, Phil grew increasingly impatient. Although the reasons for merger seemed obvious enough, logic often proved an insufficient ally against the entrenched interests of independent operators and the comfort of habit. Not only had circumstances contrived to give considerable independence to lumber producers, distant and isolated as they tended to be, there were advantages to a traditional system which allowed for separate accounting for each camp and sawmill, regardless of organizational relationships. What had worked earlier and elsewhere, however, seemed in need of adjustment in the rigorous economic climate of the Inland Empire.

The initial merger plan, which made its appearance in the summer of 1930, seemed simple enough. First, disinterested parties would make a survey to determine the current worth of each company. Next, a holding company would be organized with a capital stock equal to the total. That stock would then be distributed to the stockholders of each corporation in exchange for their separate certificates, the new holding company coming into possession of all the properties. The holding company would then be reorganized into an operating corporation. As simple as the process might sound, Phil knew that there were complications aplenty.

At the Rutledge Timber Company, Phil had an important ally in Fritz Jewett. If some had worried about Fritz's ability as a general manager, the concerns had little to do with his enthusiasm and willingness to tackle complex problems. In fact, he had just completed an effort resulting in the passage in March 1929 by the Idaho legislature of a new tax bill which would permit, and possibly encourage, selective cutting and sustained-yield programs. The new yield-tax program would defer the major portion of tax payments until the trees were harvested, thereby eliminating one of the reasons for early liquidation.

Regarding the merger of Idaho properties, in a memorandum Jewett expressed the belief that such an accomplishment could only increase the return on stockholder investment. Specialization would be one of the initial advantages: "If we had fewer executives and more experts, we would be better off." Existing arrangements contributed to loss "in executive efficiency . . . in the conflict of interest of our various groups of stockholders." That many of the stockholders, especially the Weyerhaeusers themselves, were represented on all the various boards did not alter the isolation and lack of cooperation. As Fritz correctly observed, each manager had to consider the effects of various decisions on his own responsibilities and the attitudes of his own particular board. Although there might indeed be a common interest, there was little opportunity for it to be considered, much less expressed. Fritz felt that his own energies were being foolishly expended—energies that might better be devoted to actual operation or to special projects such as the Idaho tax review.

"Duplication of efforts is another serious waste of energy," Fritz observed, noting the various questions common to all Idaho operations but necessarily considered separately by each. Then there were benefits involving equipment sharing and purchases of equipment and materials in larger and more standardized quantities. Some of the advantages foreseen by Fritz were too farseeing. For example, he remarked that under existing arrangements it was absolutely necessary that each plant be operated at capacity, whereby under a consolidated organization it would be possible to consider the closing of one or more facilities. Also, once the advantages of the larger organization were demonstrated, it might be well to consider public sale of stock. Such public financing would permit greater flexibility through increasing capital funds, would make it possible for present stockholders to withdraw more easily from the business should they desire, and perhaps make it possible for employees to invest in ownership. In short, "Successful financing of this plan would open the way to taking over other timber properties and insure our leadership in the industry."

Fritz saw the Inland Empire as the means to demonstrate the future to the coastal interests—that is, to the Weyerhaeuser Timber Company. At the moment, however, there was more than enough to accomplish in Idaho.

Phil understood, probably better than his cousin, that a studied approach to their problems was all well and good, but getting individuals to accept the results was something else again. It was too much to expect that those in positions of responsibility and authority would be enthusiastic about any scheme that would diminish their roles, and this was true for managers and owners alike.

Disagreements were not limited to the question of merger in Idaho. They continued to plague the Sales Company. In August 1930, the proposal to move the Sales Company headquarters from Spokane to St. Paul reemerged. In a letter to Phil and Fritz, F.E. reported that T. J. Humbird continued his opposition; his "chief argument seems to be that the Sales Company should be close to the mills, where it can inspect manufacture and shipments of lumber." F.E. thought it unnecessary for Sales Company executives to be burdened with that sort of detail.

Humbird had proposed a meeting on September 15 to consider the question, and F.E. also noted that Laird Bell, "who is acting as Chairman of the Idaho Merger Committee," was also interested in getting together at about the same time. F.E.'s own assessment was not optimistic. "The more I study this merger problem," he wrote, "the more impossible it seems to become, but frequently there is a simple answer to problems which seem extremely difficult." In any event, he was interested in the opinions of Phil and Fritz regarding the location of the main office of the Sales Company, the desirability of proceeding with merger efforts, and whether the Boise Payette sawmills ought to be shut down.

The meetings were called, and it was apparent to most if not all that the Depression conditions required difficult decisions. Four meetings were to be held at the mid-September gathering: (1) a directors' meeting of the Boise Payette Company; (2) the meeting requested by Humbird regarding the Sales Company headquarters; (3) the Idaho merger discussion; and (4) a meeting to consider creation of a service corporation. "Probably at the same time," F.E. thought, "we will get into a general discussion of the lumber situation and how far we should curtail our business, in view of present market conditions."

Had it not been for the hard times, the merger effort would probably have remained on the shelf, but problems and possible solutions could no longer be ignored. Many years later, Phil recalled those difficult days. Perhaps he wished to disassociate himself from the earlier times and circumstances. In any event, his choice of pronouns is interesting. "They," he began, "had a hard time making money; in fact if anybody made any money he was lucky." Indeed, that they made it at all was the result of special circumstances: "The thing that got them through was that they had an enormous inventory of lumber which they could draw on like money in the bank. Of course, they had inventory in trees, too, which they cut free. There was quite a period over there when they were operating on just about break-even cash basis, when the company would realize no depreciation and get nothing for its trees. The only people that got anything out of it were the people working there; they got some salary, some wages."

In those circumstances, even that inventory of lumber had to be used with care. Phil remembered times "so bad that some of the manufactured lumber in the yard would cost more to pick up and put through the planing mill and on board cars than it could be sold for," so one had to be very selective in what was picked up.

It would seem that the decision to shut down might have been made easily. But things were not so simple as they might have seemed at first. Some costs would continue, such as those having to do with interest, fire insurance, and protection. So if at least a portion of those continuing costs could be defrayed, it probably was just as well to keep operating, unless one was willing to declare, in Phil's words, "Not only is it no good now, but it never will be." Few seemed willing to make that declaration.

The merger committee, or Preliminary Committee as they chose to call themselves, included C. R. Musser, T. J. Humbird, Fritz Jewett, and chairman Laird Bell. For Bell, a Chicago attorney, this was his first real introduction to lumber matters, and it was no easy assignment. Laird was the only child of Frederick Somers Bell, then president of the Weyerhaeuser Timber Company, and grandson of William H. Laird, one of the most important of Frederick Weyerhaeuser's associates, especially as concerned the decision to invest in the Pacific Northwest.

Laird Bell, born April 6, 1883, was sixteen years Phil's senior. The difference in years would matter little. The difference in experience and attitudes would matter a great deal. If Phil Weyerhaeuser had learned much of his forestry from Bill Billings, he learned much about the world and worldliness from Laird Bell. Bell was a Harvard graduate, a classmate of Franklin Roosevelt. For reasons that even he had difficulty explaining, he selected law as a profession and was a graduate of the University of Chicago Law School, there a classmate of Harold Ickes, who would be FDR's secretary of the interior. Those school associations were probably less important at the time than some would later presume, although Laird is one of only two in the class of 1907 mentioned by Ickes in his autobiography. One might assume that these two acquaintances, and particularly FDR, help to explain Laird's liberal tendencies, but the fact is, Laird Bell seems to have been born a liberal.

Idaho wasn't exactly an unknown to Laird in 1930. He had made two trips west early in the century, between graduation from Harvard and his decision to go to law school. On the first of these visits, he had been introduced to the fir forest of western Washington and had been amazed at the size of the trees. As to the extent of the Weyerhaeuser Timber Company holdings, that was beyond comprehension. George S. Long had tried to put the matter into understandable terms, estimating that "if two such mills as the Laird Norton Co. [at Winona, Minnesota] were put sawing on the W.T. Co.'s holdings they would require 700 years to finish it—provided the timber didn't grow in the meantime." Laird later traveled into the Idaho country, an easterner clearly out of his element. He found the hotel at Moscow to be "a great big dirty barn"; his father claimed "he recognized the same matches on the floor as three years ago." The town itself was an "awfully ugly place," with nothing to do. Laird "walked up & down the blazing street . . . and grouched," then returned to "a miserable dinner, which you could hardly see through the flies. . . ."

The following summer, 1905, Laird returned to Idaho in something of an official capacity. The Potlatch Lumber Company was in its earliest stages of organization and young Bell was assigned a minor supervisory responsibility. As he described it to his father, "Apparently I am to keep the tab on the number of men employed by contractors and subs, to keep an eagle eye on the surveyors who have no inspectors, and to pacify the settlers generally." In any case, it was not a pleasant experience, requiring more exercise than Laird appreciated. At isolated construction camps, he complained, "it was hot, nobody hospitable, flies thick, dinner wretched." It seems likely that this brief introduction to Idaho lumbering might have encouraged the decision for law school.

In the interim, much had happened to Laird Bell. He was a member of a prestigious Chicago law firm, happily married, the father of four daughters, and already involved in public service. Still, he recognized his lumber heritage and the responsibility that went with it. When he came west in the late summer of 1930, he brought little more with him than his legal experience and his most pleasant and persuasive manner. Whatever he had known of Idaho had been largely forgotten, but he was anxious to learn anew and to be of help. It is doubtful that Bell could have accomplished more had he known more about the subject or the individuals involved. Most important, however, he became well acquainted with Phil Weyerhaeuser and these two would develop a close and lasting friendship—one significant in a business sense and of great personal satisfaction to both.

Subsequent to the initial mid-September meeting, the managers of the Idaho operations received a request for estimates to be used in determining "the relative realization values of the Companies." Thus H. J. McCoy of the Humbird Lumber Company in Sandpoint, A. W. Laird of the Potlatch Lumber Company, C. A. Barton of the Boise Payette Lumber Company, Fritz Jewett of the Edward Rutledge Timber Company, and Phil Weyerhaeuser of the Clearwater Timber Company each had considerable figuring to do. They were asked to estimate: "Present holdings of uncut timber, divided between (a) white pine, (b) Ponderosa, (c) mixed woods, and (d) cedar poles, and segregated as to amounts tributary to each mill operation. State separately timber which it would be economical to carry to mills of other companies. Also state your experience over last three years in overcut by species."

They were also asked to estimate the quality of timber, the probable cost of logging, the acreage of cutover lands, annual capacities and what percentage of these capacities had been operated over the past three years, average overruns, and many other considerations. "Since the purpose is to get at realization, and this involves only *future* cash outlays, it should not include depreciation on equipment and improvements already in." It was to be no simple matter.

The merger committee met again in St. Paul on November 14, and in a letter to John from F.E., but actually written by A. W. "Gus" Clapp, a meeting of principal stockholders was suggested in order to consider the plan. Clapp, a lawyer, was brought in to deal with one of the major obstacles in the way of an Idaho merger: the large outstanding indebtedness of the Clearwater Timber Company—an indebtedness accounted largely to the credit of the Weyerhaeuser family. As of October 1, this Clearwater indebtedness, in the form of stockholders' loans, included $7,055,507.71 owed to Weyerhaeuser family interests, $563,499.81 to Denkmann interests, and $219,700.00 to Humbird interests.

The loans had been guaranteed as far as possible; that is, the agreement with the company was that the indebtedness and accumulated interest would be paid off before any dividends or distributions could be made upon the stock. The Weyerhaeusers could hardly favor an arrangement that would make the loans to Clearwater less secure; and, at the same time, any plan for consolidation that included provision to assume the Clearwater indebtedness on a guaranteed basis could hardly be favored by the non-Weyerhaeuser interests. Chairman Laird Bell seemed on the verge of resolving the problem, or at least it seemed so to Gus Clapp. In exchange for the transfer of assets to the consolidated company, each company would receive debentures and stock of the new company proportional to the value each had contributed to the consolidated organization. Subsequently, that consolidated organization would be responsible for any current liabilities, but not for the sort of permanent indebtedness incurred by the Clearwater Company. In short, the merger would be complete in all respects except that "after the transaction Clearwater Timber Company instead of owning its present assets would own debentures and stock of the consolidated company and it would still have its stockholders' indebtedness."

So the important question for the Weyerhaeusers was whether their loans were as likely to be repaid under the new as under the old arrangement. In fact, not much had changed, for under the merger no dividend or distribution would be made on Clearwater stock until the indebtedness of that company not assumed by the consolidated organization was paid in full. Gus Clapp advised that "under the proposed arrangement our indebtedness would be as certain to be paid, and would be paid about as fast, as under the present circumstances," and the reasons were those that argued in favor of consolidation in the first place: "Neither we nor the other large stockholders would approve of any consolidation unless we believed that the properties as a whole could be more efficiently and economically operated, bringing larger stumpage returns than if the operations were continued by the separate companies." In other words, a healthier whole was more likely to be in a position to repay indebtedness than sick and struggling parts.

Admitting to the likelihood that Boise Payette would not be a party to the consolidation and that Mr. Humbird would refuse to join, the letter from F.E. advised that all subjects related to the merger effort should be treated "as strictly confidential." And he closed by again emphasizing that the one question above all others, from the Weyerhaeuser side of the table, was "whether we would consider the security for loans to the Clearwater Timber Company substantially impaired if Clearwater were to trade its physical assets for the securities of the proposed new company."

There were, of course, other questions and obstacles. Some would continue to argue that there were still legitimate reasons for separate operations, and that the individual managements were best able to respond to individual problems. Even assuming that merger might result in a higher caliber of overall leadership—no small assumption—the top management might be too removed from local circumstances to make proper decisions. The argument was neither new nor without merit. There were also dangers inherent in the tendency of a single board of directors to compare operations that might seem similar from a distance but were actually quite different. No two logging operations were the same, yet the temptation to measure them against each other statistically was strong. They might all deal in man-hours and board feet, but they also dealt with gullies, storms, and labor organizations. Managers emphasized the differences while owners looked for similarities. True enough, there was something comfortable about arguing in behalf of a "unique" situation, one that had to be judged on its own terms, thereby avoiding the pressures of comparative accounting. In any event, much could be said on both sides, and much was.

Another factor, conveniently overlooked by the Weyerhaeusers, was power. As a family and as individuals, they were as sensitive as possible to the concerns of those with whom they were associated, but fairness did not change the rules of the relationship. The number of shares determined the number of votes, and even if Weyerhaeuser shares lacked a majority, it had become expected that there would be enough loyal associates to carry the day. Grandfather Frederick had faced the problem over and over again, and occasionally he had lost. But at least Frederick could recall times when he was not in command. His sons and grandsons had no such experience, and as a group they tended to be impatient with those who wished to go another direction and especially with those who wished an early return on their investment. These two considerations most often troubled the minority stockholders—a lack of any real say, and an occasional immediate need for money. Some investors simply were not always in a position to take the long view of things. To the Weyerhaeusers, to think big usually meant to think in the long term. That may now seem an inevitable corollary to lumbering operations, but it was anything but the case in earlier days.

The merger discussions continued. Carl Stevens was invited to participate, and the firm of Mason and Stevens was subsequently employed to provide the necessary disinterested review of the figures and accounting. As the weeks passed, it seemed more likely that any merger would involve only the north Idaho properties of Clearwater, Potlatch, and Rutledge. Fritz Jewett still hoped to convince Tom Humbird that the Humbird Lumber Company would benefit from involvement, but few others were hopeful. Still, the effort would be made. Phil, looking over statistics for operating capacities and timber reserves, became "increasingly convinced . . . that it will be quite necessary for the Humbird Lumber Company to be included," or so Carl Stevens reported.

But with or without Humbird, the merger plans proceeded. Phil was already giving thought to the organization of the consolidated company, and there seemed to be no doubt in his mind—or in most minds—that he would be its leader. He was also desirous that this would be an organization with a mission, a permanent responsibility. The phrase then current was "sustained yield," and Phil hoped that the new company's title, or at least its logogram or motto, would advertise its sustained-yield operations. Uncle Fred puzzled over this idea and concluded that there was no possibility of getting "into the name of this corporation anything that will adequately suggest the sustained yield features of the operation." And almost as if he had arrived at an answer, he suggested that they manage it through the letterhead, with something like "Sustained Yield Operations Designed to Perpetuate The White Pine Forests of Idaho." Obviously the question required further thought, but it is significant that such matters were seen as important, even without the benefit of experts in advertising and public relations.

F.E. had consulted with H. J. Richardson and F. S. Bell regarding the new company's organization, and both had agreed with Phil's suggestion that "the directors, executive committee and officers of the proposed merger corporation should be made up so far as possible from the younger men in the organization." It is significant that Phil should have taken that position, which was a bit audacious on its face. He was by no means an elder of his generation, but he was clearly emerging as its leader.

Uncle Fred proceeded to offer for Phil's consideration a list of directors agreed upon in conversation with Richardson and Bell: Fritz Jewett, F. K. Weyerhaeuser, Ed Davis, Phil Weyerhaeuser, Laird Bell, George Little, C. R. Musser, Fred Reimers, and H. J. Richardson, "with T. B. Davis, Jr., and T. J. Humbird suggested as alternative or as two additional names if you wish to have a Board of 11 members." It was noted that "this drops from the present board your father, Dr. Clapp, Mr. F. S. Bell, and I think also Mr. R. D. Musser." F.E. further suggested that the officers might be: president, J. P. Weyerhaeuser, Jr.; vice-presidents, H. J. Richardson and Laird Bell; secretary, Fritz Jewett; and treasurer, Allison Laird. F.E. wanted it understood, however, that he was only making suggestions. In Uncle Fred's mind, there was no doubt that Phil's opinion mattered most. Indeed, in the years ahead it would be Phil, the youngest in his family, and F.E., the youngest in his, whose opinions were weighed most carefully in the family.

The work of merging the three companies proceeded slowly, but proceeded nonetheless. Carl Stevens was in constant communication with Phil. Basic to their deliberations was a memorandum prepared the previous fall which stated the objective simply as "the most profitable liquidation of the N. Idaho timber," with four subdivided questions: what timber was to be cut and what left; where it was to be manufactured; how fast was the cutting to proceed; and in what order. The underlying principle was to be that "the timber and plants of the various companies must be considered first as a composite whole, regardless of ownership or capital structure." Once that had been established, six steps seemed in order: (1) the allocation of the blocks of timber to the individual plants; (2) a decision on the operating life of each plant; (3) an allocation of the market demand to each plant; (4) a calculation of the gain that would result; (5) an equitable division of this gain among the ownership; and (6) the creation of an organization capable of securing the results. The principle of sustained yield was included with reference to rates of cutting and the establishment of cutting cycles.

Other than the details, which were, of course, many and complex, the crucial step was the approval of the stockholders of Potlatch, Rutledge, and Clearwater. Potlatch called its special meeting for April 29, the stockholders being advised that they would be asked to vote on

all questions which may arise at said meeting; including authority to vote for approval of plans of reorganization substantially in accordance with the plans referred to in the notice of said meeting, to authorize the change of the present capital stock having a par value of $100 per share to shares without par value, with an increase of the total authorized capital stock to 300,000 shares, to waive any right of the undersigned to subscribe for any portion of said stock which may be used for the acquisition of property, to vote for an increase in the number of the Board of Directors, and for a change of name of the corporation, to amend its By-Laws, and to consent to the declaration of a dividend payable in debentures (and/or scrip therefore), all substantially in accordance with said plans of reorganization and the notice of said meeting. . . .

Those were questions enough for any stockholder's meeting, but the section of the reorganization plan read most carefully was undoubtedly paragraph B, section 3, which stipulated the "Clearwater Timber Company to guarantee Potlatch Lumber Company against liability on any and all claims or demands, except current liabilities as per balance sheet as of January 1, 1931 . . . and stockholders of Clearwater Timber Company holding notes or other obligations of said Company to agree not to look to Potlatch Lumber Company for the payment of said notes or other obligations, with the specific note that current liabilities above excepted do not include any liability on loans from stockholders."

Not surprisingly, some Potlatch stockholders questioned the wisdom of the merger. One wrote at length, complaining that insufficient information on the condition of Rutledge and Clearwater had been provided, and charging that the Potlatch stockholders were being asked to acquire liabilities rather than assets. He closed by observing,

"The officers and directors are responsible for the welfare of *all* of the stockholders, not any group or portion thereof," and that if he were an officer or director, he would certainly oppose the merger, not wanting "to be the subject of a personal liability suit, nor the object of malfeasance or misfeasance proceedings."

But the number of such dissenters was few, at least in terms of votes, and the merger went through, although details of the final organization would drag on well into May. Even after the consolidation of the three companies, Carl Stevens and Phil continued their efforts to convince Tom Humbird that it would be to his advantage, and theirs, if the Humbird organization would also join. Stevens wrote directly to Humbird, expressing confidence that they had arrived at "a reasonable base for liquidation over a period of some length . . . if the market and output are controlled as they may be if a merger is given full effect"—a fuller effect obviously involving the Humbird Company.—And he added ominously, "Any other method of procedure must of necessity attempt to force an unwilling market with consequent severe loss to everyone." Stevens assured Humbird that the inclusion of the Humbird Company could be managed with a minimum of difficulty. And he predicted, erroneously as it turned out, that with a bit more reflection Humbird would agree with "our firm belief . . . that much is to be gained by everyone in their merger."

Stevens had long since ceased to be the disinterested consultant. He admitted to Phil and Laird Bell that he had undoubtedly overstepped his authority, but explained, "I feel the desirability of completing the merger in this manner so strongly that I cannot refrain from butting in." To Phil he added, "I live daily in the hope that your Uncle Fred will get tough on this matter before very long but, of course, realize that action may be delayed until it is pretty late to do anything." As was often the case, others without power assumed that they would act more directly if they had the Weyerhaeuser power. It took time to realize that possessing power did not always translate into its easy or wise application.

By June 5 all the legal details had been resolved and things were sufficiently in order for Phil to assume his responsibilities as president of Potlatch Forests, Incorporated. Following the death of Charles, Phil had been elected president of the Potlatch Lumber Company, a move he realized could not have set well with Allison Laird, the general manager of Potlatch. Phil later observed that Laird "looked upon me as an upstart who was scarcely dry behind the ears." But Allison Laird died shortly after Phil's election, and Jack Irwin became general manager at Potlatch. The team was complete, and Phil was responsible for the former three organizations, now Potlatch Forests, Incorporated.

In the midst of the obvious need for greater efficiency and cost accounting, Phil and the other Potlatch directors were called upon to consider whether to appropriate funds for research. A two-year research program had been authorized by the Potlatch Lumber Company directors in January 1929, and a decision was now required for continuation. Research in the forest products industry had not been a matter of much attention; indeed use of the word "research" seems excessive. For the strongest of organizations, energies and resources seldom seemed sufficient even to manage the moment. But however distant the benefits of research appeared, Phil and others recognized that greater utilization was at least as important as efforts to conserve. And sooner or later, research would be the means to increase utilization in a profitable sense. But as in any research effort, patience was the key. Fortunately Phil had plenty of patience. Usually, that is.

One notable exception occurred when Phil attempted to organize a meeting of Potlatch and Weyerhaeuser Timber Company managers to discuss common labor problems and policies. Phil was beginning to question the wisdom of their continuing allegiance to the Loyal Legion of Loggers and Lumbermen as labor's representative, fearing that a sea of unrest was building behind the dam of conservative 4L leadership. But Rod Titcomb as general manager of the Timber Company showed little interest, and in a telegram of November 2, Phil expressed his disappointment in no uncertain terms. He sarcastically concluded, "I want you to accept my apology and understand that I will not again attempt anything beyond my sphere."

During that summer and fall of 1931, it was almost a welcome relief to read of distant concerns. So it was when Uncle Rudolph reported on his recent visit to the old Weyerhaeuser home in Niedersaulheim. He had planned to pass through anonymously, merely wishing to see the Sangerhalle which "Father gave the town some 25 years ago," but everyone was so pleasant and hospitable that "Louise thought it a shame not to let them know who we were." And so they did. The hall was in need of repair, and Rudolph agreed to underwrite the expense, explaining, "it seemed to be the community center of the town and I am quite sure that Father would approve of my going ahead and doing what I personally thought was the best thing to do." Upon his return to St. Paul, Rudolph found Fred K. absent from the office, and not much doing. He did note, however, that the Sales Company was scheduled to make the long-discussed move to St. Paul the following week.

In the meantime, Uncle Fred and Phil continued to carry on their long-range discussion of forestry policy and practice, with particular reference to the increasing experience with selective logging. In June 1932, F.E. expressed disappointment in a report compiled by Earnest

J. Brigham for Minot Davis, on the subject of selective logging in Longview operations of the Weyerhaeuser Timber Company. Although Phil had no direct involvement at Longview, F.E. was anxious to have his nephew's thoughts. To F.E., the report indicated a need for stronger organization and coordination between cutting operations and marketing strategies. F.E. recalled that a year or so earlier, Tom Humbird had expressed the opinion "that there was a lot of bunk about the whole selective logging program." Although Uncle Fred was unwilling to agree with that pessimistic view, he remained sensitive to the fact that his St. Paul desk was a long way from the western forests and thus wished Phil to be of help. "I am sending this report to you for such criticism of it as you care to make." He concluded, "Perhaps recent experience has somewhat modified your views on selective logging," and added, "I have tried to champion the idea very largely because I have felt that you believe in it, but neither the management nor the Executive Committee of the Weyerhaeuser Timber Company seem to be very keen on the subject." The uncle promised the nephew that he would not mention his name in the course of any future discussion of the report, "but I do wish to know pretty definitely what you think of it, and whether you think I should continue to urge the adoption of the program of the WTC in spite of the probability that Mr. Minot Davis thinks it is largely nonsense." That F.E. valued Phil's opinion was obvious. Their experience differed greatly, but this only served to enhance the importance of their relationship.

Phil studied the report and wrote that he thought it reasonable to begin a selective logging approach in the Longview district, as adapted to the special conditions of Douglas-fir. F.E. made little headway with the Executive Committee of the Weyerhaeuser Timber Company, however, reporting that, when he raised the issue on June 29, and read Phil's letter on the subject, "Mr. Bell made no expression of interest either way," and Clapp, had he expressed himself freely, "would say that he did not believe that it was worthwhile." As a result, F.E. was discouraged. Although he knew he was no expert, he was convinced he had seen enough logs passing through the Everett sawmill "from our Skookum Chuck operation to know that we have wasted a large amount of money by our failure to understand and adopt the principles of selective logging." Phil could almost hear his uncle's sigh as he complained, "I have talked selective logging now for a long time and seem to have made no headway with our Executive Committee." Now he was willing to drop the matter, at least for the time being, "hoping that before long you . . . will be a member of the Executive Committee of the WTC and be in a position to insist on the adoption of some program that will take care of the problem." Although the

problems of western Washington were different from those of the Inland Empire, already F.E. was evidencing greater faith in Phil than in
others then engaged in the production end of things.

F.E. encouraged another use of Phil's experience and abilities. William Carson, president of the Boise Payette Company, died in July, and
Jack Mason expressed interest in having Phil as a member of Boise
Payette's Executive Committee, since the other members, George Little
and Dr. E. P. Clapp, had little practical knowledge of the business.
Uncle Fred urged Phil to accept the position if offered, "but with the
understanding that you can ask Fritz to go to Boise . . . to attend meetings when it is impractical for you to attend." Phil had his doubts, and
in response suggested that Fritz ought simply to be given the responsibility. F.E., however, felt the need for an "operating man" on the
committee, and he looked forward to discussing the matter with Phil.

The fact was, of course, that Phil had more than enough problems
and hard decisions of his own. In October 1932 the Rutledge unit of
Potlatch Forests was shut down. The announcement, over Fritz Jewett's signature as general manager, came on October 7, with the date
of closing November 1. In his statement Fritz called to the attention
of the people of Coeur d'Alene "the fact that excessive taxation is an
important factor in this economic situation," noting that "last year
Potlatch Forests, Inc., paid in taxes and fire charges, a form of taxation, almost exactly a half million dollars." Although the taxes had
been "somewhat reduced this year, we are forced to meet this expense
in December or suffer the confiscation of our property." He indicated
that they looked forward to a return of better times, but at the moment it was "economically possible to run only one operation." Phil,
commenting on the Rutledge closure, noted that the volume of business had "shrunk to such small proportions and . . . its overhead
costs, taxes, firefighting and other expenses involved in the ownership
of timberland and mill properties are so onerous that it is not a matter
of choice, but necessity, that the situation be met by every curtailment
of expense possible."

He further observed that the Elk River plant was into its second
year of shutdown, and that during the past year, 1932, it had been
brought "to a completely idle condition." It was not even shipping
lumber. The Coeur d'Alene mill was shut down "in spite of the fact
that much lumber remains there to be shipped." Finally, the Potlatch
plant had not operated during the past year, "except to ship lumber
in pile." Only the Lewiston plant continued to operate at something
of a full schedule. It must have been difficult for some to believe that
things could have been worse had the merger effort failed completely.

Cousin Ed Davis wrote to Fritz Jewett after receiving word of the
decision to close the Rutledge sawmill, inquiring whether this would

be a permanent arrangement. "You have done a fine job out there," Ed told Fritz, "and I have heard nothing but favorable comments on your work." Davis undoubtedly wrote to Jewett in sincere concern and complete innocence, but the fact was that there had been difficulties within the Potlatch organization. Fritz occasionally assumed positions on issues others in the family considered inappropriate—positions that made it awkward for the corporation, since outsiders were unlikely to distinguish Fritz's private opinions from those of the Weyerhaeusers or of Potlatch management. Phil apparently came down rather hard on Fritz in early 1933, so hard that even Ed Davis heard some of the echoes in distant Cloquet. Again Ed attempted to console his cousin, suggesting, "it would appear that Phil had used very poor judgment." Ed knew next to nothing about the Idaho situation, but nevertheless opined, "Those companies need your help badly and [I] believe you are the only man in the organization that can do the kind of job you are working on now." The Depression was taking its toll on the Wood Conversion Company as well. "Things don't look very good here and if we cannot do much better this year than last I am going to recommend that we fold up" was his own depressed assessment.

As to the most important organization—the Weyerhaeuser Timber Company—George S. Long would have been a most difficult act for anyone to follow. The economic hard times that coincided with his retirement and death were simply additional burdens to an incredibly heavy load. Unfortunately, it all proved to be too much for Rod Titcomb. In fact, it may well have been too much for anyone. It is difficult to say just what kind of leadership was required. The adjective "rock-like" comes to mind, but a great many very able managers went down with their organizational ships in the economic seas of the 1930s.

For those who had been watching with discerning eyes, Phil Weyerhaeuser had demonstrated some very impressive qualities in those difficult years of the Clearwater effort. The Clearwater Timber Company and then Potlatch Forests had been managed as well as could be expected; they had been given effective organizations and sound programs, and had been forced to mark time until general conditions improved. Throughout, Phil kept his poise, doing as much as he could each day and going home satisfied. If he had any doubts, he kept them to himself. To those around him he seemed to work in complete confidence. There was nothing fancy, nothing dramatic about him. "Don't worry about those things we can't control," he seemed to say; "let's just do as much as we can." He didn't expect miracles of himself and certainly not of others. And if Phil wasn't worried, it must be all right.

Thus only those who had not been paying attention could have been much surprised on January 19, 1933, the day following Phil's thirty-fourth birthday, when the trustees of the Weyerhaeuser Timber Company passed the following resolution:

That J. P. Weyerhaeuser, Jr., this day elected as one of the Vice Presidents of the company, is hereby designated as the chief executive officer of the company, to have full charge and control of the management of the company and of its property, business and affairs, and of the property, business and affairs of the company's subsidiaries, with full control and authority over all subordinate officers and employees and with the right and power to prescribe their duties, all subject only to the direction and control of the Board of Trustees, the Executive Committee and the President.

Although Rod Titcomb would continue as general manager, everyone understood that Phil would now be in charge, his position of executive vice-president being created specifically for the situation. Had either Rod or Phil possessed a large ego, there would have been problems. But Rod was probably relieved to be sharing the responsibility. And Phil came not as one riding a white horse but as one wishing to help things along; and he let it be known that he needed the help of everyone, Rod included.

Still there were some who would attribute the appointment simply to the Weyerhaeuser name. R. D. Merrill of the Merrill and Ring Lumber Company may have had these doubters in mind when he addressed a note to R. W. Wetmore, secretary of Shevlin, Carpenter and Clarke Company: "I suppose you know by this time that Mr. Phil Weyerhaeuser has been made executive Vice President of the WTC, effective February 1. He is the man that headed up the Potlatch Forests, Incorporated, and had a great deal to do with the merger of all of the Weyerhaeuser interests in Idaho. I am sure he is going to be a tower of strength. . . ." Time would prove Mr. Merrill right.

As Phil acquainted himself with the Tacoma office and the widespread operations of the Weyerhaeuser Timber Company, as he thought about the political and economic uncertainties, and as he looked for a home for his family—soon to be increased in size— he might be forgiven if he felt anything but a "tower of strength."

CHAPTER 5

The New Order

On January 30, 1933, Rod Titcomb, general manager of the Weyerhaeuser Timber Company, announced the appointment of J. P. Weyerhaeuser, Jr., as the company's executive vice-president. Readers of the *Tacoma Daily Ledger* learned of the appointment the following day in an article on page 2. Almost a week went by before those who subscribed to the *Lewiston Morning Tribune* read that the president of Potlatch Forests was moving to a new position, which "carries with it greater responsibilities and a wider scope of operations." The reporter might have added, "and many of the same old problems."

When Phil moved into his tenth-floor Tacoma Building office in 1933, he was, of course, familiar in a general way with the extent and nature of the company, and he was acquainted with most of its key personnel. Phil knew, for example, that it was still largely a timber company, although recently it had become increasingly involved in production activities. That was part of the immediate problem. New mills had been constructed at Longview, Washington, and Klamath Falls, Oregon, and the Longview sulphite pulp mill was not yet two years old. The construction effort had required an enormous capital commitment, and the production capacities introduced problems of their own: specifically, whether market conditions warranted operating the new plants. It was determined that the Longview sawmill was too efficient to sit idle. The Everett Mill "A," the old mill, was closed instead, subsequently to be turned over to the Everett pulp division, and orders to Everett were directed to Longview. Largely because of the arguments put forth by R. B. Wolf, the Timber Company's authority on pulp and paper matters, the Longview pulp mill also began production, although it didn't operate in the black for at least two years.

Normally, even during hard times, it was difficult for the Timber Company to lose money. It is an indication of the seriousness of the Depression that the company *did* lose money during two years; and had it not been for the manner of bookkeeping, the reports would have been worse—and more accurate. (For example, the fact that taxes were not paid on many properties failed to show up in the accounting, since the books were kept on a cash receipts and disbursements basis.) Still, given the resource base and the efficiency of its new production facilities, the Weyerhaeuser Timber Company was in a position of relative strength.

But relative strength in an industry so decimated was cause for little joy. In the coming months, Weyerhaeuser would be forced to accept responsibilities of an industry-wide nature, since there could be no single, independent approach to problems of this magnitude. How Phil must have wished things were otherwise. In the first place, by instinct he was a business conservative, although it was becoming increasingly apparent that he was to have no choice but to deal, as best he could, with greater governmental involvement in an effort to assist one and all, big and small, efficient and otherwise, in his industry and in the economy in general. Second, he sincerely wished to introduce, at least to make a start, in sustained-yield operations and methods leading to increased utilization, but hard times were simply not conducive to considering such changes. The natural response to hard times was to liquidate the resource, and to do so in the least costly way. Third, he was assuming leadership at the very time when a public role was demanded, and any public role was something he abhorred for reasons primarily personal. Yet to his great advantage, Phil accepted change easily. He was able to focus on long-term objectives to an extent that interim detours or defeats received no more attention than deserved. He could readjust and proceed, his course altered to new circumstances but his direction as before. Like his grandfather, he was basically an optimist.

Unlike his grandfather, Phil was to be denied the luxury of privacy. For the most part, nineteenth-century lumbermen worked in complete confidence of their contribution to the nation's progress. Few people saw any objections to sawmill smoke, noise, and wastes, and the isolated scenes of logging devastation were far removed from the eyes of those who might care. Such was not the case for Phil and his generation. They might claim to be private industrialists, to own the land upon which they operated just as surely as any other American businessman or farmer, but the fact was that everything they did, they did in public view, under public scrutiny. Lumbermen often pointed out that there was simply no way for them to cover up their assets and veil their methods of operation. In any event, the business of lumbering carried with it a public responsibility. To Phil's great credit, private person that he was, he early recognized that the Weyerhaeuser Timber Company could endure and might even benefit from exposure.

Phil can reasonably be called the first full-fledged production chief executive for the Timber Company. Since its 1900 beginning, the company had been managed by George S. Long, but for the most part his efforts had focused on superintending that incredible investment in timber. Blocks of land were sold, traded, purchased, and protected from fire, always with a view to eventual production. But it was hard to manage a wilderness. When Phil assumed the responsibility, it was with the understanding that any commitment over time meant management with the objective of growing trees to replace those harvested. And it was under Phil's leadership that the Weyerhaeuser wilderness gradually became an operating forest. Central to the effort was the belief that careful management of the company's resource base was the proper way to be in the lumber business. It is a belief that was—and still is—open to debate. At the same time, Phil knew that forestry did not pay for itself. How to justify careful resource management thus became one of the continuing challenges of his administration.

It should be noted that Phil had inherited a very capable office staff in Tacoma. In addition to Rod Titcomb were Charlie Ingram, assistant general manager, soon to become Phil's right-hand man; crusty and capable Minot Davis, in charge of timberlands and railroad engineering; Al Onstad, plant engineer, the planner of sawmills; C. S. Chapman, who had graduated in the first forestry class from Yale and was the company forester, although he gave a good deal of his time to matters of lobbying; Gus Clapp, the legal counsel; and E. W. DeLong, who managed the office in addition to working on taxes. It was an effective nucleus, a testimony to the good judgment of George S. Long.

Despite the leadership of Long and his central office, in many respects the Weyerhaeuser Timber Company was a collection of virtually autonomous operations held together in the unarticulated assumption that there was some advantage to association. It was, however, not automatically assumed that even greater centralization would result in increased efficiency. Indeed, Phil would quietly encourage a sort of intramural competition between branches, trusting that he would be conscious of any form of competition destructive to the whole, and would step in and put things in order.

One of the first issues demanding attention was wage policies. Each branch had been making its own determinations in this regard, undoubtedly in recognition of special local circumstances. Phil understood local considerations, but he was unhappy at the absence of any overall policy or philosophy. This he expressed in a letter to Gus Clapp concerning recent wage reductions by the Klamath Falls branch. Although he recognized that any immediate reversal of that decision, "battled . . . out with the men in their 4L group meeting," would be unwise, he also urged that "we give ear and encouragement to a group meeting called at the Shevlin instigation at Klamath to see if some higher base wage could not be agreed to by a substantial part of the production there." He then provided his reasoning:

Without going into detail of why I feel that way, I can say that I believe there is a very close relationship between the base wage paid and the price attitude of the industry, and I believe also that the lumber industry in general is today . . . paying the lowest wage of any major industry in the country. I think further, that there is a very close relationship between the wage which a company is justified in paying and the hours per week which it is at that time able to offer an employee. I feel very strongly that we are going far in encouraging the rapid downward trend of wages by going to $2.00 at Klamath.

He added that he was "very anxious" that the Timber Company "both on the coast and at Klamath . . . lend ourselves to a movement vigorously to stabilize wages at some point, literally to my mind, the higher the better." And as he would commonly do in the early days of his new responsibility, Phil inquired, in apparent innocence, whether he might be exceeding his authority. In this instance, however, he simply allowed, "I am sure that when I go too far, I shall be properly corrected."

It was not only in the matter of wages that some cooperative approach within the industry seemed worthy of consideration. The year 1932 had been so disastrous for Pacific Northwest lumbermen that the possibility of merging corporations had received serious attention. Laird Bell's contribution to the Idaho consolidation was widely recognized, and accordingly he had been called into the Douglas-fir region to direct a similar effort. If there had been frustrations in Idaho, there at least had been the advantage of common ownership. No such advantage existed west of the Cascades and, by February 1933, Bell was already discouraged. To Phil he admitted that "this possibility looks more remote now than it did in June." Things appeared so unpromising that Laird wondered whether he was wasting his time, although he saw no easy way "to let go in the present stage of proceedings."

Regarding the merger effort and its worth, Phil seemed to hold no doubts. "Certainly you can have no serious thought of ceasing at the present time," he wrote to Bell. The reasons favoring merger were as legitimate as they had been in the Inland Empire. By means of consolidation, the timber resources could be more efficiently utilized, production could be more effectively managed, and the product more carefully marketed.

One of Phil's early involvements was perhaps more closely related to the merger effort than he initially appreciated. The Clemons Logging Company had previously received relief in a timber purchase contract that permitted a reduction in the price of its logs, and competition in log prices was one of the incentives for a cooperative approach. Phil noted that he had received a plea from Minot Davis for a continuation of that relief beyond the first of April, but Phil was not convinced that the Grays Harbor mills operated at such a disadvantage as to warrant the lower prices. As he told Laird, he was about to write to Colonel William B. Greeley of the West Coast Lumbermen's Association, hoping to "smoke out" the facts of the situation. In short, Phil was unwilling simply to take Davis's word for it.

Not only did he consult with Colonel Greeley, but he corresponded with Laird Bell and Carl Stevens. "It occurred to me," he wrote Stevens, "that possibly you or Laird might like to submit a brief aimed at some particular line of action." Central to the Grays Harbor question and to coastal log prices in general was the problem of too many operators, resulting in competition that was destructive to all. A merger of the Clemons Logging Company, formerly independent but now a subsidiary of the Weyerhaeuser Timber Company, with the Saginaw Logging Company, an organization headed by A. J. Morley, seemed logical. But loggers had an independent nature, and long years of competition had hardened differences and consciences as well.

In this instance, the Grays Harbor mills argued that they could not continue to operate given current log prices. Minot Davis accepted the argument and unilaterally cut Clemons's prices. A. J. Morley learned of this reduction while in the East and rushed to pay Laird Bell a visit in Chicago, "in a state of considerable indignation." Not only did Laird wonder about the "equity in our taking a loss on timber in order to permit . . .[the mill operators] to make a profit," he also questioned the advisability of appearing to act alone. He was, however, quick to admit to being completely at a loss how to proceed. Laird had no idea what he should tell the Morleys, so he was "still playing hide and seek." Should Phil "think of any tactful way of inviting the Morleys to commit harikari, don't hesitate to send me a wire."

As in the Inland Empire matter, Laird and Phil were consulting together, confident in what each brought to the discussion. As Laird wrote, "When I start to tell a story like the above, I realize how complicated the whole thing is, and how impossible it really is to convey this sort of story by letter. I would infinitely have preferred to talk with you about it. I have felt, however, that your coming to Tacoma would change the aspect of a good many of our problems including the Clemons-Saginaw problem, and that it was just as well to wait until you were a little more firmly established."

There was another important facet to the Grays Harbor controversy: the relationship with William G. Reed of the Simpson Logging Company. Reed and Simpson had been a party to the merger negotiations, and for this and other reasons both Phil and Laird wished to maintain good feelings between managers. Regarding stumpage and log prices, Laird suggested that Phil talk with Reed. By this, Laird did not mean that Reed should set Weyerhaeuser prices:

... but I do think that if there is any justification for any such differential between the Harbor and the Sound, or if it may fairly be contended that the cut has not resulted in a slashing of prices, Mr. Reed is broad enough minded to see it and agree. If there isn't any justification, Mr. Reed can give you the ammunition to use on Grays Harbor. He would be keenly alive to the political and public aspects of the situation. And above all, Mr. Reed, like any one else, would be sensitive to the compliment of having been consulted and would feel that the new era implied a closer relationship than has existed in the past.

Indeed, a new era had arrived. Franklin Delano Roosevelt had warned the nation about fear in his inaugural address, but the times were so bad that even the Weyerhaeusers wished the Democrat in the White House good luck and Godspeed. Phil took a brief vacation to move his family from Lewiston to Tacoma. One of his first decisions after he returned to the office concerned the Grays Harbor controversy. "After as careful consideration as time would permit," Phil decided that the log prices should be raised 75 cents, or back to the levels of the previous December. He gave his reasons in a letter to Gus Clapp, but admitted that "this was not a matter on which I could convince him [Minot Davis], and as a consequence he agreed to it only under order." Phil gave early evidence in Tacoma of that willingness to do what needed to be done, and the fact that his initial adversary had been Minot Davis was lost on no one—certainly not on Minot. Not only had he faced an angry Minot, Phil had gone directly into the lion's den—to Grays Harbor—for "a meeting staged for my benefit" with the various representatives of all the mills. Although presented with "a good show," Phil remained firm in his decision, "convinced that the thing to do is to leave our prices for April as indicated, $7.00, $10.00, and $12.00."

Phil later recounted the Grays Harbor meeting to Carl Stevens, indicating that he had been informed by the manufacturers there that some 20 million feet of lumber had been booked uncut, the decision on whether to fill the orders depending on the log prices. "This made me very sad," he said with tongue in cheek, "and I realized then for the first time how arbitrary the Weyerhaeuser Timber Company was being." He might have been tempted to reply that had only the Timber Company's interest been considered, no logs of any sort would be sold on that market.

To a considerable extent, Phil was feeling his way in his new responsibilities, but as Grays Harbor evidenced, his approach was anything but tentative. Corresponding with F. S. Bell, Laird's father and president of the Timber Company, he told of making a start in familiarizing himself with past policies and procedures:

It will not be possible for me to digest the situation rapidly and I shall not try to. Coming out on the train, Mr. [William L.] McCormick showed me the minutes of the Executive Committee from its inception, and I ran through it carefully. The chief thing which remained with me as an impression was the fact that the Committee has apparently been called upon to decide on an increasing number of detailed questions. From something which you said to me when we first discussed my coming over here, I have the impression that it is not the wish of the Executive Committee to be called upon to act upon a number of detailed problems in the future. I wish, of course, to guide myself carefully in the matters which I assume for decision, and will find Mr. McCormick, no doubt, of immense help.

William L. McCormick was officially the company secretary, but more than that, he was its organizational memory. Furthermore, Phil could consult easily with Bill, since their relationship was mutually nonthreatening.

F. S. Bell responded to Phil's "pleasant" letter in a relaxed manner. He suggested that Phil judge matters freely for himself and proceed accordingly, "falling back on the Executive Committee where you do not feel comfortable to act." There were, of course, practical limitations; the members of the committee were going to be scattered for the next several weeks and Phil would be pretty much on his own. Bell observed, with an indication of past problems: "I note that you were surprised to find the number and character of things that have been referred to the Executive Committee. Privately I would intimate that when Mr. Titcomb found the Committee inclined to criticize him on two or three matters he lost initiative to a certain extent and used the Committee much oftener than he needed to." He closed by repeating the expectation that Phil would "seek counsel when you feel you need it, though for the immediate future it is going to be hard to get much." It had to be taken as an expression of confidence.

Phil had already decided to take the Klamath Falls wage question to the Executive Committee, probably because he felt it an example of a larger problem worthy of serious consideration. He remained convinced of the close relation between the base wage paid in the industry and its "price attitude," and he could not believe that the industry was "doing itself any good in repeated and continued cuts in the base wage." Gus Clapp, however, saw no need to involve the committee in the Klamath Falls matter. "I am quite sure," he wrote, "that in all details of the operation, as well as in all current matters of policy, the committee expects you to use your own judgment at all times." If there were any doubts, he added, "it was to obviate the weakness in our whole business structure which resulted from a committee thousands of miles away passing upon matters of this sort that we were so anxious to have somebody who could and would take the responsibility of conducting the business in the west." That was clear enough. There would, however, be disagreements down the road between Executive Committee and executive vice-president, and freedom of action would seem less assured and less appealing. In the meantime, the larger operators at Klamath Falls had agreed to a 30-cent hourly minimum. Although Phil had his doubts that this could be maintained throughout the pine territory, it was an effort in the desired direction.

In the spring of 1933, lumbermen could speak more surely of problems than of solutions. They saw their own depression to be the result of overproduction in the face of declining demand. Excessive production had been the problem long before the Depression. The nature of the industry admitted any number of small operators. Entry into the competition was so easy that start-ups often occurred with no apparent consideration for long-term profitability. Invariably, harder times would require that resources be liquidated, again not with any view of economic operation but simply because of an immediate need for cash to meet interest on indebtedness. If such had been the traditional dilemma, the years following the boom period of the mid-1920s gave it unprecedented emphasis.

There were, however, other causes for the tendency to overproduce. The tax rates on privately owned timber varied greatly from region to region and often from county to county. The higher the rate, or so it was often argued, the greater the incentive to liquidate, to cut and run. Thus companies formulated different and often conflicting strategies. In an industry known for its independent and individualistic personalities, the natural disdain for cooperation had been encouraged out of fear of antitrust charges. But in truth, self-regulation in the lumber industry, which usually translated into efforts to curtail production, was, as one nineteenth-century observer noted, "just so much smoke."

An additional problem, many feared, was the possibility of unrestricted sale of timber from public lands in competition with privately owned timber. Not uncommonly, a single operation would purchase timber, from whatever source, in volumes that made sense internally but failed to consider the available market. Manufacturing and sales responsibilities lacked integration. Sustaining employment was another complication, especially in communities solely dependent on lumber manufacture. Finally, natural disasters often dictated the direction and extent of operations. Timber damaged by fire or insects had to be salvaged immediately if it was to have any value.

In discussing these problems, Fred K. wrote a lengthy letter to Fritz Jewett in Coeur d'Alene. Fred had just finished reading a bulletin published by the National Lumber Manufacturers Association entitled *Forest Resources of Nation Found To Be Adequate.* The Weyerhaeusers had been stressing that point for years, primarily in opposition to the Forest Service projections of a pending timber exhaustion. The booklet had listed ten items necessary to improve the lumber business: better logging and milling methods, wider use of by-products, industrial integration, modification of taxation methods and practices, cheaper credit, restriction of public timber sales, transfer of some mature timber from private to public ownership, regulation of cutting, mergers, and modification of antitrust laws.

Fred reacted to the booklet with enthusiasm. Regarding the first two items, he thought that they might be combined as a "greater utilization of the products of the tree," involving research leading to new products as well as greater efficiency in logging and manufacturing. Cheaper credit he saw as two very separate concerns: first, a method of financing that would permit carrying timber on a sustained-yield basis—in other words, tying the rate of interest to the rate of timber growth of productivity; and second, the development of programs of credit financing that would enable contractors to build houses of wood, and families to buy them. In fact, a number of organizations were already entering the field, among them the National Home Finance Corporation of Chicago and the Lumbermen's Finance Company of Winona, Minnesota.

President Hoover had made a start in limiting the sale of public timber and in transferring timber from private to public ownership. Regulation of cutting as a part of the sustained-yield program was also making headway. Laird Bell had been spearheading efforts to achieve more economic operation by merging pieces into wholes. The Supreme Court seemed to have modified the Sherman Antitrust Law in its Appalachian Coal decision. In short, there was movement along a number of these lines, but so much more needed to be done.

Perhaps it was something of a relief for Fred K. to push aside the daily problems of the Sales Company to consider questions of a larger and more abstract nature. He seemed to enjoy opportunities for reflection, and he also accepted the responsibility of sharing his reflections with others, most notably his brother Phil. More often than not, Phil would shake his head, suggesting that Fred was interested in too many things, that he had "too many balls in the air." In a sense, Phil suffered from tunnel vision. If there was a task at hand, or a problem to be faced, it would receive Phil's entire attention. The ability to concentrate was his forte, and he had little patience for those who seemed uneven in their commitment—whose involvement was temporary or tentative. There was steadiness in his being. Thus Phil's evenings belonged genuinely and completely to Helen and family. He had earned the end of his working day and what went with it—the greeting hug from Helen almost as if the separation had been one of months rather than hours, the relaxed participation in domestic dialogue, the cool bite of a martini, and the softness of the sofa. Nothing special, but special nonetheless.

Laird Bell had not been released from his leading role in the merger efforts, and he was becoming increasingly frustrated with his lack of progress. It appeared to him that Weyerhaeuser "held the parasol over" many of their competitors by curtailing production, providing logs, and generally seeing to it that business went ahead as usual, or as best it could, while the fruitless discussions ground slowly to nowhere. Even friend Bill Reed seemed to have joined the list of growing disappointments. "He sees nothing to be gained by a merger," Laird concluded, and "prefers to go his own way." And he inquired of Phil:

Why don't we go our way, too? Can't we lick him & his pee wee logs on realization?

Lastly, we have threatened these good folks, in a polite way, with what we could, and would have to do if we can't get mergers. Why not give some point to these arguments? If our property is as good as we think we can run them ragged, always with the help of the benign principles of selective logging.

Laird was obviously in a cynical mood. He had tried to relax by playing golf with Al Raught, manager at Longview, but even that pleasure was dampened by concerns of business. He reported to Phil that they had argued about the 4L throughout the match, explaining he had defended the organization "after I found which side he was on." It was not unusual for Laird to take issue simply on general principles, usually supporting the underdog. Many years later, Robert Hutchins told of a meeting in which Bell had "vehemently defended Roosevelt," only to admit afterward, "I am against Roosevelt when I am alone."

Laird received some encouragement from Carl Stevens, who worked closely with him on the merger discussions. Laird had decided to try another tack: sit back and wait for an expression of sincere interest on the part of others. Carl had some thoughts of his own. "I don't suppose there is any reason why I should go into a long harangue in an attempt to continue what you call your education," he wrote. But he did, and among other suggestions, advised that Laird's "coyness should be accompanied by some outward evidence that there is a brick in the mitten." He went on: "That the W.T. Co. is willing to lead but not march alone with nothing but the banner; that the company proposed to have the fair share of all business and will take immediate steps to get it . . . I merely report again that this can be done to some extent without breaking the log price, and anyway, why is it always the W.T. Co. who breaks the price?"

Stevens concluded by urging that Laird not be discouraged by "failing to revolutionize this entire industry within a very short time." The important thing was that they had seen movement. There were other reasons for optimism. "With the sort of intelligent help and cooperation with Phil in Tacoma," Stevens was confident that Laird was "going to win through with a really constructive program." Speaking as an outsider with feelings of an insider, he allowed that it seemed to him that the Timber Company was being too reticent. Now was the time "to start showing some teeth . . . and show just how thoroughly tough a proposition that Company can be if the others continue to expect it to carry the banner alone." Such a display would inspire courage in the others and they would shortly enlist in the cause. "They will, if only because they must, come to time and be good dogs." But as Stevens must have known, that would not be the way.

Aside from business concerns, these were extremely difficult days for Phil and his family. They had arrived in Tacoma on the first of March, and more than the usual domestic responsibilities devolved upon Phil, since Helen was approaching the end of her pregnancy. There was a good deal of hired help, of course, but there was much that simply could not be delegated. Elizabeth Hunt was born on April 19, 1933, and she had none too easy a time of it for the first several weeks. Only four days after the arrival of Elizabeth, or Wiz as she was soon called, Anna died. It had not been an easy life, but she must have taken tremendous satisfaction in her boys and their accomplishments.

Phil was required to leave Tacoma almost immediately after the funeral to attend an Executive Committee meeting in Chicago May 1. On the agenda was a report from Laird Bell. He opened with the simple statement, "I have to report lack of progress or worse as a result of my April trip to the Coast." He explained in detail where matters stood in each of the four merger efforts—northern Washington, the Portland district, the Willamette Valley, and Klamath. All in all, Bell could not recommend that the efforts be continued. "There is no use pretending that I am not very much disappointed in the developments," he said. "I hate to let go." At the same time he could not in conscience advise further effort. In a manner so typically Bell, he concluded, "The results to date consist very largely of a pleasant course of education for one of your stockholders, and that would be rather an expensive policy if widely applied."

But as they approached the summer of 1933, much was happening in the world to place the merger questions, however important to Laird and Phil, in some perspective. Fred K. had gone to Chicago to attend meetings at the Drake Hotel May 24 and 25. Called together by John Blodgett, president of the National Lumber Manufacturers Association, the assembled lumbermen would discuss Senate Bill S–1712, "To Encourage National Industrial Recovery. . . ." Although only recently introduced, this bill was thought to be "one of the cornerstones of the program of the Roosevelt Administration," or so Fred described it in a letter of May 26.

It was with a mixture of hope and foreboding that the Weyerhaeusers viewed these developments. After noting that for as long as he could remember, Weyerhaeuser interests had attempted "to fix prices and to control unruly competition in some way but have been prevented by fear of the Sherman Antitrust Laws," Fred K. proceeded to outline what he thought the National Industrial Recovery Act proscribed. The bill would suspend the antitrust laws for industries that adopted an approved program. Thereafter any who violated that trade agreement, "whether in the matter of wages, hours of labor, exceeding of production quotas, or cutting of prices," would be held in violation of the law. Apparently, he concluded, "not only may we break the Sherman Law, but we are compelled to do so."

Despite the many uncertainties, two things seemed obvious: there would soon be some curtailment of the manufacture of lumber, and prices would be raised to allow for an increase in wages. Accordingly, from strictly a company consideration, it seemed desirable to produce as much lumber as possible before any production controls took effect and at present costs, since the resulting inventory would be "good property." As president of the Sales Company, Fred K. took the occasion to announce that Weyerhaeuser was raising prices "$1.00 per M straight through, on all items, in practically every market and in every species." Furthermore, and for the moment, "we are inclined to discourage orders in the belief that lumber will be better sold a month or two months hence."

The National Industrial Recovery Act became law June 16. Envisioned as the basis for a healthier business climate, it was indeed intended to be one of the cornerstones of administration policy and programs. Title I of the law detailed the method by which "codes"—rules and regulations—could be established for every type of industry. Representatives of each industry would write their own code; and provided that the administration gave its stamp of approval, each code would become, in a sense, a charter. It was only under those terms that operations would be permitted. Although the act was specifically designed to contribute to economic recovery, there was much of reform in the plan. Section 7a encouraged collective bargaining, designated maximum hours and minimum wages, and attempted to eliminate child labor. By any definition, it was a monumental effort. General Hugh Johnson, accustomed to difficult assignments, was given the responsibility of heading the National Recovery Administration, a task he likened to "mounting the guillotine on the infinitesimal gamble that the ax won't work." Within two years the Supreme Court would declare the National Industrial Recovery Act unconstitutional in *Schechter Corp. v. The United States*—the famous "sick chicken" case—but few if any could foresee that development with certainty in the summer of 1933, and everyone was expected to work hard and make the best of the situation.

Phil was soon attempting to exert some influence in the consideration of quota formulas to be used for production allocations of the lumber code. The formulas suggested were many: smaller operators argued in favor of a determination based simply on production capacities in an eight-hour day, while the larger producers maintained that other factors deserved to be included. Early on, Phil thought he was achieving some success in injecting taxes and timberlands into the quota-making process.

F.E. had been invited to sit as a permanent member of the Emergency National Committee for the lumber industry, although word of his appointment was delayed and he arrived late for the July meeting in Washington, D.C. When he reached the scene, he found that the "members had pretty well worn themselves out in discussion." His initial contribution was to suggest that Laird Bell serve as "the Drafting Committee," to settle impasses regarding the wording of resolutions. This "resulted in speeding up our work tremendously." Getting persons to serve would prove to be another problem. It had been "pretty well accepted" among lumbermen that Harry Kendall of the Weyerhaeuser Sales Company would be asked to serve as the executive of the Emergency Committee, but he had informed both F.E. and Fred K. that he preferred to stay in the Sales Company. F.E. expressed the hope that John Tennant, vice-president of Long-Bell, would take "more and more kindly to the suggestion that he accept the position, though I can scarcely see how the Long-Bell Lumber Company can afford to let him do so."

Regarding the code of trade practices, the wholesalers had been attempting to delay consideration until the general code had been filed. What was necessary, according to F.E., was "to get it adopted and in such form that all questionable trade practices will necessarily be brought out into the open." His own thought was that this could well prove to be "the most important thing that we can hope to accomplish"; minimum prices would mean little if dealers were "permitted to mix grades, substitute species, or give unusual concessions in the way of commissions without all this information being brought into the open." F.E. concluded his letter to Phil with a prediction that they could expect a considerable offensive to be "made by our emotional forester friends" who view this as "a rare opportunity to force upon the lumber industry all of their theories and imaginings in relation to the maintenance of our forests." In that prediction, he was entirely correct. But, as events would prove, this was one of the happier results.

Keeping board members current with the affairs of the Timber Company without overburdening them was a delicate problem. Uncle Fred offered mild complaint in late July that those in St. Paul were much concerned about a strike in Klamath Falls; the only information they had received had come by way of their competitors. He reminded Phil that they were "a long way from your operations and of course are anxious to learn what is going on." Phil reacted, sending a lengthy letter to F.S. Bell concerning the labor situation. Central to the problem was the anticipated wage increase, which would be effective with the official enforcement of the NRA lumber code. The situation varied from plant to plant. At Klamath Falls, the AFL leadership called a strike in late July, demanding more pay and shorter hours. Following a meeting with company representatives, the union officials agreed to halt the strike, but IWW interference prevented a sufficient number from returning, so the sawmill remained shut down. On August 4 the work force returned, the Timber Company having announced that it would pay according to code wage scales retroactive to August 1 and would adjust the workday to what the code prescribed.

Clemons had also been struck for some three weeks, as had all the Grays Harbor operations. But for Phil, the greater immediate problem was how to make the adjustment for those on salaries, a problem complicated by the difference in the workweek between woods and sawmill personnel. He indicated to F.S. Bell:

There will be some inequities whatever we do if we assume a general policy. . . . As you know, none of this is related to earning power of the company. The government has simply asked us to pay in the hopes that as a result of it we can maintain our earnings, or increase them. My analysis of the question, therefore, is based entirely upon what to do in view of the past relationship between salaries and wages in this Company. Were I left to my own devices, I believe that I should now, even in the face of further advances in the near

future, raise all salaried men 10%, effective for the month of August. I say
this with no conviction, but simply for you to have something to shoot at.

The question may have lost some of its urgency in the miles that
separated St. Paul from Tacoma, but Phil knew that a decision would
be required very soon after the approval of the lumber code.

President Bell was supportive in his response, but as usual indicated
that it was really a matter deserving Executive Committee attention
and, as usual, the Executive Committee was difficult to get together.
In the meantime, Phil was to feel free to use his own best judgment
regarding an increase for those who had experienced salary reductions, "somewhat equivalent to the wage cut in common labor." No
final decision was forthcoming on the code, and the pressures for a
company determination continued to mount in the woods and at the
plants. In view of this, Phil had decided that the "politic thing" was
to restore wages to levels prior to the last reduction, again retroactive
to August 1. The action meant a general increase in salaries of about
15 percent. He had, of course, expected that by mid-August the details
of the lumber code would have been known and approved, but having
no word by the end of the month, he deemed some action necessary.
F. S. Bell's response was as before, and Phil in turn responded, "It does
not seem reasonable ... to ask you to do more than tell me to take
the responsibility, which you did and for which I thank you."

Two days later, on August 19, the president approved the lumber
code. As had been expected, the basic workweek was set at forty
hours for both woods and mill employees, with a 42.5-cent hourly
wage scale, the latter allowing for some regional differences. Operators could show their acceptance of the terms by going to the local
postmaster and signing the president's reemployment agreement, thus
indicating their intention to comply with the code. There they could
pick up their "Blue Eagles," decals that symbolized their cooperation
with the program.

Phil would learn of the NRA developments from many sources, but
without doubt he most looked forward to Laird Bell's report, to which
he received an introduction in an August 22 note:

From time to time during the late madness in Washington, I tried to crystallize
my ideas as to what this whole business of the NRA and its codes might mean
to the Weyerhaeuser Timber Company and thought that I would favor you
with a summary of my valued views. I decided, however, that there is no place
so bad as Washington for forming an opinion on anything and that I had
better wait in the North Woods awhile to see how my ideas jell. The thing
may work. As I feel about it at present, and as the Recovery Act is being
administered, I think the chances are the other way. But that is not a very

valuable contribution to the solution of your problems and for the present you had better assume that my views are unsettled but apprehensive.

A lengthier and even more pessimistic assessment came from Gus Clapp. Gus tried to prepare Phil for what might be expected in the days ahead, particularly concerning the leadership of Colonel Greeley, whose West Coast Lumbermen's Association administered the code for the region's producers. He noted that each district or division would be required to submit to the Lumber Code Authority its own formula for allocating its quota of production between the various member plants. In the interim, the business would simply be allotted on the basis of hours of production, which would probably be construed "to require everybody getting equal hours." The problem was to prevent the interim arrangement from becoming the permanent solution.

The divisions could consider any one or more of five factors, giving them each the proportional value agreed upon, "the only limitation being that they shall not give more than 10% to taxes and not more than 15% to timber owned." Greeley's position, as Phil had understood from the beginning, was to ensure that every mill be allowed to operate "at a reasonable rate," and Clapp assumed that in Greeley's mind a reasonable rate amounted to a forty-hour week. Such a general allocation would probably use up the entire production quota for the division. In other words, Greeley would give full consideration to the first factor—hourly capacity—and this, in effect, would permit all the small mills, "none of which had ever run more than one shift," to operate as they always had, while those double-shift plants would have their production reduced by at least half.

But criticizing Bill Greeley was no easy matter. No one commanded greater respect, and even Gus Clapp was willing to acknowledge that the colonel was a man of "great value to the West Coast industry, and . . . to the industry throughout the country." Nonetheless, in this instance, Clapp saw "a real animus toward the larger operators." Greeley had argued that unless all the mills were given the opportunity to continue operations, there would be "hell to pay" in the West Coast Lumbermen's Association. But Gus wondered that there would not be just as much "hell to pay" if the large operators were treated unfairly.

The course seemed clear enough, although it promised to be difficult for any one company. Thus Gus advised Phil: "If your ideas with regard to what is fair are in agreement with mine, and if you see no internal or local reason why you should not raise a fuss, I suggest that you start out and get together a group as large as you can of people who will not get what they are entitled to under a 'soup bowl' kind of formula for control of production." (The "soup bowl" referred to

Greeley's desire to divide the quota kettle to ensure that everyone received a portion.)

Clapp thought the issue was of such importance that past relationships should be forgotten. He suggested that the group might include, for example, the Weyerhaeuser mills, Long-Bell, Bloedel-Donovan, St. Paul and Tacoma Lumber Company, the large Portland mills, and perhaps Coos Bay. As if to stress the seriousness of the situation, Gus sent his lengthy letter by a new means—air mail—in hopes that Phil would have it by the time Greeley reached the coast. Gus emphasized that it was important that Phil manage the business himself, noting that "one of the embarrassing things to Tennant and myself was the fact that . . . Rod [Titcomb] had agreed that Col. Greeley's idea was right." In Clapp's view, "If there is going to be a firm stand taken in this matter, there should only be one person speaking for your company, and that is yourself."

Phil received another side to the story from Laird Bell, who acknowledged: "It is quite true that I came to have great confidence in Colonel Greeley. He was clear-headed, forceful, always on the job, and, so far as I could see, entirely honest with all of us. He was not, of course, representing the Weyerhaeuser Timber Company. He would not have been honest if he had done so. He was representing the West Coast Lumbermen's Association, which, whether we like it or not, is an association of individual units, small as well as large, and controlled by the small units."

Laird said that he did not think it fair to charge Greeley with being overly concerned with the small producers. After all, there were more small operators than large, and perhaps the "emphasis should be upon the protection of the small unit." Without saying it directly Laird was confident that Weyerhaeuser would endure the moment with or without Greeley's help. The same could not be said of its smaller competitors. In any event, he felt that there was "legal justification . . . and plenty of political justification" for the colonel's position. Of the other association leaders, Laird was less certain, although he did note that they were very fortunate in having Arthur Bruce as executive officer of the Lumber Code Authority. That he was writing to Phil so openly on what was obviously a delicate subject indicates that Laird recognized Phil as a kindred spirit. Even if there were differences in opinion, they were not beyond discussion. Laird seemed confident that the two of them had advantages not shared by the preceding generation: an ability to respond with flexibility, to modify the instinct.

As if there had not been sufficient worries during that 1933 summer, word reached Tacoma in mid-August of a terrible fire in northwestern Oregon. Apparently it had started on August 14 in the Crossett Western logging operations along Gales Creek. According to State Forester

Cronemiller, it had probably started from friction when a log was dragged across a low windfall. On August 26, Phil's information on losses was still sketchy. But it was already clear, as he reported to Laird, that the fire was "without doubt the biggest fire that ever occurred in the state of Oregon and will leave several billion feet of timber to be salvaged." It would be known as the Tillamook burn. The losses were disheartening. So were the attempts to rearrange existing plans with a view to salvaging as much as possible as efficiently as possible.

Although those in St. Paul could hardly comprehend the extent of the Tillamook loss, Phil did receive an expression of sympathy from F. S. Bell. "This fire will create one of your major problems," the president of Weyerhaeuser wrote, "but it is too early to discuss at present." He did add, "I am sorry on your account that it had to come." Little else could be said. Gradually the details began to arrive. The losses in three counties—Tillamook, Washington, and Yamhill—were estimated at 14 billion feet, more than the previous year's output of softwood and hardwood lumber, paper pulp, and other wood productions for the entire United States.

The Weyerhaeuser interest involved was the Wilson River Company. Substantially all the company holdings were "burned thoroughly." Reminding the Weyerhaeuser directors that they owned 70 percent of the Wilson River stock and held notes of more than a million dollars, Phil assured them that the opportunity to conduct salvage logging operations in the burned area would receive "the most serious consideration."

With that in mind, Laird Bell addressed a committee of owners from the burned-over region in early October. Bell was convinced that given the extent of their mutual tragedy, they would be ready to consider a collective approach. As Laird saw the situation, for the benefit of operators and the affected communities, the salvage effort ought to be approached "as a social and economic problem rather than a problem of the individual owners." Given the deteriorating condition of the timber, the most fundamental question would be the market: could it absorb 300 million feet of burned logs? The effects of the lumber code on the problem were as yet unclear, but certainly would not "make the disposition of the logs any easier."

According to Laird, the owners had only two choices. Individually they could "rush for the exits, with every owner scrambling to salvage what he can in competition with every other owner," or they could join together in some form of unified action. Such action might involve an outright merger of properties or simply the pooling of excess logs—those not used by the sawmills of the owners—for sale. Arguing for a unified approach, Laird pointed out that regardless of the

The Frederick Weyerhaeuser family on the porch of their Rock Island home, the House on the Hill, ca. 1890. From left to right: Margaret, Frederick E., Rudolph M., Elise, Frederick, Charles A., John Philip, Sarah, and Apollonia.

(*Above*) John Philip Weyerhaeuser, ca. 1925; (*left*) Nellie Anderson Weyerhaeuser, ca. 1898.

Frederick and Sarah Weyerhaeuser with grandchildren Elizabeth and Frederick King, 1895.

Phil Weyerhaeuser modeling the fashions of the day. Being five years old was obviously not all fun and games.

Young Phil seems a bit doubtful about his driving skills, but sister Elizabeth and brother Fred appear reasonably confident.

Dominoes was a serious game, and even more so when posed for the photographer.

The fish of Lake Nebagamon seem in no present danger at the hands of Phil, Fred K., and their father J. P. Weyerhaeuser.

Lake Nebagamon provided many pleasures, not the least of which was just fooling around in the water. Doing the fooling: Phil, Miss Aimee, Elizabeth, Lawrence Noyes, and Fred K.

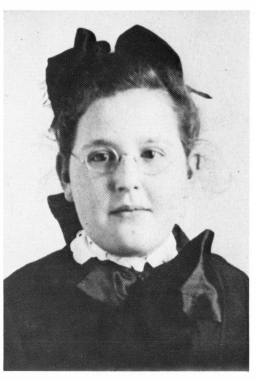

(*Above left*) Elizabeth, age thirteen; (*above right*) Frederick K.,
age ten; (*right*) Phil, age six.

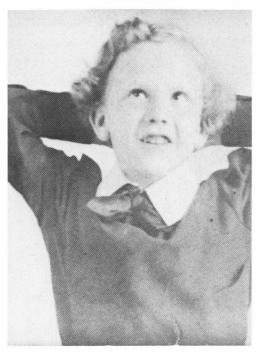

Anna Holbrook Weyerhaeuser with her two young knights, Phil and Fred K.,
1907.

An elderly Frederick Weyerhaeuser, neat and attractive, momentarily absorbed in a letter that doubtless involved either family or business matters.

(*Above*) The male cousins Phil, Fritz Jewett, Fred K., and Ed Davis on a Mississippi River trip aboard the *F. Weyerhaeuser*, ca. 1908; (*left*) Phil prepared to fight for the honor of the Hill School, 1915.

(*Above*) Members of John Markham's cruising party in the summer of 1916: H. F. Johnson, W. F. Fullenwider, Phil, and Fred K.; (*left*) Phil Weyerhaeuser, an obviously proud second lieutenant in the artillery, in the summer of 1918.

A family gathering, ca. 1920. Seated in front: C. Davis, Fred K., and Frederick. Frances Maud Moon Weyerhaeuser is seated with fan. Center row, standing, are Anna Holbrook Weyerhaeuser, Sarah Maud Weyerhaeuser (in white dress), Louise Lindeke Weyerhaeuser, Harriette Louise Davis Weyerhaeuser, Phil, James Richard Jewett, Margaret Weyerhaeuser Jewett, Apollonia Weyerhaeuser Davis, Elise Weyerhaeuser Hill, John Philip, and Rudolph M. Standing in back are Charles A., Frederick E., William Bancroft Hill, Margaret Louise Weyerhaeuser, and George Frederick Jewett.

The second generation Weyerhaeusers, ca. 1920: Apollonia Davis, Elise Hill, and Margaret Jewett; Frederick E., Charles A., John Philip, and Rudolph M.

John and son Phil pose on the porch of Haddaway Hall, Tacoma, 1922.

The happy angler. Phil Weyerhaeuser somewhere, sometime in the 1920s.

Helen Hunt Walker, age eighteen.

Father Phil and baby Ann, 1923.

Phil and Helen during an automobile trip to California in 1928.

John and grandson George enjoying each other's company on the grounds of Haddaway Hall, ca. 1930.

C. L. Billings and Phil pose by some unimpressive logs, about to be dumped into the Clearwater. Logs like these contributed to the early cost problems of the Clearwater operation.

code, liquidation would lower prices, meaning less realization and fewer logs that could be salvaged profitably. Furthermore, they were not simply talking about a decrease in log—and lumber—prices in the Columbia River district. "It is in a small way the situation of the lumber industry as a whole," Bell observed, with "pressure for realization, excess of productive capacity and markets which do not respond to lowered prices."

Less likely to be considered in the salvage question were freight costs. All the railroads serving the district, Laird pointed out, were common carriers, and all imposed a stiff log rate. Individually the owners were helpless to deal at advantage with the rail operators. "United, however, salvage operations could be concentrated on either road and might conceivably warrant building a road," Laird suggested. "Certainly the group together could negotiate to better advantage a lower log rate of trackage rights." It soon became apparent, however, that the tragedy had brought little change in attitudes. Once more Laird reported his lack of progress to Phil, somewhat apologetically. What they had done was to appoint a committee to gather information, so at the very least each owner would have some idea how "his own property stacks up in comparison with the others."

Laird was also feeling apologetic about the overall situation, allowing that he didn't feel he had been as helpful as he should have been. In truth, of course, Laird was of great help, and his concluding sentence indicated just the sort of assistance that he alone seemed able to provide, although he typically managed to make the contribution seem minor: "I feel a little guilty when I see the problems that you are facing, and, so far as it will help you to talk them over with an outsider, I have hoped that you would feel free to use me as a wailing wall or otherwise."

In the meantime, the Production Committee, to which Phil was trying to contribute, was moving slowly in its consideration of a formula for quotas. Phil reported their glacial progress in detail to Gus Clapp. The West Coast men who had participated in the Washington, D.C., deliberations, he observed, acted a good deal differently on their home turf: "They are distinctly more impressed with the fact that they cannot simply ride the will of the majority through in defiance of reasonable economic principles." The essence of the opposing positions remained as before: the small mills generally favored the idea of a forty-hour minimum before anyone shared disproportionately in the business to be allocated, while the larger operators generally wished to reduce that minimum hourly percentage, thereby allowing for a greater portion of the allocation to be based on other factors. They appeared to be at an impasse. But Phil was not totally discouraged, retaining a hope that there was "a little ingenuity left in the world" and that they might yet be able to work things out. At the very least, Phil was getting to know others in the industry, most of whom had very different problems from those confronting the Weyerhaeuser Timber Company.

In his December 4 report to the company trustees, Phil indicated that it seemed as if most of the Tacoma organization had "been busy constantly on Code matters since my letter of October 2nd," and the crucial question of a formula for allocation of production in the West Coast Division was still unresolved. He thought that they had been successful in getting greater consideration for investment properties, but admitted that the final resolution was "still much in doubt." There was better news concerning the allocation under the Western Pine Association formula, Klamath Falls receiving 50 percent in excess of what had been granted under the hourly formula. All the Douglas-fir operations of the Weyerhaeuser Timber Company and its subsidiaries had run thirty hours a week during October and November, "and rather surprisingly registered operating profits in all cases for the month of October," although the Willapa Harbor Lumber Mills and the White River Lumber Company carried a tax and interest burden that resulted in a total net loss for the month. The pulp division continued to show promise.

Such was not the case regarding cooperation in the merger efforts. Laird's stay in the West came to an end on December 13, and he addressed a note to Phil while heading homeward by rail aboard the Empire Builder. Laird apologized for having seemed to take his leave on "rather a sour note." He assured Phil that while it seemed "a little patronizing of me to keep telling you . . . I do believe you are doing a fine job." And he added (mixing metaphors somewhat), "It is a shame that you were pitchforked into these Code squabbles on top of trying to get on top of the W.T. Co. monster but except for the antagonism to the Co. that you have uncovered, I see nothing to worry about." Phil replied in kind: "You always succeed in bucking me up, one way or another, and I wonder if I begin to have a sort of defeated air in order for you to feel that this is necessary. I hope not, but regardless of that, thank you very much."

Upon his return to his Chicago desk, Laird took the time to report at length to Phil on all the attempted mergers; and all of them, except the Klamath survey, were practically at an end with no very discernible results. The reasons for failure varied from region to region, but as Laird saw it, "inanition" was the principal cause. Even in the Tillamook timber district, where "the fire accomplished what unimpeachable logic failed to accomplish," the possibility of a merger seemed unlikely. Laird did not see that he could do anything more. As he concluded, however, he tried to put a better face on the matter:

Perhaps from the depths of my modesty I might add a word on what I have supposed were some by-products of this enterprise. I am chagrined to have so little to show in the way of concrete results. Of course, I started with the chances against any form of success, and probably it was a forlorn hope at best. The Company evidently felt, however, the need of making a genuine move toward taking the leadership in promoting mergers, and I hope that from that point of view I have really done the Company some good. This is a little inconsistent with the antagonism which you have encountered in your efforts to get allotments. But I believe that I have made some contacts on behalf of the Company which it did not have before which may in the long run prove useful, and whatever these personal contacts are worth will of course inure to the benefit of the Company as well as compensate me for some imponderables I have lost through my long absences from the office.

On reading the foregoing over I am impressed with the fact that I have whined too much about my absences from the office. Like my long absence on the Lumber Code, which was of course on my own time entirely, the experience has been highly educational to me in a field which I am probably bound to have to know about before I get through, and if I had no partners I might well feel that the education was worth all the time.

As a matter of fact, both Phil and Laird had learned a great deal in the course of 1933, in the process growing in their appreciation of each other and in their mutual desire to be of help in moving along what was gradually becoming more and more their own enterprise. At the time, however, had Phil been asked about the year, he might have said, "It's over, that's the best part." It was over, and after two years of losses, the Weyerhaeuser Company showed a slight profit and distributed a small dividend to its shareholders. Whatever the reason, things were beginning to look a little more promising—or not so completely discouraging.

CHAPTER 6

Life under the NRA

At first glance it seems curious that the great and lasting benefits of the New Deal legislation to the lumber industry had as much to do with forestry as with production, prices, or wages. But the problems of forestry or conservation were, at heart, problems of an economic nature, and problems clearly beyond the ability of any single operator to resolve, regardless of interest or commitment. Simply put, an individual operator could not assume the costs of intensive forestry practices and remain competitive.

On October 24, 1933, the opening conference on the subject of forest conservation had been held between representatives of the forest products industries and public agencies. On January 25, 1934, they met again, and out of these discussions Article X of the National Recovery Administration's Lumber Code came into being, the purpose of which was to encourage forest practices aimed at the conservation of resources. It was one objective with which few disagreed, at least publicly. Only the means of collective action was needed.

Although Phil took more than a little interest in these proceedings, most of his attention was directed at concerns of the moment. He had continued his lonely battle on the question of production quotas, allocations that would affect both loggers and sawmillers. As to the loggers, Carl Stevens urged Phil to take a firmer stand. Stevens was convinced that "those particular men require indirect leading." He added, "I do not know anyone else up there who can give it intelligent direction excepting yourself." He recommended that Phil "go around, put your feet up on these gentlemen's desks and sit there until they talk." Sooner or later, "some of the group will think of what you want them to. The mill men may come later, but, even here, I think it can do no harm to scratch some of the paint off their desks as well." He concluded by observing, "I am completely out of patience with your own view of yourself because I know how tremendously effective you are in small meetings." Phil was no doubt pleased with this expression of confidence, but what his friend was suggesting was not his style. Even within his own organization, his methods were primarily those of quiet but persistent persuasion. Rather than running into obstacles, he leaned against them, and in time they moved.

On January 5, Phil had gone to St. Paul to attend the annual meeting of General Timber Service, Incorporated, and to visit with various Sales Company personnel. Following his midwestern stops, he planned to go east "to have a thorough visit with Colonel [James] Long and become as well acquainted as seems justified with the Eastern Yards situation aimed at recommending management changes which may prove to be rather far reaching." The most important of these involved the position of manager of Eastern Yards, the East Coast distribution arm of the Weyerhaeuser Timber Company. Bill Peabody, then manager at Everett, was selected to replace Colonel Long. The internal arrangements for this are not evident in the company's table of organization. Eastern Yards was primarily a Sales Company responsibility, and although Peabody would meet with Horace Irvine, a large Timber Company shareholder and increasingly active in policy matters, and F.E. in St. Paul before any formal announcement of the change, it was Phil's decision. The complicating factor was an additional responsibility belonging to the Eastern Yards manager: managing the Weyerhaeuser Steamship Company. In the 1920s, the Timber Company purchased merchant ships that had been used in World War I, with each vessel constituting a separate company. Thus the USS *Hanley* became the Hanley Steamship Company, the USS *Pomona* the Pomona Steamship Company, and so forth. Prior to the construction of the Longview plant, the Everett mill possessed the company's only deepwater port facility, and the manager at Everett thus had responsibility for overall direction of intercoastal shipping. Part of the confusion was clarified in 1933 with the organization of the Weyerhaeuser Steamship Company, which included all four vessels then in service. With the appointment of Peabody as Eastern Yards and Steamship Company manager, Phil hoped to eliminate whatever confusion remained.

Following his graduation from Williams College and a brief enrollment at the University of Chicago law school, where fortuitously he had made friends with Laird Bell, Peabody had come west apparently in search of a job involving some physical activity and a share of excitement. He seems always to have been in need of proving his manhood. He found the activity and excitement he was looking for, and, being able and aggressive, soon advanced within the Everett management. Although they had little in common, Phil and Peabody took great delight in each other's company. Phil may have taken some vicarious pleasure in Peabody's gruff, tough, but consistently effective manner. Peabody apparently deferred to only one man, Phil Weyerhaeuser. Phil was well aware of this; and if on occasion Peabody seemed to exceed good judgment in dealing with subordinates, Phil could, good-naturedly, quickly, and effectively, remind him just where the larger authority rested.

Peabody's discussion with Fred K. and Horace Irvine was mostly about his salary, which, as Fred subsequently reported to Phil, had finally been settled "by meeting Bill's ideas entirely." In any event, Phil had his man in charge of steamship and Eastern Yard operations, Fred indicating that Phil would "probably have to break the bad news to the Colonel. . . ."

One of the more interesting facets of the Timber Company's history was the impact of its immense timber resource base on policy. In a sense, every company decision was made in the shadow of the company's vast timbered estate. All that timber provided a profound sense of security. Without doubt, the mere possession of the resource base encouraged a conservative approach. There was little inclination to take chances, to experiment, because there seemed no real need to do so. At the same time, however, that advantage provided the security that would permit a consideration of forestry practices. Few other organizations could indulge in the luxury of long-range planning, much less deferred profits. The Timber Company could also engage in research; and while it would be inaccurate to make great claims for such efforts in the early years of Phil's administration, Weyerhaeuser was a leader in private forestry research. This, however, was not the case in matters of forest products diversification, even in the most basic of related involvements. The Timber Company had been a reluctant and tardy participant in the pulp and paper field even though they had wood chips—the raw material—piled on every available open space. Entry into the plywood field also came surprisingly late, considering their plethora of peeler logs. In the years ahead, the company would also miss opportunities to add to its properties, although in some of these instances the fear of charges of monopoly, or at least "bigness," was as much a factor as conservatism. In short, the company personality was a complex one: some of its actions were farsighted, some shortsighted; some wise, others unenlightened. There was a good deal of truth in a common observation: the Weyerhaeuser Timber Company was a "sleeping giant."

A specific example in early 1934 concerned plywood, by this time no new item in the industry. Fred K. had suggested to Phil that perhaps the Timber Company should employ an engineer knowledgeable about the manufacture of plywood, with an eye to exploring possibilities. Although Phil was not unreceptive, he was convinced that such a study should certainly involve the sales end of the business: "Of course, we want somebody in our organization who, if possible, is familiar with the Plywood game if we are going to be induced to manufacture Plywood ourselves as opposed to buying it. But, isn't this problem, like all others approached in a conservative fashion, one of building our market first, if possible?" The differences may seem slight, but, in truth, they were significant.

If there was security in the resource base of the Weyerhaeuser Timber Company, there was also security in the Weyerhaeuser family. Of the second-generation brothers, it was Uncle Fred who had assumed the greatest responsibility concerning the boys of the third generation. It was F.E. who had remained in St. Paul, initially managing his father's widespread interests. Subsequently he endeavored to respond to opportunities as he assumed his father would have wanted. Thus he became not only the manager of the family resources, largely expressed through the Timber Securities Company, but also the conservator of family tradition. Over the years F.E. had developed a special feeling for Phil and Fred K., no doubt in part because it was apparent that Phil was to become the business leader and Fred K. seemed likely to assume the role of family leader. True, the lines between business and family were seldom clear. For example, in later years, if Phil stated an opinion regarding a family matter—not a very common occurrence—that opinion was likely to be accepted. The fact was, however, that maintenance of family tradition and cohesion was of less importance to Phil than to his brother.

In the 1930s, F.E. assumed a fatherly role to both Phil and Fred K., wishing not only to help them in the course of their growing responsibilities but also to pass along just what it was to be a Weyerhaeuser. Phil had written to his uncle regarding plans for a St. Paul visit in 1934, and in response F.E. indicated that he too would be in St. Paul at that time. F.E. looked forward to the chance "for a real visit" with Phil. "I should like to sit down quietly by ourselves," he wrote, "without interruptions, and have a couple of hours of conversation on a number of things which seem to me to be important." Although there is no record of the ensuing discussion, one can imagine the tenor of things.

On a business note, Phil was consulting with general manager and brother-in-law Rod Titcomb regarding the Timber Company's response to Article X of the Lumber Code. C. S. Chapman had recommended that the Timber Company proceed with "a complete plan of reforestation," to which Phil indicated entire agreement. This commitment occurred in advance of the Lumber Code Authority's formal approval of Schedule C, which took place on May 17. Operations that established themselves on a sustained-yield basis would be permitted to increase their production allocation by 10 percent. In the case of the Weyerhaeuser Timber Company, the 10 percent consideration, coupled with the desire to manage the thing anyway, was more than enough encouragement. Indeed, the company published a new field book in May, the introductory statement of which read, "The Weyerhaeuser Timber Company thoroughly subscribes to the aims and purposes of Article X." There was to be no question regarding that.

As expected, not everyone was equally enthusiastic about these developments. Minot Davis, responsible for the overall supervision of logging and land management, was one who dragged his feet. In discussing the response to Article X, Davis observed that one of the most important elements in reforestation was "our program of strip logging," that is, leaving strips of trees standing along the borders of the clearcutting operations. He noted that the practice had evolved for at least two important reasons: to isolate slash-burning activities to limited areas, and to allow natural reseeding of the logged areas. But Minot also wanted it understood that the practice should "be confined to leaving occasional strips of areas of inferior or defective timber," or timber that they just could not reach with their logging equipment. There was no point in leaving sound old-growth timber on each forty acres, "because . . . such trees are almost always blown over within a short time after they are isolated." In short, Minot was opposed to any dramatic change in procedures. The established method of logging "should be played up for what it is really worth, which seems to me considerable." Like many others, Minot was very good at doing things the way they had been done. He was less able to imagine how they might be done more effectively.

Labor complications loomed during the early NRA days. Such problems were not new to the company. What was new was the atmosphere in which they were to be considered. To the company, laborers were to be seen—working hard—and seldom if ever heard. There had been, of course, unwelcome expressions of pent-up frustration, the most notable involving the radical Industrial Workers of the World organizers. But lumbermen assumed that the Wobblies were not representative of the labor force in general. For the most part, managers in the Northwest continued to support the comfortable arrangement with the 4L, hoping that the old organization could endure the battles sure to come.

Perhaps the earliest evidence of change, as concerned Weyerhaeuser, occurred in late January when A. G. Hanson of the White River Lumber Company received a letter from Charles W. Hope, executive secretary of the Regional Labor Board, to which was attached a petition for recognition from the Executive Committee of the Loggers, Timber and Sawmill Workers Union. Hope's letter announced a hearing date of February 9 on the petition, and Phil knew that the manner of his response held more than passing importance.

Thus it was that on February 1 he addressed a note to Gus Clapp, then in Washington, D.C., requesting some advice. First, just who should appear, and what should the attitude of the company be? Article V(a) of the Lumber Code was a repeat of the famous Section 7(a) of the National Industrial Recovery Act, which guaranteed employees the right to organize and bargain collectively through representatives of their own choosing. The AFL hoped to use the National Labor Board to organize the lumber industry, and Phil saw this as an attempt to do so "along the lines of a vertical union or an industry union, comprising all branches and classes of employees, without reference to the craft, or kind of employment . . . or other specialties which require skilled labor." Furthermore, he feared, along with Roy Morse and Judge C. H. Paul of Long-Bell, that this was simply a prelude to other efforts; and Longview would soon have similar citations. Since the White River Lumber Company already had a significant AFL membership, their citation had been the first put forward.

Phil tried to keep the Executive Committee of the Timber Company informed during the rapidly developing situation. On January 23 the 4L met to consider requesting a raise in the base rate for the lumber industry. Phil had been certain that they would ask for a 50-cent minimum hourly figure, but instead they settled on 45 cents, effective February 1, "coupled with a resolution to petition the Code Authority for a 50¢ minimum. . . ." Even Phil found this overly timid, and expressed concern that such a position would weaken an already weak organization. On February 10, he was called "to attend a hearing of the Regional Labor Board as to why a petition of the American Federation of Labor locals at White River and Longview asking for an election among our employees of representatives to bargain collectively . . . should not be granted." Phil could think of lots of reasons. At Longview, for example, if the mill and woods employees were combined, 4L membership would total a small percentage and a "militant campaign" on the part of AFL organizers would probably meet with success. But in his sober manner, Phil concluded a report to the Executive Committee by observing, "We don't today know that answer nor exactly how to meet this, but wish to report it as being of interest."

On March 20, Phil and Helen left Tacoma to spend a couple of weeks at Del Monte, California. Before departing, he wrote a detailed letter to F. S. Bell describing the labor situation. He noted that under the Lumber Code, compliance boards were to be established in the various regions, each responsible for enforcing the labor, price, and trade-practice provisions of the code. In the meantime, the president had created a National Labor Board which in turn had appointed regional labor boards. These, as Phil understood, were without authority other than a responsibility for advising and assisting in the settling of labor disputes. In the Pacific Northwest, however, the board had been "attempting to assist the American Federation of Labor to organize our industry." Phil then told of the hearings and of subsequent plant elections. The elections had been called "in spite of our protest, which protest was based mainly on the statement that it was not necessary to have an election because no one knew what the issue of the election was."

The elections were held, and in each instance AFL representatives were successful. Both the Weyerhaeuser Timber Company and Long-Bell refused any official recognition of the results, but Phil admitted the likelihood of continued difficulty. "The A.F. of L. organization attempts to strengthen itself, the introduction of the Wagner Bill in Congress which would necessitate the withdrawal of our support of the 4L, and the almost daily newspaper publicity on the part of the President and Gen. Johnson to the point that wages must be increased and hours shortened" implied that the company was "going to have some serious labor troubles."

But labor relations were not the only issue during life under the NRA and the Lumber Code. The membership of the West Coast Division received a letter from W. B. Greeley, dated April 30, in which they were given, collectively, something of a lecture. The colonel's remarks were directed at those who seemed determined to get around the provisions of the code. He maintained that success depended on "the honest support and unflinching adherence of the great solid bulk of the industry." He went on to say:

The Lumber Code is not an edict handed us by Congress or the President. We went to Washington and asked for it. We asked for power from the President to govern ourselves; and he gave it to us. Are we now going to destroy our own charter, or undermine it by secret violations, or pass the buck for honest, sincere enforcement to the Association officers and the Trade Practice Complaints Committee?

We deliberately wrote this Code to pay fair wages to our labor, to protect our cost of production, and to stop or greatly reduce the destruction of our capital assets. Whatever miracles the Code has failed to accomplish, just compare the situation of the West Coast lumber business today with what it was a year ago or what your common sense tells you it would be tomorrow if the president cancelled the Code. After that comparison, I wish every operator would ask himself this question: "Can I afford to do one single thing that, through loss of confidence and honor within the industry, is going to break down this Code?"

One can almost picture Phil and Laird Bell reading Greeley's letter. Probably they sighed, shook their heads, and said, "Good luck, Colonel."

In the midst of such considerations, reminders often occurred that served to maintain perspective. Even seemingly minor problems could be distracting if not downright annoying. One such was introduced in an April 25 letter from Ernest N. Hutchinson, secretary of state for Washington. The subject was a strip of timber along the Snoqualmie Highway, the Naches Pass portion. Secretary Hutchinson wrote that the governor and others had been trying "to think of some way in which we could help the women and the nature lovers" preserve that particular stretch of timber. After noting that "the name of Weyerhaeuser is already a monument," the secretary observed that he had been advised by persons "who know you intimately" to "simply put this matter up to you."

Phil would have none of that approach. After acknowledging receipt of the letter "telling me that the ultimate solution to the problem ... rests entirely with me," Phil pretended innocence. He stated that he was "a comparative newcomer to these parts," and therefore knew nothing of the history of the problem, although he found it impossible to believe that its resolution rested entirely in his hands. He concluded by suggesting, "perhaps you could find the opportunity to tell me more of what is in your mind and whether or not it is really something which must be put up to me."

If Phil thought his response would end the matter, he was mistaken. On the evening of June 15, forester C. S. Chapman attended a meeting of the State Federation of Women's Clubs to present the company's proposal to log selectively the area east of what was called the Women's Park. Those assembled deemed this insufficient, and a resolution was offered "which had been previously prepared commending the acts of the state officials and calling upon the Timber Company and Lumber Company to refrain from cutting . . . and also providing that copies of the resolution be sent to the state officials, to the companies and the press." Undoubtedly this was not the first time that Chapman had felt ambushed, but he could not help feeling a bit abused: "While I pointed out that they had omitted to mention anything along the line of selective cutting and that the Weyerhaeuser Timber Company mentioned in the resolution was out of place as the Snoqualmie Falls Lumber Company was the one involved, nevertheless the resolution was unanimously adopted."

Indeed, the Naches Pass controversy was another clear example that insisting that land was privately held did not necessarily forestall public involvement. Consulting forester Carl Stevens, about as progressive as any lumberman of the day, sympathized with Phil's dilemma. He knew that Phil wished to see things as right or wrong, and in this instance it seemed wrong for those who possessed little or no information to insist on altering arrangements already made. But Stevens also knew that being right in this instance was of little solace. As he wrote Phil, "I just hope that bunch of wild women beard you, in your secluded office, and I hope that I may have the privilege of being around to enjoy the fun. In the meantime, may your troubles multiply and wax fat."

The labor situation was a much more serious concern. In mid-May Phil had reported to the Executive Committee regarding the problems along the coast. A stevedore strike had completely stopped shipping from Seattle, Tacoma, Everett, and Portland. There had been some talk of calling out the militia, but this threatened to trigger sympathy strikes among boat crews, tugboat operators, truckers, and perhaps others. After telling of some reports of violence on the Seattle and Portland waterfronts, Phil noted that two of the Weyerhaeuser Steamship Company vessels were tied up awaiting the end of difficulties.

Even though production allocations for the month of June were equivalent to only eighty-two hours of operating time, large stocks of lumber, particularly the upper grades, had accumulated in the course of the year, and all mills were congested. In short, the volume of business was not sufficient to cause any worry about a week or more shutdown in lumber. Phil went so far as to suggest to the Executive Committee, "it would be discreet and worthwhile to avert trouble by shutting down Everett, Willapa and Longview completely before the end of this week, which we plan to do." The Longview pulp mill was an exception to the plan, for "as you know, shutting down the Pulp Mill is a real cost."

Bill Peabody, now head of the Eastern Yards and Steamship Company, bothered Phil more than necessary, but in this instance Phil seemed not to mind. New organization and procedures were being implemented and Phil was, at least initially, more than a little interested that progress be made. There was also a certain romance connected with the Steamship Company that appealed to Phil, though he never directly admitted it. And despite all of Bill Peabody's faults, Phil genuinely liked him. One might say that Peabody was undeniable evidence of Phil's capacity for camaraderie. As was later observed, "Phil gave Peabody credit for being a shrewd old rascal."

Phil was pleased that Bill seemed to have taken hold so quickly. "I hear happy reports about everything that has happened since you have been down there," he wrote on May 18, "except as to the debates which you apparently lost to Al Raught" (the Longview manager). Phil informed Peabody of the West Coast dockworkers' strikes, adding that if they were able to "effect a complete shut-down promptly on the part of the lumber industry and others, I believe that public opinion will militate against the strike."

On June 5 a delighted Phil was able to inform Laird Bell of his election as vice-president, executive committeeman, and director, all of which "went through without very much politics." He also expressed the hope that Laird's father "was pleased at the result. . . ." F. S. Bell was now chairman of the board and an ex-officio member of the six-member Executive Committee, which Phil assumed would permit him to participate to the extent he wished. "He has been so considerate of me throughout this past year," Phil noted, "that I have a lot of personal feeling, in addition to regret for the Company, that he is no longer actively at the head of the Company." F.E. was now the president of the Weyerhaeuser Timber Company, as well as the chairman of its Executive Committee. Laird replied that while nothing appealed to him more at the moment than living the quiet suburban life and practicing a little "regular law," he imagined that he would soon be able to rouse himself to lumber matters, "mergers, and what not."

Concerning the other changes, F.E. agreed with the contents of a recent letter from Phil to the Executive Committee that plans should proceed for the development of a pulp mill at Everett, but he wanted it understood that neither he nor Horace Irvine favored anything more than the development of plans at this stage. In other words, he was not yet convinced of the wisdom of such an investment. On the subject of national affairs, F.E. reflected on the passage and signing of the Farm Mortgage Bill, this seeming to him "to be a President's last word in an effort to wipe out all Constitutional rights," and he could only hope that "the Supreme Court will have something to say on the subject."

There were some interesting activities in the woods, especially work by Carl Stevens in developing a report on selective logging and the Everett-Vail operation. Stevens was enthusiastic. "I think that you have chosen a particularly appropriate time to initiate this program," he wrote to Phil, "and I hope that your decision will be to go ahead right away." In recognition, however, that little could be accomplished without the cooperation of the branch managers, Stevens noted that he had "taken the liberty of contacting enough of your managers to assure you (as was implied that I must) that we will not only carry them along with us, but will be filling a long felt need with each." In short, Phil was assured, "we shall never start on any job until sure that the managers are with us." He added, "You have enough to make the start you need and the rest are certain to see the force of these illustrations."

One of those who failed to see the "force of these illustrations," at least in theory, was Minot Davis. Minot, who viewed the forest and logging through experienced eyes, could hardly imagine an effort that did not involve old-growth timber. Thus he was skeptical about the Stevens report. He indicated to Phil that he saw no possibility of profit in a second cycle of logging at Vail: "Entirely aside from the likelihood of fire and wind damage to lightening the stand, I should say that the logging of the second cycle would be so very expensive as to be entirely uneconomical."

Minot appeared to recognize that selective logging was itself not unsound, if it simply meant leaving trees that had little value. But Minot was thinking more of effective liquidation than selective logging. He described his understanding of the latter: "We try to indulge in this form of selective logging by leaving in the woods as many as possible of those logs which are of minus value." That was clear enough. He continued: "I am sorry to have to say that I consider the action recommended in this report, however correct it may be theoretically, to be entirely impractical to put in effect excepting insofar as we might analyze and check constantly on the possibility of leaving worthless areas and worthless logs. While we, of course, try to do this in a rough way, yet there will doubtless be plenty of chance for continued improvements in method."

Needless to say, that isn't what either Carl Stevens or Phil had in mind. At the same time, it was of great importance to Phil and to the organization that Minot and others felt free to disagree, especially when such disagreement was unpopular. In the meantime, he would wait for the evidence to build, all the while leaning in the direction he thought would prove out. He knew that the Timber Company had grown dependent on the security of its mammoth wood pile, that it was in a position to break out of the old warehouse management philosophy of timber into some form of active management. He also knew that the appeal of the original investment and subsequent involvement of many of the managers and most of the directors had to do with the old-growth forest, and they had difficulty seeing beyond it.

At the moment Phil was having difficulty seeing beyond the labor problems. The only reassuring aspect, as he reported to F.E., was that "the constituted authorities" in the port cities were doing their best to protect the facilities, and it was hoped that the ports would soon gradually reopen. Public opinion seemed to be swinging away from the stevedores, although there had been a brief walkout at Longview by the sawmill workers. "No demands were presented to either ourselves or Long-Bell," Phil noted, and the other unions, including the Pulp Workers' Union, refused to participate.

Politically, Laird Bell was far more liberal than most of his associates. Although he was willing—some of the Weyerhaeusers thought too willing—to give the Roosevelt administration a fair chance, he did allow that "the administration has created a situation, or permitted it to be created, where the trouble-making element have a wonderful chance, whatever their economic and social views." If there were specific difficulties down the road, he suggested that Phil's "competent young men" had better be duly impressed with the new depreciation provisions of the income tax law.

Article X of the Lumber Code became effective in the summer of 1934, and the first report from divisional forester Russell Mills clearly reflected the enthusiasm of the Weyerhaeuser organizations for the program. Although more than one hundred operators had submitted outlines for restocking and slash disposal, only five completed cutting and restocking schedules for areas to be logged in the coming year—and all five were Weyerhaeuser companies or subsidiaries.

But if the opportunity to initiate some forestry practices seemed one of the benefits of code policies, to many it seemed the only benefit. While Phil did not despair, he also did not approve of the course of action fostered by the NRA. Politicians restricted his company's ability to operate to advantage. In late August the West Coast Code Administration adopted a production formula that Phil described as institutionalizing the "thirty-hour soupbowl." The decision had been made "over the protest of several individuals including ourselves." In addition, the formula for log allocation seemed to operate to the disadvantage of the Timber Company. To drive home the seriousness of this development, Phil resorted to the extravagance of sending a lengthy telegram on the subject to F.E.: "Price control features are operating . . . to get us a continually smaller percentage of the business available, and it becomes apparent that the method of voting by individuals in the industry is more and more dangerous to us as the industry becomes more conscious of its power." Each operator had a vote, and there were more small operators than large. Phil indicated that the only option remaining was to appeal, and "in this particular matter we would be joined by Long-Bell, the Reed group, Bloedel and the Columbia River discontents." On price matters as well, "there is a growing group that would join us."

Phil had decided that the time for patience had passed. "It seems to me," he told F.E., "that we have reached the point where there is no gain in continuing to mark time and that we should very definitely get all the support we can and proceed to fight on all these scores." His uncle applauded this indication of conservative feistiness. "Horace [Irvine] and I fully agree with your suggestions," he telegraphed in reply. "In fact I personally favor withdrawing from all associations."

Phil began preparing a petition to the trustees of the West Coast Lumbermen's Association even before he received F.E.'s encouraging response. The document raised matters specific and practical as well as philosophical. Beginning with the assertion that the present formula, adopted in December 1933, had proved "discriminatory and unfair, and not in accord with the spirit of intent of the Lumber Code," the argument proceeded. Phil noted that the formula had caused "undue and unnecessary hardship on those persons whose overhead in the form of depreciation, taxes, insurance, timber expenses and timber taxes, and general overhead is far above the average, per unit of production." He asserted that mills built and equipped for continuous operation on the basis of their own timber holdings and markets were limited by code allocation to operate at about 30 percent of normal, while other mills were not similarly limited. Indeed, some were operating above normal production levels.

Phil also charged that the formula "encouraged and induced the establishment of new units of production" with little or no regard for consideration of high cost and lower efficiency:

The only reason ever given for the present formula is that all labor should be permitted to work the same number of hours. This has never been true during normal times, as will appear from the striking variation in operations during 1927–1928–1929 and 1930. Furthermore, the present formula is resulting in all men working for less than a living wage; in most cases ... for a lower weekly wage than during the worst of the depression period. The N.I.R.A. and the Lumber Code was [sic] not designed, nor is it within their purpose and scope to put all laboring men on exactly the same footing, any more than to put all industry on the same level. To accomplish the real purpose of the Act and the Code, it is necessary to take one man's property or business and give it to another, as is the effect of the present formula.

The petition closed by noting that it was not the intention "to demand or even request any particular formula" and that there was agreement that "production should be controlled," but that there must be a method of providing for controls "on a basis much more proportional than under the present formula."

When the request for reconsideration was denied by the West Coast Lumbermen's Association trustees, Phil sent letters to most of the major producers in the West Coast Division, calling for a meeting in Tacoma on September 12. The timing was important. Their appeal was scheduled for a hearing before the Control Committee in Washington, D.C., on September 17. The Weyerhaeuser position received support from sixteen others, including Long-Bell, the Bloedel-Donovan Lumber Company, and the Reed Mill Company, so that in addition to the five Weyerhaeuser organizations, twenty-one signatures appeared on the petition.

As a result of the protest, the Lumber Code Authority resolved that "the present method of allotment is not equitable and is not substantially carrying out the purpose of the Act and Code." Accordingly the West Coast Division was ordered to submit a revised formula that included a factor of hourly production "at not in excess of 40%." The balance was left for the division to determine according to other factors, although if no agreement was possible, the Lumber Code Authority provided a formula that included yearly production, employment, and taxes to be considered at 30, 20, and 10 percent respectively.

The victory, if it was a victory, was anything but easily effected. Harlan Watzek of the Crossett Western Company had tried his best as chairman of the Lumber Production Control Committee but had found the responsibility a thankless task. A recent decision to forgo minimum price controls had completely demoralized the executive. On October 31 he wrote to E. W. Demarest of the Pacific National Lumber Company, explaining why he wished to resign: "I can't see daylight through the maze of troubles ahead of production control after the Trustees decided this week to forsake [setting a] price. With the Courts refusing to issue more injunctions, our price is gone today in reality. If we had started without price we could have continued to control production but not now. Without price you throw more load on production than it can carry. You can't sell lumber cheaply unless you produce it cheaply and you can't produce it cheaply at 12 to 20 hours a week. Moreover, our Code morale went with the price."

Noting that the new formula for production would be "impossible for such a large majority of our mills" and that enforcement would also be unlikely, Watzek observed, "You can't enforce anything against a reasonable majority." The lesson of Prohibition was clearly remembered and often quoted. Watzek had been hopeful to compromise on some problems, "but not on all at once plus the loss of price." Phil took note of Watzek's "self styled swan song" in a brief but friendly letter. "Needless to say I am sorry that apparently our interests are forcing you to give over," he began, and he concluded by expressing the hope that present differences would be no more lasting than those of the past. Watzek immediately assured Phil that there was nothing personal in his decision: "I can see your necessity and your position." The problem remaining, however, was holding the other 525 operators in line "on that basis."

Watzek's resignation was not immediately accepted, and he subsequently addressed a letter jointly to John Tennant and Phil on November 16. He began by expressing his hope that they would attend the meetings scheduled to begin on November 21 in Portland. He wished to know, before those meetings, whether Long-Bell and Weyerhaeuser were going to accept Colonel Greeley's latest idea of a "so-called permanent formula, viz., two-thirds on hourly and one third on annual [production], let the chips fall where they may, with no adjustments up or down for any plants." He also wanted to know if Phil was going to continue to insist "on two shifts annual rating" for his new plants, "which have never run two shifts."

The answers from John Tennant and Phil Weyerhaeuser were predictable. Tennant saw no reason to accept an unfair formula merely to ensure temporary harmony. He maintained that a "correct and fair formula" could be created "if all of us will consider the subject from a point of view as to what is really equitable." Phil's answer was the briefer of the two, but it left no doubt about his position:

I have tried to express frankly to you in the past that I do not see how a contribution to political expediency can be argued as just. The proposed lumber production formula, which Colonel Greeley said to me in open meeting . . . was not fair, can not be considered so by anyone who will make a study of the facts. You have never expressed yourself in any other terms than that you thought the will of the majority must rule. Consequently, a fair formula was impossible. The formula proposed, if permanent, would of course deal such a blow to the plants with which I am familiar that I do not believe we could long continue to exist. If, in spite of this, there is a refusal on the part of the West Coast Association to recognize the rights of new plants, as definitely provided for under the Code, in reference to their annual ratings, the situation is just that [much] more aggravating.

Phil was not a stubborn man by nature, but he could become a bulldog if he felt his company was being treated unfairly. In matters of its continued existence and integrity, there was no room for compromise.

On December 1, Phil wrote a lengthy letter to Laird, responding in detail to questions regarding the November elections and their possible effect on Timber Company plans. Phil seemed unperturbed, although enigmatic might be more accurate. He indicated to Laird, "I was satisfied that the Democrats would be in power for several years anyway, and to find that it is to run until 1940, or after, is not much of a shock." Then he added a significant observation: "In spite of knowing this to be a fact, I cannot help feeling that the general business situation in the country is good and going to improve." Although he could wish for better treatment at the hands of government, he maintained that this should not discourage them from making the "well justified investment" which will "give us the earning power to do the things which will be required of us." Phil gave his blessing to plans for a new pulp mill at Everett and was prepared to call an Executive Committee meeting early in the new year so that the members could "express themselves on this matter."

Regarding Laird's possible appointment to the Lumber Code Authority and his misgivings about such a responsibility, Phil saw no problem, indicating to Laird that a "free agent" role "would go without saying":

I don't think there is anyone in the group who does not agree with your feeling that the industry should control minimum wages and the conservation movement to the extent it can in any future code set-up. Gus [Clapp] is here and I have discussed this with him, to some extent. He and I agree that with a fair formula for individual allotments, production control would be desirable. Both of us, and Rod Titcomb, cannot help feeling, from our experience to date, that political strength of numbers in associations as today constituted, is always going to be against us and that as a result we will always be in the position of accepting a compromised formula which will be economically unfair to us.

Phil acknowledged that there were differences about whether the Weyerhaeuser companies stood to gain more than lose in these compromises, noting that F.E. maintained that nothing could be gained from production controls, while Gus and he weren't that certain. But that need not concern Laird. "If you can be elected as a member of the Lumber Code Authority," Phil asserted, "it will be because you are looked upon as a man of broad unbiased opinion, representing no one to the exclusion of your considered personal judgment."

A couple of days later, Laird received a far different letter from F.E. It seemed to F.E. that no one on the Executive Committee thought it important to consider the unbleached pulp mill question at the present time, since he had heard nothing on the subject from "Mr. Clapp, Mr. McCormick, or Phil Weyerhaeuser." Obviously he was feeling a bit testy. After all, he *was* the president. Regarding Laird and the Lumber Code Authority, his reaction was interesting if not unexpected. As F.E. saw things, the world was going to hell: "The present Administration has not been altogether consistent in its policies. In the face of the highest wage scales in the world's history and the shortest hours of labor, with resultant high costs, there seems little probability that we can build up an export trade, not even with those nations who are friendly to us, if any can be discovered, nor do I see any particular virtue in decreasing the demand for labor in this country because of importations. It all seems to go around in circles like the second hand of the clock I am looking at."

Phil had previously written to F.E. concerning Laird and the Lumber Code Authority position, and now he admitted that perhaps he had said more than he should have regarding code matters, noting the likelihood that his uncle felt differently about them. Still he wanted F.E. to understand that he continued to believe it was desirable to have uniform wages and hours and felt "quite strongly" that Article X, or something even more forceful, should be encouraged: "Whether Laird agreed at present in many of these matters or not, I would still feel it worth our while to have him as someone whom we could contact with a large influence on Lumber Code Authority and I would want him to take the job as a 'free agent.'"

On December 28, 1934, Phil Weyerhaeuser did something he had rarely done. He spoke publicly, at the annual dinner of the Tacoma Chamber of Commerce. In part because he hated to perform, his preparations were painstaking. He would write out in longhand a detailed outline of what he wished to say and then circulate it among those most likely to suggest improvements. There were upwards of 350 in the audience, eager for their first chance to hear this young leader speak. Apparently they were not disappointed. Although Phil detailed, as suggested in the invitation, the importance of the lumber industry to the local and state economy, most of his remarks were given to a look into the future. He used the occasion to review those recent experiences that seemed to place the industry in a position to take advantage of the better times that were coming. For example, he talked about Article X of the Lumber Code, and the shared hope that they would be able to attain a forest management objective "whereby there is a balance between yearly or periodic cut and the growing capacity of the land." He observed that this effort "must be applauded and assisted by all of us, since it is frankly not in the power of the industry itself to accomplish without substantial assistance from the government and the public."

Phil acknowledged that a pessimistic attitude had been a pretty easy thing to come by in recent days, "because vexatious matters claim such a disproportionate amount of time," but at the same time it was possible to extend a "Happy New Year" greeting quite honestly, and the "best way to be cheerful about 1935 was to consider 1934 to some extent." For all of their much discussed problems of the past year, there had been progress. For example, never before had the leaders of industry had such opportunity for study and discussion of common concerns—a study and discussion that would not have occurred without the public insistence. As a result and, of course, dependent on numerous other factors, Phil suggested: "If the much advertised wedding of industry and government can take place, and the disturbance of constant drastic reforms can at least be soft pedaled, our optimism would be real, and we could see the lumber industry, together with many others, working its way into real prosperity." In closing, he allowed: "We are living today in an 'ordered' economy and to show my acquiescence I have followed instructions . . . and done my best to dwell on encouraging signs." Phil took his seat to loud applause, perhaps hoping that it was not simply because he had kept well within the time allotted.

The end of the year saw a temporary truce between the Timber Company and the West Coast Lumbermen's Association. The compromise was reached in the course of discussions in Washington, D.C., before the Lumber Code Authority. Gus Clapp reported in detail to Phil. He noted Colonel Greeley's long presentation "with figures and charts," repeating his old position that when it came to equities between "the larger of the small mills and particularly the medium sized mills . . . and the larger companies to have a production large enough to carry their overhead, he thought weight should be given to the former." The debate had continued on and on, and in an evening appeal, Greeley "came to me and wanted to know if we would not consent to a certain adjustment—substantially the one that was agreed upon the next day. . . ."

The compromise involved a minimum weekly work rate of eighteen hours. As Gus Clapp indicated to Phil, "Personally I do not regret my decision because of two things." The first involved both Greeley and the other operators, Clapp believing that "unless we made some concession we would have alienated a majority of the division who, after we made the concession, would be behind us in getting control of production for the next three months." A second reason favoring the agreement, and probably the more troubling, had to do with confusion regarding the "attitude of the Weyerhaeusers on production control." Apparently Rod Titcomb had made a statement before the Lumber Production Control Committee that was misunderstood, intentionally or otherwise. Clapp did not accuse Titcomb of any wrongdoing in the matter, "However, as you know, he has not the faculty of expressing himself clearly," and, "In fact, he hasn't the faculty of keeping quiet at a time when a red flag of this kind, no matter what he means, should have been kept furled." As a result, Clapp had been questioned along lines that he had not understood and had given answers that seemed to indicate a contradiction to what Titcomb had stated. And so it had gone, and now they should work to make the best of it.

Phil undoubtedly agreed. They had made their point as best they could and had received some adjustment in the desired direction. Total victories are seldom worth the cost.

CHAPTER 7

Never Business as Usual

The Executive Committee of the Weyerhaeuser Timber Company met early in the new year, 1935, and approved plans for the construction of an unbleached pulp mill at Everett. There followed negotiations with the city of Everett and Snohomish County for the purpose of arranging a water contract and obtaining a more favorable tax rate, the company being reasonably successful on both counts. By mid-February, details had progressed far enough to arrange for the purchase of the major items of machinery, dryer and digesters, and it was hoped that the plant would be operating before the end of the year.

Another item of discussion at the January Executive Committee meeting was the continuing survey of the desirability of entering the plywood manufacturing business, a discussion that provided further evidence of the conservative tendency that had become traditional. Clearly the most fundamental factor involved was that, given the size and quality of its resource base, the Weyerhaeuser Timber Company could continue to do what it had been doing and show a profit. Although Phil was far more willing to experiment than his "board of uncles," he was guided by two basic principles: first, there had to be an economic justification for a new or different involvement (in the case of new products, market feasibility came before the development effort); second, by and large the company ought to keep its efforts focused: it should continue to do those things with which it was familiar, and do them better than anyone else. Time after time, when offered some new opportunity, Phil would respond, "but we just don't know much about that." To many of the bright young men around him, this must have seemed an unimaginative stance at best. But to many others, such a considered approach had its merits.

Indeed, for the Weyerhaeuser Timber Company in 1935, there seemed to be more than enough developments. As Phil wrote to the Executive Committee, the Klamath merger, "off and on for months," finally looked as if it would be completed: "the Kesterson Mill of the Great Northern, and the Shaw-Bertram Mill of the Southern Pacific will be merged with some of our timber, and as a result we will be in the control of another operating company in pine." What with these railroad timberland mergers, the interest in plywood production, and the construction of the Everett pulp mill, Phil admitted that it probably appeared as if they were expanding very rapidly, but none were new fields. Nevertheless, for a depression year, the policies of the Timber Company surely expressed hope for better days, and soon.

The announcement of plans for the new pulp mill made headlines in the *Everett News* of February 14: "Weyerhaeuser to construct Pulp Plant on Mill A Site." This amounted to the best economic news the citizens of Everett had received for some time, the reporter noting it constituted "the most progressive move in the city since the outset of the depression and indicated that industry has regained enough confidence to go forward again." In the midst of this expression of cautious optimism, Phil directed that the company budget be redone to include the Everett pulp mill expenditures, $300,000 that would be required in connection with the Klamath merger, and $100,000 for a possible investment in a plywood plant, while maintaining the commitment to a one dollar dividend per share for September and December. Phil needed to know how much in the way of bonds they would have to sell to finance the Everett expansion, and the extent, if any, that short-term borrowing might be required. That he would even have considered short-term borrowing is interesting. It was a most unusual consideration for a company that traditionally expanded by using its own capital.

But there was nothing unusual in the antagonism that existed between representatives of the U.S. Forest Service and the lumber industry leaders, a condition that seemed endemic. For the Weyerhaeusers, who possessed long memories, their disaffection with federal involvement certainly dated back as far as January 1905, when Frederick had been invited to address a session of the American Forest Congress in Washington, D.C. This was only the second such meeting to be held in the United States, and although Gifford Pinchot was the principal organizer, it was understood that President Theodore Roosevelt was taking great personal interest in the proceedings. F.E. was on good terms with Pinchot, and when he indicated that Frederick was not available by reason of ill health, Pinchot invited F.E. to read a paper in his father's stead. Frederick used his influence to encourage many of his friends and associates to attend the conference, assuming that there would be some expression of mutual interest aimed at future cooperation between federal officials and leaders of the industry. Certainly F.E. had shown a commitment to long-term solutions—a commitment that Pinchot welcomed, admitting that here was a lumberman cut from different cloth.

F.E. was Pinchot's house guest. The evening before the conference opened, he shortened his paper at his host's request, and also read the speech that Pinchot had written for President Roosevelt, later recalling that "Pinchot's statements were very fair and would have been accepted by lumbermen." Roosevelt addressed the afternoon session on Thursday, January 5, with some two thousand crowding into the National Rifles' Armory. The speech as reprinted hardly seems provocative, and most heard nothing very unexpected from the president, but the performance proved to be one F.E. would never forget, or forgive. As he described the event many years later, Roosevelt discarded the Pinchot text and launched into a diatribe of his own invention:

Many of the most prominent timber owners and lumbermen were there and all were invited to sit upon the stage to hear the President's speech. The opera house where the Congress was held was packed. With a grin and show of teeth, Roosevelt hurried onto the platform, acknowledged the plaudits of the crowd, and then fairly turning his back on the audience, began a tongue lashing of the lumbermen and their methods, calling them "skinners of the soil," "despoilers of the national heritage," and using other characteristic epithets. . .

F. E. Weyerhaeuser was more than hurt; he felt betrayed. Afterward in a sense he and his family retreated to their forests, quietly resenting what they came to call "Forest Service propaganda." Indeed, the file in Phil's office on the subject was so labeled: "Forest Service Propaganda."

In the mid-1930s the leader of the opposition was Chief Forester Ferdinand A. Silcox. For the most part, the propaganda took the position that the lumber industry continued to cut and run, leaving economic and social devastation in its wake, depleting a great national resource and public treasure. The message may have sounded old to Phil and his associates, but its seeming logic found public support. When Silcox addressed the annual meeting of the Society of American Foresters on January 28, 1935, his remarks were well received by many, but they could hardly have pleased the president of the Weyerhaeuser Timber Company or its executive vice-president. Silcox was advocating an expanded responsibility for the federal government, meaning his Forest Service, not only in the management of public timberlands but also as concerned the lumber industry itself. The New Deal seemed about ready to force its entry into the private forest. Silcox described the need for such entry:

This new philosophy, which is really the old philosophy of this country, imposes upon us, as foresters, new tasks. The forests of the country must regain and hold permanently their place as sources of employment in every forest region. They must become centers around which communities may be assured a stable existence. Human welfare, opportunities for useful employment, permanent communities, and all the other social benefits that flow from productive forests must be our goal. In the past, we have laid much stress on forestry for timber production, without much regard to its immediate benefit to the surrounding communities. The lumber industry was concerned merely with the extraction of logs for the immediate profit that might be made, and gave little or no consideration to the social consequences of timber depletion.

At the very least, the chief forester got the attention of the leaders of the industry. Phil heard from many of them, most of whom shared his misgivings. One who wrote was Henry F. Chaney, who observed that the address was "full of the same type of misleading information that characterizes the general propaganda of the Forest Service since Pinchot's time." Chaney wondered, on the basis of a remark that Phil had recently made, whether it wasn't time for the lumber industry to employ "somebody of capacity" to make "an actual study of the facts" and then publish that study, "perhaps in the *Saturday Evening Post*." Exactly what Phil had said is unknown, but it must have been to the effect that it was time to do some of their own talking. Phil's tendency was to be open, but being open was only a small step toward taking the stage and competing for the public ear.

Chaney, however, was a lumberman of the old order, one unlikely to debate successfully with such as the chief forester. For example, in objecting to Silcox's use of "the old theme of abandoned lumber and sawmill towns," Chaney argued that by their very nature such towns were "never considered anything but tools in the rescuing of the timber and would be discarded just like a worn-out hoe or a plow or any other piece of equipment whose purpose had been served." As if to prove his reasoning, he asked, "Outside the rescuing a timber body in some pestilential swamp in Louisiana or pine flat in Wisconsin or Michigan, what other purpose would be served by maintaining a town there?" Obviously, this lack of compassion would not be acceptable in New Deal or subsequent times.

One who was more importantly involved was Fritz Jewett, chairman of the forestry committee of the National Lumber Manufacturers

Association. Fritz had assumed an active role in the public discussions on the subject of "private as opposed to public ownership of the forests," although he seemed far more ready for accommodation than many thought practical, including most of his family. Phil tried to be supportive of his cousin's efforts, but it wasn't always easy. He preferred to be more selective in the battles to be fought. One of the areas of difference was Fritz's opposition to the Copeland Report, which had favored federal acquisition of marginal timberlands. Phil maintained that there was little purpose in trying "to block the well-started steamroller," and that they should limit their efforts to insisting "in every way possible upon the government's actually purchasing marginal lands only."

The next salvo from Silcox occurred in a March 13 address before the National Control Committee of the Lumber Code Authority in New Orleans. There were few surprises, and there were few industry leaders in the audience who could feel much encouragement from what they heard. The chief forester had attempted to emphasize the commonness of the problem, observing that "as your interests extend beyond forest lands in your own ownership," so does the public's interest "extend far beyond the areas which are today in public ownership." The immediate question, of course, was how "far beyond." There followed the inevitable lecture: "In frankness I must say, however, that as far as I can see after traveling widely over this Country, a large portion of the lumber industry is still operating on the basis of quick liquidation, draining off the new remaining reservoirs of virgin timber, with the usual inevitable result. There are notable exceptions to this general statement, but, unfortunately, the exceptions are all too few."

Certainly the "exceptions" disliked to be treated like school boys on a subject about which they felt they knew much more than Mr. Silcox. It is perhaps understandable that they tended to view the chief forester and public policy more as a part of the problem than of its solution.

Lumber owners and operators in the audience found more to concern them when Silcox got to that portion of his remarks dealing with the possibility of the government logging its own timber. He stated with apparent confidence that even "if carried on fairly extensively," such logging would not seriously compete with private enterprise, noting that less than 5 percent of logs came from national forest timber. Although he claimed to understand the nature of local markets, for others it was hard to imagine that direct government sales would fail to have a significant impact on a log marketplace. As to the construction of government sawmills, Silcox saw this as likely only for the purpose of "testing and demonstrating better methods of milling and utilization."

By the time of the New Orleans address, copies of the *Journal of Forestry*, which included the paper presented to the Society of American Foresters' annual meeting by the chief forester, had been distributed. Many reacted, among them Carl Stevens, who wrote letters to Phil, to H. H. Chapman of Yale University, then serving as president of the Society, and to Silcox himself. To Phil he sent copies of the other two letters, indicating, "You are, no doubt, familiar with Silcox's 'Pinchot-like' effulgence . . . and that will be enough background for the present." To Professor Chapman, whose own remarks had pleased Stevens, he wrote, "I wish that more of these foresters who have their heads in the clouds knew how earnestly no inconsiderable part of the lumber industry has been striving with us to bring order out of chaos," adding that the effort had involved "the expenditure of no small amount of money, when money was very hard to get."

In his letter to Silcox, Stevens disdained the indirect attack. "A few foresters have continued to work at forestry, in the woods and with the trees, with and through the economic catastrophe of the last five and one-half years," he said by way of introduction. He then offered the opinion, "American foresters will never secure American forestry for American forests by shooting with large calibre guns from behind the smug security of governmental bulwarks," suggesting that the proper "function of the government forester . . . is to help and not threaten." While there was "a foundation of truth" for much of what concerned the chief forester, Stevens was positive that Silcox had "not yet reached the cure." He closed inquiring, "May we not have moderation and intelligent cooperation?" Phil must have applauded enthusiastically.

While Silcox was holding forth in New Orleans, Phil and Helen were vacationing in California, meeting Dave and Kay Winton in San Francisco, and then motoring south by easy stages to Pasadena. Upon his return to Tacoma, Phil came down with chicken pox, extending his time away from the office by a few days. As always there was much to be done when he finally returned to work. One of the letters awaiting a response was from Ralph J. Hines of the Edward Hines Lumber Company. Ralph wondered what action Phil was advising on the matter of sustained-yield certification under Article X of the Lumber Code. If he had been paying attention, he would not have needed to ask. In any event, Phil made it clear that the failure of the code "to continue to function" should not be allowed to destroy its advantages. In this connection, he observed, "It occurs to me that the industry is going to have to recognize a responsibility placed upon it by public opinion and especially the Forest Service which is in a position to deal us a lot of misery." Phil's own analysis of the situation was that "wherever possible . . . the industry should go on with this kind of work," if for no other reason than that "we gain tremendously in public appreciation if we can point to sustained yield operations." Many things had to be done by the public if timber owners were going to be able "to carry on the financial burden of ownership through the years," and few of these had as yet been initiated. Nevertheless, he contended, "we are being continually put on the defensive by such men as Silcox and I believe we spike his guns to some extent by cooperating in the face of difficulties."

Of far greater immediate worry was the deteriorating labor situation. On the last day of April, Phil sat down and tried to summarize it for his Uncle Fred. He reported that Clark and Wilson Lumber Company had just gone out on strike and that E. P. Marsh, as on-the-scene representative of Secretary of Labor Francis Perkins, was in Portland seeking interviews with operators. The previous day the wage board of the 4L had met and determined to advance the date of their regular meeting and to seek an increase in the minimum wage rates from 45 cents to 50 cents an hour. Phil observed that there were as "many opinions among operators as there are individuals" as to the best course to follow and added, "Many who have not yet their tail in the gate still advocate methods which refuse to recognize the union or have anything to do with it."

In agreement with Long-Bell, Phil indicated that they would be meeting together or separately, "but in close conjunction" with union representatives. If progress resulted, then the thought was "to reduce the matter to writing after substantial agreement has been reached, instead of offering a memo before hand." Noting that most operators "shy at written agreements," Phil saw no reason to refuse "to outline on paper" what they were willing to do. Indeed, they had been willing to do as much for the 4L.

That very morning they had also received notice that the National Labor Board was calling for an election at Willapa Harbor. It was, of course, not the most propitious time for an election, at least not from Phil's vantage. The only happy news to report was that business had "been pouring in," that they had a large order file, and that the prices were advancing "on the strength of the strike talk."

At its annual convention in San Francisco in October 1934, the AFL had designated the United Brotherhood of Carpenters and Joiners as the union to assume jurisdiction for the forest products industry. Active involvement of the new union was delayed until April 1, although prior to that a joint Northwest Council had been formed in the Douglas-fir district among the loggers and sawmill workers. The shingle weavers and the plywood and veneer workers had organized two separate councils, the three maintaining some semblance of coordinated effort by means of a joint executive board. When A. W. "Abe" Muir, a general executive board member of the Carpenters Union, arrived to direct union activities in April, he found a fairly militant leadership already in place. Although the organizational effort was only beginning, the demands seemed to have already been decided. These included, in addition to union recognition, a six-hour day and a minimum wage of 75 cents an hour. In mid-April a convention of union representatives from all lumber-related industries was held in Longview at which those demands were adopted along with the call for an organization offensive. Most important, a deadline of May 6 was established, each local then to report its success or failure to the joint Northwest Council. Discipline was going to be a difficult matter within the union, as evidenced by strikes that took place prior to the agreed-upon deadline; the workers at the Bellingham plants of Bloedel-Donovan struck on April 27, followed shortly by a walkout by the laborers of the Clark and Wilson Lumber Company in Portland.

Given the fragmented nature of the Pacific Northwest lumber industry, it is understandable that union effort concentrated on Long-Bell and the Weyerhaeuser Timber Company branch at Longview. If those negotiations were successfully managed, unions throughout the fir district would be greatly encouraged, and indeed many other organizations would be likely to settle along the lines accepted by these two "giants." The representatives of Long-Bell and Weyerhaeuser could not be called enthusiastic about participation in the negotiations, but they approached the table more realistically than their adversaries. Across the table from Abe Muir at the Monticello Hotel in Longview sat John Tennant and Roy Morse of Long-Bell and Al Raught and Harry Morgan of Weyerhaeuser, with Charlie Ingram from the Tacoma office looking over their shoulders.

With the exception of Abe Muir, this was a new experience for the union representatives. That was probably unfortunate. He had difficulty convincing the rank and file that it was serious business—a serious business that demanded preparation, a willingness to exchange, and discipline. At the same time, for the rank and file it had to be exciting to think in terms of power, even of picket lines. These were tough men who believed themselves to have been hoodwinked in the past. Never again. And they had come to believe their own rhetoric. Muir knew that the 75-cent hourly minimum wage demand was ridiculous, but he had little success convincing those around him.

One of the things Muir had trouble understanding, for good reason, was the nature of the Weyerhaeuser Timber Company organization. He had inquired a number of times whether the Longview settlement, whenever reached, would automatically be accepted by the other company branches. Although the answer to the inquiry was a definite "no," there was nonetheless a recognized relationship. Indeed, Phil thought that the fact of the Longview negotiations was probably the reason that none of the other Weyerhaeuser operations had struck. In a May 4 letter to F.E., he reported rumors that Willapa, Snoqualmie, and Everett all had been on the verge of striking over the past three days, but they had been held in line by the union leadership. Furthermore, the news of the Longview talks seemed to be encouraging. The hope proved short-lived. The following day, May 5, a large meeting was held at the Labor Temple in Everett, and a walkout resulted. The union leadership in Longview "confessed that they were out of control of the situation at Everett and suggested that we not try to operate there until the situation has cooled off." All plants in Portland, Tacoma, and Olympia were also closed down. At Grays Harbor the sawmills continued to operate, although the boom men had walked out. As yet, only one mill in Seattle was struck, and all the Willamette Valley mills were operating.

In the meantime, Phil could report that the Longview negotiators had "reached the point where all features of the working agreement have been agreed to except wages." That was a colossal exception—75 cents! Thus no one was predicting a successful conclusion. E. P. Marsh, the Labor Department's observer, later described the developments to Secretary Perkins:

On May 10 an agreement was reached bearing modified union recognition of 40 hour week and fifty cents an hour minimum wage, with five cents an hour increase to all other classifications. This proposal was approved by not only Mr. Muir, but by a local committee of 25 employees of the five operations of those two companies [Long-Bell and Weyerhaeuser of Longview]. Mass meetings of the entire membership, both in the camps and mills, were called to discuss the terms of the proposed agreement and ballot on the same. Terrific objection to the terms of the agreement arose, mainly centering on the wage increase. It should be borne in mind that the men everywhere were striking for a minimum wage of seventy-five cents an hour, and the difference between seventy-five cents and fifty cents offered by the company was so wide that the men could not reconcile themselves to accepting the same. A later analysis of the wage structure of these companies disclosed that while they were paying the same minimum as most companies, namely, forty-five cents per hour, in the higher classifications they were paying far in advance of nearly all their competitors. As a matter of fact, the highest wages paid in the lumber industry in the world were then being paid by these companies, but this economic fact was that they were being given a nickel an hour when they asked for thirty cents. The result of this ballot was a rejection of the proposal, and these camps and mills did not open the following morning.

Marsh further believed that if the agreement had been accepted by the Long-Bell and Weyerhaeuser Longview locals, it would have "influenced settlement of the entire industry within a week." Such was not to be. Phil was able to report a clean slate on the morning of May 13, "a complete shut down in all operations on the West Coast." As to the immediate future of negotiations, there seemed no cause for optimism: "It looks as though this would be a continuing condition inasmuch as there seems little with which we can compromise."

The disappointment attached to the failure to resolve the labor disagreement was accorded a different perspective with the death of John Weyerhaeuser on May 16. A cold had worsened to become pneumonia, and he was old and very tired. John died in the morning at Haddaway Hall. The *Tacoma News Tribune* reported the event, acknowledging his ties with "the huge timber company and its affiliated concerns," but at the same time noting with complete accuracy, "Mr. Weyerhaeuser might rightfully be said to have been one of the least personally known of Tacoma's citizens." The reason was clear enough to those few who had known him: "He was modest and retiring and preferred to remain as inconspicuous as possible." The fact is that had not F. E. Weyerhaeuser been in Tacoma on business, the paper would have been hard-pressed to provide any details of John's life.

In the meantime, one of those strange and tragic webs of circumstance was in its conception. A month earlier, a curious trio arrived in the vicinity of Raymond and South Bend, Washington. Harmon Metz Waley and William Dainard had known each other in the Idaho State Penitentiary in 1930, and mid-April of 1935 found them, along with Waley's wife, Margaret, in western Washington and in need of money. It was the banks of the two coastal towns that interested them, but robbing a bank was only one of several possible means to quick money. On May 1, Waley and Dainard were in Seattle, and apparently they had decided that kidnapping was the easier and safer course. Dainard went so far as to dig a hole, in a remote section south of the hamlet of Issaquah, to hold their still unselected victim. They also began to prepare a number of ransom notes for possible use.

In the midst of these plans and preparations, Margaret Waley came across the obituary of John Philip Weyerhaeuser in the *Seattle Post-Intelligencer* of May 17 and called the article to the attention of her husband and Dainard. The deceased was identified as one of the four sons of Frederick Weyerhaeuser, "billionaire St. Paul lumberman." Thus two sets of people were introduced for the first time. Dainard and Waley spent much of the week of May 20 in the neighborhood of the Phil Weyerhaeuser home at 420 North Fourth Street in Tacoma, to acquaint themselves with the children and their habits in going to and from school. The kidnapping of eight-year-old George took place a few minutes before noon on Friday, May 24. George was walking home from Lowell School for lunch. He never arrived.

A special delivery letter containing the first ransom note was received at Phil's house that evening at about 6:30. The police had, of course, been notified in the meantime. But it was the Federal Bureau of Investigation, building its own reputation as it provided careful and considerate assistance, that proved decisive in this as in so many other kidnapping cases of that troubled decade. W. K. Bolling, Department of Justice agent from Seattle, was at the Weyerhaeuser home within two hours of the arrival of the ransom note. Public announcement of the boy's kidnapping was made that same evening by Charlie Ingram, in behalf of the family.

For any family it is difficult to imagine a greater tragedy than to have one of its members at the mercy of unknown others, and to be totally helpless. The sudden harshness of the public spotlight was an added agony for Phil and Helen, so anxious to raise a family "simply," as Phil's mother used to say. All of that changed, was lost, from the moment they realized that George's disappearance was a kidnapping. In the days ahead, Phil and Helen would learn far more than they cared to know of the gamut of public interest and attention, from those whose expressions were sincerely sympathetic to those whose only possible excuse was morbid curiosity. They had known sadness and worry before, but there had been nothing to prepare them for this ordeal.

The original ransom note had demanded $200,000 in unmarked bills. Five days were given to satisfy the demands, and a number of conditions were included, such as the impossible "Keep it out of the papers." That first typed note concluded, "SO JUST REMEMBER A SLIP ON YOUR PART IS A SLIP BY US. DON'T DO IT," and it was signed, "EGOIST. EGOIST." It would be unfair to ask on whom the pressures and heartache bore most heavily, but it was Phil who would be required to act, to respond to the kidnappers' demands and directions. The second note arrived on May 29, ordering him to go to Seattle and register at the Ambassador Hotel under the name of James Paul Jones. He left that same afternoon, accompanied by Rod Titcomb, the two driving in Titcomb's black Pontiac sedan. In Seattle they got in touch with Charlie Ingram, who had been handling the arrangements by which the $200,000 ransom money had been obtained from the First National Bank of Seattle. With the money "in a large black suitcase of cheap construction," Phil went to the Ambassador, where he registered according to instructions and was assigned room 602. There he waited, alone, until he received two messages, these in a single envelope which was delivered to the hotel by a cab driver.

Following the new instructions, Phil took the suitcase and drove Titcomb's car to a spot at 64th and Renton avenues in Seattle. Having no idea what kind of people he was dealing with, he had to believe that his son's life depended on his ability to follow the directions exactly, but the directions seemed vague and the area was dark and unfamiliar. Nonetheless, he located the first spot, where he found two sticks driven into the ground to which a small piece of white cloth was attached, and nearby he found a can which contained another note. This merely directed him some 700 feet distant where he again found two sticks with a piece of cloth attached. But here he found nothing else. Reluctant to leave without having made any contact, he sat in the car at the second location for about two hours, until after midnight, or the early morning of May 30.

Phil spent the rest of that night at the Olympic Hotel, returning to the Ambassador the following morning. At 11:27 A.M., he received a phone call, the substance of which was as follows:

KIDNAPPER: What happened last night?
WEYERHAEUSER: I did as told and waited.
KIDNAPPER: Didn't you find those notes?
WEYERHAEUSER: I didn't find any more.
KIDNAPPER: You were supposed to go in the side road.
WEYERHAEUSER: There were no directions.
KIDNAPPER: Somebody must have taken the can. Have you the demands ready in full?
WEYERHAEUSER: Yes.
KIDNAPPER: We'll give you one more chance tonight. If not made by 12 o'clock tonight we're through with the case.

That same evening at about 9:45, Phil received another phone call, advising him to go to 1105 East Madison Street and step inside the gate at that address, where he would find a note. The kidnapper warned Phil to make certain that he was not followed, and when Phil admitted that being alone at night in these remote places made him nervous, the kidnapper replied, "Maybe you are as scared as I am." Phil went to the spot, located a can containing a note which directed him to a location about fifteen miles south of Seattle along the Pacific Highway toward Tacoma. There he was supposed to turn around and head north again, turning right on the second dirt road. Some one thousand feet down this road he spotted the now familiar sticks and flag and located another can with its note.

Following the new instructions, Phil returned to the car, where he sat for five minutes with the dome light on and then proceeded on down the road to another set of sticks, another can, and another set of directions. This time he was advised to leave the car, "motor running, dome light on," and to leave the suitcase containing the ransom money on the seat. This he did, proceeding to walk on down the road. After going about a hundred yards, he heard someone crashing through the brush and then heard the car being driven away. It was nearly midnight when an exhausted Phil was picked up on the highway by Rod Titcomb, the two returning to the Olympic Hotel. It was already Friday, May 31. It had been a week since George's disappearance.

The car was discovered on Saturday morning, June 1, but that discovery was not regarded as significant, at least not by Phil and his family. George was already safely home, having arrived in a taxi at about 7:45 that morning. There were, of course, many related stories, not the least of which had to do with the experience of victim George. The fact was, however, that although he must have been terribly frightened and fearful throughout his ordeal, he was not mistreated. The fact also was that, with the resiliency of youth, he returned to a normal life almost immediately. What was undoubtedly more difficult was not so much their son's return to his routine but the decision required of Phil and Helen in allowing him to do so. The only public statement they made following George's return, given out that Saturday morning, read in part:

The terrible ordeal he has gone through has brought him back a badly-shaken little boy. We request that further details regarding his frightful experience be withheld from publication to reduce any bad effect on his future life.

We are overjoyed that George is back, and the awful suspense is over.

We are very grateful for the many expressions of sympathy and offers of help.

Despite their best efforts, however, Phil and Helen could not protect George. Like it or not, he was a public figure, for the moment almost as well known as Shirley Temple; and from then on and for years to come, he would be George Weyerhaeuser, the kidnap victim. The notoriety was evident in all manner of ways. Within minutes after George had been permitted to go outside with his friends, Phil and Helen noticed a small tent erected on a neighbor's front yard which featured a poster prominently advertising the attraction within. "See George Weyerhaeuser, 5 cents," an enterprising playmate had lettered. Given the circumstances, things were as normal as could be expected.

As the events unfolded, it was not long between George's release and the apprehension of the Waleys. On June 8, Margaret Waley was purchasing a twenty-cent cigarette case and the clerk at that Salt Lake City store routinely checked her five dollar bill against the ransom money list. Harmon Waley subsequently led agents to the cache where more than $90,000 of the money was buried. Their trial began a month later in Tacoma, and on July 9 Phil took the witness stand, giving his "own story of the agonized efforts whereby he obtained the release of his nine-year-old son," this according to the *Seattle P-I*. Noting that Weyerhaeuser was the third witness called, the report described the courtroom scene:

The young heir to one of the world's greatest timber fortunes had been sitting in a front row seat with Ingram, unrecognized by a vast majority of the courtroom spectators, and there was a stir of interest as his name was called and he strode slowly to the stand. Dressed inconspicuously in brown, he gave no outward indication of his wealth. His demeanor was deeply serious, but his face was completely expressionless. He spoke in a calm monotone, and he seemed to be striving to avoid looking at the defendant, who twisted a handkerchief that she knotted through her wedding ring. . . .

The Waleys were found guilty. She received a sentence of twenty years and he one of sixty.

Another side to the story was the hundreds of letters received from those offering sympathy, and the few from those who sought to reap some personal advantage from the affair. Such tragedies inevitably elicit expressions of faith, and faith from a variety of sources. One of the first letters received was the combined effort of four of George's Sunday school classmates at the First Congregational Church. Even the obvious assistance of teacher Annie B. Moore could not hide the basic statement of childish concern. "We will ask God every day to take care of him in the stillness of the night and even in the daytime," their letter to Phil and Helen read. "We don't want him to be afraid."

The procurement of the ransom money was another story within the story. Phil, of course, could not have managed it alone, and the initial solution involved his brother and sister. At the time of the kidnapping, Uncle Rudolph had been in Lewiston. He and Bill Billings arrived in Tacoma on Monday. That evening Rudolph was at the Titcombs for dinner, and following dinner Rod Titcomb and Charlie Ingram had told him about their plans for raising the money. Rudolph allowed: "I thought it was a family matter and that we should get behind anything they did." This position was subsequently reaffirmed in a meeting that included Uncle Fred, Fred K., Ed Davis, and Fritz Jewett. Rudolph agreed to carry that message to his sisters and to the Walter Rosenberrys, who represented the estate of brother Charles. Walter Rosenberry, Jr., was the husband of Charles's only daughter, Sarah Maud.

In the meantime, the children of John Philip and their spouses had sent their own letter to the family members. It was signed jointly by

Phil and Helen, Rod and Elizabeth, and Fred K. and Vivian, although it was probably Fred's composition:

Our kidnapping experience is now over except for the terrible publicity and the efforts of the government to catch the kidnappers and recover what money it can. This last phase of the matter still makes necessary absolute silence by the members of the family in regard to the details of the kidnapping, payment of ransom, etc.

We are writing you all this letter, first, to tell you of the great feeling of gratitude in our hearts for the instantaneous offer of financial help as well as sympathy from all of you. No one can express what this meant to Helen and Phil and to the rest of us who joined in the week-long vigil, waiting and hoping against hope for George's return.

In the second place, we want to set up a financial understanding with you in regard to the $200,000.00 ransom money. We want this to be a loan to Father's three children to be repaid out of his estate as soon as possible. Three individual notes each signed by one of us are enclosed herewith. Our reason for wanting this is simply that we [the J. P. Weyerhaeuser children] do not wish to be in the position of causing financial loss and deprivation of material things to the other members of the family. Please accept these notes in the spirit in which we offer them. We want to do our part and not be a drag on everybody else. We will feel better if this is done.

To Phil and Helen and many others it must have seemed as if the world had stopped during that terrible week of George's absence. It only seemed that way. One heartening aspect of the experience was that although the kidnapping occurred during the West Coast lumber strikes, there was little suggestion of any possible connection—that strikers might have become kidnappers.

As a matter of fact, concurrent with the week of the kidnapping, meetings were going on between the representatives of the union and the branches. Within both organizations, the Timber Company, as expressed through its Executive Committee, and the union, there was disagreement on how to proceed. Uncle Fred told Phil of the Executive Committee discussions. Reports had been received indicating that the workers at Longview might be willing to return to the job if the offer previously rejected were made again. Apparently Gus Clapp and Laird Bell had argued in favor of doing so, but F.E. had, in his words, "objected very strenuously . . . on the ground that we had fulfilled all of our commitments under the code and that our men had rejected an agreement approved by their Washington representatives, and that we should not weaken our position by making another offer to sign an agreement with them." Laird, described by F.E. as being "quite excited about my suggestion," had countered by proposing that nothing be done until it was possible to consult Phil. Uncle Fred agreed that Phil was the one "finally to pass on this labor problem." Still he wanted it understood that he regarded the Longview locals as "a lot of irresponsible members of a Union who will not respect agreements made by their officers . . . and that we are merely letting ourselves in for a lot of trouble when we invite ourselves into the American Federation of Labor as it exists on the Pacific Coast."

Regarding the position taken by Laird Bell, Uncle Fred saw this simply as a result "of his support of the movement for social justice somewhat as expressed by Mr. Hutchins, president of the University of Chicago, of which Mr. Bell is a director." Although F.E. did not declare himself to be in open rebellion, assuring Phil that he would support "the general ideas of this group," he did warn that they must be practical in their approach and "must remember that our stockholders also have some interest in the business we are directing"; and while it was all well and good to give employees "all they are entitled to, and more, we cannot allow them to ruin our industry."

Interestingly enough, Laird's letter of the same week mentioned not a word of the Executive Committee disagreement. Rather, he apologized to Phil for his inability to express himself about the recent tragedy. "I am afraid I left Tacoma without a word about how I felt for you & Helen, before and after," he began. "I seem talkative enough in ordinary things but I go dumb when it comes to the personal & real matters." In this, Phil understood exactly what his friend was saying. Had Laird's family been the sufferers, Phil would have experienced the same difficulty.

On June 19, Phil wrote a letter to the Weyerhaeuser family, observing: "Aside from finding it difficult to concentrate on anything so prosaic as business, I am back to normal." He reported that they had just sent George and Flip off to camp. George had been undergoing an experience that was necessary but worrisome, at least to his parents. He had been accompanying FBI agents around the area, identifying places and people, and Phil acknowledged that he and Helen were "delighted to have him away where we hope he will forget it all." Regarding Helen, Phil thought that she might have acquired a few more gray hairs, but he allowed that she had been "perfectly wonderful throughout." As for himself, he was scheduled to appear the next day before the federal grand jury for the purpose of indicting the Waleys. The mail continued to arrive at a rate that was "appalling," Phil noting that "yesterday we received about a thousand letters, fifty of them bearing foreign stamps." He further noted that they were now "on every 'sucker' list in the world and are asked to show our gratitude in a multitude of ways."

The publicity and its results were indeed difficult to accept, and it is hardly surprising that Phil and others in the family held the press largely to blame. Phil complained that reporters were "one class of animals which never seems to be apprehended"; in connection with the recent experience, "They stooped to *any* device to get something to write about." Elizabeth had been sufficiently disturbed to promise that her "next major effort is going to be directed against the newspapers," and Phil wished her the best of luck. Still, "with the exception of the newspapers, all the world has been exceedingly sympathetic to us," he wrote, and "we are benumbed with kindness." Phil closed by recognizing the family sense of togetherness, an infrequent admission on his part. "I cannot express the extent of our feeling toward you all," and he concluded, much in the manner of his father and grandfather, "The Lord has been good to us in numberless ways."

That same day, June 19, F.E. was writing to Phil, acknowledging the joint letter of June 5 in which the three children of John Philip had attempted to assume full responsibility for the ransom amount. Uncle Fred trusted that his nephews and niece, and their spouses, would not "object to our taking the position that this particular incident is a family affair," adding that "one of the best things that can be said of Father's family is that they have always stood together with perfect loyalty and devotion."

Evidence of Phil's return to business as usual was his June 21 complaint to brother Fred regarding some of the policies and personnel of General Timber Service, Phil charging that certain procedures were being forced down the throats of western branch managers. General Timber Service had been organized to provide various services required by all the associated companies; but like the Sales Company, what seemed a logical approach in theory was not so easily managed in practice. Phil well understood that his managers were an independent and occasionally cantankerous lot, but he also understood that it was crucial that he be loyal to them. Anyway, he, too, tired of these St. Paul "experts" in a hurry.

Fred K. responded to this complaint in fairly typical fashion. "I am sorry to get your hand written note of June 21," he began, "indicating a seething and dangerous spirit of revolution and I am sorry the actions of anybody that I have anything to do with is [sic] the cause of this unhappy situation." Then he tried to put things back together again. Although not wishing to blame Phil "for being wrought up," Fred maintained that "we have a number of situations where there is a sort of dual authority and it is only by keeping our 'shirts on' and working together that we can get things done and work effectively." He closed by assuring Phil that nobody in St. Paul had "any desire to cram anything down the throats of any of the Companies."

All of this raised several questions, but since they had all been discussed previously at one time or another, raising them again would serve little purpose. Needless to say, Phil's view of the matter had a western skew to it. Unless he worked hard at telling himself otherwise, he simply assumed that what was truly important was what was going on in the woods and mills; that those on the production end of things were producing as best they could; and that then it was up to others to support those production efforts and to sell the results, at a profit. In a sense, the differences that developed were those typically of staff and line. Phil and Fred K. were unwittingly a part of an inevitable schism, made all the worse by the organization and physical separation of the Weyerhaeuser Timber Company and the Weyerhaeuser Sales Company and General Timber Service, between Tacoma and St. Paul. Phil must have been tempted, in moments of particular pique, to regret the cumbersome geographic split. Only Phil and brother Fred could have made it work at all.

In this instance, Phil seemed willing to accept Fred's explanation. "Your letter of June 24th reprimanding me for my spirit of revolution is at hand and I accept the reprimand with humility," he began. But Phil was unwilling to pretend that the issues were without basis of concern, again stating his belief that the General Timber Service auditors were taking on more than they could do "to the detriment of everybody at interest." He suggested that at the very least they be more selective in the responsibilities they accepted. That would require some rearranging, he acknowledged, "but let somebody do that shifting right or wrong, and if other jobs which cannot be undertaken are urgent then let the Timber Company or anybody requesting them do the jobs themselves."

July came and the labor problems were still in a state of turmoil. National guard troops were assigned duty at various locations, and the threat of violence hung depressingly in the air. Phil had written to Lawrence Ottinger, president of United States Plywood, suggesting that they continue to postpone consideration of any joint venture. He did so in no apparent sense of despair. Times simply were not propitious. But there had been bad times before, and better times would return, no doubt bearing some changes. Uncle Fred was far less able to accept an optimistic view of the world and its future. He *was* despairing, and the more things changed, the more he reminisced. Aside from FDR, few things bothered F.E. more than the aggressiveness and accompanying success of organized labor. Certainly there had been excesses and examples of irresponsibility on the labor side. At the same time, it seemed impossible for F.E. and many others to see beyond such disappointments, to admit the possibility that relations with labor had been imperfect, lacking a maturity and even a mutuality of respect. This view is hardly surprising. The second-generation Weyerhaeusers had come to shun even shared partnerships—that is, partnerships with outsiders. And if one worried about cooperating and compromising at the owner-manager level, how much more difficult was it to involve workers in the decisions that had to do with "running a business."

In a long and rambling letter written on the eve of the Fourth of July, Uncle Fred defended his position on the company's labor policies. He told Phil that while he did not object "to negotiating with our own men, whether they are members of the A.F. of L. or any other organization of their own choosing," he did object to making any written agreement. In part, this objection was based on his belief that insistence on a written agreement was the result of "interference from political sources in Washington," and that such an agreement would have an adverse effect on the industry as a whole. There certainly was some justification for the second concern. Al Raught would later recall that "the whole industry was sore at us for being such damned fools as to sit down and even talk to the union representatives." Other than the appearance of weakness that the willingness to negotiate implied to some, there was the real worry that the details of settlement at Longview, involving the two most efficient operations in the fir region, would be forced on the majority of Northwest operators. In the case of F.E., however, one has the feeling that he viewed the negotiations as just the first step down the road to socialism or worse.

Again he talked specifically of the division existing within the Executive Committee of the Timber Company. Gus Clapp and Laird Bell were in favor of allowing Al Raught to offer again the same written agreement that the Longview employees had previously refused, with Lyn Reichmann, manager of the Everett branch, given the same authority. Since F. S. Bell would "naturally" agree with his son Laird, "clearly three of our Executive Committee are in favor of a written agreement with the A.F. of L. Horace [Irvine], with whom I have briefly discussed this matter, feels very much as I do. Accordingly, if after considering all the facts, you are in favor of making a written agreement with the A.F. of L., covering our employees, the vote would be at least four to two in our Executive Committee. . . ."

Although he would not say so directly, it is apparent that F.E. looked upon Laird Bell as being an unfortunate influence, too willing to accept change and too deficient in knowledge of what had gone before. Laird wasn't a lumberman. Worse, he was a lawyer. The occasion seemed appropriate for Uncle Fred to offer "one of my usual digressions." True, one had to read between the lines to get the message, but Phil was an old hand at this, as F.E. knew. The digression went as follows: "Mr. F. H. Thatcher died quite a few years ago. You probably remember that he and Mr. Bell managed the Laird Norton Company interests. Mr. Thatcher told me that he had asked Mr.

151 Never Business as Usual

George S. Long to liquidate the Weyerhaeuser Timber Company in ten years. This statement must have been made at least fifteen years ago and illustrates fully how little Mr. Thatcher comprehended the extent of the assets of the Weyerhaeuser Timber Company. It is probable that Mr. F. S. Bell feels as Mr. Thatcher did. . . ."

He next indicated his own feeling that he agreed with the liquidation of timber at a reasonable rate, but he did not believe a fifteen-year supply was excessive for any sawmill operation, although he would distinguish between operations east and west of the Cascades. Then F.E. commented on a recent letter from Laird Bell in which Laird had again expressed disappointment in the fact that "we did not merge our timber in Idaho with the Wintons." While acknowledging, almost proudly, that he had played no part in the Idaho merger negotiations, Uncle Fred also claimed that it had seemed "absurd for us to buy an interest in the old Winton sawmills with timber while we ourselves had one or two idle sawmills, one of which at least could manufacture the timber in question." And from this he had concluded that Laird was "exceedingly anxious to liquidate timber today. Perhaps he is correct but I don't see the problem as he does. Of course if the political and industrial situation in this country goes as it did in Germany, and under the leadership of our President I think it may, there isn't much purpose in our building up organization and plants looking toward future liquidation of timber. On the other hand, if we have converted our timber into other securities, when the crash comes there will not be much gained."

Clearly the outlook was gloomy as viewed from F.E.'s desk, whichever way one chose to leap. And just as clearly he failed or refused to understand Laird Bell and, in a sense, Phil Weyerhaeuser—neither of whom favored liquidation, in the old sense of the word, but rather looked forward to circumstances when liquidation of timber was no longer necessary. In the meantime, it might be true that one had to schedule the realization of profits and the decrease of liabilities in a manner sufficiently balanced to permit operation over the short term. Perhaps the gap in their understanding involved that continuing focus or fixation on the old-growth timber as being all important in the fir region. If indeed that was the only resource of value, the only manner of operation was liquidation. Everybody, including F.E., knew that trees grew, but growing trees for profit was still a subject for dreamers. There was a lot of the old and traditional in Phil, but he thought he could see movement in a desirable direction. And unlike his uncle, he did not despair.

Perhaps some things simply seemed less confused closer to the scene of activities. In this instance, one thing was definite, as Phil would report to Uncle Fred: "The 4–L has done us no good whatsoever and is completely dead at our plants with no members at Snoqualmie or Longview." Although he had not yet discussed the matter with the various managers, he saw no reason for attempting to continue any pretense anywhere of a 4L relationship. There was really no choice other than to deal with the unions representing "our employees at our plants." As to the problem of a written agreement, "when the time comes," Phil argued, "we should be willing to make a written statement of what our agreement with them is, if we can reach an agreement." As a matter of fact, things were beginning to look up. In Everett they had hopes of starting operations the next week, although there was still considerable tension in that community. He thought it might help if they were to publish in the Saturday edition of the paper an announcement that employees could return to work on Monday, with an accompanying statement recognizing the "union as representing the men of our plants who are its members."

To some of the older generation Phil may have seemed overly willing to accept the union position, but others saw in him the unyielding and coldhearted stereotype of the American capitalist. It is true that it was difficult for him to have any real understanding of the personal hardships occasioned by unemployment, the effect of strikes, or even of limited income. It is also true that in the course of the kidnapping and its aftermath, Phil deeply resented being portrayed as an extremely wealthy man, and there is no question that he and his style of living were grossly misrepresented. At the same time, he had never experienced want, and he could only imagine what it entailed, no matter how sympathetic he was by nature. Regarding the strike of the summer of 1935, he probably did not feel as estranged from "our men" as they did from him, but neither side had much opportunity for dialogue beyond the specific discussion of proposal and counterproposal. Any exchanges beyond those issues were rare indeed. One such did occur, in a letter to Phil from the wife of a Longview laborer, the effect of which we can only guess.

"Is there no other way to settle this trouble?" the worried wife and mother asked. "I think my husband and many others of your old employees are out of work because they *won't* go to work thru a picket line." She then tried to share something of her family's situation. It is an interesting letter, and one can picture Phil reading it slowly, then reading it again, wishing that he could talk personally with the couple, and perhaps feeling nearly as helpless as they.

We owe some other bills too, about $300.00 in all, but he has lost that much in this strike. Do you not realize Mr. Weyerhaeuser that if you would come over here and talk to your employees like man to man you would gain more ground than by force and if you would pay a living wage every or nearly every man would work for your interest, and you would very soon win back what you lost. We have a family of 8 to look out for and God only knows what the end will be if we don't get work. Just stop to think $300.00 to you is nothing and to us it would pay all we owe, so we could look the world in the face. We are all willing to work, but not by police protection. . . .

Did you ever stop to think that if it had not been for the working people, you would not have what you have. My husband was born in Rock Island, Ill., 48 years ago today, he remembers your Grandfather's first mill there. He is 48 today and we can't even afford a nice dinner for him. It is also J. D. Rockefeller's birthday. What a difference in our lives. . . .

I read the papers thru when little George was gone. I like the looks of yours and family pictures. George was surely a brave little fellow, but what I liked best of the whole affair was the way you and your brave little wife prayed and then when George was returned, in all your gladness you did not forget to give your thanks to Him, who knows all our troubles.

Please don't give this letter to any reporters, perhaps I am doing wrong in writing it, but I just feel so full that I must do something.

Please give this a thot [sic], also your employees and I know they will co-operate for better and happier times.

In fact, the conditions for settlement suggested were those originally offered and rejected. Things weren't simple, and wanting it so did not make it so, whether for a worker's wife or a Weyerhaeuser.

The labor situation finally broke. In the first week of August, the employees of the Willapa mills returned to work, the company providing "a statement on the basis of which they went back to work." Snoqualmie and White River had also arrived at a written agreement. The Everett and Longview employees decided to return in advance of any formal written statement but with the assurance that such a statement would be forthcoming at the conclusion of negotiations. As with most such battles, it was difficult to determine who had won and who had lost. Certainly the unions had achieved recognition, but the manner of the achievement had been costly to the workers. The negotiations which had reopened on May 30 had seemed successful, and union leader Abe Muir had "formally ordered the men to return to work, which they did." The troubles, however, were far from over. E. P. Marsh summarized the developments:

A few days later, the shingle weavers who had not effected a settlement, placed a picket line on the plants which were again closed. The second shutdown of the mills resulted in revocation by Mr. Muir of the Union Charter, and in its stead the installation of four new charters, one at each plant and logging camp. Mr. Muir again ordered the men to return to work in a letter explaining in full the whole situation, mailed to every employee of the Company. Upon a given date the plants announced they would again receive applications for employment, and gradually the mills and plants resumed operations. It took some few days to bring them back to normal production and there was considerable desultory picketing and guerilla warfare between disgruntled ex-employees of the company and employees who were members of the newly chartered unions.

At the time of his report, August 22, Marsh noted that the mills were "running 100% with union crews in all branches."

But while these settlements were occurring, other developments were taking place far to the east that would shortly alter the labor situation in the Northwest. The Committee for Industrial Organizations (CIO) seemed to exude strength from its inception. Increasing numbers became caught up in the evangelistic fervor of John L. Lewis. Sermons intended originally for miners obviously had a general appeal to laborers, and soon those in the woods and mills would be facing a difficult choice as to representation. There would, of course, be complications for management as well.

At the August meeting of the Timber Company Executive Committee in St. Paul, Phil had been directed to review the cash situation of the company, partly to be able to consider the possible effects of stock distribution in subsidiary corporations, particularly regarding the tax effects. At this time the Weyerhaeuser Timber Company was still a very small organization in number of stockholders, the total being only 301. Although it was somewhat out of character, Phil occasionally welcomed opportunities for organizing information in a statistical way, no doubt in part because it seemed to accomplish the purpose with few accompanying words. More important, however, Phil was committed to sharing more information with more people. There were at least two reasons for this commitment: he believed that accurate information, even if not always of the most favorable sort, was to be preferred to rumors and fears based on an absence of information; and he became increasingly convinced that news of what the Timber Company was doing deserved to be shared, in short to be advertised. The changes came slowly, despite considerable opposition. Many of the directors opposed any unnecessary exposure—an understandable stance, given what seemed to be long experience of abuse. Phil later recalled the evolution:

When I first came over in '33, if you came to the annual meeting, you were handed one sheet of paper, a balance sheet, and an earnings statement to take home. But no statement was mailed to the stockholders at all. No effort was made to explain the company or its objectives.

During all the years of Mr. Long's regime he used to make out a fat annual report, which I guess he gave to the directors. He'd come to the stockholders' meeting with a lot of pieces of paper stuck in here and there where he'd read excerpts. But you had to come to the meeting to get any information about the company. Now some would say we're rather blatant about announcing to people our earnings and lots of other things about the company. It's a great change anyway—that and the advertising. We go around the country making speeches about how good we are, how swell we are for the communities in which we operate.

The "now" referred to was 1953, but the changes were already becoming apparent in 1935.

The statistics that accompanied Phil's review in accordance with the Executive Committee's directions are of interest in themselves. For example, he employed two five-year periods as a basis of inquiry, 1925 through 1929, and 1930 through 1934, and it was evident that much could be concluded. There had been a revolution in company practices, this involving a shift from liquidation through timber sales to liquidation through operation. In the first five-year period, the Timber Company had reduced its stumpage by 11.7 billion board feet, all but 434 million of which had involved the sale of timber. In the second five-year period, stumpage reduction had fallen to 4.2 billion feet, but more than half of this total was the result of Timber Company operations.

Profit and loss statistics were also revealing. Net profits for the first five-year period, not including noncash items such as depreciation and depletion charges, totaled $20.3 million, with 1926 being the best single year, with a profit of $5.2 million. From 1930 through 1934, losses amounted to $2.1 million, the years 1931 and 1932 losing $1.4 million and $1.7 million respectively. In 1931 and 1932 no dividends had been paid. Slight profits had been managed in 1933 and 1934, of $254,000 and $315,000. It is of interest, however, that the program of capital investment, while affected, did not fall at the same percentage. For example, in the first five-year period nearly $20 million was expended on additions, replacements, plant construction, and equipment, and although this figure declined over the second period, it still amounted to $13.5 million.

One of the advantages of looking at statistics over time is that they provide an indication of trends and also a sense of continuity. As Phil looked ahead, he maintained his optimism. There were many problems, but most of them had answers, or so it seemed. For example, the subsidiaries were problems insofar as their surpluses became "sources of taxable distributions" to the Timber Company and thence to the Timber Company stockholders. Consolidation was a reasonable objective, for reasons of administration as well as taxation. This effort would involve the Snoqualmie Falls Lumber Company, the Clemons Logging Company, the White River and Willapa companies, and the Yards Securities Company.

In September, word finally arrived that the Great Northern officials had reconsidered their position on a Klamath merger. The issue was pronounced dead. The Executive Committee met in Tacoma in mid-October, and the members traveled down to Oregon to view the Klamath timber and discuss options in the wake of the merger breakdown. After so much effort expended, there was a natural letdown at the ending of what had once seemed such a promising and logical solution to a difficult problem. Laird Bell, who had personally assumed responsibility for the effort, felt especially bad, sharing those feelings in a letter written while heading homeward on the Burlington. Phil's response was as expected: "There is no reason that I can see why you should feel that you are of so little use . . . from my point of view your help has been tremendous." He continued, "both of us, and perhaps all of the Committee, had a sort of defeated air about the Klamath conference and I suspect nobody was satisfied. At any rate, we arrived at a policy which will be all right."

Phil also took the opportunity to raise a subject he claimed to have forgotten to bring before the Executive Committee: what position should the company take concerning the legislative consideration of the new federal proposals on Social Security and unemployment benefits? He thought they might be able "to exert an influence in Oregon," attempting to get the legislature "to lay off the passage of an enabling act or try to influence that body toward the passage of a good enabling act." His own preference was "to be as helpful as possible toward the latter end," but he would feel better having Laird's ideas on the subject. Not surprisingly, Laird supported his inclination.

In the midst of his normal routine, Phil was called upon to summarize the Timber Company's "forest policy" by I. N. Tate of the Weyerhaeuser Sales Company. Dr. Wilson Compton of the National Lumber Manufacturers Association had recently composed a suggested policy statement to serve "as a basis for the industry to stand on in future legislation." It was thought, what with the end of the National Recovery Administration, that new approaches to problems would be developed, and in Tate's words, "we must either contribute our part or take whatever is dished up for us in Washington." It should be noted that because of the nature of the organization and its contacts, the Sales Company was assuming a public relations responsibility for the Timber Company. Thus the request was reasonable enough.

Nonetheless, Phil didn't much care for assignments such as this, even though he realized there was more than a little merit in what Tate was saying. Although he knew better, Phil may have wished that it could be considered enough that the Timber Company was doing a good job in the management of its responsibilities. The best he could do was blame his brother Fred for Tate's request. Thus he began his response to Tate by wondering just what he had said or done that had caused Fred K. to point the finger at him. In any event, Phil was not going to pretend that the Weyerhaeuser Timber Company possessed any grand design in terms of what might be called, in a very small voice, a forest policy. He did remind Tate that in the days of the NRA the company had fallen in "wholeheartedly" with the requirements of the code "in both fire protective measures and silvicultural matters aimed at stimulating a regrowth on our cut-over lands." He also enclosed the pamphlet that the company had produced and distributed, "evidencing our whole-hearted cooperation."

Since the code's demise, the West Coast Lumbermen's Association had maintained its forestry committee and a forester's position, and, of course, the company supported the association's efforts and involvement. As noted in the pamphlet, Weyerhaeuser, "together with many others, has stated its policy as being in favor of continuing living up to the requirements established under the Code and we are doing so by making definite cutting plans, leaving seedling areas and protecting from fire, going to the expense of leaving commercial trees to some extent where necessary for seed areas, and protecting those seed areas from slashing fires, also, cutting snags for fire protection."

Phil acknowledged that these efforts had been accomplished at no great expense, that they had been reasonably effective, and that the company should surely be willing to go that far. Furthermore, although it could not "be applicable to our timber generally," he looked forward—"it is our hope and ambition"—to early establishment of sustained-yield operations at Longview, White River, and perhaps at Klamath and other locations. That was no theoretician talking but a practical lumberman for whom the balance sheet divided the reasonable from the foolish. Phil made it clear: "When I say this I mean that we should dedicate our efforts toward working out a plan of sustained yield operation which will commit us only so long as it is economically feasible." Forestry had to pay its own way.

Compton had suggested many approaches in that area of common interest and concern between public and private management of timberlands. Phil recognized that there were instances when cooperation with the Forest Service might be desirable, but he certainly didn't want to make any unnecessary commitments. When such occasions occurred, "both parties should go into a well thought out plan . . . and both parties should have the privilege for cause of withdrawing when it appears impossible." On the whole, however, he thought Compton's program was "harmless," if it was rather more detailed than the moment called for. "I do have a lot of hesitation about, either as an Association or as individuals, getting so involved in discussions with New Dealers that we can be said to be on record in favor of any policy on which they can easily misquote us," he concluded his letter to Tate.

In the meantime, things generally seemed to be on the mend. Phil reported to the directors that all operations were "producing at an expanded gait," and double shifts were working at Everett, Longview, and Snoqualmie Falls. The Clemons Logging Company had been shut down again briefly as a result of labor problems but had resumed operations, and at the end of October labor relations seemed "to be getting along quietly." Pulp mill construction was progressing, with an expectation of the start of production moved back until February 1. Phil also noted his recent authorization by the Executive Committee to seek a plant manager to design plans for a plywood operation at Everett with a view to building early in 1936, although he cautioned that "this information should be withheld until an opportune moment for announcement."

The day after Christmas, Phil sent another informational letter to the Timber Company directors, and for the most part the news continued to be encouraging. He called their attention to figures indicating that, at the current rate of production, "we are piling up an inventory at the fir plants which has seemed the wise program." He further noted that December orders exceeded those for any December in recent years; in fact, there had been almost no seasonal decline in demand, "which seems to us a very encouraging sign." The second shifts were still operating, and even if there were labor problems, it appeared likely that there would be "a nice volume of business at a good price" in the coming years. Indeed, logs were likely to be so scarce that it would require them to make lumber out of hemlock, which would probably mean "that the low hemlock log prices which the pulp consumers have enjoyed will be corrected." It is interesting that it was only the pulp consumers who enjoyed low log prices and never the lumbermen. But Phil was, at heart, a lumberman.

CHAPTER 8

Timber Is a Crop

I f facing independent and aggressive union representatives across the bargaining table required some getting used to, so did the growing publicity as to the value of Weyerhaeuser Timber Company stock. From its organization in 1900, the Timber Company had been in effect a closed corporation, increasing its shareholders mainly to include new descendants of the original investors. Little thought had been given to disposing of shares, and if ever there was a need to do so, it was supposed that the exchanges would be made within the ownership circle.

But with the passing years, some attitudes changed, and the allegiances of former days were not as certain. Furthermore, unless there were occasional open sales of stock, who was to assign it a value? The fact was, however, that only a few stockholders cared to know what value would be assigned on the competitive fields of the marketplace. But like it or not, there was a good deal of outside activity along those lines in January 1936. Phil expressed surprise at the inquiries they had been receiving, indicating in a letter to Laird Bell that brokers had begun "to be a little bothersome asking us for information as to the value of the stock." He also reported hearing of a number of sales, one at eighty-one dollars, another at eighty-four, and Dave Winton had recently mentioned that a member of the Hamm family in St. Paul had made a purchase at eighty-five dollars.

Phil was still harboring a grudge against the Hearst *Seattle Post-Intelligencer*, which, as he reminded Uncle Fred, had "published the sensational stories about father's wealth at the time of his death which story was the inspiration for George's kidnapping." And on the morning of January 23, that newspaper's financial page "offered us another indication of their friendliness." Details concerning the financial circumstances of the Timber Company were featured, including the number of shares, dividends per share for the past two years, and related data which seemed to paint a very healthy picture. Although Phil was willing to reveal much, there was much that he considered privileged information. Also, the timing of any such revelations could be important. It seemed so in this instance, Phil reporting to F.E. that these statistics "in the hands of our Union Committees will be embarrassing." He added, "the time is most unfortunate in that the plywood mills as of January 1 have raised their wages 5¢ an hour; and demands of all kinds are being presented to operators, ourselves included at Willapa, most of them being for wage increases and others of course embracing closed shop agreements, requests for the check-off system, etc."

Regarding the stock sale situation, Phil was uncertain what to do. He could threaten the brokers involved, at least to the extent of their losing business. He could cajole. He could even cooperate, by providing "more complete information upon which to base their ideas of values and future purchase or upon which to base their selling talk." It would continue to be a puzzle.

So too would labor relations. As he tried to look ahead, Phil presumed that it would be to the company's benefit to take the initiative and suggest the likelihood of a wage increase, thereby taking some of the wind out of the sails of union leadership. There had been too much optimism expressed regarding an improvement in business, and this coupled with the publication of the Weyerhaeuser Timber Company stock distribution and dividend record encouraged assumptions that were difficult to refute. An additional complication was the radical labor organization, the National Lumber Workers, especially active in Grays Harbor. Although it was too easy to blame these "communists" for any and all frustrations, there is no doubt that they were a disruptive element, not only to the owner-managers but to the elected union leadership as well. E. P. Marsh had earlier reported as much to Secretary of Labor Perkins: "This element, while not numerically strong, was an active influence in several localities in poisoning the minds of workers against Brotherhood officials, and in upsetting wherever they could well-defined trade union policies and programs and in promoting internal strife and dissension, and no doubt had a prolonging effect on the strike."

It was clearly in the interest of the company to support the more conservative union leadership. In particular, Phil worried about the spread of radicalism. "We fear the extension of the Aberdeen communistic activities into the union relationships at our other plants," he informed Uncle Fred. In early February he merely noted, "The labor situation is disquieting," then added, "It is our belief that before the year is out we will find it expedient to again raise wages."

Although it was to be expected that some of the more conservative members of the board would question the advisability of another appearance of weakness by suggesting a possible wage increase, Phil was probably counting on Laird Bell's unqualified support. He got support, but it was hardly unqualified. After indicating, "I like the maneuver," Laird expressed worry on two counts. First, he wondered whether the management initiative might not weaken that very element of conservative union leadership they were interested in encouraging, particularly as concerned Longview. Second, "won't you get more cursing from the industry than benefit from your relations with your labor?" These were simply questions asked, and Laird admitted, "I can't get a clear picture in my mind." He seemed far more certain that the Executive Committee ought to be meeting more frequently, and that if two or three meetings could be scheduled on the West Coast, he claimed "it would be a comfort to me." In a sense he was only supporting what Phil had been proposing, but their reasons were different. Phil thought they should meet more often on the Coast because more could be accomplished there, "getting the reaction of the men in the field, than can be accomplished by my going to St. Paul to discuss things in a necessarily second hand fashion." His preference was always to have the responsible individual make the presentation and answer questions. It was a policy that worked well, and of course sharing the stage was something Phil did gladly. Laird's interest in increasing the number of meetings was less specific. He noted that other large corporations had regular meetings of the Executive Committee, some as often as monthly. As he reasoned, "The more we get to be a public company the less I think we can rely on the traditional custom of having eighteen meetings in two days in St. Paul in January." A meeting had been called for February 24 in Tacoma.

The planned start-up of the Everett pulp mill had been long delayed. Originally scheduled to begin production in the fall of 1935, that date had been extended a number of times, and it was apparent that the delays would continue beyond the time of the Executive Committee meeting. Phil understood the problems of pulp production only to the extent that others took time to explain them. Although he appreciated the importance of the involvement from an economic consideration, the process still seemed strange. Sawing a log into boards made sense, but converting that log into an entirely different substance was the work of specialists. In any event, there was little he could do but look interested and a little anxious.

One of the continuing subjects of controversy in the lumber industry through the years has been tariff policies. In the mid-1930s, many were concerned about the internationalist tendencies of Secretary of State Cordell Hull. These tendencies achieved expression in the Trade Agreements Act of 1934. Under the act, the president could alter existing tariff rates up to 50 percent, provided there was reciprocity. Northwest lumbermen generally feared the possibility of an increasing Canadian share of the American market while American producers were being limited in their entry into the British Empire marketplace. Colonel Greeley had been active in behalf of the West Coast Lumbermen's Association in opposing any reduction in tariff schedules for Canadian forest products, a position Phil apparently accepted without question. He had, however, forwarded to Laird Bell the materials on the subject, asking for his opinion. The response is perhaps less interesting, or at least less important, in its particulars than in the manner of presentation.

Laird Bell and Phil Weyerhaeuser were both systematic thinkers, although they usually thought about very different matters. The truth was that Phil had given little consideration to the tariff question, and certainly not in any general sense. Laird obviously had, and he was more than willing to share his thoughts with friend Phil, at the same time begging that they not be shared with other members of the Executive Committee. He also apologized "for this dissertation," admitting, "I am a little like the single taxer at the funeral, once I get started on tariffs."

Laird began his "dissertation" by noting the decline of lumber exports from 1929 to 1934 of some 44 percent, although he wondered whether that was not about equal to the general decline in lumber production for the same period. It was, of course. Then, noting Greeley's use of the "conservation argument," Laird suggested that such use had to involve a "tongue in the cheek." Greeley contended that with fewer imports there would be better utilization of the forest because there would be increased production of lower grades that could not be transported at a competitive price. Laird might accept that, but he could not understand how an increase in American exports could be managed without a corresponding increase in "the rate of exhaustion of the forests as a whole."

But such questions were almost beside the point. Laird proceeded to explain his position philosophically, using as his example the automobile industry—an example that seemed far more appropriate in the mid-1930s than it would a half century later:

It is probably unnecessary for me to confess that I am a low tariff fan. I genuinely believe in a pretty untrammeled flow of international trade. You probably know all the standard arguments. My favorite example is the automobile. If there were no tariffs, or if there were tariffs for revenue only, automobiles would in the long run tend to be made in that country where, by reason of a combination of easily accessible raw material and skill in mass production they could be made cheapest. If, on the other hand every country insists on making its own automobiles, there will be that much less volume for the American product, and inevitably the cars made in the ill-favored countries will be expensive. That must mean that less people, the world over, can afford cars, and that less cars will be made.

"Well, you asked for it," Laird concluded several paragraphs later. Some might have been offended by the academic form of the discussion, but Phil was not. Quite the contrary. He was delighted that Laird had taken the time. Phil promised not to publish the commentary, "although it is worth it," and he closed sincerely, "Thank you a lot."

However important, the tariff question was generally beyond the reach of individual operators. More often than not, so was the labor question, but it at least could be considered in everyday terms. As Phil and his associates discussed policies to be adopted, they made increasing use of statistics and charts. Some of the information assembled was more than a little revealing. If it seemed that labor had made impossible demands and incredible advances over recent months, a glance at figures from the Everett plant indicated that the minimum hourly wage settlement in the summer of 1935 of 50 cents was still 10 cents below the figure for 1920. It is true that the figure had bounced back and forth before settling at about 43 cents for several years, then declining to its low point of 28.5 cents in 1933, but the fact remained that 50 cents was not as exorbitant as some claimed. Furthermore, the minimum weekly wage of $20 was just about average over the period, with the exception of 1920, 1932, and 1933. Much larger ranges were apparent in the average sales figures. At Snoqualmie, for example, the sales average per thousand feet in 1920 had been $47.24. This figure had fallen to $15.04 in 1933 and had climbed back to a $24 level in 1935. Minimum weekly wages for those same years had been $28, $12, and $20. Longview statistics indicated that there had been little actual change over the past six years. In 1930, Longview's first year of operation, the average sales figure was $19.28 and the minimum weekly wage $21.60. In 1935 the sales figure was $19.34 and the wage $20.

But while they studied their statistics, most were aware that the issues were likely to require answers not readily apparent. There would be principles involved, and principles are difficult things to compromise. Of less immediate concern were discussions regarding the responsibility of directors. Without saying it in so many words, those involved in governing corporations were becoming aware of increasing complexities. By default, at least in part, managers were assuming greater responsibilities. The trend may have been as desirable as it seemed inevitable, but still there was the worry that always accompanies change—the concern that something important was being lost, and lost forever. Many suggestions were passed about. Ed Davis wrote a lengthy discourse on the subject, addressing it to Uncle Fred. Among other things, he charged that "most directors are not familiar with the details of the business which they are directing, and have not the time to devote to them." He also noted the difficulty of keeping directors interested even when attending meetings, that they were "more or less impatient to adjourn in order to hold another meeting or get on to something else."

Phil probably didn't have his cousin's concerns in mind when he set his trap for O. D. Fisher at the March 6 meeting of the Snoqualmie Falls Lumber Company directors. Rather it was just his way of making the most of an opportunity. It had long been evident that O. D. talked more than he listened and was only incidentally aware of what was going on. Thus when Phil announced that each of the directors was required to sign an "oath of office," O. D. did so without hesitation. The "oath" read as follows:

The undersigned, each being sworn on oath, deposes and says that he is a citizen of the United States and of the State of Washington . . .[and] that he will faithfully comply with, support and observe all of the constitutions, laws, rules and regulations of all Labor Unions in the State of Washington, and elsewhere within the jurisdiction of the United States of America; that he will vote the Democratic ticket; that he will cause all earnings of the corporation to be distributed to its employees; and be personally liable for all obligations of said corporation: So Help Me God.

Needless to say, O.D. did more than a little stammering and sputtering when his awareness returned. Even F.E. thought it a worthy exercise, writing to Phil, "I should like to have seen OD's face when he realized what he had signed." He thanked Phil for the "good laugh."

Phil reported to the Timber Company directors at the end of March, informing them of some modifications that had been instituted in organizational administration. He told of having just completed the round of annual meetings of the subsidiary companies, "and this year [we] instituted the practice of holding what corresponds to Annual Meetings at each of the branch operations, giving the manager a chance to report and discuss his problems." Phil was pleased with the results, noting that the discussions had been more specific than usual, "centered to a large extent upon the desirability of making timber purchases in some cases, in other cases improving kiln facilities and spending considerable money toward woods equipment and other equipment to enable the plants to efficiently maintain the present comparatively high operating schedules." He also was able to report that he felt "reasonably safe" in predicting that the Everett pulp mill would be operating "to some degree by the first of May." The labor situation remained unsettled, and although no announcement of a wage raise had been made, it seemed likely that such an adjustment would be forthcoming.

The first strike action occurred almost as Phil was describing the situation as being unsettled. To no one's surprise, it took place at the Willapa Harbor Lumber Mills when the night crew, "without any discussion of the matter with Company officials . . . pulled the whistle at 9:30 in the evening and walked off the job." Apparently the issue involved a millwright who had reported at that time but did not belong to the union. As Phil informed Uncle Fred, there never had been any understanding regarding a closed shop; in fact, there had been no discussion of the grievance. But pickets were in place the next day and the mill was shut down. A few nights earlier, Aberdeen operators had decided to offer a five cent an hour increase, effective the first of April, and voting was taking place on whether to accept the offer. It applied to both loggers and mill men, and Phil was certain that the entire district would soon be offering the same increase. At the Willapa Harbor mills, of course, the closed shop question would have to be resolved first.

Phil also reported the visit of some fairly prominent guests. Dr. C. A. Schenck, the German forester who had formerly headed the Biltmore Forestry School, and Dr. Hellmuth Muller-Clemm, one of the directors of the Waldhof Paper Company, were expressing an interest in building a pulp mill, and the two were shown possible locations in Willapa. Bob Wolf was enthusiastic, describing them as "the ablest people in the game," and the very tentative plan envisioned a "semi-partnership whereby we take care of the timber and logging investments and they attend to their own knitting." Phil foresaw some problems, but he looked forward to informal discussions. The real problems of such a joint venture had little to do with log prices and sharing profits. In a March 29 plebiscite, a reported 98.7 percent of German voters had cast votes approving Hitler's foreign policy. The citizens of Austria were apparently less approving of those policies, for they began planning for conscription. In the meantime, Schenck and Muller-Clemm had gone north to inspect pulp plant possibilities in British Columbia.

Perhaps one of the accompanying benefits of the improvement in pulp production was the encouragement it provided research activities generally. There had, of course, been some effort at new product development through the Wood Conversion Company activities at Cloquet. But it was not until mid-April 1936 that any separate commitment to research had been made by the Timber Company itself. In a letter to his branch managers warning them of a pending prorated assessment to cover the $18,000 cost, Phil announced the plans to conduct research "into the fields of Wood Waste Investigation, Lumber Treatment and Preservation, and Hemlock and Fir Bark Waste." The survey was formally the responsibility of General Timber Service, but it would be conducted at the Longview pulp plant by R. W. Hatch, research engineer with that division. Al Raught, general manager at Longview, was already aware of the plan, thus merely noted Phil's "warning that we may expect an additional charge on this account." Tip O'Neil at Snoqualmie expressed his "hearty approval," observing that if anything was accomplished "in the wood waste investigation alone, it will be a great benefit to this plant." The opportunities for selling waste wood were fast disappearing, what with the increased use of oil and the cheaper power that was then becoming available.

Like the number of Timber Company stockholders, the Weyerhaeuser family had increased in numbers. But the family was still small enough that when gatherings were planned, they could be managed within the homes of those hosting. In the fall of 1935, the third generation had enjoyed a family gathering in Cloquet; but, as Phil would suggest, that "memorable meeting . . . left some unfinished business, both social and otherwise." Thus an invitation was offered in behalf of the "western contingent," inviting the rest of the family, "to the exclusion of all else," to Tacoma for "another meeting of the Clan." This was scheduled to begin on Sunday, May 31, to last four days. "Our plan is that Fritz and Mary Jewett will take over the Titcomb American Lake residence where they will be hosts; Elizabeth and Rod, and Helen and Phil will extend their hospitality at their town houses." The meetings would be held at the American Lake house, from which it would be convenient to take meals at the country club. Phil closed the invitation by urging them "to take this time and attempt to continue what was started in Cloquet."

Although the affairs of business were not quite so lighthearted, there did seem more reason for optimism, and satisfaction, than had long been the case. Toward the end of April, the Timber Company announced a 5-cent hourly wage increase, effective April 15, to all employees except those at Klamath Falls. Phil estimated that this would increase costs by about 60 cents per thousand feet. Volume of production was increasing at more operations, and the pulp mill would be ready for inspection if not actually operating at the time of the annual meeting.

But not everyone was happy. One who was suffering at least a temporary fit of pique was Snoqualmie manager Tip O'Neil. He had just read a memo from a Weyerhaeuser Sales Company representative, intended for Harry Morgan at Longview, which had been delivered to him by mistake. Morgan and Longview had been congratulated for shipments for the week ending April 23 of nearly 8 million feet. "This certainly is hitting them on the nose and we want to compliment you," the representative observed in good sales company lexicon. After pretending an apology for reading another's mail, Tip angrily inquired of Phil why it was that Longview was receiving congratulations while at Snoqualmie they had been forced to send their shipping crew home. "Now, there are one hundred and one excuses that the Weyerhaeuser Sales Company can give why this should happen," Tip continued, "but the fact remains that we have not turned down any business at this office and have had to send our shipping crew home." There is little doubt that Phil enjoyed such expressions of spirit, especially when the Sales Company was indicted. His response to Tip was a mixture of sport and business. "I don't blame you for gnashing your teeth and any other evil feelings which you may have had," Phil began. He was forced to observe, however, "I think the best defense that the Sales Company will be able to make will be that for the year-to-date Snoqualmie has shipped 101 percent of its cut, and Longview 97 percent." Tip was reminded, ever so pleasantly, that Snoqualmie was a part of the whole.

One source of great relief must have been the San Francisco capture of the last of the kidnappers, William Mahan, alias Dainard, whose subsequent confession made a trial unnecessary, a most welcomed development. On receiving the news, Laird Bell wrote a note to Phil. "It must be an immense relief," he understated, "and I trust the public will be allowed to forget about it too." The public had a longer memory than Laird imagined, but the worst of the experience was certainly over.

There is little doubt that what interested Phil most during the summer of 1936 was a survey of cutover lands to determine whether the Timber Company should pay the taxes owing and retain the properties or simply let them revert to public ownership. Although the survey was undertaken at Phil's request, Dave Weyerhaeuser was primarily responsible for it. A cousin, the son of F.E., Dave fell between generations, the last of the third generation, ten years younger than Phil and ten years older than Edward Rodman Titcomb, who was the firstborn of the fourth generation. Trained in forestry, Dave had for several years been uncertain whether to work for the Timber Company or follow a career in the church. Phil probably didn't understand that particular dilemma, but for the most part he was patient, and after various other experiences Dave was given the opportunity to work with Minot Davis. The two were probably about as different as could be designed. Minot moved about with great authority, his manner the product of long experience, temperament, and power. He managed the lands for the Weyerhaeuser Timber Company, and to a large extent this involved the sale of parcels to other operators. They came to Minot, and he decided. It was seldom necessary for him to ask favors of others. Dave was relatively new to the business and was gentle and sensitive by nature, but the chance to work in forestry seemed ideally suited to him.

The Logged Off Land Company had carried its unromantic designation around without much enthusiasm. It had been created to dispose of the cutover lands to the best possible advantage, and to separate the liability for those lands from the Timber Company responsibility. With the passing years it was increasingly apparent that there was little demand for such lands. As had been the case with much of the forested region of the Lake States, there was no real agricultural option for future use. What the land did best was grow trees.

Prior to 1928, the Timber Company had always paid the taxes on its properties, forested and cutover, but in that year the land values and taxes reached levels that seemed extreme. It was decided that no taxes would be paid on those parcels that had no immediate value in terms of trees or sales, the hope being that within the five-year grace period, taxes might decline to a more reasonable level. Normally the lands delinquent since 1928 would have been foreclosed in 1934, but because of the Depression, emergency legislation had been passed in 1932 to extend the grace period. In 1936, however, that emergency legislation had run its course and the first foreclosures were scheduled. The question could no longer be deferred. Either delinquent taxes would have to be paid or the lands would be given up. Dave Weyerhaeuser, Fred Firmin, who had general responsibility for the logged-off lands, and Ed Heacox, a young Iowa State forestry graduate, fought their way through the brush of the lands in question, drawing crude maps and taking notes on soil and other pertinent details. The final report was based on their field work, calculations of taxes owed, interest penalties and any other fiscal considerations, older surveys, and growth and yield data from the Forest Service.

As was stated, "The purpose of this report [was] to briefly review the problem of future land ownership and to form a basis for intelligent management of these lands and to more clearly define a policy which will maintain or dispose of them to the Company's best interest." Phil was pleased with the results and requested Dave to present the recommendations to the Executive Committee at its June meeting. The response was not enthusiastic, but the committee did authorize the funds necessary to pay the back taxes on some of the properties, specifically the Longview and Pacific blocks, delaying a decision on the Vail and Elbe blocks.

Phil addressed a covering letter to the report to Rod Titcomb, Charlie Ingram, and Minot Davis, in which he indicated his personal commitment:

This report is so interesting that I wish you would take the time to study it. We are, in paying up the back taxes, definitely spending some money for positive instead of negative or defense reasons with the expectation of getting something back on the investment. That being so it is also suggested, and I think with merit, that in logging, in our own operations in the future and in logging through contractors, that we try to do something affirmative toward insuring a good cover on lands and we will hereby be launching on a program of growing trees. . . .

Nothing could more clearly state Phil's interest and intentions. Still he knew that the distance between saying and doing was considerable and crucial, and orders alone would not accomplish the objective. He knew, for example, that it was the logging superintendents or contractors who would have to take charge of seeing that the snags were cut and the slash properly burned, and he also knew that they were "going to do these operations in the cheapest way possible." Accordingly he wanted to provide some incentives "whereby the operator can be induced to protect seed areas, perhaps leave more of them, and protect burned over slash from reburning . . . the expense of which is to be borne as part of the investment in the lands and not as a cost of operation."

It is always dangerous to read backward in time, assigning importance to actions and events largely on the basis of the way things turned out. In any detailed and systematic study, for example, one is struck with the expenditure of time and energies for purposes that never achieved realization. Much of life is spent following paths that lead nowhere. In Phil's recent experience, a case in point was the Klamath merger effort. It never came about so it was not important after all, but neither Phil nor Laird would be willing to dismiss it as a nonevent, at least not for many years. Nevertheless, it would be difficult to overemphasize the significance of Phil's position regarding the 1936 problem of delinquent taxes and cutover lands.

Although there had been a good deal of discussion of forestry practices and management of "sustained yield," little had been accomplished. Foresters might be employed, but they soon found themselves doing jobs anyone could do. They might "talk a good game," but they seemed to play about the same as everyone else. Certainly the company had assumed more than its share of responsibility for fire protection through the Washington Forest Fire Association and the county protection associations in Oregon, but those needs were obvious. It simply had not been demonstrated that there was any economic basis for attempting to produce a new forest on private cutover lands, particularly when one was required to think in terms of one hundred years between seedlings and merchantable timber. In 1936, with such demonstrations yet to be made, Phil, his foresters, and even a reluctant Executive Committee, had decided that the time had come to force the issue. It may have involved a revolution in attitudes for some, but not for many. More accurately, it was the first step in a direction long desired but never before deemed possible. Phil had concluded his letter as one in charge:

It is suggested that the management for these growing lands ... authorize operators to spend definite sums of money for definite purposes; the suggestion being 50¢ an acre as cut, in an attempt to create more trees on cutover lands quickly.

I wish you would think this matter over and after you have all read the report I would like to have a conference with you and the authors of the report to discuss its practicability.

That conference would be the first of many on forestry matters, and although progress would often seem slow and uncertain, the direction of movement was clear. In a sense, what followed was merely the result of those 1936 decisions which the question of tax delinquency had demanded.

One of the immediate results involved a reassessment of the purposes of the Weyerhaeuser Logged Off Land Company. Following some discussions, Phil wrote to Gus Clapp on the subject, noting that some 47,000 acres of land valued at $130,000 were presently owned by the Logged Off Land Company in the Pacific and Longview reforestation areas, which amounted to about one-third of that company's remaining ownership. It was suggested that the Logged Off Land Company be disincorporated and that the Weyerhaeuser Timber Company, "for reasons of general convenience and because the taxes and expenses of the reforestation areas can be an expense item of advantage to it," officially acquire the assets of the Logged Off Land Company. The current income tax law permitted 100 percent subsidiaries to be dissolved without being taxed at their book value. Even assuming the fire risk that they had theoretically been escaping, there was no doubt that the Timber Company ought to be managing any and all lands growing timber.

Tax policies were also providing an incentive to reconsider the corporate arrangements, particularly concerning subsidiaries. It seemed that the dividends of a subsidiary, even in the case of complete ownership, were taxed because they were readily identified. Fred K. was reflecting on the organizational problems from another angle, and he shared some of his thoughts in a letter to Uncle Fred, a copy of which was sent to Phil. Fred K. had covered a "multitude of things," among them a suggestion that "proper policy direction of various of the companies requires common ownership through a holding company." In a sense what Fred K. was expressing was an extension of the Sales Company and General Timber Service philosophy. Here were all of these organizations, more or less involved in the same sort of activity, yet there seemed to be no overall direction, no centralized authority.

Phil thought the idea of a "holding company" would prove to be a very expensive proposition. He noted that the Timber Company was trying to get rid of corporations, "mainly on account of the present actual and probable tax on intercorporate dividends." A case in point was the Clemons Logging Company, "in which there is no difficulty of control or management . . . but by the mere form of having a separate corporation, the Timber Company is paying . . . about $10,000 per year in intercorporate dividend taxes."

Of greater importance, however, was the institutional effect of such a central committee management effort. Phil suggested that his Timber Company responsibility had provided different experiences from those available elsewhere. The Timber Company had "many subsidiaries which it controls, and on many problems I believe it is just as difficult for us to arrive at a policy which is fair to all parties as it is in your case in dealing with various corporations in which, basically, the ownership is the same." By that he meant that "common ownership . . . does not iron out the problems to the degree it would appear to on the surface." The fact is that Phil had faith in his managers, but that did not mean that he was always in complete agreement with their decisions and policies. He was reluctant, however, to offer objections or complaints without considerable thought. Part of it involved his personality. A decentralized organization was more in keeping with his temperament, but that was merely complementary to his certainty that the experience and opinion of those on the ground was deserving of respect. It was a combination of faith and accountability, and perhaps it came more easily to one whose own experiences at Clearwater and Tacoma were so distant from the St. Paul offices.

Phil did express his willingness to get together with his brother, possibly in company with cousin Ed Davis, to discuss the questions raised. He heard shortly from Fred K., who had just returned from a Canadian fishing trip. Fred gave as his "chief complaint" the fact that each year they seemed to spend a great deal of time talking about details "and almost no time talking about fundamental things." Phil might even have argued that point, observing that in his view far more than in Fred's the details were the fundamental things. Still he knew what was meant, and he undoubtedly welcomed Fred's plans to head west a bit in advance of the September 28 Executive Committee meeting, so that they could take a brief fishing trip and "have a chance to talk some of these things out."

There were many things to talk over, not all of a pleasant nature. The recent changes in tax legislation seemed to place the Timber Securities Company in jeopardy, at least from a consideration of fiscal feasibility. Fred K. wrote to Phil that Uncle Fred was more than a little disturbed by the lack of concern family members had shown regarding the matter. Fred K. was willing to think about it. One of the pressing problems was that before the Securities Company could be dissolved, the indebtedness of the estate of John Philip Weyerhaeuser to that company had to be met. It appeared that this would amount to nearly a million dollars. That was enough to get Phil's attention. But brother Fred had other worries as well. What he saw as being "the most serious part of the problem" was that if the Timber Securities Company was dissolved, family unity was likely to suffer, as would "the advantages of voting such a large amount of stock as a unit; also, the advantage of having a large central financial pool on which to draw for new investments or in the development of present investments." Phil decided that the questions were sufficiently serious to call for his presence in St. Paul. He went immediately.

The results were complicated, and it was Phil's responsibility to try to explain them to sister Elizabeth. The John Philip Company had been created to assume their father's indebtedness on account of his guarantees of Rock Island Plow Company notes. With the assistance of money advanced to the John Philip Company by the Timber Securities Company, the Rock Island Plow Company obligations had been resolved. But the Timber Securities Company could not proceed with its own dissolution until the indebtedness of the John Philip Company had been satisfied, and that, of course, involved Phil, Fred K., and Elizabeth, the stockholders of the John Philip Company. Phil's letter to his sister is interesting. He explained matters in considerable detail, well knowing that she would be looking over the figures with great care. Their responsibility was large, it was true, but he also wanted her to understand that many benefits had accrued along the way. For example, he closed by reminding her that she had coming down from her Aunt Elise's trust, to be distributed at the time of Uncle Bancroft's death, one-tenth of one half of her share in the Timber Securities Company, which had a present value of approximately a quarter of a million dollars. "Please gather, therefore, that you are rather well heeled," Phil had closed.

If there were not enough things to occupy one's attention between matters of business and family, there was always politics. The presidential election of 1936 provided considerable entertainment, but not much in the way of hope. Any temptation to become involved would be easily restrained in Phil's case. It was to be officially restrained according to a resolution approved by the directors of the General Timber Service at a St. Paul meeting July 15. On a motion of Laird Bell, the managements of all the affiliated companies were advised to make "no attempt whatever to counsel or influence employees in political matters during the coming Presidential Campaign." As things turned out, it was just as well.

The Executive Committee meeting of September 18 was held as scheduled in Tacoma. In addition to the usual items for consideration, Rod Titcomb offered his resignation as general manager of the Timber Company. Phil announced that decision to the directors in a letter of October 2, noting that "neither his health nor his inclination would permit him to go on much longer carrying a heavy load." The resignation was accepted, and Charles H. Ingram, who had worked with Rod at the Snoqualmie Falls Lumber Company before coming to Tacoma to serve as assistant general manager, was appointed to take his place. This proved to be a most important appointment, providing as it did the nearly perfect complement to Phil's interests and abilities. Charlie was the grandson of Orrin H. Ingram, one of the associates of Phil's grandfather Frederick. As a matter of fact, in Wisconsin logging interests, Orrin had assisted Frederick in a manner not much different from the way Charlie assisted Phil. Both Ingrams were bundles of energy for whom attention to detail came naturally. With the assurance that Charlie Ingram would be checking everything that could possibly be checked, Phil could feel freer to look further into the future and to assess those things that seldom showed in the accounting.

Phil also notified the directors that the Sales Company management had offered a budget that foresaw an increase in production of some 18 percent on the part of the stockholding mills. In short, "the outlook seems quite optimistic," and "order files around the circuit are rather plump and we anticipate that the balance of the year will continue to show reasonable volume."

If there had been any disappointment in connection with the Executive Committee, it was a lack of opportunity for Phil and Laird to discuss things in private. Laird wrote a long letter when he returned to Chicago indicating his disappointment and suggesting that next time he was "tempted to come early . . . ahead of the general migration." In this instance, however, Laird had some specific suggestions that he had wanted to discuss before offering them for a more general review. His immediate concern was over public relations and the possibility of appointing a new assistant general manager with strengths in that area. As Laird reasoned, "It seems to me that there is a chance in that to improve our situation in a sphere in which I am afraid we are weak."

He wanted it understood that he referred to public relations in a general sense, not only involving relations with competitors but also including "relations with our timber and other customers, with labor, the local press, governmental bodies (non-political) and the public generally." The trend was clearly in that direction, at least for "most corporations in conspicuous businesses," and "certainly those in public service or in quasi-monopolistic businesses are doing so." Although the Weyerhaeuser Timber Company was no monopoly, it was "the biggest thing in sight in Washington. . . . We own a natural resource and the trees stick up for all who care to see." Phil agreed entirely that the criticism of the organization was justified and that steps should be taken to overcome this weakness.

The public relations question narrowed itself in the course of subsequent discussions. Charlie Ingram was given the responsibility of managing the search for a person with particular strengths in labor relations. This seems to be the first time that the Timber Company had sought outside assistance in recruiting qualified candidates: Charlie wrote to Carl Hamilton of Booz, Fry, Allen and Hamilton of Chicago, listing the qualifications deemed important. Obviously more labor problems were foreseen, and in order to handle them Charlie indicated that the candidate "should be experienced in dealing with labor and merit its confidence; have access or acquaintance with higher union officials; have some ability as a speaker before groups of either employers or employees; and primarily must be convinced of the merits of our present capitalistic system and its maintenance." It seems a rather innocent statement in retrospect, but one must remember that the step seemed large in itself.

But the big news of the coming winter had to do with the Weyerhaeuser 4–Square Special Train. During January, the Weyerhaeuser Sales Company usually held three separate meetings for its personnel—on the West Coast, in Chicago, and in New York City. Plans for January 1937 involved sending all the salesmen by special train for a visit to the mills. The 4-Square Special was scheduled to leave St. Paul the evening of January 4, then stop at Cloquet, Coeur d'Alene, Potlatch, Lewiston, Emmett, Klamath Falls, Longview, Snoqualmie Falls, and Everett, arriving in Tacoma at noon January 20.

General meetings would be held at the headquarters of the Weyerhaeuser Timber Company prior to a departure for St. Paul Friday evening, January 22.

This had not been done since the summer of 1922. In his announcement of the plans, Fred K. noted that it was only the change in the market situation that had permitted consideration of such a trip. "We believe this expense is justified by the improvement in morale to be expected from the trip and by increasing the salesmen's acquaintance with our products and facilities, and with the situation being created at the mills by business which they have sent in," Fred had stated in his December 16 announcement.

End-of-the-year news was fairly matter-of-fact. The monthly figures reflected the effect of a Pacific Coast shipping strike, and there was no certainty when it might end. Despite the strikes, Longview had been able to maintain its production figures, using rail markets that previously had never consumed more than 50 percent of the output. With tongue in cheek, at least partly so, Phil told the Timber Company directors that the Sales Company management was "so apprehensive about the large order files and broken stocks that they are bringing the salesmen West to be off the road most of the month of January." He also reported that the Steamship Company had purchased a 9,000-ton ship, the *Exporter*, and renamed it the *Winona*. As he explained, "this was justified in our opinion as an investment but mainly because our west-bound tonnage necessitated a certain frequency of pick up." The Clemons Logging Company minority interest had been purchased, and that company would be dissolved at the year's end. Similarly, the Yards Securities Company was in the process of dissolution.

The 4–Square Special ran into unexpected difficulties when many of the salesmen were struck by a serious flu virus. Phil joined the group at Lewiston, where he found them "coming down one after another." But despite bad weather and sickness, the special train arrived in Tacoma on schedule with most aboard. Phil had made careful plans for the banquet honoring the visitors. As evidence of his seriousness, he indicated his intention to serve as the master of ceremonies at the banquet in the Crystal Ballroom of the Winthrop Hotel on January 21. The program was the usual mixture of business and pleasure. On the pleasure side, Minot Davis and "chorus" were to render an "old Sea Chanty," no doubt ribald in the extreme. Phil also asked Tom Murray, president of the West Fork Logging Comany, to accompany Minot and his chorus at the piano, although he had assured his friend, "please don't think this is our only reason for inviting you on this occasion."

Intended to be informative were presentations by R. B. Wolf of the pulp division, R. S. Hatch, also of the pulp division though currently involved with the engineering effort, and special guest, Colonel Greeley. It is of some interest that Phil included these particular individuals, as it surely indicated his own concerns. Colonel Greeley, of course, deserved the honor of the invitation, and his remarks on the general conditions of the industry had to appeal to salesmen as well as those engaged in production. But the inclusion of Wolf and Hatch on the program had more significance than just general appeal. Phil wanted to share what was happening in some of the lesser-known and lesser-appreciated efforts. Bob Wolf entitled his remarks, "What Is in a Hemlock Tree," suggesting, of course, that the time of considering the hemlock a weed had long since passed. Ray Hatch spoke for twenty minutes on "Our Adventures in Research." It may have been a slight exaggeration to label it "research," but the adventures part was accurate. In addition, the salesmen got to meet all of those on the Tacoma office staff of the Timber Company who had previously been names without faces. After returning to St. Paul, Fred K. wrote a note of thanks to Phil, noting that the banquet had been "ably toastmastered," and that "the whole affair did more to build up the morale in the Sales Company organization than anything that has happened in a great many years."

Almost coincident with the visit of the salesmen, the new Research Building was completed at Longview. By almost any standards not an impressive structure, it was likely to be mistaken for a small grammar school building, but at least the research group had a place to call home. Fred Weyerhaeuser, Dave's brother and older son of F.E., was administratively in charge for General Timber Service, although Ray Hatch continued to run the program. "Long" Fred, as he was known for reasons obvious and to distinguish him from the other Freds, had earlier proposed the organization of a research committee to give direction to the program and also to encourage an interest in the results of research. He had suggested, in a letter to Phil, that the committee might include either Phil or Charlie Ingram as the representative of the Timber Company. In his reply, Phil was all encouragement, expressing his willingness to serve and also assuring that Charlie too would be willing. He also expressed his happiness with Ray Hatch, satisfied that they had "a very able fellow to do most of the work."

Aside from the shipping strike, the labor situation seemed misleadingly settled. In addition to the ever-present issue of wages, however, there remained many points of disagreement. Chief among them, and one that would present problems for many years to come, was the question of a closed shop. This issue became something of a cause célèbre, the apparent principle of the thing obscuring the real situation. Both sides came to believe their own rhetoric: to union members, victory was incomplete until a closed shop was achieved; to the Weyerhaeusers, acceptance of a closed shop was un-American, violating the constitutional principle of freedom of choice.

Charlie Ingram described the situation to an inquiring Ed Davis. "At none of our operations do we have what might be called a closed shop," he observed, "at least to the extent that they recognize the union as the sole bargaining agency, give the check-off, hiring hall, or any of the incidentals which are attendant upon the closed shop." Snoqualmie Falls had the largest percentage of union membership, and Charlie admitted that the workers there "might term it a closed shop, as they are quite insistent that any new members affiliate with them." Still, "it is not recognized as such by the management."

Wages varied considerably, from "the lowest paid trackman who gets 55¢ per hour to the skilled head rigger who gets $1.22½." In the woods the average hourly rate was 80 cents. The logging camps operated on a schedule of a five-day week, eight hours a day, with most of the men coming out of the woods for the weekend. Meals were assessed at $1.20 a day and lodging at 15 cents a day, for an average weekly deduction of $6.75.

One of the most welcomed bits of news came into Phil's hands in a February 1 letter from brother Fred. That very afternoon, Ed Davis had called Fred advising him that the J. I. Case Company had just delivered a check in the amount of $500,000 for the purchase of the Rock Island Plow Company plant, inventory, and assets. As Fred K. wrote, "I know this will give you a big kick, as it does me." At long last, the headache that had been inherited was relieved. Another family problem seemed on the verge of resolution. Although the Timber Securities Company had been dissolved, the question how best to manage family interests and investments remained. Fred K. noted that he had spent most of the day with Uncle Fred, Charlie McGough, and Walter Rosenberry discussing the whole investment problem. F.E. had agreed to hiring a person to assist Charlie, perhaps putting him on the payroll of the F. Weyerhaeuser Company. But this would be more a secretarial or clerical assistant. What was also needed was access to an organization skilled at investment counseling. They had almost decided to send their securities to the Fiduciary Trust Company; but after talking with the president of the First Trust Company, they thought they might give that organization a trial. In any event, there would be some family approach to a service providing fiscal management.

In the meantime, Phil was making plans for the pending Executive Committee meeting. According to his schedule, the committee would meet in Tacoma Monday, February 15, for a general discussion, then go to Everett Tuesday where they would receive a report from the managers of the Everett plant and the Vail woods operation on last year's results and this year's budget planning. Wednesday would be spent back in Tacoma, Thursday in Klamath Falls, and Friday in Longview, again with reports from managers and key personnel. Rather suddenly, the old, relaxed days of Executive Committee membership had ended. The members might occasionally disagree with the decisions made by the executive vice-president, but at the very least they were in a position to understand the reasons for those decisions.

The shipping strike ended at most points February 5. The Executive Committee went much according to plan, and Phil and Helen departed Tacoma the evening of February 20, heading directly for New York, and then to enjoy the Panama Canal passage in a westerly direction. There would be some business mixed with the pleasure. Charlie Ingram had made some progress in his efforts to find a labor relations assistant. Roderic Olzendam was one of the early candidates, and Charlie suggested that Rod should feel free to get in touch with Phil in New York. Charlie wrote to Phil, half in apology about bothering him. He reported that Bill Peabody and Harry Kendall were in Tacoma, discussing the reorganization of the shipping department. Apparently they had decided that Roy Rogers should be in charge of shipping matters and another person in charge of sales. Captain L. C. Howard was also there, and he was making his report at that very moment. The next day all the general managers were scheduled to meet and talk about labor policy. After mentioning a possible Olzendam call, Charlie concluded, "I presume it is a rather cheap trick to write you regarding these business matters when you left here Saturday evening hoping to entirely forget them for at least a month," but he added, "I think possibly to cut off business too suddenly might be too severe treatment, so I am giving you this parting shot which will be the last that you will receive for a month."

For the most part, Charlie kept his word, and Phil and Helen made the voyage in a happy and relaxed state, indulging themselves for a change. The problem, as always, involved the return to work and the realization that much had accumulated in the interval. Phil's initial effort was to complete preparation of the final statements of 1936 for the Timber Company and its wholly owned subsidiaries. The figures were encouraging. The net profits were $5.1 million compared with the 1935 total of $2.2 million. Although the shipping strike had again interrupted the business of the last quarter, this interruption was in part offset by the firmness that it provided to the market. Dollar sales of major products came to nearly $30 million, "an increase of 53% over 1935," while dividends of $1.3 million represented an increase of $559,703. He also noted that the Weyerhaeuser Logged Off Land Company had been completely liquidated in October, its assets transferred to the newly created Reforestation and Land Department. The

14 percent minority stock of the Clemons Logging Company had been bought out and the corporation liquidated as of December 31, its future operations continuing under the designation "Clemons Branch." Finally, the 33 percent minority interest of the Yards Securities Company had also been purchased prior to its dissolution.

Phil did take time to respond to John Musser of the General Timber Service regarding a suggestion that they set up "a centralized research corporation for profit." As one would expect, Phil was not enthusiastic. Research for the sake of research interested him not at all, and the possibility that it could be done at a profit seemed remote indeed. He stated his position clearly: "I am in thorough sympathy with the idea of trying to find the answer to certain specific problems through research and I have the feeling that our present start at Longview is the right approach." He also indicated, "somehow having the research studies going on immediately adjacent to operations appeals to me a great deal more than setting up an independent laboratory in which everybody is interested but nobody is close at hand to keep the program on earth." Although Phil tried to be gentle in his rejection, expressing a willingness "to talk to you sometime about the whole matter of research," young John Musser probably wondered what there was to talk about.

Phil did not intend to needle Musser. He merely wished to state his position as one opposed to the suggestion. It was, however, his intent to needle Bob Wolf of the pulp division in a letter of April 1. Phil wished to call Bob's attention to an article in the current issue of the *Architectural Forum* concerning the Everett pulp mill. Phil took delight in quoting from that article: "It is a perennial architectural paradox that industry recognizes the functional approach in its production buildings but immediately reverts to sentimental traditional forms when it shelters its office personnel." Phil suggested that Bob might wish to send a rebuttal "inasmuch as I remember some rather heated arguments between us as to the office." The fact was that Bob Wolf was very adept at presenting his side of an issue, and more often than not the subject under discussion was one in which few others had any real understanding. In short, it was unfair, and this was probably one of the few opportunities Phil had enjoyed to question the authority of the Timber Company's resident expert on pulp and paper.

As the Timber Company established a distribution network, it occasionally made use of outside organizations. One of these was the Santa Fe Lumber Company of Stockton, California, and Phil soon developed a close relationship with its owner-manager, A. J. "Gus" Russell. Gus thoroughly enjoyed the company of the lumber executive and offered to sponsor him as a member in the Bohemian Club. This was an ultraexclusive organization with a beautiful camp, or "Grove," located in the midst of the redwood country some seventy-five miles north of San Francisco. Typically, Phil was uninterested. In his reply he indicated that he would "like nothing better than to bask in your glade," but explained, "my wife tells me that I am in danger of being 'clubbed' into insolvency and if there exists a club which I can get along without I should do so, and for that reason I have never taken you up on your suggestion that I might make the grade." In a more serious vein, he indicated an unwillingness to use up the few vacations he could manage "without wife and without family, which doesn't really seem the thing to do."

Following his meeting with Phil in New York, Roderic Olzendam, director of the Social Security Bureau for the Metropolitan Life Insurance Company, came to Tacoma to look the situation over and to be looked over. Apparently he left with a favorable impression. Phil received a letter following Olzendam's return to New York which read in part, "To team up with you and Charlie in an effort to help fulfill your ambition as you put it to me in New York—to provide steady employment to the largest possible number of persons under the best conditions—is something I am looking forward to with keen anticipation." Phil subsequently wrote members of the Executive Committee, informing them of the developments. To Horace Irvine he noted, "Charlie and I have taken a Brodie and agreed with a man by the name of Roderic Olzendam to come here and act as Labor Relations Counselor." To Laird Bell he wrote that they were convinced that Olzendam was "not only able but will accept direction and not sell us out," although he did qualify that confidence: "That, of course, is a matter of opinion based on short contact."

In a way it is not surprising that Laird's original suggestion for the appointment of a public relations expert had been narrowed to a concern with labor relations. That did seem to be the most pressing problem, although in the spring of 1937 it was still unclear whether a settlement was possible. Phil had reported to F.E. in early April that negotiations were continuing in Longview, somewhat complicated by the need to wait for Long-Bell. As Phil explained matters, "the nature of the labor set-up" had placed Weyerhaeuser's Longview operations and Long-Bell together, "and our rate of speed is dependent somewhat upon them before a finally approved agreement can be signed." Furthermore the terms were not identical. For example, during the past year Long-Bell had maintained a 50-cent minimum wage while Weyerhaeuser had gone to 55 cents. Despite the complications, "we feel the matter is going reasonably well." But it was not simply a matter of wages. Laird had attempted to share what he thought were some valuable insights into the labor question earlier in the year. He had been discussing the matter with several experienced persons and was

apparently convinced that they were "witnessing a sort of mass phe-
nomenon in that there is a more or less unconscious and unreasoning
claim by laboring elements that they are entitled to assert a large influence on their own destinies." He told of a story, passed along by an
industrial relations executive with a steel company, which involved a
representative of the bricklayers. The company had made a voluntary
offer of a wage increase, but the union representative was unhappy:
he would have preferred the increase to come after two months of
negotiations.

The story could well have been apocryphal, but Laird thought he
understood the moral: "it is that management must go in for genuine
collective bargaining." It seemed to him, "Rigid hostility certainly will
provoke dangerous reactions." The best policy would be a "slow strategic retreat," which he thought pretty accurately described what Phil,
Charlie Ingram, and Bill Billings of Potlatch had been doing. Thus,
"my remarks are little more than an endorsement of your action."

The "slow strategic retreat" appeared to be working. Agreements
were reached in Longview the third week in April, primarily involving
a 7.5–cent wage advance "straight through." The negotiations at the
other operations had been largely marking time to see what the Longview settlement would be. There was other encouraging news. Plants
had been running to capacity, and additional log purchases had been
necessary for the Everett and Longview mills. Klamath Falls shipments for March had broken all records, and the Everett pulp mill had
performed profitably for the first time.

But 1937, which had started in such a promising fashion, soon
proved disappointing. Indeed, things reached the point where the West
Coast industry was discussing the possibility of curtailing production.
Phil had heard more than a few expressions of curtailment talk before,
and he was not altogether certain that he wished to join in any cooperative effort at reduction. As he indicated to Uncle Fred, "It seems to
me that we should be as quick to drop off production during sags in
the market, except for the fact that everyone regrets it and dislikes it,
and also the fact that our actions in the matter can never take care of
the difficulties in the situation unless other producers also do their
part." Still there was always the hope that others might follow their
lead, and Phil was convinced that the industry did not serve its own
best interests or those of the public "if it so governs its production as
to have a graph of its average price full of peaks and valleys."

In the midst of these concerns, Phil had taken time to sail with his
sons Flip and George on the *Winona* from Everett to Longview, along
with Charlie Ingram and Charlie's son Erskine. Everyone had a good
time, Phil telling Laird afterward that the *Winona* seemed worthy of
her name. More important, however, Phil had used the occasion to

have a lengthy discussion with Captain L. C. Howard. Fundamental to the Weyerhaeuser Steamship Company's chances for profitable operation was the arrangement for westbound cargoes, and this was Howard's responsibility. His Pacific Coast Direct Line was the agency involved, but it all seemed rather too casual an arrangement to Phil, and he had been urging Bill Peabody to reach a formalized contract. As a matter of fact, there was much about East Coast shipping arrangements of which Phil was uninformed, and to some extent that was probably just as well. It was a different world. Getting to know Captain Howard, however, was in itself reassuring. He was a man of wit, intelligence, and surprisingly long experience, with a seagoing career that included sailing-ship voyages around the Cape. Years later he would publish the *Log of the Edward Sewall, 1911–1912*, recounting his initial experience, 127 days, New York to San Francisco. Phil was, of course, much interested in the captain, but he was more relieved to ascertain that here was a person of integrity. The agreement between the Weyerhaeuser Steamship Company and Captain Howard would be arranged without difficulty, and the captain would prove to be vital to the future of that involvement, hard-working and responsible in his business dealings, and patient and encouraging to all those amateur sailors who increased in numbers with the passing years. At the moment Phil was anxious to get the understanding on paper. Thus he wrote to Peabody following his conversations with the captain, "If you can reach some meeting of the minds on the subject I hope you will call in Gus Clapp to put it on paper as he can do that sort of thing to the Queen's taste."

Phil and Helen had purchased property on American Lake and built a small cottagelike home to serve as a summer retreat. In any spare moments, they were there not for relaxation, at least not yet, but to work at clearing the landscape. If Phil had not known Scotch broom previously, he and his hands and back got to know the shrub that summer. As he pulled, one of the things he thought about was the matter of curtailment. Uncle Fred had advised against acting in other than self-interest, in other words to refrain from any cooperative involvement. It isn't clear whether the decision to go to a four-day week involved any industry considerations. As Phil would write to Laird, his reasoning was "difficult to explain by letter," but he was convinced that they had "done the wise thing and probably stopped the market from going down as rapidly as it appeared to be." On the brighter side, Phil reported that they had moved into the American Lake house and that he was looking forward to working less and relaxing more.

In addition to reduced production as a result of the four-day week, it seemed likely that strikes would again become frequent. Earlier in July, the Willapa Harbor woods operations were shut down for two weeks because of a strike, although the crew returned without any concessions being made and there was no loss of sawmill time as a result. The major complication was beyond the province of the company. The CIO organizers were active in the Northwest as elsewhere, and votes were being taken to determine whether locals would stay with the AFL or align themselves with the CIO. There was also the threat "on the part of the Carpenters & Joiners to boycott lumber made by C.I.O. mills." Thus Phil foresaw the likelihood of "some involuntary curtailment which will further correct the balance between production and orders."

In that same letter to the Timber Company directors, Phil enclosed a copy of a full-page Weyerhaeuser advertisement that had appeared in the *Seattle Post-Intelligencer* of July 25, 1937. In retrospect, this would seem an insignificant item, but at the time it was viewed as a major change in policy by everyone and a foolish expenditure of money by some. And a few probably viewed it as dangerous. But as Phil explained, not only did he wish to educate the editor of the *Post-Intelligencer*, "it is the kind of a story which we must . . . try to tell to the public in general." The advertisement featured the phrase "timber is a crop," and the text read: "Timber is a crop, like any other crop. When harvested and protected under sound public policies it will provide continuous employment, furnish adequate cheap supplies of lumber and add materially to the national wealth."

Thus was born, at least in a public sense, the national advertising campaign of the Weyerhaeuser Timber Company, and to a considerable extent the basic approach has varied little over the years. Also born, or at least announced, was the expression that would become identified with the company, "Timber is a crop." One of the subsequent internal squabbles had to do with just who came up with the phrase originally. Rod Olzendam took claim—a claim that Phil never disputed. But Charlie Ingram, interviewed in 1978, would recall a different origin. Olzendam had been readying himself to make a speech, and Charlie and Phil were sitting with him. In the course of their dinner conversation, Rod had mentioned that he was going to say "timber is a farming industry." As Charlie remembered, Phil had said, "No, say 'timber is a crop.'" According to Charlie: "'Timber is a crop'—that came from Philip, I'd swear to that, which Olzendam picked up." In truth, the Weyerhaeuser Timber Company's first general manager, George S. Long, had used the phrase "Timber is a crop" when addressing the annual meeting of the Pacific Coast Lumber Manufacturers' Association at Seattle's Commercial Club on January 30, 1909. Whoever thought it up, it proved to be effective and enduring.

Phil heard immediately from Laird Bell concerning the *P-I* advertisement. Laird was, of course, enthusiastic, and thought the cross section of hemlock that was pictured was "very impressive." All was not perfect, however: "I suppose, to keep my record right, I should complain of a split infinitive in the text, but maybe you had to do that to get it into the Hearst paper." That was vintage Bell, and he would have been doubly amused had he witnessed the results of his observation at the Tacoma office. It is strange how the smallest of things can register. Years later, George S. Long, Jr., then serving as the assistant secretary for the company, recalled that Phil came into his office, Laird's letter in hand, wanting to know just what a split infinitive was. If the question seems surprising, it is far less so to those familiar with Phil's prose style. If he knew the rule, he chose to violate it recklessly. But to Laird, his reply was as casual as the observation that occasioned it. "Thanks for your thoughtful criticism," he wrote. "We are still looking for that split infinitive."

CHAPTER 9

The Great Depression Is a Long Depression

It is not clear whether Phil Weyerhaeuser ever heard directly from his uncle Rudolph regarding the entry of the Timber Company into the field of national advertising. The fact is, however, that Rudolph was willing to admit that the time had come for that change. In the summer of 1937 he had written as much to Bill Billings at Lewiston. Rudolph was serving as president of Potlatch Forests, and some articles had come to his attention which praised the policies of the company in the matter of providing assistance to the citizens of Coeur d'Alene in those difficult days. He expressed his pleasure to Billings at reading these. Then he noted, "The publicity end of the business is something that we have let go by default for a great many years, and have begun to realize that we made a mistake." He added, "That may be the cause for a great many people seeming to think there is some mystery in the lumber business." Perhaps it only seemed simpler, less mysterious, as Rudolph became less involved. There was, however, evidence that a new pride was influencing the positions assumed by Bill Billings, Phil, and others.

The Timber Company Executive Committee met again in Tacoma in late September, Phil thinking it especially important to have it on the scene since Minot Davis had a series of presentations to make concerning timber matters. There were other problems. Phil wanted consideration given to a stock split, not so much for purposes of sale but because of the possible effect of stock prices on labor negotiations. He also wanted the question of an increase in the capital stock of the Weyerhaeuser Steamship Company to be discussed, as well as consideration of possible purchase of the stock of the White River Company and the Snoqualmie Falls Lumber Company. Regarding the first stock question, the committee recommended a four for one split.

Despite the reduction in the work week to four days, the balance between market demand and production failed to improve. On October 14, Phil addressed a note to Harry Kendall of the Sales Company, telling of a visit just that morning from Colonel Greeley. According to Phil, the Colonel had arrived "with a worried look, to state that he was again on the thankless mission of trying to save an industry which did not wish to be saved." He was convinced that "our prices were in a tailspin and that business would not again be forthcoming until the bottom had been reached," although he "felt an artificial bottom could be put in the market by such people as ourselves." Phil was less certain, but he was prepared to seek information and advice from Kendall and Sales Company associates. One of the complications noted was that they were facing an "inflexible labor cost," which meant that the choices were reduced. One could not reduce costs while continuing to operate. "A Willamette Valley mill tried to do that the other day and all his crew walked off the job." In the meantime, the week's industry figures were "most discouraging," showing a production figure of 95 million feet and sales of only 83 million. Thus Phil inquired, "Do you think that we should take the pressure off . . . by further reducing production and that if we do so you could justify a firm price for its effect upon our competition?" What Phil wanted was for Kendall to indicate a willingness to lower prices. Kendall had replied, "it makes no difference what we do—let's sell each day and keep running at present rate."

Equally puzzling was what should be done regarding the growing struggle between the CIO and the AFL, the tendency of some obviously being to wish them both ill. The presence of Rod Olzendam had apparently failed to broaden the views of many in management. Laird Bell, writing to Phil October 14, saw part of the problem in specific terms, perhaps seeing what Charlie Ingram and Phil also saw but preferred to ignore. Laird feared that either they were using Olzendam poorly or he wasn't filling the role as planned. He also objected to the newspapers referring to Olzendam as an "expert" and thought that a title of either director of public relations or director of labor relations would tend "to put both the public and labor on their guard a little." Furthermore, he warned, "If he continues to make speeches avowedly as a public relations man, I am afraid he will either degenerate into an entertainer or hamper his ability to have a real influence on public relations."

Laird's observations, in a letter of October 21, on the labor situation were insightful: "Especially since my return, I have been impressed with what seems to me the fatuity—no extra charge for the word—of the attitude of a good many employers on the Federation—C.I.O. quarrel." The employers tended to think that the CIO was further to the left and therefore the worse of the two evils. Laird believed that if they were to have unions, "we are better off with industry unions than craft unions." He was not advising that they immediately "climb into Mr. Lewis' lap"; he was advising, "we should 'watch our step.'" He closed by expressing the assumption that "one justification for my salary is giving you the benefit of ideas I get in other contacts, and this is submitted for what it is worth on that basis."

Phil responded October 23 to both letters, acknowledging that he and Charlie had talked about the Olzendam situation, but had "not reached a conclusion." He promised that they would talk again, giving consideration to Laird's observations. Regarding the CIO and AFL matter, Phil told Laird, "I have no quarrel with anything you say on that subject either," although he admitted, "Just how to interpret the thought into a line of action, however, is difficult." In any case, he was passing Laird's comments along to Charlie and Rod Olzendam.

In the meantime the Timber Company, largely through the promotional schemes of Rod Olzendam, was going public in several ways. A film was being produced; and a speech given by Olzendam at the Pacific Logging Congress in Seaside, Oregon, entitled "Timber Is a Crop," was reprinted by the company for distribution. This found its way into the hands of their old antagonist, Forest Service Chief Ferdinand Silcox. Olzendam heard directly from Silcox, the chief beginning with the observation, "this is the most effective forest industry presentation I have seen." None of this, however, had much altered his opinion of the problems and their resolution. He maintained, for example, that "nowhere in the world has private initiative succeeded, of itself, in substituting sustained yield forest management for forest exploitation generally." Perhaps slightly more agreeable was his observation that "public regulation offers real protection not only to public interests but also to those private owners who, recognizing inherent social obligations, must without it inevitably be confronted by unfair competition from other owners who for one reason or another elect to continue forest exploitation."

Phil shared Olzendam's letter from the Forest Service chief with others. To Fritz Jewett, he remarked on the "very illuminating letter from Silcox, who I suppose sums up the voice of public opinion for us as much as any one person, and against whose propaganda we are advancing the movie under current production." Fred K. had replied that it was indeed "a most remarkable letter," adding, "it certainly indicates a great improvement in the attitude towards our Company."

Of more immediate concern was the continuing decline in business. On November 10, Phil reported to Horace Irvine that the "market is dropping away from us so fast it makes my head swim." Having received no very satisfactory answer from Kendall, Phil wrote directly to Fred K. concerning the Sales Company's attitude and policies. He was as specific as possible in describing the problem:

It is almost impossible to get across ideas by mail, but in response to my letter of October 29th in which I said: "If our statement to you that we are not going to produce in excess of our percentage of the industry sales would result in a different price outlook on your part, we are willing to give you that assurance," to which you answered: "Do you approve of the policy I am trying to outline, or do you think it would be wiser for us to freeze our present prices and adjust production to orders?"—I did not think when I was writing that I was suggesting the latter policy. I was simply trying to suggest an approach by which you would remain free as to price but we would not pile inventory. That is, to my mind, the major consideration at the moment.

The problem was all too familiar: they were producing more than they were selling. Phil reported: "In the last week, our fir production exceeded orders received by three million feet," and if they accepted the orders received for the last two weeks as a standard, it would suggest a monthly rate of production of 16.6 million feet for Longview, 11.1 million feet for Everett, 6.1 million feet for Snoqualmie, and 11.4 million feet for Klamath. Further computations using current cost and price figures, including the "best guess as to the average price for a typical log," indicated profits at Longview of 75 cents per thousand; at Snoqualmie, 50 cents; at Klamath Falls, $3.00; and an outright loss at Everett of $3.25 for every thousand feet of lumber produced. Phil continued: "At some point in this process we can decide for ourselves that the bottom of the market is reached and interpret that into a price policy. Perhaps as long as there still is some profit margin at some of the plants we should not do this, but, of course, viewed from any cold-blooded business angle, we are not, under present conditions, realizing any sort of a satisfactory return on investment, and at one plant we are losing our shirts."

He concluded with about as frontal an attack on one of their organizational problems as he could mount against brother and uncles: "I regret the distance which separates us because at times like this it seems to me that we should have a very thorough understanding of all the factors affecting the situation." That regret seemed corroborated by Fred K.'s telegraphed reply: "Lack of information here makes impossible answering yours fourth which contains figures astounding to us."

Phil heard shortly from Harry Kendall. There was, however, no very satisfactory answer forthcoming. Kendall pointed out that the Timber Company inventories were still some 42 million feet below what they had been the previous January. "Someday," he continued, "business is going to open up, and we have got to be ready to take care of it." In the meantime, it seemed impossible to please anyone: "Our competitors will tell you we pressed the market," and "our customers will tell you they can't buy from us except at great sacrifice." In short, it was a long, long depression.

Kendall did offer to come to Tacoma in order that they might consider the problem with the greatest possible care. Phil wired back: "Rome is not burning and although we are not agreed, do come west at your pleasure." Kendall correctly took "at your pleasure" to mean at the earliest opportunity, and he was soon aboard the Great Northern heading west. Fred K. was happy that Phil and Harry had decided to get together, but his own prediction was that there was little they could do. "My impression is that '38 is going to be a bum year with no basic improvement in sight until early in '39," he wrote to Phil. "We are going to have to economize and play it safe for the next twelve months." In any event, Phil and Harry felt better for their discussion.

There were specific results. The Sales Company revised its plans for the coming year, committing itself to a volume equal to 1937. The question of price, of course, was more difficult, but it was assumed that prices would average somewhat lower. Phil refused to accumulate inventory. Thus by the end of November, White River's operations had been shut down. Willapa was also closed, and Everett's production reduced to about 35 percent of capacity. Longview was scheduled to go to 80 percent of capacity, and Snoqualmie Falls somewhere in the neighborhood of 60 percent.

Although Laird tried to follow the developments, he felt somewhat at a disadvantage, or as he put it, "my information on lumber is always quite a long way after the fact." Perhaps because he knew less of details, he was able to take a broader and longer view. To Phil he indicated, "I still think there is a combination of depression psychology and a sort of morbid delight in blaming the President which makes everybody bluer than they ought to be." And even though there did seem to be a temporary imbalance between production and consumption, that was likely to be corrected in fairly short order, and the basic factors looked encouraging: "There is no great debt structure that has to be liquidated, labor troubles certainly ought to decrease, and, so far as the lumber business is concerned, we seem to be in line to become beneficiaries of whatever there may be that the government can do by way of stimulating building." Phil could only hope that his friend's view of things was accurate.

Phil was soon on his way to Hollywood to participate in the final editing of the promotional film, *Trees and Men*. As he described it, the film was an attempt "to portray the history of the lumber industry in relation to the history of the country to show the growth of the conservation movement and the change of the industry practice with the change of economic and social conditions in the country." Although it had been aimed at the Timber Company employees and communities, he was hoping that it would also be useful in more general terms.

In addition to the movie, which would be the first in a series of such productions, other Timber Company employees were contributing on the public scene. Bob Wolf had written a paper entitled "West Coast Pulp," which received wide distribution, and C. S. Chapman delivered a paper at the Society of American Foresters meeting in Syracuse, New York, December 17, entitled "Industrial Problems of Forest Practice in the Northwest." In his Christmas letter of 1937, Dr. C. A. Schenck took special note of Wolf's contribution in a footnote, calling it "the best description, in word and in picture, of Western logging!" For the most part, however, the letter seemed a pained attempt to find justification for the events in his country. "Is there a religious war in Germany?" he asked rhetorically:

If there is—as some Americans seem to think—I am not aware of it. Both protestant and catholic bells are chiming, day by day and notably of a Sunday, in my own village of Lindenfels, and there is nothing to prevent me or any other Lindenfelsian from doing and believing what I or he wants to. If there be any heathens, I am one of them. Anyhow, neither the christian nor any other religion can be killed by any sort of a government. A religion may die, however, from old age. History proves it.

Dr. Schenck recognized that Hitler was "misunderstood" if not "despised" in America. But he seemed convinced that "Hitler's regime has done . . . more for good forestry and for good game laws than what was done by all imperial and democratic governments before him," and he penned in on Phil's copy, "And labor is fully satisfied, for the first time in History."

Somehow the possibility that Hitler may have been an advocate of good forestry and game laws seemed strangely insufficient. Recent months had introduced the word "Lebensraum" into the American vocabulary, and in response the American president had talked of "quarantine" in a political sense. War continued in Spain, Japan had invaded China, and on December 12 Japanese planes sank the American gunboat *Panay* on the Yangtze River. Herr Schenck might walk his "domain" in relative calm and security, but the world looked anything but calm and secure.

Possibly because he received it as a Christmas gift, Phil started keeping a diary on January 1, 1938. His first entry was typically short and to the point: "New Year's party, 4 o'clock on, no casualties." Fred K. had come west to attend some sales meetings at Longview—meetings that Phil also attended. For their first evening there, the diary noted a poker game with "Billings, Graue, O'Connell, Kendall, O'Neil, and FKW." The following evening the word "Rotten" was inserted following reference to dinner and the showing of "Trees & Men." Doubtless the comment referred to the movie, since meals were seldom of importance.

But apparently the movie was not so "rotten" that the plans to share it had to be shelved. On February 1, Phil told the Timber Company directors that it had already been shown "to all the salesmen and several thousand interested parties across the country." The response had been "favorable," although there were certain changes being made. A long introductory section showing Rod Olzendam lecturing to a group of interested workers was being cut, undoubtedly the portion to which Phil had objected. That was just too paternalistic to stomach, and "rotten" probably was an appropriate assessment.

Some improvement in the "barometer," as Phil called it, seemed evident toward the end of the first quarter of 1938. White River, which had been shut down since December 1, resumed operations, soon to be followed by Willapa, "and the other plants are operating at a slightly increased gait." Prices, however, remained low, averaging some three dollars less than in 1937. As a result, pressure was being placed on the Weyerhaeuser Timber Company by other producers to join in an industry effort at collective labor negotiations. By and large, Phil's position was that such "entangling alliances" should be avoided, except for the pulp division. Laird Bell was quick to agree: "I suppose we have to balance the good will of our competitors against the good will of our labor, and I should say that you had chosen to favor the right end." Laird was not convinced that leaders in the industry had made any headway in labor relations, and "if we subjected ourselves to industry influence we would constantly be urged to take the lead in unpopular moves—and also be left holding the bag." Gus Clapp was even more vehement in his support, noting, "Frankly, I don't believe *our* labor has received more than their share of our capitalistic enterprise during the past two years and I think it is up to us to stand by them for a time at least and see if we don't pull out of these doldrums."

Much of Phil's time was being spent on the annual report for 1937. Perhaps it seemed ironic that in the year the Timber Company had produced *Trees and Men* and published the booklet *Timber Is a Crop*, so little continued to be done to inform stockholders of company affairs. Phil was convinced that they should do a better job of sharing information with the stockholders and others by means of the annual report. He was not at all certain that F.E. would be supportive.

Previously the annual report had included only a brief letter over Phil's signature, a generalized statement of assets and liabilities, and a listing of directors and officers. Before Phil's administration, there had been no annual report but what was called an annual statement, which was very detailed but with an extremely limited distribution. For example, only seven copies of the 1932 report had been prepared for the stockholders' meeting. The changes that had occurred were not simply the result of changes in office technology. For the 1937 report, Phil suggested that in place of the condensed balance sheet there should be the balance sheet as prepared by the General Timber Service, along with a verification statement by certified public accountants, and also a profit and loss statement. Accompanying the letter, which was, of course, a summary of the year's activities, he recommended that there be nine charts illustrating various aspects such as the source of revenues, the distribution of costs, payrolls, plant additions and improvements, and taxes over a ten-year period. Recognizing the extent of the change he was recommending, Phil circulated it "in tentative form" to F.E. and the other members of the Executive Committee for approval:

You may think that we are going too far in our ten year historical data. My reasons for wanting to do so are, briefly, that I have the feeling strongly that in one way or another much information about the Company, the amount of its dividends in particular, will be known to the public either through the publication or duplication of the report, such as occurred last year; through the giving of information to statistical bureaus; through the necessity of reporting to the Securities and Exchange Commission in reference to over-the-counter sales of stock. . . . That being so, it seems to me prudent to explain the situation in the way outlined, the more so because the story is a good one.

He also wanted to go a step further and share this information with the managers of the various operations, and, assuming the willingness of the managers, with groups of foremen.

Uncle Fred was not convinced, acknowledging, "You are a long way ahead of me in presenting this program." But he was unwilling to oppose in an arbitrary fashion something Phil favored. He did offer two general predictions: "First, you will be disappointed in the amount of good that will come to the Company because of making the information public; second, there will come much less harm from doing so than Tom Humbird and I expect." He also expressed the hope that Phil was not being overly influenced by Rod Olzendam and worried that he was not getting "an honest expression of opinion from men like Minot Davis." Finally, F.E. had found that "labor leaders and politicians rarely, if ever, make honest use of any information that comes to them."

Phil could only assure his uncle that he had discussed the question fully "with everyone in our organization here, including Charles Ingram, Minot Davis, Bill McCormick, Dwight Orr, George S. Long, Jr., and all of the managers of the branches and major subsidiaries," and was convinced that everyone had had a fair opportunity to criticize, and all were in favor. Laird Bell and Gus Clapp had responded by letter, and Horace Irvine had been in Tacoma, and all supported the change. Still, Phil allowed that he was "sorry to go on with the program with you expressing the doubt which your letter implies." But the program did go forward.

The week of May 23 was exceptionally busy, with meetings of the directors, the Executive Committee, and the annual meeting. There were fifty-one stockholders present and, as Phil noted, "many complimentary things said." The directors' meeting in the afternoon was not quite so easy and relaxed. "Long and difficult," was Phil's assessment, noting that Ed Hayes and George Little were present for the first time. The appointment of Ed Hayes as a director would prove of great benefit. A grandson of Orrin Ingram and cousin of Charlie Ingram, Ed had considerable experience as an independent operator in the West Coast lumber industry, and he brought to the board his knowledge of business and a progressive view of forest management. The election of George Little was in recognition of the wishes of the Laird and Norton interests.

One of the disappointments in the course of the recent meetings was the board's refusal to proceed on a pension plan. At the March meeting of the Executive Committee it had been determined that Gus Clapp and Laird Bell would serve as a committee, to offer a recommendation to the full board at the earliest opportunity. As presented, the plan would apply only to salaried employees earning over $3,000 a year, and the total cost to the Timber Company would be less than $50,000. Phil was satisfied that the recommendation was entirely reasonable, but the more conservative members decided otherwise. As he reported to Fred K., "The matter hung really upon each individual's notion of whether the ability to pay would continue to exist, and it was voted down." Still he was reasonably certain that the matter would come up again, and he concluded on the positive side: "I think we have progressed to the point of having a satisfactory introduction plan worked out."

And still the economic situation refused to improve. In late June, notice was given at Longview, Everett, Snoqualmie, and White River that the Timber Company had decided that a change in the wage provisions had become necessary. As Phil noted in a letter to F.E., "Other points are operating without contracts and will step into negotiations, with the exception of Klamath Falls, which goes as Pine goes." They had tried to outlast the depression within a depression, and the duration had exceeded their ability to withstand. "We felt that the time had come when we must discharge our responsibility in this respect, both to ourselves and the rest of the industry." That did not mean, however, that the rest of the industry would be satisfied. Phil indicated that he was unwilling to follow the suggestions offered by many on the amount of the reduction: "we believe it would be desirable, if possible, to reach an agreement which sets 55¢ as the minimum, being a present 7½¢ cut, which is the size of the last raise." Although he admitted that conditions warranted "more drastic treatment," he still believed that sharper fluctuations were not desirable, "preferring to go through the agony of more frequent negotiations, if necessary, than take too big a cut at one time."

Indeed, other members of the industry would "undoubtedly be resentful, as usual," when the Timber Company's plans became known. Phil noted that the strategy that had been encouraged by the National Labor Board of collective bargaining involved a "give and take" approach, which meant that the initial offers or demands were always less or more than what would be acceptable. Thus their offer of "the wage which we are willing to pay" would be attacked, Phil wrote to F.E. "This seems absurd to me, nevertheless it is the procedure to settle the point." In short, he saw no need to be devious, and if labor negotiators could not agree with the reasoning, at least they appreciated the directness. As one observer would later remark, "Weyerhaeuser meant what it said."

But it would not be easily managed, either by the Timber Company or its competitors. Phil noted the lack of progress in a July 7 letter to Uncle Fred: "Apparently the sections of the industry banded together under John Tennant's committee have gotten exactly nowhere in their attempt to negotiate a wage reduction," and "many meetings have resulted in a lot of waving of hands and promises" but little else. Phil had about concluded that everyone was waiting for Weyerhaeuser to do something first. To Laird Bell he also noted that things were at "a complete standstill with everyone saying 'Let George do it' and when we get all through I suppose George will be the Weyerhaeuser Timber Company." Fred K. and Vivian were spending the summer in Tacoma, so there was opportunity to do some sharing of problems, and also some fishing, golfing, and general relaxation.

One of the matters they discussed was Al Raught's decision to retire. No one seemed in favor of this, not even Al, but he was eager to be done at Longview, and if nothing appropriate was offered, there was little doubt that he would retire. Phil was uncertain just how much pressure was desirable. He wrote to Laird, "It seems to me that our purpose has been accomplished in letting Al know that we all regret his retirement." What was desired was for Al to come into the Tacoma office and help Charlie Ingram in the management of his growing responsibilities, but Laird wondered whether he would accept a position of "Assistant General Manager." In a conversation with him, Laird said he had tried to avoid reference to being the number three man, although that was really what was in mind. Laird had not been able to think of a better title, "anything like 'Assistant to the Executive Vice-President' would be a little on the comic side."

By late July it appeared there had been a turn in the market and that lumber prices were strengthening. This, coupled with lack of progress in negotiations on wage reductions, seemed to point in the direction of no change. Of much concern, although no great loss had been experienced, were the fires that had been burning in recent days. The air was full of smoke, and several large fires were burning out of control over the cutover lands. The weather conditions were unusually hazardous. Phil and Fred K. and the boys had gone down into Oregon to fish the McKenzie and do a bit of camping. They slept at the 4,000-foot level, and even there the night was hot, temperatures never falling below the mid-eighties. During their drive home, it was 106 degrees in the Willamette Valley.

On August 3, a decision was reached to extend for thirty days the existing labor contracts, primarily for two reasons. The first was the expectation that within that period the interpretations of the Fair Labor Standards Act would become available and, of course, would be implemented in any new contracts. Second, although justification for wage reductions could still be made, business prospects looked more favorable for the rest of the year. The first six months of 1938 had been bad, revealing a decrease of almost 80 percent in net profits over the same period in 1937 and dollar sales off by one-third. The order files as of June 30 had indicated a total of 44.5 million feet compared with 70.4 million feet the previous year.

But the days were passing. The summer was at an end, and paddle tennis and badminton at the Ingrams would soon give way to other activities. On September 6, Phil started the furnace at the Tacoma house. The following day the family moved back into town, Phil attempting to ease the transition by taking them all to dinner at the Tacoma Club. September 6 was also Nick Genta's first day as Phil's personal secretary, and some of the afternoon was given over to showing Nick around and explaining procedures.

Phil and Helen had decided to send Ann to the Masters School in Dobbs Ferry, New York. They planned to go together, spending some time in St. Paul on the way and arriving in New York September 15. They would stay there for a week before returning, again stopping over in St. Paul.

Dave Winton joined the party at Spokane, and there was a good deal of pleasure in that. Phil's diary entry for Friday, September 9, merely noted that they were on the train at St. Paul, "Much dominoes, etc., Ann sick." While in New York, they toured Radio City and saw their first "television," and got Ann ready for school. Her "last day aboard" was September 21, Phil noting that "she and Helen did some frantic last minute packing and shopping in the morning, lunch at the hotel and shoved them off for Dobbs Ferry at 2:00," after which he went to Captain Howard's office to follow the news of the coming hurricane.

Charlie Ingram tried not to bother Phil in the course of his eastern travels. He did write a letter care of the Waldorf-Astoria on September 17, observing that it just didn't seem possible that Phil had been gone a week, and that "nothing of particular importance" had taken place. There had been a strike at Willapa, the plant closing down on September 13. The planing mill had continued running on accumulated lumber and they were still shipping a little, "but I understand that in a few days the whole operation will be cold." Although they were preparing for an extended shutdown, Charlie thought it likely that "the fallers and buckers will shortly have enough pressure exerted on them by the rest of the crew so that they will accept the proposition as made." As to the question of wages, the managers had met the previous day and decided on a third thirty-day extension, hoping again that before its expiration things would be sufficiently clear to permit the negotiation of a regular contract. In general, however, business had changed little.

The other news concerned a visit by Chief Silcox. They had spent a day at the woods operation at Longview. As Charlie reported, "I am very pleased to report that Silcox descended to earth, and much to the surprise of all of us, talked in a sane and moderate manner. There was nothing in any of his remarks with which, I think, any of us could argue." He concluded that perhaps Silcox "figured that we had all finally been impressed with his knowledge and position, so at this time he had come to talk sense, which, I must confess, I think he did."

Doing business continued to be more an act of treading water than anything else. Phil reported to the directors in late October that they had been drawing "rather heavily" upon the order file and had been able to keep up too easily in shipments. Of less worry but still irritating, John Boettiger, publisher of the *Seattle Post-Intelligencer*, had apparently "taken up the cudgel!" and was addressing the Pacific Logging Congress then meeting in Tacoma, calling for a stop to the "ruthless practices" of Pacific Northwest lumbermen. Phil also mentioned Silcox's visit to Longview, indicating that the chief had been "so impressed that yesterday I was waited upon by his Regional Forester, C. J. Buck." The regional forester wished to undertake a study of the Longview area for possible designation as a sustained-yield area, "with consequent advantages through the reservation of Forest Service timber." Phil was unconvinced of the advantages: "It remains to be seen whether there is any possible way of setting up a contractual relation with the Forest Service with the foregoing end in view without mortgaging our future."

One of the subjects that had been handled rather casually through the years was the corporation's responsibility in the area of philanthropy. The practice of the Timber Company was to decentralize the responsibility, allowing the branch operations to make the decisions, accept the credit, and pay the costs. In general that meant that few donations were made, and those that received support probably had such community-wide benefits that the good will engendered was obvious or, read the other way, that refusal to contribute would have had detrimental effects. Fred K. posed a question to Phil concerning the problem of contributions, specifically concerning the response the St. Paul office should make to the appeal of the St. Paul Community Chest. They had never made any corporate contribution, and it was the feeling of many in St. Paul, and many in the Weyerhaeuser office, that they were not doing their part. But there was disagreement within. Uncle Fred was opposed to such a contribution, while Gus Clapp and Horace Irvine favored it.

Phil's answer provided a clear statement of his and, therefore, the Timber Company's feelings on the subject. Just as clearly, there was no stated policy:

Corporate contributions to the Community Chests are, to my way of thinking, simply not justified on any score, except to keep ourselves in a defensible position with the people among whom we live. The WTC has for years, on account of a precedent set so far back that I know nothing about it, given substantially to the Tacoma Community Chest. In many other cases, corporations come much closer to being personal givers, and, therefore, the solicitors seldom draw the kind of line which it seems to me should be drawn between the individual and the corporation.

For us, as officers of a corporation, to give away the stockholders' money requires a very complete justification, and the only justification which I have been able to find is the public relations angle.

The Executive Committee began its sessions on the afternoon of November 8, but F.E. did not arrive until the following morning, and it was then that the pension plan proposal was reintroduced. Phil's presentation was matter-of-fact and, he presumed, effective. He remarked, for example, that "the proposal has much interest inasmuch as the company will, with a pension plan, definitely have discharged what, in the minds of some modern thinkers, is an obligation, and will have greater freedom of action in the retirement of older employees when their efficiency declines." Perhaps the latter observation was a mistake. His diary entry for the day indicated, "Session of Executive Committee, with violent reactions by F.E. supported by RMW at pension suggestion. Lunch Tacoma Club."

The Executive Committee had also taken time to pay a visit to the Snoqualmie Falls operation, and, for the most part, this outside experience was beneficial to the group. But there had been some criticism. As Phil would later write to Tip O'Neil, after thanking him for his hospitality, "the only criticism—which must be considered constructive—came in the form of a question as to whether Snoqualmie was doing well to bring in the Hemlock mixed with its Old Growth Fir stands." F.E. had raised the question, and Rudolph had immediately launched into a lecture about what had gone wrong with Potlatch. Since the period of the Potlatch overview was the period of Phil's involvement, he could not escape responsibility on either score. The point concerned Potlatch's realization of ten dollars per thousand on its white pine stumpage, at the same time it was losing from three to five dollars a thousand harvesting ponderosa pine, fir, and larch. The reasoning was that the white pine could not be marketed by itself, the other species being necessary to fill out orders. As Phil suggested, there was also the thought "prominent in the minds of the management that they were continuing their operation over a longer life and providing jobs." Phil assumed that Tip was eager to respond to this criticism, and he was personally convinced that "over a period of years you can demonstrate that you have been on the plus side of the hemlock brought in." In any event, Tip was invited to give the matter some thought and then to provide him with "an analysis on this subject."

The thinking that had governed procedures was soon put into words by the Snoqualmie manager. Tip would not argue that they should prolong the operation to make jobs, "nor do I feel we need Hemlock to sell our Fir." He would note, however, that extending the length of operations was worthwhile, because the timber tended to increase in value with each passing year. Actually the problem was much the same as Phil had faced on the Clearwater. Although the figures seemed to indicate a loss on mixed woods or, in the Snoqualmie case, hemlock, that was only because the costs of logging were averaged over all species. Thus what seemed to compute as a loss on hemlock was a gain on fir: if no hemlock was logged, the costs of logging fir would be substantially increased. As Tip explained: "We would have an additional charge for construction costs against the Fir if we left the Hemlock," adding, "that, of course, is true of overhead, taxes, depreciation, etc." In short, they were justified in taking out hemlock when it was mixed with fir. Phil understood, of course, but when he discussed the question again with F.E., he found his uncle still unconvinced. As he would write to Tip, "we expect to hear more of it in the future." Things could seem so clear when viewed from a St. Paul desk.

If the uncles had been less than enthusiastic in the course of their recent visit, the Timber Company management had apparently done much better in the case of Ferdinand Silcox. On November 17, Ralph Hines invited Fred K. to a luncheon given by officers of the First National Bank of Chicago for the chief forester, and the guest list included Laird Bell. It was clear, according to Laird's report, that what Silcox most wanted was "to talk to a Weyerhaeuser," and next he wanted "to get along the road on sustained yield." He "says he can't go far without us." At the same time, Silcox maintained that Weyerhaeuser couldn't go very far down the road without the government: "and he has his eye on the Longview area as a nice place for a sustained yield unit! He sees government's contribution in (a) contributing timber, (b) buying reproduction land, (c) putting pressure on local governments to keep the tax load bearable, and (d) setting up some form of insurance against loss by fire (a new idea to me) which he considers might be possible with government's resources and the spread of risk in many places."

To this Laird had responded, making "a speech about how close to your heart forestry is, how much progress you made in Idaho, what a change had occurred in the thinking of all the group in five or six years, and how I felt you wanted to go as far and as fast as good business will permit." As to a sustained-yield cooperative unit involving the Timber Company and the federal government, Laird indicated that Phil would want to be certain that he could extricate himself if he didn't like it. All in all Laird thought the situation warranted an effort by Phil to meet with the chief forester. "I should like to see you go to see Silcox in Washington, and talk, or at least be talked to," Laird wrote. "He's not wild all the time—in fact, I should like to go along with you."

Fred K. also reported on this meeting and another on the following day in Minneapolis, hosted by Dave Winton. He told of Silcox's plan to create operating units in which Forest Service timber would, in effect, be the pawn in encouraging sustained-yield management in cooperation with the private producers. This would, of course, involve contracts between the Forest Service and the individual operators. While he admitted that he knew little about such matters, Fred K. did offer "the impression that the Forest Service is anxious to cooperate and that a series of conferences between ourselves and the Forest Service . . . might be very productive of good results for us."

As it worked out, a trip east was convenient. Charlie and Phil had already made plans to go to Chester, Pennsylvania, to visit Scott Paper Company representatives regarding the possibility of a cooperative effort. Phil also wanted to meet with Bill Peabody and Captain Howard, and pay daughter Ann a visit. It was church again on Sunday, November 27, where Phil heard Harold Long give a sermon on the Jewish situation, later remarking in his diary how "very interesting" it had been. That afternoon he and Flip played golf and "Helen walked around with us." In the evening Charlie and Phil took the Milwaukee Road east. They arrived in St. Paul on Tuesday evening. The next morning, November 30, following breakfast with Fred K., the two brothers attended what must have been a sobering meeting. According to Phil, the meeting had been "called by the uncles of the family to discuss extravagance," and "All were smacked down, especially me [on] account [of] having said I favored a pension plan." That evening they had dinner at Aunt Maud's where the governor-elect of Minnesota, Harold Stassen, made a call "and impressed everyone."

Monday morning they took the train to Chester, where they saw the Scott Paper Company plant and were introduced to key members of the corporation. Phil later noted, "an impression of a very live organization." Tuesday, December 6, Phil met with Bill Peabody and Captain Howard, and that evening he and Charlie went to the theater to see Phil's old artillery instructor, Raymond Massey, starring as Abraham Lincoln. Wednesday, Phil went to Newark for more discussion with Peabody, and following a luncheon which included the Eastern Yards department heads, Phil noted a problem already perceived, and one that would long trouble them. The talk with Peabody had been frank, "including [the] suggestion that young Bill would do better elsewhere." "Young Bill" was Peabody's son, who had recently been hired by the Steamship Company. The suggestion had not been taken. "No impression on big Bill," Phil admitted.

The rest of the week was largely devoted to more discussion of the Scott Paper Company proposition, specifically whether to make a 1940 commitment. It was finally decided that Keve Larson would be given the responsibility of proceeding with caution. And on Friday evening Phil went to see *Abe Lincoln in Illinois* a second time, in the company of Laird Bell, who had just arrived. Following the play, they boarded a train to Washington, D.C. After breakfast at the Metropolitan Club the next day, they met with Silcox and Assistant Chief Earl Tinker for some three hours. Phil observed that the session had provided "Interesting listening." The chief forester repeated his wish "to cooperate in sustained yield units all around the circuit," to which Phil had responded that he too wished to cooperate, but wanted "to feel our way." In his subsequent report to the Timber Company directors, Phil simply indicated that he and Laird had met with Chief Silcox "and listened to a long story." The chief "has much on his mind about cooperation to insure sustained production." Phil suggested that "perhaps something constructive can be worked out of it."

Back in Tacoma, Phil found a stack of mail awaiting him. One letter was from Burton F. Vessey, of the Charles W. Sexton Company, concerning pension plans. Phil's reply was to the point: "Thanks for the retirement plans, which revive in my memory a very dead subject." Not unrelated was a note received from Ed Davis, a participant in the recent St. Paul meetings with the uncles. Ed had gotten together with F.E. and Rudolph following the stormy session, and he had predicted that the Weyerhaeuser Timber Company would double its profits in the new year, at which time "the conversation shifted to making an adequate return on your capital and surplus, which would again amount to approximately twice that figure." In some ways, it must have seemed that the second generation was expecting more of the third than they had themselves managed. Ed seemed to imply that: "Personally, I think we are all doing a darn good job under the conditions that exist today. While it is not flattering to have someone prove that this group has not made a dollar in the lumber business since 1914, the third generation can not be held responsible for that. If we can set up so we recognize a bad job more promptly in the future and know when to let go of the bull's tail, I am sure we can do as well as the average."

After the St. Paul dressing down, it is not surprising that Phil went directly to F.E. with a problem of long standing, but given some immediacy as a result of a visit from a group of operators on December 21. Phil described his visitors as "a sincere and inquiring committee of the industry" seeking to determine the position of the Weyerhaeuser Timber Company on the current wage base. Two basic questions were posed: "Were wages of the West Coast industry too high?" "Did we see, as they thought they saw, an opportunity now to effect a reduction in those wages?" To Phil, the answer to the first question was an easy yes, but the answer to the second was less certain. It was apparent, however, "that the industry will endure the grief necessary to accomplish a reduction in wages if we will."

Following a meeting of the Weyerhaeuser managers, a consensus was reached that "we should lend our support to an effort toward general wage reduction to be accomplished as near the first of February as possible, if we can get satisfactory assurances from a substantial group in the industry that they will pursue a similar course." It was by no means a simple decision. Phil had wished to follow rather than to lead, but apparently that was impossible, and conditions simply would not improve. Districts that had been shut down for a long period were beginning to receive requests from employees to reduce wages if that was what was necessary to start up. In any event, Uncle Fred was being given the opportunity to register his opinion.

Before opening presents on Christmas Day, they went to church. Phil had recently responded to a request from his good friend Corydon Wagner for a donation to the First Congregational Church. He had contributed in the past "because I attended occasionally and the boys went to the Sunday School." But in the past year, he noted, "I have more definitely affiliated myself, as have they, with the Immanuel Presbyterian Church." And he closed, "I am, therefore, declining your invitation."

Perhaps the increased interest in church was simply the result of the aging process and a growing appreciation of the value of Christian theology and the natural desire that one's children at least be exposed to such teachings and associations. But the fact that Phil and Helen had decided to attend a new church indicates that their involvement was not simply for the sake of tradition or example. Phil seems genuinely to have appreciated Reverend Long's sermons at the Immanuel Presbyterian Church, many of them having to do with issues of current interest. And certainly, developments the world over encouraged the practice of churchgoing.

No doubt one of the more depressing moments of that holiday season was the reading of the Christmas letter from Dr. C. A. Schenck. Recent months had witnessed the Munich decisions regarding Czechoslovakia and Japan's withdrawal from the League of Nations. The "Crystal Night" of November 9 had left no question about the anti-Semitic policies of the Nazi government. Dr. Schenck agonized over the growing separation between Germany and America, all the while trying to justify what was taking place: "While my fatherland was crestfallen, she was liked by all my friends in the diaspora; since she began to be a factor in the world, she came to be despised." He assured his American friends that he did "not applaud everything in Germany any more that you approve of Indian massacres and of lynchings—that you know." In short, "loving both countries, I feel like a boy whose parents got a divorce." And in his handwritten postscript, Dr. Schenck invited Phil to come and visit him in Germany. "Come and see!" he wrote. "I shall show you, incidentally, that *sane* regulation by an autocracy isn't bad at all for the timberland owner: On the contrary!! It is sad but it is true that a democracy has never seen the way clear for private forestry conducted profitably for the benefit of labor, of consumer, and of the nation."

In his reply Phil agreed that the misunderstandings between their countries were a source of worry, "but I do not think they should affect our friendship, nor do I think we will settle the merits of democracy versus What-Have-You at this distance." He did suggest that perhaps Dr. Schenck would return to the United States, at which time they could give the matter the attention it deserved.

The new year began with the "usual party at home," although Phil described it as being "more successful than usual." His January 1 diary entry also noted a "beautiful home thanks to Helen's taste." But the new year did not end old problems, the most pressing continuing to be the need for wage reductions in the face of declining business. The Executive Committee had granted Phil authority to move as he best determined, but the solution was not evident. On the more positive side, Al Raught had informed Charlie that he would come to work at the Tacoma office following a vacation of six months or so. Phil wrote Laird that they expected Al to "be back in the fold" in July, and "meanwhile we must figure out a sphere of activity for him which will tend to divide the load." Charlie had gone to Longview that day, January 6, to announce that Harry Morgan was to be the manager replacing Raught, and Sid Lewis the assistant manager.

Many meetings failed to form an industry approach to the wage question. Phil told of attending a January 10 gathering, the object of which was to get a cross section opinion of the situation, but the results were "inconclusive in that no action of any kind was taken, except to appoint a committee which would recommend a course of procedure." While everyone "stressed the need for action . . . all felt the usual distrust for their competitors." Phil was at a loss to know just "what kind of assurances could be exchanged which could be both satisfying and within the spirit of the legal restrictions now upon us." Rod Olzendam, by job description, ought to have been heavily involved in these deliberations; but there must have been some unhappiness with his work, Phil's diary entry for January 12 indicating: "All afternoon with Rod Olzendam discussing his job and how he was doing it," an unlikely expenditure of time if all was going well.

Phil and Helen were planning to spend the week prior to the Executive Committee meeting on February 27 in Sun Valley. They were also making plans to go to Sweden in the summer with the Dave Wintons, "the thought being those of us interested in forestry matters would spend most, if not all, of the intervening time in Sweden, and the wives would pry loose enough time to spend a day or two in Paris, as well as London." Phil wrote to Laird, inviting the Bells to join up. But Laird had other commitments, hoping, "without too much confidence," to have two daughters graduating in June, one from Bryn Mawr and another from Milton. Probably at Phil's suggestion, Laird had, in the course of one of his eastern swings, tried to talk to Bill Peabody about his son, again with no apparent success: "He knows some of the troubles but everybody pulls his punches & tells him whatever good of the boy they can think of, naturally enough." Laird judged that Bill Sr. had concluded that someone was intent on "spreading a lot of poison, and has a natural instinct to fight to protect his son." Captain Howard understood the problem, wanted to help, but it was difficult. Laird and the Captain agreed that it was up to Phil, Laird concluding, "I can't think of any answer, but there must be one short of breaking old Bill's heart."

One of the continuing discussions involved the possible entry of the Timber Company into plywood production. It seemed reasonable from nearly every consideration, but the initial outlay and the prospect of entering competition with old, established firms was enough to make Phil drag his feet. Brother Fred was eager for a plywood product with a Weyerhaeuser identification. In early February he had attended a housing conference in New Haven and had come away more convinced than ever that they should take steps leading to a plywood involvement. As usual, Fred K. shared his feelings with Phil.

Phil agreed that they should be giving plywood their attention, possibly designing product improvements that could result in a plywood identified as their own, but he remained unconvinced that this meant that "we need to get into the game of manufacturing plywood." As he understood the situation, the Sales Company was experiencing no difficulty in placing its orders for plywood at rates that allowed profit in its sales, and the mere threat of Weyerhaeuser production would seem to ensure a continuation of favorable treatment. Furthermore, they had built relations with plywood suppliers over the years that might permit an eventual production of a "Weyerhaeuser" plywood and even for an involvement leading to product improvement. In addition, and a factor that Fred K. probably didn't consider, there was the demand for plywood logs, or "peelers" as they were then called. With the growth of the plywood industry, that market was continuing to improve. In short, "As long as we do continue to find a satisfactory market for our logs and a willingness on the part of the existing operators to sell us at a price which nets us a sales profit, I think we should be quite hesitant to jump into the field with additional manufacturing facilities." Fred K. argued "we cannot afford not to move in the direction of plywood manufacture." Phil clearly had yet to be convinced.

A question that received considerable discussion at the February Executive Committee meeting was the minority ownership of the Willapa Harbor Lumber Mills. The Weyerhaeuser Timber Company owned two-thirds of Willapa Mills, and although outsiders tended to assume that Willapa was one and the same as Weyerhaeuser, such was not the case. In fact, freedom of action was simply not possible given the large minority ownership, or as Laird observed while riding east toward home, "I am impressed with how much influence on the situation the fact of a different corporation owning part of the timber & plant makes." He recommended that "serious thought" be given to eliminating that minority ownership: "I'd like to see those outsiders out of the way, if it could be brought about in such a way as to avoid the appearance of squeezing, & at a realistic price." He was also disappointed that the committee had been of such small help to Phil in the matter.

Phil replied, indicating general agreement. But the matter was even more complicated than Laird could know, because on the evening of March 6, J. W. Lewis, the general manager at Willapa, had unexpectedly died. As Phil noted, it was "not only a great shock, but a great loss to the company," and it seemed now "that short of buying out the minority stockholders . . . the program for Willapa must be one of waiting and of basing operating decisions upon the assumption that those mills will be liquidated against the timber now in their ownership and immediately tributary." Phil was not convinced that it would be wise to make any large capital investments there as long as there was a possibility of using the timber in the district in some other way. He suggested that perhaps their "best bet is to wait until an offshore market develops, as it probably will when the Oriental war is settled, more or less marking time in the meanwhile."

Phil was not marking time in terms of staff. On March 23, he addressed a letter to F.E. concerning the possibility of getting Gus Clapp to move to Tacoma; apparently Gus had indicated a willingness to do so. The problem was that lawyer Clapp had responsibilities in St. Paul, Phil mentioning "the so-called Legal Committee, the nature of which I do not pretend fully to understand." In any event, because of the work that Gus had done for the family through the St. Paul office, it was necessary for Uncle Fred to give his approval to any such change. Phil felt the need for Gus's presence, but he also knew that such an appointment might be viewed as just another example of extravagance. The question was complicated by the arrival, sooner than expected, of Al Raught, rested and ready to assume his new responsibilities in the Tacoma office. Phil explained the situation carefully: "I have some fear that we may be getting too top-heavy with the addition of Al Raught, Olzendam, and such others as are coming into the Tacoma Office picture, and above everything else, I do feel that our strength lies in decentralization. Speaking in general terms, I instinctively lean away from a large central office organization for fear it will tend away from decentralization."

Phil also recalled from many past conversations that Uncle Fred "felt that decisions of policy in our company were already too much dominated by lawyers" and thus might feel that a Gus Clapp in Tacoma would "accentuate that condition." But despite these considerations, Phil was convinced that Gus would be a valuable addition if he could join them on more or less a full-time basis.

The response from F.E. was short, to the point, and confidential. He had shared Phil's letter with Horace Irvine, who had suggested that the matter should be considered at the next Executive Committee meeting, although F.E. stated emphatically, "It is your responsibility to build an organization." Then he added, "My guess is that you have one member who would not be missed," although he also noted that he had already expressed himself fully on that point. Nevertheless, he said again, "I believe that each man's talents should be used in the field of his qualifications." Phil understood.

If Phil was being noticeably circumspect regarding relations with his Uncle Fred, Chief Silcox was receiving similar treatment. The Forest Service had put together something of a "fact sheet" on the Weyerhaeuser Timber Company about which there was possibility for considerable complaint, but Phil was willing to dismiss those differences, or so it seemed. He wrote to Silcox on April 3:

We serve no good purpose by debating nonessentials when our aims coincide at least to the extent of desiring more permanence in our industry.

As a company, we face the task of removing in orderly fashion an oversupply of old-growth stagnant timber. We progress toward permanence of employment and production as we improve the condition in which we leave the remaining land from which these stands are removed and with the addition to our ownership and the preservation of all classes of second-growth stands. All this implies increasing effort in planning to insure restocking, perfection of fire protection, adoption of selective logging where practical, and many other things. Our company is doing these things and its personnel is well alive to problems needing answers. We will welcome aid from you in finding right answers.

Phil noted Silcox's expressed interest in Klamath Falls, and he was willing to agree that there might be a "real opportunity for cooperation between public and private timber owners in that district." But taking things one step at a time, he offered to meet with the chief either in Tacoma or Klamath Falls at his convenience. He also shared his plans to go to Sweden with Dave Winton, "this in anticipation of no war."

Laird Bell had recently met with Earl Tinker and Lyle Watts of the Forest Service in something of an off-the-record discussion. Laird left with the impression that Tinker believed that good logging practices were more important than the sustained-yield enterprise, the latter being viewed "more or less as Silcox' baby." Tinker admitted that the Forest Service had internal disagreements on the correct approach for the Northwest, although they "ought to have a definite and determined policy," and that "he would like to work out that policy in conference with the well disposed operators." He also indicated that they had been looking for a letter from Phil. Phil sent Laird a copy of his letter to Silcox assuring that if "Mr. Silcox wants to talk to me, or to Al Raught, or to Minot Davis, or to Ralph Macartney, we will all of us make ourselves available." Laird replied that he thought Phil had "come out to where Silcox would like you to, without climbing into his lap too ardently."

But Silcox could wait. The report to the stockholders could not, and much time was being given to its preparation. In the meantime there had been brief strikes at Wallapa and Snoqualmie Falls. Bill Turner, the new Willapa manager, had his "baptism of fire" when the woods crew demanded that a bullbucker be discharged at one of the camps. Picket lines formed immediately and everything was shut down. Bill suggested that the complaints should follow the grievance procedures, and then he "would endeavor to iron it out in negotiations, with them." After a week, the men returned to work. The strike at Snoqualmie was also over in one week. Apparently it had to do with the collection of dues, but Phil seemed uncertain as to the real causes. To F.E. he indicated that he and Helen were still planning to go to Sweden in June, "But if we had to sail today, I think we would not go." Laird wrote on the same subject, saying there were uncertainties about whether they should plan on European travel. "I just can't believe that there is going to be a war," he wrote, "but neither can I see how it is to be avoided," adding, "with which helpful remark I close."

The annual report did come out on schedule, Laird offering his congratulations on its style and supposing "there is some turning in graves going on, but the times are what they are." The Swedish trip also came about on schedule, with Phil and Dave Winton trying to visit as many companies and meet with as many industry people as possible. But as Phil noted in a subsequent letter to Silcox, "the time was altogether too short for us to do most of the things which would have been instructive and enjoyable." But he thought the trip had been worthwhile and thanked Siicox for his encouragement and suggestions on what to see and do. "Other than being a sort of look into the future, there are, of course, a few things of immediate application resulting from such a visit." Probably the six weeks' absence convinced him that he much preferred to stay at home. The family, however, thought the return voyage aboard the *Queen Mary* made it all worth the effort. Phil was impressed by the speed of the homeward crossing but found an "uninteresting crowd on board."

If the trip had seemed rushed and some times unfulfilling, Phil clearly appreciated the opportunity to meet new people and explain what his company was trying to do. Upon his return he addressed a number of letters to his Swedish hosts, enclosing materials that he hoped would be of interest. With one, he had even left a copy of the film *Trees and Men*. To another, he continued a discussion of the subject of public prejudice toward American lumbermen. As he explained: "[It] arises out of the fact that, as in Sweden, in the past we have cut our forests with little thought to their replacement. The time has arrived when it is apparent that there is an opportunity to replace the old-growth timber which we are removing with a young forest, which we hope can, as an effort by private initiative, end profitably; and we are engaged upon an effort to justify our industry and our company in this aim, and also to shoulder other responsibilities in our existing social and economic order."

Apparently Chief Silcox was becoming convinced of the Weyerhaeuser sincerity of purpose. Lawrence Smith, manager of the firm that published the *West Coast Lumberman*, noted in a letter to Phil that he had recently heard Silcox speak at a Seattle meeting, and from the tenor of those remarks concluded that "Weyerhaeuser has more than a 30 year head start in its program of establishing perpetual timber operation." Smith also called attention to an article in the June issue of the *Lumberman*, the substance of which Phil had provided by sending along the annual report. Phil was pleased but was unwilling to accept Smith's invitation to write a few comments for publication regarding his trip to Sweden. It was "for pleasure only, accompanied by family," he replied, adding, "what few impressions I got of that country's methods of conducting their forest enterprises were so hastily absorbed that it would be silly for me to try to give you any for publication."

On their return home from New York to Tacoma, Phil and the family had stopped off in St. Paul, with a side trip to Cloquet for a brief visit with Ed Davis and his family. Phil was able to attend a meeting of the Research Committee, which he found quite interesting, writing subsequently to cousin Ed, "I am especially impressed with Clark Heritage." Phil was a little concerned that Ed assumed that others were not much interested in a commitment to research: "You repeatedly have expressed to me the fear that there will be no inclination to follow up any program indicated by our research disclosures, and I think that you are entirely wrong in assuming such to be the case." Phil assured him, "There is every reason to expect the Weyerhaeuser Tim-

ber Company to be searching continuously for places to invest its liquidation, in new ventures, some of them even highly speculative, especially if those ventures appear to be developing markets for its raw
materials, either present waste or currently valuable material." Those
at the Wood Conversion Company undoubtedly felt left out on occasion, dealing in matters of seemingly small consequence. It was true
that Phil insisted on looking carefully before making any leap, but he
was not opposed to change, as any brief look backward would sub-
stantiate.

As Phil noted in a letter of August 2 to F.E.: "It is fine to be home
and enjoying a glorious summer." The weather was indeed beautiful,
but the sunny summer skies meant that the danger of fire was on the
increase. There had been a couple of fires reported, one at Klamath
Falls, but nothing very serious as yet, and the air was still clear. Logging operations, however, had been stopped several times because of
the low humidity "and are all operating on the hoot-owl shift." Upon
his return, Phil was pleased to find that Al Raught had assumed his
new responsibilities, "handling the industry and the company labor
matters," which relieved Charlie Ingram's burdens a good deal. He
was also pleased to pass along news regarding Dave Weyerhaeuser,
specifically that Minot Davis had told him "that Dave is doing a great
job." Perhaps the most welcomed news was the financial statement for
the first six months of 1939, Phil allowing that "it looks more encouraging than I expected."

Labor problems began to reappear as the summer wore on. In the
midst of negotiations at White River with the newly elected CIO representatives, the union began picketing and closed the plant down.
Writing to F.E. on September 2, Phil admitted that he didn't know
what the result would be but felt that things might be back to normal
soon. Problems were also developing at Longview, and the stevedores'
contract was due to run out at the end of September. The news of the
invasion of Poland had been received and Uncle Fred, recalling their
experiences during the First World War, supposed that they "must
expect a lot of lawlessness on the part of labor agitators in the near
future." Laird Bell offered congratulations to Phil "on the timing of
your European trip" and observed, "I have been trying to get some
idea of the effect of the war on the lumber industry, as well as the law
industry, but to date my mind is a complete blank." They both knew
the effects on the lumber industry would be considerable.

Already Bill Peabody had been approached by brokers representing
"British interests" inquiring about possible sale of the four largest
ships of the Steamship Company. The second week of September had
witnessed lumber orders averaging about 3.5 million feet a day at the
Newark office. As Peabody wrote to Phil, "No one knows how long

this situation will last, but it is crazy for the moment." By the end of the month, operations at White River had resumed, Phil noting that this was their first written contract with the CIO.

In the midst of all the war news and worries, Phil and other members of the Executive Committee were reconsidering the plywood question. Although most seemed reluctant to change their opinions, Phil was definitely becoming more interested in Timber Company involvement in plywood production. Thus he was seeking permission to undertake serious negotiations with Ed Westman and other representatives of the Washington Veneer Company directed at some joint venture. But as he wrote to Laird, F.E. had acknowledged his memorandum "rather noncommittally," and apparently Horace Irvine was not enthusiastic, "nor was Gus Clapp; and unless I hear something within the next few days to the contrary, I will have no option but to tell the Washington Veneer crowd that we are not interested." As it turned out, Laird wasn't much interested either, noting, "I gather that I very nearly make it unanimous." But it wasn't unanimous as far as Phil was concerned. He had obviously given the matter much thought, and he explained his reasoning to Laird:

... for a long time we relied on the log market or the timber market to liquidate our forests. Our customers worked themselves into unsound financial situations, and, by and large, because they were always in a position to quit, did not adopt long-range programs. I feel that the company is in far better situation today in liquidating its own timber, building for the future with advertising, and all the things which we are doing, than it would be were we back in the position of selling trees or logs only. To the extent that we will in the future depend upon the plywood business to liquidate a part of our forest, we will be depending on others to build for permanence, and the bigger the industry becomes and the more dependent we become upon it, the more danger we will run of a repetition of what it seems to me we can clearly see has happened in the lumber end of the game.

In connection with that particular issue and other matters supposedly put to the Executive Committee, Laird had been studying the procedures being followed, and he was not convinced of their correctness. Indeed he had inquired of Phil where or to whom he should be expressing his opinions. "Your question ... bothers me," Phil had replied. He then recalled that in years past he had often addressed communications to the individual members of the Executive Committee, and that process had resulted in their individual replies coming back to him. "Although nothing was ever said to that effect, I sensed some resentment on the part of Mr. F. E. Weyerhaeuser, because the result was to rather short-circuit him as chairman of the committee." Accordingly, Phil had taken to posing questions to be considered by the committee directly to F.E., sending copies to the individual members. This had not meant that he, in turn, polled the members individually for their opinions, and Phil admitted to having arrived at the answer "by induction." He could, of course, request that each member communicate his feeling to F.E., but he feared that procedure might encourage stalemates requiring more committee work than should be necessary. Democracy and efficiency are seldom partners.

The Executive Committee, minus Laird, met in St. Paul on the morning of October 21 to approve the purchase of some timberlands, Gus Clapp communicating the decision to Phil. Included in his note was reference to the plywood question. F.E. had mentioned at the meeting that Phil seemed to have been, in Gus's words, "somewhat disappointed that the response . . . was as it was, as you would have liked to have started more intensive dickering with Mr. Westlund [*sic*]." As a result, the matter had been discussed again, and it was agreed that there would be no objection to continuing discussions provided they were not of "such a character as to embarrass you if it is decided not to buy into this particular plywood company." In short, although they were not yet convinced, they were willing to allow for the possibility that they might be at some future date.

One of the most appealing attractions at the Timber Company was its official greeter and tour leader, Eddie McIntyre. Ed was the son of Will McIntyre, friend and companion to John Philip, and it is curious that at the time of his employment by the Sales Company, specifically by Fred K., for responsibilities unknown in Tacoma, Phil expressed considerable resentment. Although he subsequently apologized to Fred, allowing that they would find something appropriate for Eddie to do, Phil could not then imagine just how important the son of his father's friend would become. It was soon apparent, however, that Eddie had much of Will's ability to entertain, and a good deal more energy for work. In a short time, Eddie McIntyre *was* the Weyerhaeuser Timber Company to many who visited, and just as important, he provided much in the way of genuine happiness to all about him. Phil may have tended to overlook such matters in the course of his own devotion to duty, but testimonials arrived often enough to remind him. One such was sent by an Illinois lumber dealer following an October visit. It was typical.

Eddie McIntyre was singled out, and Phil was congratulated for "having chosen a gentleman of his perfection to greet your distributors, one who enjoys such vast knowledge of the industry." The recent visitor then proceeded to speak of all the "public scorn" that had been heaped upon lumbermen, admitting that he himself was on the side of those who advocated "conserving and perpetuating our natural resources." Thus "it was a happy revelation to learn and view with my own eyes the care exercised in your timber operations to conserve and perpetuate timber for the use and comfort of oncoming generations." His only regret was that the public was uninformed of such efforts "to make for everlasting timber." Phil took time with his answer, indicating "it is my hope and expectation that our organization can be helpful in bridging the gap which has so long existed between an ideal forestry theory and a practical economic application." And he closed, thanking him for the letter, "for having come, for having stayed long enough to form real impressions, and for the business with which you have favored us over the years."

Another pleasing development involved the small nursery that had been started at the Snoqualmie Falls Lumber Company. In its second year of operation Tip O'Neil counted more than half a million Douglas-fir seedlings, and seventeen other species, from western redcedar to tung trees. For the most part, these were used either for experimental plantings or beautification projects. It was with the latter concern in mind that Phil wrote to Tip, inquiring about the availability of seedlings for use by the White River Lumber Company along the Naches Pass highway. Tip was glad to give them away, "as we have no particular use for them." The real purpose involved the experience of nursery work. It would soon become increasingly important.

Phil had wasted no time in proceeding with his plywood negotiations, given the permission to do so by the Executive Committee. The discussions soon reached the point of decision. As Phil described the situation to Horace Irvine, "With an investment of approximately $613,000, we would gain a bare majority of the common stock in Washington Veneer, which, in turn, would own two-thirds of the stock in the new plant at Springfield [Oregon], erection of which is just starting." Phil was confident, "all things considered," that they should proceed, and indicated that if he received an offer, he would take it. He acknowledged that this was "obviously in excess of the authorization granted by the committee somewhat reluctantly last week," but the opportunity to acquire control of both plants seemed too good to let pass.

A couple of weeks later, Phil heard from Uncle Fred. It was a curious note, closing with a thinly veiled complaint: "I have been hoping to hear something from you about negotiations with Mr. Westman but not having heard from you I suspect that no progress has been made in carrying on negotiations." Phil began his reply with an apology, and then proceeded to explain in detail just what had been done and what remained to be done. The lawyers were working out the details, and the plywood deal awaited the results of their efforts.

As the holiday season approached, Phil reflected on the situation of his Swedish friends. Given the currency and production circumstances in Scandinavia, the American pulp and paper industry was booming. Phil admitted as much to Stig Kempe in Stockholm, noting, "The pulp mills are busy and prices are too strong." He added, "We all wish that we could return to a peaceful and normal existence, as there can no good come to us or to any one from the kind of thing now going on." Stig had observed from his end, "I hope you are well and happy and the pulp situation is better because of the poor Finns. 'The one's bread the other's death,' we say here. It is really horrible." And what was already horrible would soon become even worse.

CHAPTER 10

A Time for Tree Farming

As had become the custom, Bob Wolf and Phil received Christmas messages from Dr. Schenck, although the 1939 greeting came in card form, with personalized handwritten thoughts attached. Bob inquired of Phil just what his message from the German forester meant: "Try and find flowers at the edge of the desert." Phil assumed that their friend was expressing his unhappiness in a manner that would pass censorship. Herr Schenck's rationalizations of previous years were not repeated.

Far more cheering were the birthday greetings to her "Philip" from Aimee Lyford, now an elementary school principal in Elgin, Illinois. Almost forty years had passed since Miss Aimee had joined the family at Lake Nebagamon, and she recalled those days with fondness. Elizabeth wrote to her at least twice a year, and Aimee expressed pleasure at having received "Christmas greetings from all you three children—you are still children to me."

At the end of January 1940, Phil reported to the Timber Company directors that the final steps had been accomplished, and the company now had a controlling interest in the Washington Veneer Company of Olympia "on a basis which we believe will make it a good investment." Business had generally improved far faster than even the more optimistic projections, and the cash balance grew substantially. Laird Bell foresaw trouble in this and suggested that they consider "putting it away in governments where it doesn't look so big and tempting." Phil interpreted this as an indirect objection to the plywood deal, responding, "it may be that too much money on hand provokes attempts to spend it—and evidently you consider the plywood venture in that category." But Phil assured him that he was convinced it was "a good deal, and hope that you will think so, too."

Early April was a busy time. C. S. Chapman, the first graduate of the Yale Forestry School and chief forester with the Weyerhaeuser Timber Company since 1924, died suddenly on April 3, his sixtieth birthday. Negotiations were under way to purchase some 36,000 acres of Northern Pacific land for $400,000. As Phil explained to Uncle Fred, this was a "fine area of reproduction," and the ownership would "give us the logical preference in acquiring intermingled sections of Forest Service timber." It was located conveniently to "our Upper Deschutes railroad," and was a logical investment in every way. Within the week Phil had received word from all members of the Executive Committee, all in support of the purchase, and the thing was accomplished.

The war had first been felt in a direct fashion in the shipping end of the industry. Bill Peabody had been approached by brokers representing the British Ministry of Supply, and in early March Phil heard directly from a representative of J. F. Rafailovich and Company, whose cable address was ONEMIND. The message was short and to the point: "to find out whether you would entertain an offer to sell the S.S. *Pennsylvania*, or any of your steamers." As Phil would admit to Bill Peabody, "my thinking is always confused by the realization that we are necessarily going out of business in five or six years anyway because our boats will then be too expensive to maintain and operate."

Instead of selling vessels, the Steamship Company purchased two steamships, the *Narcissus* and the *Jallapa*, from the Maritime Commission. Phil seemed uncertain of the wisdom of that decision, writing to F.E., "I am hopeful that this will turn out to be the reasonable thing to have done." As it turned out, the successful bids were entirely reasonable, but to bet on political and military developments was hardly the preferred course. Laird Bell was one who foresaw the likelihood of storms on the seas. "It is only a month or two ago that we talked about selling all our ships," he wrote and observed that "the wide fluctuations in demand and supply make me wonder whether we should not forego some profit and keep our capital investment down." He recalled that in 1937 "Peabody was all steamed up to purchase more tonnage and a year later we had too much." Laird suggested that they should only "buy more bottoms" if they were certain of getting their money back "in a very short time."

Laird would subsequently apologize for his lack of optimism or faith, noting that he had worried all week that his letter "about new boats was just another case of dragging my feet." It was difficult for him to justify his attitude: "I have puzzled a good deal as to what use a director is and one possible use seems to me to remind the management that times have been bad and may be bad again." Phil surely smiled at that. He immediately responded that there was no reason for Laird to apologize. Indeed Phil had requested a "frank expression," and "in spite of the lack of enthusiasm on your part and, in fact, on everybody's part," he had authorized Bill Peabody to make the bid on the two vessels.

In the midst of the steamship discussions and deliberations, Phil heard from F.E., then vacationing in Pasadena. Uncle Fred was apparently feeling more positive about things, no doubt as a result of the improvement in the Timber Company's business over the first quarter; "much better returns than I dared hope for," he admitted to Phil. Along with numerous other items, F.E. made passing reference to Laird's suggestion that "he thought we would do foolish things if we hold our present cash balances." Although F.E. would not object to investing in short-term, "very low rate governments," he would oppose getting rid of their cash except "for very promising investments." But as he wrote to Fred K., in a letter of the same date, "who can tell what tomorrow will bring forth in the New Deal," adding, "I never did think much of poker." And to Phil, he dismissed Laird's worries. "If you knew [Laird Norton Company] history, you wouldn't be surprised," he wrote. "They have objected to most new things we have undertaken." Again Phil must have smiled. Although he and Laird occasionally disagreed, they never bickered. The decision made was the decision accepted. Thus Laird wrote on May 4, "I can hardly wait until I see Admiral Peabody on the quarter-deck of the *Narcissus* and *Jallapa*. I shall expect to be mollified by a nice trip."

Phil was making plans for a different sort of trip. Largely because of the preparations and persuasiveness of his college roommate, Peavey Heffelfinger, Phil had decided he would attend his twentieth reunion at Yale. He joined the old gang in Columbus, Ohio, at the home of Art Vorys, after which he, Peavey, Art, Spider Reinhardt, Egbert Driscoll, and Pudge Heffelfinger, the immortal Pudge, headed on to New Haven. Following the reunion festivities, Phil went to Newport, Rhode Island, where he, Fred K., Laird Bell, and Gus Clapp joined Bill Peabody and Captain Howard for the maiden voyage of Howard's launch, the *Quickstep*, from which vantage they watched the famous races.

While at Yale, Phil had become reacquainted with former classmate Paul Graves of Spokane, and he accompanied Graves to Watertown, Connecticut, to visit the Taft School where another classmate, Paul Cruikshank, was headmaster. Phil was so impressed with Taft that he decided to see about enrolling son Flip there for the coming fall semester instead of at the Hill School. Probably the most difficult task concerning that change was the letter to James Wendell, Hill School headmaster. In explaining the decision, reached only "after long family discussion," Phil indicated that it was because Flip's "two best friends here in Tacoma" were going to Taft, adding, "It seems disloyal, unpatriotic, etc., etc. Nevertheless, the die is cast."

The terrible concerns that summer in western Washington were the heat and low humidity and the resulting fires. By the end of July, it was estimated that the Timber Company had spent more than $120,000 in fire-fighting efforts, and that losses of equipment, logs, and timber brought the total to nearly $440,000. Logging, of course, was stopped. But if fires were a worry, the state of business was not. The first six months of 1940 had been so favorable that Laird Bell admitted, "It scares me a little," although he thought that the "excess profits taxes will correct part of the excess prosperity."

The excess profits tax was just one indication of the revolution that had been taking place in relations between business and government. Since the demands made on corporate managers like Phil Weyerhaeuser were invariably time consuming if not downright aggravating, one can only imagine the resentments that accumulated during the years of the Second New Deal. In the spring Phil had been responding to requests of Leon Henderson of the Securities and Exchange Commission in behalf of the Temporary National Economic Committee. "We enclose in triplicate your Form B, showing the distribution of our capital stock by size of holdings" was the first of four items. In late spring Phil had been visited by a representative of the Department of Justice in connection with an antitrust investigation of the building trades. It was, as the representative acknowledged, a "fishing expedition," but if permission for access to the records was denied, those records would be subpoenaed by the grand jury in session in Los Angeles. The "fishing expedition" commenced. In early June the National Labor Relations Board determined that the Timber Company had dismissed an Everett employee "on account of his union activities," Phil wrote to the directors, "and the company was ordered to return him to work with back pay for the period—which is a great shock to us all." The "fishing expedition" continued through the summer. Harry Kendall reported to Gus Clapp July 12 that the examiner had requested "a complete list of all our customers throughout the United States for the years 1935 to June 30, 1940, inclusive, showing the amount sold, the basis sold, etc." Then there was always the Forest Service and its perennial campaign for authority to regulate the lumber industry.

At the same time that these involvements were occupying the time and energies of many, Edward R. Stettinius, head of the Industrial Materials Division of the National Defense Advisory Commission, was attempting to organize for cooperation within the industry and between government and industry. A Lumber and Timber Products Defense Committee had been appointed, along with a five-man Executive Committee chaired by M. L. Fleishel of the National Lumber Manufacturers Association. John Watzek, Jr., had been appointed chief of the Lumber and Forest Products Division of the Defense Commission, and it was his wish to procure Al Raught's services to aid in the effort. On July 29 Phil wired Watzek as follows: "I have talked with F. E. Weyerhaeuser and Raught about your recent request. Although I think it extremely unlikely that he will do the job, neither F. E. Weyerhaeuser nor I wish to induce you to refrain from offering it if you wish." Phil wrote to Uncle Fred, "I am perfectly sure Al will not take it under any circumstances."

Laird Bell was none too pleased with the apparent disinterest of Phil and others concerning Al Raught's possible involvement with Watzek's commission. Part of the problem, Laird surmised, was that "while the East Coast may be too jittery, I really wonder whether the West Coast is jittery enough." Laird felt that the war situation and threat to the hemisphere were more serious than Phil and his Tacoma office colleagues cared to admit. "I suspect that something may break out in South America, and particularly around the Canal, which will result in our finding ourselves in great need of war facilities," he continued. Admitting that he might be "one of the over-jittery ones," he did want Phil to know "the way it looks to me, and if you are disposed to think that I am soft-headed at least the foregoing will give you my reasons." And he closed by noting, "I am for Willkie—unless the Republicans make a fool of him before November."

Phil's response was quiet and considered, which was the attitude he wished to convey regarding the war threat. "It seems to me we could make haste more slowly," he wrote, "with profit both to the defense program and to the nerves of the country." He quickly admitted, however, that he supposed that "same attitude was reflected in France and in England and I may just be another one of those simple isolationists." He assured Laird, however, that he had played no part in Al Raught's refusal to go to Washington, D.C. This, of course, was Laird's objection in the first place: Phil should have played a part.

One of Phil's concerns was that war hysteria would result in rapid increases in lumber prices. Although this might seem to be an attractive development, it carried with it too many problems. First, there would be charges that the industry was taking unpatriotic advantage of the circumstances. Second, as he would write to an associate, the industry would be so swamped that it would be unable to meet the demands and could thus be charged with failing to meet the emergency. Third, an overdemand would probably be followed by a sudden decrease in demand, to no one's benefit. Finally, labor was likely to assume that higher prices were permanent, justifying a corresponding increase in wages.

Related to these concerns was a letter from Corydon Wagner of the St. Paul and Tacoma Lumber Company, also president of the West Coast Lumbermen's Association and currently serving on the Executive Committee, the liaison group between the Lumber and Timber Products Defense Committee and the National Defense Advisory Commission. Although Corydon placed the blame for the "runaway market" on "conditions beyond our control—a large volume of forward buying by the commercial trade, stimulated by the prospect of heavy orders for national defense," he was advising manufacturers of West Coast lumber to take steps that might alleviate the situation. He suggested that "prices be maintained for sixty days at current levels on those items most important to the national defense" and that "they use their influence to seek similar action on the part of their wholesale, commission, and retail outlets."

Phil was uncertain how or if to respond. To Fred K. he noted that Cordy had recently appeared before a group of lumbermen in Tacoma, preaching much the same doctrine, and he had received "quite tepid interest." Perhaps, thought Phil, "the realization that an emergency was upon us did not seem to be in the minds of many." There was certainly a serious problem, of that he had no doubt, and "some gesture of this kind might be wisely made independently, but taking a group action might be unwise." Indeed, he was uncertain whether Cordy was writing as an officer of the St. Paul and Tacoma, as president of the association, or as a member of the Defense Committee. In short, what was needed was some specific direction from an official source, namely the National Defense Advisory Commission. Fred K. replied, wondering about the antitrust problems of such a cooperative approach in the matter of prices and suggesting that before they got an answer to that question, they had best proceed individually.

Despite the uncertainties, it was soon decided that some sort of positive action was required. Thus on September 17 Fred K. made an announcement as president of the Weyerhaeuser Sales Company concerning the products of the Weyerhaeuser Timber Company, Snoqualmie Falls Lumber Company, Potlatch Forests, and Boise Payette Lumber Company. Customers were informed that the prices of those items of Douglas-fir, western hemlock, and redcedar that were crucial for military camp construction would be held at the September 9 levels unless costs, "or other reasons beyond control," required an increase. In the same announcement, "old customers" were informed that the government and government contractors would be given preference in distribution. Two days later Charlie Ingram attended a meeting of the

West Coast Lumbermen's Association at which the subject of voluntary price controls received much attention. During that discussion it was suggested that the various groups ought to agree on a price policy and submit it to the government. Charlie took the occasion to inform the gathering of the recent action by the Sales Company, and reported that the "reaction to this was that they felt this to be a noble gesture on our part, but that most of them would prefer to go along without any limitations on them."

As something of a distraction, John Boettiger, publisher of the *Seattle Post-Intelligencer*, was continuing his campaign to point out "the grave need in the Northwest for a national forest policy" and was urging "the federal department of agriculture to outline its idea of what such a policy should include." Thus Henry A. Wallace had been invited to write on the subject, and the first of the secretary of agriculture's two letters was published in the Sunday, August 25, 1940, edition. Phil, of course, distributed copies of the articles. Laird Bell admitted that he had delayed reading "Wallace's letters because I thought they would make me mad," but instead he had been "pleasantly surprised." There were things to complain about, including the "assumption that regulation would always be virtuous, intelligent and reasonable," Laird contending, "This seems the hardest of all to take."

Regarding an appropriate response, Laird suggested a temperate approach, talking of the difficulty of "regulations imposed from without and the dangers of bureaucratic control." But more important, Laird wished that they had a "more specific basis for pointing with pride to what we have done and are doing." He was sure there was a story to tell, "all the beauties of continuous employment, avoidance of ghost towns and the sins of others, of which at the present time we can't be very justly accused." Phil agreed on all points, that Secretary Wallace's letters "were more temperate than I expected," and that the Timber Company should be able to make presentations in its own behalf that "will become more and more effective." The problem, however, "lies in the fact that there are so few definite, positive facts upon which to hang a story that one is in danger of overstating the case when talking about it." Phil obviously thought it was too bad that actions could not speak for themselves. He told of their work on the sequel to *Trees and Men*, the new film entitled *Trees and Homes*. As Phil reported to Fred K., he had recently stopped off at Longview to watch some of the filming, finding "Rod [Olzendam], as usual when in the midst of a job . . . full of enthusiasm and simply bubbling over."

Labor negotiations, now largely directed by Al Raught, had been going better than expected. Laird expressed much satisfaction in this, adding that in those matters they did well "to keep in step with the rest of the industry." As he reasoned, "With our published annual

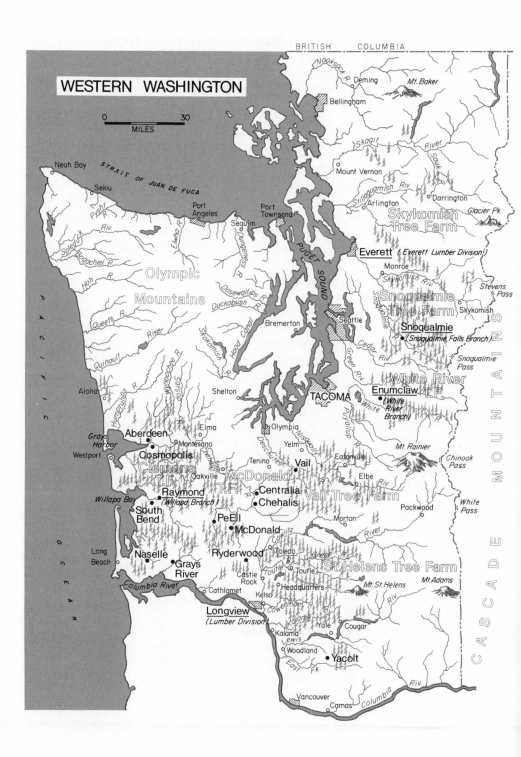

WESTERN WASHINGTON

0   30
MILES

BRITISH   COLUMBIA

Nooksack R.

Deming

Mt. Baker

Bellingham

Skagit

River

Sauk

Mount Vernon

Stillaguamish Riv.

Arlington

Darrington

Glacier Pk.

Skykomish
Tree Farm

Neah Bay

STRAIT OF JUAN DE FUCA

Sekiu

Pysht R.

Port
Angeles

Sequim

Port
Townsend

Elwha R.

Dungeness R.

Soleduck

Riv.

Bogachiel R.

Hoh

River

Olympic

Mountains

Dosewallips R.

Duckabush R.

Skokomish R.

Hood Canal

Everett *(Everett Lumber Division)*

Monroe

Skykomish Riv.

Stevens
Pass

Snoqualmie
Tree Farm

Skykomish

Snoqualmie
● *(Snoqualmie Falls Branch)*

Snoqualmie
Pass

PUGET SOUND

Bremerton

Seattle

Cedar Riv.

Green Riv.

White River
T. F.

Queets R.

Quinault

River

Aloha

Shelton

TACOMA

Enumclaw
● *White
River
Branch)*

White

Puyallup

Mt. Rainier

Chinook
Pass

CASCADE MOUNTAINS

P
A
C
I
F
I
C

Grays
Harbor

Aberdeen

Montesano

Elma

Olympia

Yelm

Niscually R.

Eatonville

Elbe

White Riv.

Packwood

White
Pass

Westport

Cosmopolis

Clemons
T.F.

Oakville

Tenino

Deschutes R.

Vail

McDonald

Vail Tree Farm

Morton

Chehalis R.

Willapa Bay

Raymond
(Willapa Branch)

McDonald
T.F.

Centralia

Chehalis

O
C
E
A
N

South
Bend

PeEll
● McDonald

Cowlitz R.

River

Long
Beach

Naselle

Ryderwood

Toledo

Toutle R.

Toutle

Green R.

St. Helens Tree Farm

Mt. St. Helens

Mt. Adams

Grays
River

Castle
Rock

Headquarters

Cathlamet

Kelso

Columbia River

Cowleman R.

Longview
(Lumber Division)

Kalama

Lewis

Kalame R.

Yale

Cougar

Riv.

Woodland

● Yacolt

East Fk.

Vancouver

Camas

Columbia

Riv.

statements, etc., and our unfortunate tendency to make money, we would be a very bad mark standing by ourselves." Raught had indeed stepped into a responsibility much in need of managing, especially when it became clear that Olzendam was neither much interested nor effective in labor relations.

Filling the position formerly held by C. S. Chapman was not as easy. As Phil noted, much of what Chap did, such as representing the company on industry committees, "he grew into and no one can fill his shoes." But September 23 he announced to F.E. that they had finally decided on a replacement. An early Timber Company employee, Clyde S. Martin, had recently been forester for the Western Pine Association, and he was coming back to the Timber Company November 1. In Phil's words, "I think you will be pleased with him. He is quiet and unassuming, has his feet on the ground, and will, I believe, be a conservative influence."

In matters of defense, although lumber products had been important, one of the industry's first and most significant contributions had involved its manpower. Thus it was reasonable to consider such matters as policy regarding employees likely to be called to active service. Phil suggested that the matter of seniority maintenance ought to become a part of the negotiated settlement with the union, since it seemed likely that the union would favor the policy in theory but oppose it when the time of return arrived. The more basic problem, however, would have simply to do with ensuring that sufficient manpower was available should the demands of active service reduce the present work force by any large amount. As of November 1, 1940, of the approximately 11,000 employees of the Timber Company, 4,525 or 41 percent were registered, and 1,408 of these had no dependents. But the labor problem closest at hand involved wage negotiations. Although the year had been relatively quiet, in late October things came apart. Phil wired Fred K. October 29 that Snoqualmie, Everett, and Clemons were all shut down, also most of the Tacoma mills. As far as he could tell, the "underlying union drive for closed shop seems the basic reason," and he maintained that they had compromised just about as much as they could. At the moment, he feared any government involvement: "we might as well fight this out without having a bee on us from Washington if possible."

An Executive Committee meeting was held November 11, and one of the chief items on the agenda was the appointment of Gus Clapp as general counsel for the Timber Company. He had, of course, been doing much of the company's business from his St. Paul office, but the new arrangement would have him head a legal department in Tacoma. This was agreed to. Phil and Helen went east following the meeting for a Thanksgiving reunion with Flip and Ann, and a football game at New Haven with them and their friends. Upon his return to Tacoma, Phil found the labor situation more confused than ever. As he wrote to F.E. on December 10, "I have not been able to catch up on a three-week absence from the turbulent labor situation, and probably never will." Still, he reported that Charlie and Al thought that things would shortly be resolved. Part of the difficulty continued to be the necessity of negotiating with two separate organizations: "The problem of what will satisfy the C.I.O. and not put the A.F. of L.'s nose out of joint (and vice versa) is completely baffling. I think it likely that a substantial part of our competition will grant as much as 70¢ an hour minimum, or its equivalent through a week's vacation with pay. I say this because the prices of fir lumber have skyrocketed to such a silly point that profitable current operation for many operators can be sustained at this rate."

As matters developed, within the week Phil was able to report that CIO representatives had agreed with representatives of some sixty operations to recommend that for the first quarter of 1941, "the additional wages over and above the basic 62½¢ should be the 4% and 5% which has been in force for the last quarter of 1940, plus 2½¢ straight across the board." That brought the minimum for the CIO to 65.5 cents, with no mention of vacations. This was the same minimum that the AFL had negotiated in Tacoma, Seattle, and Portland, with one week's vacation with pay. But since the levels of pay were somewhat higher in the case of the CIO and there had been no percentage increase negotiated in the AFL settlements, Phil thought that any relative advantage was minuscule. And although he was uncertain whether "the constituents to whom the committees recommended this adjustment will accept it," as of December 16 the only operation still on strike was the Snoqualmie Falls Lumber Company.

Christmas of 1940 was anything but joyous from a larger perspective, but the sadness and unsettled circumstances gave an added meaning to family occasions. Phil had taken time to construct a set of figures in his woodshop—Santa with sleigh and reindeer—which brother Fred proudly displayed on his Summit Avenue front lawn. Fred K. said that the scene stopped traffic. Ann and Flip came home to Tacoma for the holidays, but all celebrations had something of an air of distraction about them.

In January 1941, responsibilities involving the extended Weyerhaeuser family were called to Phil's attention. He was interested, but less so than Fred, and would usually have preferred to allow Fred to act in his behalf. That, however, was not in the spirit of things, especially since Phil, and the Timber Company, held the greatest interest and importance. In short, even if he declined a leadership responsibility in family affairs, on those occasions when Phil expressed an opinion it was likely to be decisive. Thus Uncle Rudolph wrote to him January 13: "Of course, Phil, it is not for me to say whether you should come or not, but personally I do feel that you ought to come and we will give two days strictly to family matters." Saying no to such an invitation was next to impossible, and Phil was in attendance in St. Paul January 20–25.

Apparently nothing of great import took place at the St. Paul meetings. In addition to those involving Weyerhaeuser family matters, there were board meetings for the Wood Conversion Company, the General Timber Service, and Allied Building Credits, the latter organized to facilitate making home loans and mortgages as encouraged by the Federal Housing Administration. As Phil reported to Laird Bell, "They were all interesting and instructive, although matters were already so well jelled that nobody had much to contribute." And if family meetings were not of great substance, they were important in the sense and spirit of family. Uncle Fred was obviously trying to convey something of this, writing to Phil after the fact: "I am very appreciative of your taking the time to come on to Saint Paul for a conference with your several cousins," he began. "Such meetings, I believe, are worthwhile and I am sure are helpful in keeping the family together, and of course we always have many problems for discussion."

Another family diversion, obviously much more enjoyable for Phil, was Ann's thesis project at Masters School. The subject was forest conservation, and Phil sent her a bundle of materials that he thought might be of use. She had also inquired about the possibility of showing *Trees and Men*, uncertain about the availability of the necessary projection equipment and if it might not seem to others that "I was bragging, etc." Specifically she was undecided whether to show it only to her biology section or to the entire school, fearing the latter would seem "rather ostentatious." In response, Phil said he thought she should go ahead and see about involving the whole school: "It is good entertainment. You need have no fear that the name 'Weyerhaeuser' is prominent in the film, because that is not the case. At any rate, it is the name of a company in which we are comparatively small shareholders. So don't feel there is any ostentation in your showing this picture to the whole school." He closed by thanking her for her good letters, trusting that "you wrote a good thesis on conservation after all the dope which I sent you."

Phil and Helen had planned a vacation in Palm Springs following the February 24 Executive Committee meeting in Tacoma but decided otherwise at the last minute. The weather in Tacoma was not all that unpleasant, and the time just didn't seem right. There was much sadness, at home and elsewhere. Al Onstad, who had designed and supervised the important plant construction and remodeling efforts through the years, died. Like C. S. Chapman, Onstad was one of the original old guard bequeathed to Phil from the staff of George S. Long.

The daffodils and crocuses were coloring Tacoma lawns by the end of February, and Phil and Helen decided they might enjoy just working at the American Lake property, cleaning up around the new addition and having "some fun together building a fence and pulling up Scotch Broom." As he wrote to Uncle Sam Davis, "This was a compromise after planning to go to California and is an experiment, as far as Helen is concerned, as she insists I will sneak off to the office too much."

Apparently the experiment worked. At least Phil claimed it had in a March 25 letter to F.E., noting that "Helen and I retired to our place at American Lake for two weeks, and got a wonderful rest out of it." In the meantime, the strike situation at Snoqualmie Falls continued, unchanged except that it had finally come "within the purview of the new 11-man Mediation Council recently appointed by the President." Although he noted that they had not committed themselves to abide by the decision of the board, Phil acknowledged that such a decision "will be of sufficient weight to be rather binding upon us." Phil also indicated that at the annual meeting of the Snoqualmie Falls Lumber Company, O. D. Fisher had argued that they ought to accept a closed shop, and Phil seemed ready to believe that "something of that nature will be the practical answer for us if a decision of the 11-man Board goes against us."

Al Raught and Tip O'Neil went to Washington, D.C., to be present for the mediation meeting on April 9. Phil was, of course, anxious for a settlement one way or another, and Raught called "every few hours" to report. In the meantime the new film, *Trees and Homes*, was being seen by audiences. Laird Bell wrote to tell of having showed it to some seventy people and that everyone in attendance was "very well impressed." Afterward one of Laird's daughters had said that she "just loved" the Weyerhaeuser Timber Company and was very proud of it. Laird wished there had been somewhat more emphasis on reforestation, but all in all it was a "beautiful picture." And he added, "Perhaps these things don't go to the essence in the making of money, but I think in the long run they are valuable." In reply Phil agreed that they were doing something important, "not, as you say, making money," but perhaps contributing to conditions whereby the owner of a private enterprise could afford to have a "continued interest in his properties." Then Phil included an interesting aside, evidencing his growing frustrations in trying to work with Rod Olzendam: "I hope, as I told you before, that we can do much more, and perhaps more effective things—all of which seem quite hard for me to engineer because it involves certain prima donnas who think more of their own personal relationship to the program than of the success of the venture in toto."

The opportunity to do more, "and perhaps more effective things," was close at hand. While there were continuing concerns with the fir market, with the labor settlement at Snoqualmie, with the future of the Steamship Company in the aftermath of the creation of the Division of Emergency Shipping, and, of course, with the war developments in general, work had gone forward, but there were always reasons to keep things as they were. It was frustrating for those involved, for the foresters. Phil was genuinely interested, although he was not totally acquainted with all the facets. For example, he was probably more interested in a program of sustained yield, because that appeared to have more general application, than he was with the possibility of tree farms. But he was also willing to be educated, to be convinced, and he was certain of one thing: unless the Timber Company assumed a leadership of the industry in the area of resource management, there was increased likelihood of governmental regulation. In other words, it was crucial on two counts that they proceed: the company was committed to continued production, and continued production depended on managing the resource base in a manner that allowed it to be self-perpetuating; and the opportunity to continue operations depended on the public willingness to allow them to do so. In short, the forestry program was important in business terms, and it was important that it be advertised.

But how to translate this "importance" into action was another matter. It was too much to expect that a manager of one branch would be willing to accrue forestry costs that would negatively influence his balance sheet. After all, he was in competition with managers at other branches; and although it was easy enough to say that many variables influenced the reports, when matters were reduced to figures on a page, judgments inevitably followed. Thus not until everyone was doing it would anyone do it with any real purpose. In part to compensate, or at least to clarify matters, expenses that were clearly the result of fire control and reforestation activities had begun to be separated from the branch accounts and charged to the Reforestation and Lands Department. But in truth there was no separating the concerns of timber and logging from reforestation and lands.

Even with maximum effort and cooperation, progress would have been slowed simply because of the uncertainties involved. It was one thing to say what would be done and quite another to say how it should be done. If forestry was a science, it was only recently so. When the Timber Company foresters first began meeting together, they did so in isolation, involving no one outside their own group.

That was easily done. It wasn't until 1940, when Ed Heacox went to Longview, that any of the branches had a forester. After Clyde Martin's appointment, they began to include others in their meetings— branch managers, logging superintendents, and any others who were interested. Phil made a point to attend whenever possible, and so did Ed Hayes when he was in town. Years later, in an interview, Phil recalled something of the discussions: "So sustained yield is an ideal, but the measurements to govern our actions in order to keep to that ideal have been sketchy from the start and still are. It's our constant effort to improve them and arrive at more precise knowledge of what we can do and what we can't do. But if you could sit in on our forestry meetings, you'd be constantly amazed at the decisions that are based on hunches. . . . You have some terrific arguments among foresters."

But if the forestry meetings often involved disagreements on how to proceed, the disagreements were always concerned with the practical questions. This was no classroom. There was no talk about things that had no chance for application. Furthermore, although Phil was interested and supportive, he was unwilling to give orders except in rare instances. If forestry was to gain acceptance within the Timber Company, the foresters would have to sell the program themselves. That was a slow process, or at least it seemed so at the time. Some managers would have none of it, while others such as Ralph Macartney, Hugh Campbell, and Harold McCoy at Klamath Falls were willing participants. But even with the most reluctant, resistance gradually eroded— if Phil didn't give orders, he made his desires known—and eventually one could note that pride was being taken in the new practices. Like anything else, until those directly responsible became concerned with the results, little progress could be expected.

Probably the single most important contribution to forest management practices west of the Cascades was Richard E. McArdle's Technical Bulletin No. 201, *The Yield of Douglas Fir in the Pacific Northwest*. Published by the Forest Service in October 1930, it became the bible for the region's foresters. The variables remained as always, but at least they had a basis for planning. And when Ed Hanzlik of the Forest Experiment Station in Portland translated the McArdle formula to show annual yield or allowable cut, the foresters could make presentations to groups like the Timber Company board of directors and offer sustained-yield statistics in a format that could be shared.

The Hanzlik formula was $ya = \dfrac{VM + 1}{R}$ (ya = annual yield or allowable cut; VM = mature volume, based on 160 or more years of growth; 1 = amount of annual growth on the immature trees; and R = rotation, or how many years to cut the entire region). Even if the Timber Company directors might nod approvingly when figures were inserted into the formula—they could hardly refuse to listen and give tacit support to plans for growing trees and harvesting second- and third-growth timber—for the most part they would be happy to leave to others the unromantic job of translating that forest into products and profits. Even Charlie Ingram had trouble imagining the new order, at one point commenting that when it became necessary to cut timber the size of that being contemplated [on an eighty-year rotation], "it would be time to shut her down." Phil thought otherwise, and as long as the directors and others allowed his foresters to work and plan ahead, he was satisfied.

Among those working and planning ahead were W. H. Price, Mike Grogan, and Paul Meyer. Bill Price was in charge of the Reforestation and Lands Department, and Grogan did the overall planning for the Clemons development. Grogan likened the needs of a tree farm to those of city fire fighting: it had to be possible to get water on fires in a matter of minutes. Thus he designed road patterns, water holes, and equipment to permit the most rapid access and application. Paul Meyer was responsible for overseeing the on-site work and offering recommendations on the management of an area of largely cutover land, much of which had formerly belonged to the Clemons Logging Company. Therefore the name Clemons Tree Farm, and reference to it as such, became commonplace in the spring of 1941. The "tree farm" part of it was something of a catchword; as Phil noted, "Everybody understood what you meant immediately when you said, 'tree farm.'" Catchword or not, it well described the plan for management and utilization. Trees on the Clemons Tree Farm would be raised and harvested on a rotational basis, allowing for annual cuts year after year. One could describe the process simply. For example, if it were determined that the growth cycle required one hundred years, then one-one hundredth of the timber could be utilized, on an average, annually. It wasn't of course that simple. One had to have reasonable assurance that fire losses could be minimized. And in the case of Clemons, parcels of land had to be purchased and the cooperation of other owners assured, cleanup and slash burnings had to be accomplished, and a network of roads had to be constructed.

Rod Olzendam was anxious to advertise the Clemons plans, and in early April he drafted letters to Washington Governor Arthur Langlie and to area newspapers announcing the Timber Company's Tree Farm. Phil squashed the initial publicity, informing Olzendam, "it seems to me there are many unfinished details which might well call for delay in such public and detailed announcement," and he wanted to make sure that they kept their reports factual.

Official announcement of the Clemons Tree Farm, or "the reforestation and protective project," was made in April. Among those noti-

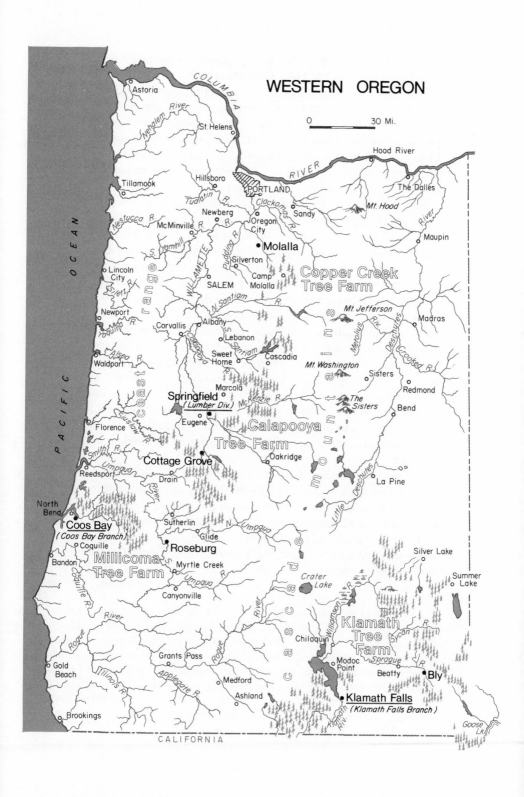

WESTERN OREGON

0   30 Mi.

PACIFIC OCEAN

Astoria
St. Helens
COLUMBIA River
Nehalem River
Hood River
The Dalles
Tillamook
Hillsboro
PORTLAND
RIVER
Mt. Hood
Nestucca R.
Tualatin R.
Newberg
Sandy
Maupin
McMinnville
Oregon City
Clackamas R.
S. Yamhill R.
Molalla
Lincoln City
Silverton
Copper Creek Tree Farm
WILLAMETTE range
Camp Molalla
SALEM
N. Santiam R.
Mt. Jefferson
Madras
Newport
Siletz R.
Corvallis
Albany
Lebanon
Metolius Riv.
Deschutes
Crooked R.
Yaquino R.
Coast range
Sweet Home
Cascadia
S. Santiam R.
Mt. Washington
Sisters
Waldport
Alsea R.
Marcola
Redmond
Siuslaw R.
Springfield
(Lumber Div.)
McKenzie R.
The Sisters
Bend
Florence
Eugene
Calapooya Tree Farm
Oakridge
Cottage Grove
Deschutes
Reedsport
Umpqua River
Drain
Little Deschutes
La Pine
North Bend
Sutherlin
N. Umpqua R.
Coos Bay
(Coos Bay Branch)
Coquille
Glide
Silver Lake
Roseburg
Millicoma Tree Farm
Myrtle Creek
Crater Lake
Summer Lake
Bandon
S. Umpqua R.
Coquille R.
Canyonville
Williamson R.
Klamath Tree Farm
Chiloquin
Sycan R.
Rogue River
Sprague R.
Beatty
Bly
Gold Beach
Grants Pass
Rogue River
Modoc Point
Medford
Applegate R.
Illinois R.
Ashland
Klamath Falls
(Klamath Falls Branch)
Brookings
Klamath Riv.
Goose Lk.

CALIFORNIA

fied was the community of Elma, neighbor to the project. Phil soon heard directly from the Elma Community Chamber of Commerce officers, who expressed their "sincere appreciation" and also their "hearty commendation for this great far-sighted enterprise, that will be of tremendous benefit to future generations." In his reply Phil emphasized the importance of cooperation, encouraging the people of Elma to consider it a "joint undertaking." He expressed the hope that "our progress, as time goes on, will warrant your continued satisfaction with the promotion of the project."

May 28 was the day of the official "opening," featuring a tour of the farm by a group of invited visitors. Phil obviously wanted some notice to be taken, but he didn't want to oversell. Bill Price assumed responsibility for managing the affair, notifying Phil, "we are making plans to receive you and to have on our best bib and tucker for the occasion." It was all very woodsy and quaint, lunch planned at Weikswood for between fifteen and thirty: "In the afternoon the visitors can have a chance to observe the protection headquarters and various sized tanker trucks in operation and other features around Weikswood. Then we have arranged transportation for a trip to Minot Lookout. On the way up we hope to demonstrate the operation of several portable pumps in successive boosting of water for a considerable distance and elevation. We also hope to demonstrate building a fire trail by hand by what is known as the 'one-lick.' The new metallic telephone line can also be observed on the way to the lookout." Price was eager that credit be given Paul Meyer for all his work in preparing the area.

The public opening of the Clemons Tree Farm was held June 12, and, as Phil expressed to Fred K., he thought it had been "interesting and, I hope, significant." It was not simply a matter of modesty that prevented any certainty about significance. For example, in a memo to Charlie Ingram, Clyde Martin attempted to explain the figuring that had gone into the Clemons annual growth calculations, indicating that much remained to be done:

If we expect to develop the Clemons area we should start preparing a management plan which will go into all of these factors in detail; show in addition to fire protection how much land should be planted each year and at what cost; figure the present and expected annual growth; and prescribe whether any current income can be obtained from thinnings or improvement fellings of the 60–90 year old hemlock stands on the area, from older stumpage, or from selling some of the mature hemlock from time to time. All of these things are important if we are to know more accurately what it will cost to develop the tree farm and what return we may expect.

The fact was that Clemons was far more an idea than a reality, more a demonstration area than a tree farm. It was, however, the place to start, even though it had to be difficult to explain to some why anyone would want to plant seedlings, with a questionable rate of survival, at a cost of from $12 to $15 an acre, when it was still possible to purchase land with fifty-year-old timber in tax sales at the Cowlitz County Courthouse at from $2 to $4 an acre. But then planting a tree is in itself an expression of faith. In this instance, the faith proved well placed.

The agreement between the Snoqualmie Falls Lumber Company and the Lumber and Sawmill Workers local had finally come to a mediated settlement on April 14. As Phil reported to Laird Bell, "the settlement was worth waiting for, although I am disappointed that some concession to the Union had to be made on the score of membership." The company had to agree that as a condition of employment union members must keep themselves in good standing with the union, and also "to recommend that all new employees . . . join the union certified as the sole collective bargaining agency." It may not have been a closed shop in the strictest sense, but there was no doubt as to the effect.

Business continued at a fever pitch through the summer, and this was both good and bad. Clearly the manufacturers were going to have to increase production. A year or so earlier, some consideration had been given to the Timber Company operating on Saturdays, paying time and a half. At that time, "we demurred," recalled Phil. To F.E. on August 5 he wrote, "Now we are faced with the rapidly jumping prices of the industry, a probable continuation of undersupply, and an investigation by a Committee of the National Mediation Board on the relationship between price and wages." It seemed advisable to "make every effort to make more lumber." Accordingly, the decision to run Saturdays at Willapa, Longview, and Everett had been made, and would soon be made for Snoqualmie Falls, with a complete second shift organized at White River. To Uncle Fred he stated, "I hope that you will think we have acted wisely in this matter." F.E. agreed that they had acted wisely "in order to help take care of the government's emergency demand for timber." It was certainly preferable for existing plants to work overtime than to encourage any new operations to start up.

In the meantime, the Clemons Tree Farm continued to receive its share of attention and occasionally, Phil thought, too much. It was surprising how enthusiastic those in the area were, as well as those who went out of their way to see for themselves. One who came from Seattle to see for himself was sufficiently impressed to write to Phil.

"After seeing this project," he began, "I wanted to write you to say that I feel such work is very much worthwhile and that private companies, in this day, can well afford to take such steps to improve your relations with the public and to inform them of your long range policies." Phil replied that he also got "a personal lift out of a visit down there," and added, "I trust that the venture can be successful in itself on its own right, regardless of the public relations angle to which you refer." But whether he cared to admit it or not, tree farming and public relations were two sides of the same coin.

Just as pleasing and perhaps more important was the cooperation the project was receiving. Phil wrote to Fred W. Conrad, president of the Montesano Chamber of Commerce, expressing his appreciation for the help given "to our experiment—The Clemons Tree Farm." Phil gave special note to the contributions of K. C. Kerstetter and Chapin Collins "for their untiring work during this vitally important organization period. Seldom have I personally been associated with any project which has been more heartening than the manner in which the people of Grays Harbor County have united to help us keep fire out of the Clemons Tree Farm. This job I know you realize, as well as any one, is a long-time proposition. We are very hopeful for the future in the light of the manner in which a beginning has been made."

The cooperation did indeed continue, especially from Chapin Collins. Much later, Phil received a strange little admission of sin from Chape, then managing director for the American Forest Products Industries, Incorporated, an organization supported by lumber and pulp and paper industries primarily for public relations purposes. It was the AFPI that had assumed the responsibility for certifying tree farms the country over. In the summer of 1948, years after the fact, Collins was ready to confess. "Incidentally," he inquired of Phil, "did you ever hear about the rather narrow squeak the Clemons Tree Farm had as being listed as Tree Farm No. 1 in the United States? When I got back here in '43, I discovered that actually the first officially certified tree farm was in Alabama. Since there seemed no poetic justice in this, we managed to get Clemons referred to in all our publicity as No. 1. Don't let the south hear about this." Phil had known nothing about the "narrow squeak," and he thanked friend Chape, promising that the South would not learn of it through him. In a public relations sense, Collins was doubtless right. Clemons served the purpose well.

Complementary to the interest in growing trees was that of utilizing a larger percentage of what was grown. That was obvious enough, but experience would make it even more so. For example, lumbermen were not happy to be forced to leave so much of the tree behind. Slash was certainly unsightly and, more important, created problems in and of itself. Unless it was burned off carefully, the fire hazards were increased many times. Furthermore, slash accumulations made the job of reforestation all the more difficult. The answer was to find ways to use more of the tree at a profit. It was another problem of economics, and when times were hard, lumbermen left more slash in their wake. They knew what they were doing.

The path to greater utilization was through research, but research was incapable of showing profit. Thus it tended to get slighted, even in the best of times. In other times it was likely to be forgotten altogether, although some would argue that it is in the off periods that research efforts should be increased. If not, producers are likely to find themselves with pockets full of money and no intelligent investment plan. For Phil and the Weyerhaeuser Timber Company, another problem with research had to do with the nature of the organization. Almost as an adjunct to the pulp division, but actually responsible to General Timber Service, was the research facility at Longview. The larger affiliated research activity was at Cloquet under the auspices of the Wood Conversion Company, headed by Clark Heritage and responsible to Ed Davis. Phil was convinced that someone ought to be giving more direct attention to the research requirements of the Weyerhaeuser Timber Company.

Just how to accomplish a greater effort posed some sensitive questions. Phil wrote to Fred K. offering his view of the problem:

F.E. indicated, without rancor, that he felt his son Fred had been slighted in something which went on in St. Paul with regard to his research program. I am sure you know about it, and I sympathize with you in your problem. I discussed with him and R.M. my sense of frustration at being unable to get down to brass tacks with Ed Davis on the Weyerhaeuser Timber Company program. In connection with that discussion, F.E. suggested maybe it would be a good idea to put the GTS program improvement research out west also. I don't have much idea about that, but thought I would repeat it to you because it might offer an out if you feel that progress under the present setup has been too slow.

Certainly Phil was convinced that progress had been too slow, especially on the new plywood effort. They had recently been approached by a government representative about producing an all-fir plywood airplane using vertical-grain plywood and veneer.

Phil could, of course, announce an intention to proceed separately with a Timber Company research effort. That would raise the question and get the attention of F.E. and others, but it would also announce his dissatisfaction with the research effort as presently organized. It was for that reason that he invited Ed Davis to come west to consider the problems together. "I do want to sit down and talk with you about it at some length and to arrive at conclusions both for the

Washington Veneer and for WTC as soon as possible," he wrote to his cousin in Cloquet. Davis agreed to come.

In early October, Ed Davis, Clark Heritage, F.E.'s son Frederick, and Fred K. sat down in Tacoma, as Phil observed, for the purpose of "discussing the nature and scope of a development or research program for Weyerhaeuser Timber Company." After much talk, a consensus evolved and Gus Clapp was called in to draw up a contract that would be presented to the directors of both the General Timber Service and the Timber Company. Phil reported to Uncle Fred that they had agreed on the "fields in which the effort should function," assigning priorities, and "we have outlined the relationship between that program and the Wood Conversion Company program and the program conducted for the benefit of the whole group by General Timber Service." If the group headed homeward feeling the Weyerhaeuser Timber Company was something of a tyrant, there could be no doubt that Phil's approach was preferable to a frontal attack, or that he was very much committed to the research effort.

An Executive Committee meeting was scheduled for the week of November 10 in Tacoma, but Phil indicated a willingness to change the site to St. Paul. He was, for reasons of the agenda, interested in attending some of the sessions of the National Lumber Manufacturers Association meeting in Chicago at about that time. He also wanted to check in with Bill Peabody. The reasons for his interest were suggested in a letter of October 10 to Fritz Jewett. It seemed likely that the Chicago meeting of the NLMA might degenerate into a feud between contesting views on the subject of industrial forestry, the results of which would be very damaging to industrial public relations. As Phil saw the situation:

We have just reached the most encouraging stage of industry action leading toward a concerted movement by timber owners and operators to give intelligent care to their forest lands whether such lands are to be kept under permanent management or not. This movement could be crystallized and implemented through organizing tree farm groups and associations, not restricting membership to members of trade groups, and joining local groups into a regional association, the regionals into a national association of tree farms. All could join who would agree to certain minimum practices such as protection, providing for regeneration, cleaning up unsightly messes along roads, etc.— This organization work could well be done by the N.L.M.A. Forestry Division under the guidance of your committee. It would encourage all timber owners to do those things they could do and understand. From such efforts more technical management would develop naturally.

Phil would never have described himself as a missionary for industrial forestry. That would have been far too presumptuous and would indicate an interest in activities other than those involving the business of the Weyerhaeuser Timber Company. It just so happened, as he tried to look into the future, that the interests of the Timber Company were inseparable from the need for a larger industry effort at improved timber management. If the public was convinced that the lumber industry had not "changed its spots," as Laird Bell phrased it, all operators, progressive and otherwise, would be the losers. Furthermore, Phil was a believer. He didn't have to remind himself of the reasons for the commitment. The reasons were not theoretical; they had to do with the objectives of the Weyerhaeuser Timber Company.

Phil was probably at his best as a spokesman for the company and the industry in general when he was speaking informally to small groups. Even for those who approached such exchanges cynically, assuming that what they had long heard about the Weyerhaeusers was fact, there could be no question that here was a plain person who believed sincerely in what he was doing. Phil took all such discussions seriously. Evidence of this is a letter he wrote following a social function at which the question had been raised about the possibility of harvesting alder and maple—species traditionally of little market value—in some sections. One of the wives present at the affair had turned to Phil and said, "I should think that the Government would force you to save this material!" Phil had obviously been dissatisfied with his response, because a few days later he wrote to the husband:

I don't think she was adequately answered, because in the first place, we are still operating under the free enterprise system, though we have less of it every day. I wish you would tell her that it is our effort, selfishly and for other considerations, to save everything that is worth saving in harvesting our timber and that it does not require a Government edict to bring this about. The utilization of what is left on the ground in our Old Growth Fir district is increasing year by year. Someday, given the population surrounding us that surrounds the German forests and given the scale of labor rates comparable to the Germans, every twig can be picked up and used; but when that comes about and there are no longer surpluses of all kinds, our way of life will be at a great deal lower standard than it is today.

He closed the letter by expressing the hope that "sometime you and your wife will be able to take time out to visit one of our operations to look for alder and maple and other wastes, while we are trying to show you some of the things which we think we do well."

One encouraging development was the decision of the West Coast Lumbermen's Association to establish an industry tree nursery on the Nisqually River flats along the main highway between Tacoma and Olympia. The purpose was twofold: to provide seedlings to participating companies, and to publicize industrial reforestation efforts.

Clearly visible from that much-traveled section of highway, the location was ideal from a public relations standpoint. But as a place to grow young trees it proved to be less satisfactory: the rich soil encouraged too rapid growth and the area was something of a frost belt. In the fall of 1941, however, it seemed promising on all counts. Phil informed Uncle Fred of his decision to cooperate, the Timber Company joining with Crown-Willamette, St. Paul and Tacoma, and the Simpson Logging Company, contracting to order 15 million seedlings to be delivered over a period of six years at a cost of four dollars a thousand. The Timber Company would abandon its Snoqualmie nursery "in favor of this cooperative industry-nursery," and there would be "considerable public relations benefit." Phil committed the company to an expenditure of $60,000 in the effort. Despite its problems, the Nisqually nursery, later dedicated to Colonel Greeley, produced millions of seedlings.

The Executive Committee met in St. Paul November 10, and one of the more important items to be considered was the report of the research meeting in Tacoma. The essentials of that report involved the creation of a Weyerhaeuser Development Committee, Ed Davis serving as chairman, with Phil, Fred K., and Frederick as members. The main purpose of the committee was to coordinate the research activities taking place within the Wood Conversion Company, Weyerhaeuser Timber Company, and General Timber Service group. It had also been decided that the Timber Company development work would become the responsibility of the Wood Conversion Company "to be handled in general as though the Wood Conversion Company were an outside agency brought in for this purpose." No doubt most pleasing to Phil was the agreement that Clark Heritage would assume responsibility for directing the Weyerhaeuser Timber Company development work, and he was assured the availability of any necessary company personnel in the management of that responsibility. No decision had been made on how much money should be budgeted to support the increased activity, although a commitment to at least a five-year period had been made. Writing to Ed Davis on October 28, Phil suggested that they ought to have a definite figure in mind to present to the Executive Committee, and he proposed that "the sum of money which we should spend, exclusive of laboratory equipment, is one-half million dollars." He also thought that if Ed could be present at the meeting, "an understanding can be reached which will be satisfactory to all parties." The action taken by the Executive Committee approved the details of the research organization and allocated a first-year appropriation of up to $100,000; and it stipulated that "the Wood Conversion Company would bill the Weyerhaeuser Timber Company for its organization salaries and expense, at cost plus $700.00 a month beginning the first of December 1941."

Other decisions being made in other places would alter priorities and perspectives beyond any Executive Committee's ability to foresee. In the days immediately following Pearl Harbor, concerns became increasingly personal. As Phil wrote to Uncle Fred regarding his son Davis's draft situation, "Of course, none of us know how our war effort will be translated into an army. If the numbers reach five to ten million men as indicated in today's comments from those who ought to know, all of us who are eligible and physically fit will undoubtedly be called."

CHAPTER 11

"Wood Goes to War"

The Weyerhaeuser Timber Company had been in the war since the summer of 1941. Four of its Steamship Company vessels had been drafted, for the most part in the Red Sea trade supplying British military needs in North Africa. In the third week of 1942, Bill Peabody advised that the Maritime Commission probably would soon take the three remaining ships they had in the intercoastal trade, the *Hanley*, *Hegira*, and *Klamath*. Indeed, the *Hanley* and *Hegira* were already at Baltimore being armed and fitted out for military transport service. Regarding the other vessels, after an extended silence, they had finally heard from the *Heffron*, in port at Wellington, New Zealand, having last been reported departing Singapore on December 2. The *Winona* had just completed a Red Sea voyage and was at dock in Baltimore, and the *Pennsylvania* and *Potlatch* were then on Red Sea voyages. Whatever plans had been made to move lumber east and general cargo west were clearly to be subordinated for the duration.

All manner of other considerations were suddenly important. There were air-raid instructions to be published and subsequently practiced at the Tacoma Building. There were credit unions to be established at the branches, the one at Longview being a typical example. Its brochure listed the objectives, the first being "to win the war," and the second: "We pledge cooperation in the sale and purchase of war fund securities and in every other service for our country." Lumber prices continued their upward climb, although, as Phil noted in a letter to the Timber Company directors, their large contracts with the government had been made "generally at prices under the ceiling." The fir plants were running a Saturday shift and the order files were large again, "mostly made up of defense business." And there were many questions awaiting an answer in those hectic days when the pages of newspapers were filled with accounts of battlefield losses on every front. As an example, Phil wondered, "Should we duplicate our irreplaceable records because of bombing and invasion threats, and what can be done to coordinate city, state, federal, and private fire-protection agencies to combat incendiary fires by fifth columnists or airplanes?" Laird Bell could be excused if he wondered for the moment just who was the jittery one now, but he probably didn't. Everyone was jittery.

There was also continuing uncertainty on the question of Weyerhaeuser Timber Company stock, specifically whether to provide all the information requested by those who wanted to sell it. Laird wasn't eager to get "very chummy with the investment banker group," but both he and Phil realized that information on the company and its status would be circulated regardless of source or accuracy. Laird had been in communication with one broker and had informed him that at present the Timber Company was uninterested in any help regarding its stock. In reply, Laird had received a letter which he shared with Phil, which began: "On the basis of probabilities and percentages, I feel sure the time will come when the Weyerhaeuser stock will find its way to the public. When that time comes, I hope that the circumstances will be such that we can do something to help."

Phil recalled an occasion when he mentioned to F.E. a purchase of nine hundred shares of Timber Company stock by R. Stuyvesant Pierrepont, who had, in a letter to Eddie McIntyre, indicated a desire to purchase more "and had also expressed himself most enthusiastically about the prospects for our Company and its setup—to which F.E. volunteered the feeling that it would be very unfortunate to have an interest developed in our Company by the Wall Street group." Laird's friend was, of course, correct that the time would come when Weyerhaeuser stock would go public, but that time was not at hand.

One issue whose time had come, after a long incubation period, was the approval of an arrangement for a retirement trust program. This had occurred at the November 1941 Executive Committee meeting, and Phil wanted to make sure that Laird knew that "every recipient is extremely happy about the trust." He also wanted Laird to know that he knew who was responsible: "The credit belongs to one Bell, who pushed it through." And he added, "I think you should feel considerable personal satisfaction."

But Laird Bell was not always the exponent of change. He counseled caution and a conservative approach in the current negotiations for the purchase of sizable tracts of Oregon timberland. His concern had nothing to do with the lands themselves or the prices being considered but what he understood to be the objective of "locking up the timber we buy" in the Willamette Valley, noting that there seemed to be "dynamite" in such a situation: "The Valley is full of little fellows who furnish employment and have local influence." Then he added an interesting observation:

I have been brought up in the belief that Mr. Long made the Company palatable to the State of Washington by being fair in his sales of timber, and the policy seems to me sound. I know you have a feeling that it got us nothing because fellows like Demarest, to whom we think we have been decent, knife us at every chance and because in the code days we found we did not have a lot of friends. Nevertheless it seems to me the situation might have been much worse had Mr. Long's policy not been followed. In tax assessments, in timber regulation and the like, an aroused opposition could make lots of trouble for us. The Long policy seems to me to have been worthwhile even if it only made our competitors a little less antagonistic.

Laird admitted that when he heard Minot Davis talk about "the Roach-Musser timber and getting control of the Avery-Richardson-Green timber, etc., I can't resist the feeling that we are going too fast." Indeed, that was always a consideration in timberland purchases, especially in Oregon. The company was conscious of its bigness, or at least its impression of bigness. It was one of the penalties of success.

There were, of course, many concerns related to the war emergency. Phil noted in his early March report to the directors that they were losing workers to military service and to some of the war industries, "and we face a severe shortage of manpower in certain lines." They could only presume that these problems would increase as time passed and that efficiency would necessarily decline. Although understandably concerned about the ability of the organization to maintain its level of operations given the loss of experienced personnel, Phil nonetheless felt a need to question the value of his own contribution. He shared this anxiety with Laird Bell, who had subsequently been "mulling a good deal" over it. While he could appreciate that Phil did not want to ask "any special consideration," Laird failed to see what purpose would be served with Phil in the service: "I am hanged if I think it would help to win the war by making a second-rate quartermaster out of a first-class executive."

The late March report to the directors indicated the various ways the war was affecting the affairs of the Timber Company. The prices for lumber shipments for the first quarter of 1942 exceeded those of the first quarter of 1941 by $5.58 per thousand feet, and shipments totaled 58 million feet more. The plywood plant, the log-buying sawmills, and the pulp mills were all complaining about log shortages. Loggers were generally operating on a 48-hour week, and men were so scarce that "added hours seem the only method of increasing production." Phil further noted that telephones were busy, "with officers of all descriptions calling in about orders not shipped quickly enough to suit them," and in some instances there were such shortages that the government was buying retail stocks. "Our steamships are still afloat, as far as we know." All of the Steamship Company vessels were operating under time charter to the government, and four other vessels, three of them new Liberty ships, had been accepted under an agency operating agreement.

Laird Bell, for one, worried about the continuing high prices. Not only did labor have a tendency to view such increases as permanent, thereby "creating a rigid obstacle to readjustment if the war is ever over," but he supposed there were "many other ways too in which high prices lead to extravagance and carelessness in operation." Phil shared these concerns and admitted in his letter to Laird that he had no ready answers. Any attempt to go it alone in pricing simply didn't work. All during the last year the effort had been to maintain high production levels in order "to depress all that we could and our price policy was consistently on the low side." But there seemed no chance to control the present market. As to investing present dollars for future benefits, he pointed to the research program and the need to gain the approval to build a laboratory at Longview. "The second method by which our current expense dollars are building for the future is in the creation of our fire protection and forestry program," and the third involved the public relations efforts. He closed by noting, "All, or a substantial part, of these expenditures may come under the category of 'extravagance and carelessness,' to quote from a recent letter from Laird Bell as to the effects of high prices." Laird had to smile at that, but doubtless felt considerably better for the discussion.

Organizational questions concerned the need for governmental management and coordination. Under the War Protection Board was created a Lumber Advisory Committee of twenty-five on which Fred K. finally agreed to serve. He asked if Phil had some concerns to pass along. He did. Although it was apparent that efficiency was on the decline as a result of a loss of skilled men, Phil didn't think that the situation "should call for action by the War Protection Board," except that draft deferments ought to be considered for those whose skills "are now absolutely irreplaceable—such as sawyers, skidder levermen, et al." Phil believed that the government would do well to avoid "any drastic actions," because the industry "is thoroughly anxious to give the Government every bit of lumber that it can use." As a final thought, he advised Fred K. not to let the responsibility get him down: "I think you are eminently fitted to carry it on and that you are the one in the organization to do it."

Summer was rapidly approaching. Any hopes for a short war had long since faded. The Battle of the Coral Sea was history, and the Battle of Midway yet to come. Corregidor finally surrendered on May 6. Phil and Helen had gone east to be with the children during spring vacation. Three were now in eastern schools, George having joined Flip at Taft.

With six months of 1942 nearly completed, Phil summarized the situation for the Timber Company directors. All operations were continuing on a six-day schedule, and lumber had been declared a "critical material," and the order files continued to bulge. Shipments from Timber Company mills totaled more than a million feet in excess of the 1941 figures, although that comparison suffered in light of the 1941 strikes at Snoqualmie Falls and Everett. Logs continued to be scarce, and some governmental action was expected. Peabody reported that they had contracted with the Army to handle between 5 and 10 million feet of lumber a month at Newark and 10 million feet at Baltimore, "and to this extent, we have the camel's head in our tent—it is our endeavor now to keep the whole camel from coming in."

At first glance, it would seem surprising that Phil would express an interest in producing another film in the summer of 1942. Complicating such considerations was the growing antagonism on the part of others to Rod Olzendam. It was almost fashionable to oppose anything that Olzendam proposed or for which he might take credit. Phil attempted to explain the reasons for his interest to Fred K., convinced that "the last film we made has been the most powerful instrument for molding a sympathetic opinion toward our Company, industry, and free enterprise in general." Fred K. did not always appreciate the accountability that Phil often felt; at least such a possibility seemed likely to Phil. Thus he wrote, "I spend a great deal of time—perhaps erroneously—in fussing around with ministers, trying to convince them our system, our industry, and our Company are square with the world, as it should be." Nevertheless he knew, however able he was in such discussions, that he could reach only a few, and convert only a few of those. Written presentations enjoyed very limited circulation. But Phil believed that it was possible "to get almost everybody in the country to look at a movie once in a while; and when you have one which tells a story well, it gets a disproportionate degree of attention." Furthermore, he was tired and in a rare state of depression, fearful that the pressures of war requirements would bring on more governmental regulation. Although he well realized that it could not be business as usual, it did seem likely that those who made the rules would give too little consideration to long-term plans and needs. And long-term plans were the essence of progress in Phil's view of the forest products industry, particularly the Weyerhaeuser Timber Company. As he wrote Fred K.:

Now we are being told every day something new which we have to do by some Government bureau. Probably we will be told to give some of our logs to other manufacturers and some of our timber to other loggers, and no one can see the end of it. Our order files are full and apparently are going to be for a time yet. Little or nothing can be accomplished by merchandising efforts at this time; the best we can hope for is a future return on those expenditures, and that future return will avail us nothing if we aren't operating under a free enterprise system. If we are spending any merchandising money, I can imagine that I'd rather convert that to out-and-out public relations aimed at preservation of the [free] enterprise system.

The war occasionally came especially close. One such instance was the loss of the Steamship Company vessel, the SS *Heffron*. She had been engaged in the Murmansk trade and July 5 was attacked and sunk off the coast of Iceland by German submarines. The captain, Edward D. Geddes of Tacoma, and most of the crew were picked up the following day by the Free French Corvette *Roselys*, but as Charlie Ingram would write to Peabody, "It brings one closer to the realities of war when such things happen."

A constant worry, war or no, was forest fires, and now there was the added danger of enemy bombing or sabotage, a danger that seems remote only in retrospect. The subject of war risk insurance accordingly received much attention. As Laird Bell reasoned, "We have a number of baskets, but they are quite large ones and very full of eggs, and the eggs are highly inflammable." Not only were the plants vulnerable, but the timber as well. "We wouldn't have to worry so much about estate taxes if the Longview block burned up," he observed, before suggesting that they would be wise to get the best possible protection. Phil agreed entirely. This was an area in which government involvement seemed appropriate and was appreciated. The rate was fifteen cents per thousand dollars of insurance, clearly too good a bargain to pass by. The Washington timber of Weyerhaeuser was roughly estimated, as of June 30, 1942, to contain nearly 30 billion board feet, valued at over $75 million, which translated into an insurance premium of $113,880. The war risk insurance became effective July 9, 1942.

Phil's fears of government intervention in logging operations and timberland management were somewhat allayed when Donald Nelson announced in mid-July the appointment of a committee to assist F. H. Brundage, the western log and lumber administrator of the War Production Board. Appointed were Edmund Hayes, Truman Collins, Ed

Stamm, Colonel Greeley, Lyle Watts, who was regional forester of the U.S. Forest Service in Portland, and two CIO and two AFL representatives. Part of the effort was directed at convincing loggers and sawmill workers of their importance to the war effort. Phil was especially pleased at the inclusion of Ed Hayes on the committee, and he hastened to assure Ed of his willingness to cooperate, asking Charlie Ingram to inform Ed fully about the Timber Company's recent efforts to increase production. Actually the report was not very encouraging, Charlie admitting that aside from a percentage increase resulting in increasing the workweek by eight hours, there had been no increase in production, "nor does an increase seem likely." As he described the situation, "You know what the story is regarding the shortage of fallers and buckers and rigging men generally, so I will not repeat it to you other than to state that the situation common to others prevails in our woods operations." With all the problems, Phil was able to report to the directors that in June the Timber Company mills had shipped, "under Government directive, almost 131 million feet of lumber," an all-time record high. More surprising was that the production figure of 115 million feet had been exceeded only twice.

The second loss at sea occurred when the SS *Potlatch* was sunk, and Captain John J. Lapoint and forty-seven survivors negotiated 990 miles in thirty-two days in a single lifeboat before a landfall on Great Inagua Island, neighbor to the Bahamas. In the course of their journey, they caught some forty fish "which they ate raw," and were without any water for the last five days. On Great Inagua "they found a water hole by tracking wild donkeys" and also "found some berries and made a broth out of some conches." Eventually they were located and taken to Nassau, "where they were well treated by everybody," including the duke and duchess of Windsor. Captain Lapoint was subsequently commended by the American consul general at Nassau: "The behavior of your crew in Nassau due to your tact and example was excellent and the best of all such survivor crews."

Phil was moved by the account. As he wrote to Peabody, "I find that I get completely emotionally upset by the experiences of captains Lapoint and Geddes, especially the former, of course." Phil was convinced that there was "something to be gained for all of us by a recitation of such experiences in the dispassionate way in which you've written about them and in which the Captains have themselves recorded their experiences." He wondered if they could get permission to share the stories with company personnel, perhaps by means of the Tacoma Office lobby display case, or in their publication, *Weyerhaeuser News*. It seemed to Phil that these contributions ought to be noted, in the process perhaps reminding those on the home front of their responsibilities to contribute. In that connection, he continued to look on the sacrifices that others were making as greater than his own. In an August 18 note to Paul Cruikshank at Taft School, Phil mentioned two of their 1920 classmates who were in military service, "making quite a record." In his reply, Paul sensed that Phil was "having 'stirrings' about enlistment" but argued as others had and would that "your present work is so vital and so closely connected with our war efforts you will have to 'stifle' whatever urge you may have."

As the weeks passed, it became increasingly apparent that the long-term plans of the Weyerhaeuser Timber Company must give way to the immediate requirements of the government and the needs of competitors. It was hard. Phil tried to describe the situation in a series of letters to brother Fred, Uncle Fred, and Horace Irvine. To Irvine, he noted, "all of our competitors, of all descriptions, view everything which we own or acquire with a jealous eye these days," adding, "I am sure there is much talk about us as an octopus and that some of it has been engendered by our timber purchases." They had tried, he said, "to take the bull by the horns and increase the production of logs from our own operations," but there weren't enough men; at present they had "twenty-two sets of fallers instead of fifty!" It seemed as if they were being penalized for their foresight: "As a matter of fact, all of the pressure of our competitors and requirements of the war effort combined is going to result, no doubt, in some timber and logs being more or less arbitrarily taken away from us. The best we can do, as I see it, is to use our production and facilities as to aid the war effort regardless of whether in so doing we assist our competitors or not."

One of the complications had to do with the recent purchase by the Timber Company of some 40,000 acres of timberland in Douglas, Lane, and Linn counties in western Oregon. Although the purchase had seemed reasonable enough, it was difficult to counter the impression of the land-grabber, especially where small, independent operations seemed threatened as a result. That communities might benefit in the long run was a possibility hard to sell. Ed Hayes had suggested that "some of the various criticisms of the Weyerhaeuser Timber Company through their holding large amounts of timber in Oregon might be partially offset by a forestry policy of which the public is aware," stressing that "the timber is being handled not only for the benefit of the Company but as a reserve for essential use of the public." A statement to that effect, "Plans for Continuous Production of Forest Crops," had been drafted and circulated for comment. Uncle Fred commented that in general he liked the article "to the extent that it appears to be your language," but "where it seems to be Rod Olzendam's I begin to question whether it is goo." Horace Irvine objected to the statement, "the trees were ripe and ready for harvesting at the time the Pilgrims landed." That probably was Olzendam. At best, the thing would have been a rearguard action, and probably it was just as well that Phil decided to let the matter rest.

Norton Clapp made a personal decision. The son of long-time Timber Company director and president of Boise Payette, Dr. E. P. Clapp (no relation of Gus Clapp), Norton had been elected Weyerhaeuser's secretary in 1938. Now in the summer of 1942 he resigned and enlisted in the Navy. As Phil reported this to Laird Bell, a bit of envy was apparent: "Maybe Norton is wise after all, because it must be rather comforting to forget all your worries and responsibilities and say, 'I will be patriotic and let somebody else tell me how to serve my country.'" Regarding a replacement, "I hope we can elect Bill McCormick," Phil wrote, "as Bill is willing and anxious to be the universal secretary while he remains in the harness." More difficult to deal with was the departure for school of the children after an enjoyable summer at the American Lake home. Phil wrote again to Paul Cruikshank of Taft on September 9, indicating that George and Flip were heading in that direction the following evening. "It is a tug to have them going away again," he admitted.

If any doubted Phil's frustrations in trying to direct the Timber Company in the midst of what seemed to be unceasing orders and directives, forever changing, they had only to skim over his late September report to the directors. After noting that August production had dropped, as had shipments, "slightly," he talked of other developments:

The labor freezing order has caused quite a lot of talk. It is hard to guess now whether it's a help or a hindrance. Wage dispute hearings start October 12. Meanwhile, government pressure is to stabilize existing wage rates.

Office of Price Administration [Henderson] has ordered ceiling established on stumpage prices. Tentative schedules presented would be quite untenable, but may be imposed.

Timber Company has been requested to submit statements to the Price Adjustment Board of the War Department, preliminary to a general renegotiation of contracts under an Act passed in April of this year. Unless the Act is amended, it will be necessary either to demonstrate that no excessive profit is being realized on account of war contracts or to make restitution to the Government.

It was all very complicated and unrewarding, especially the paperwork and the accounting to those who seemed so far removed. Something of the frustration was also evident in Phil's note of October 9, concerning the pending Executive Committee meeting. Phil assumed that the committee would meet as scheduled on November 9, although he acknowledged that there was little "on the program requiring its being held, but it affords a good chance for everyone to reorient himself to the changing conditions."

One of those changing conditions was the cash situation that placed the Timber Company in a position to purchase timberlands at a time when there were severe restrictions on most capital investments. Despite the recent reactions to such purchases, Phil had, "when under some pressure—the nature of which I do not now remember," told Minot Davis to proceed with negotiations to purchase some 1,500 acres containing 52 million feet of fir timber. As Phil reported to F.E., Minot had informed him that they were now committed to a price of $60,000. Phil said he had intended to inform F.E. of the negotiation, "but evidently I neglected to do so." Therefore he was placed in a position of reporting the acquisition "with an apology, for we have not previously ever committed ourselves without authority on such a long-range purchase."

F.E. wrote that he had no complaint regarding the purchase, although he suspected that "the other members of the Executive Committee may think that we have bought enough timber for this year." All in all, he doubted there would be any criticism. He did wonder a little about Phil's use of the word "authority": "I suspect there never has been any real granting of authority to pass on many of the subjects which come before us, but with the approval of Mr. Bell as president of the WTC, Rudolph as president of Potlatch, and the approval of such officers and directors as are in and about Saint Paul, it has never seemed altogether improper for us to act when there was full agreement of those within reach."

The war came close again with the news that the SS *Winona* had been torpedoed off the east coast of South America. The ship had been carrying coal to Brazil and was due to return to the United States with a load of bauxite. Although the torpedo struck her abreast, she was able to reach Port of Spain, Trinidad, under her own power without any loss of life. And in early November, having received permission of the Navy Department, the Weyerhaeuser Timber Company published thousands of copies of a pamphlet entitled *Nothing Sighted Today*, which told the story of the lifeboat adventure of the survivors of the SS *Potlatch*.

One of the more encouraging developments was the completion of the research laboratory at Longview. Phil wrote a pre-Thanksgiving letter to Ed Davis describing a recent visit there. He had gone through the laboratory with Helen and Harry Morgan and his wife, guided by Bob Pauley. As he told cousin Ed, "It is a thrilling experience to be allowed to wander through those corridors." A few days later he reported the visit to Laird Bell, observing that the laboratory was "quite inspiring, it seems to me."

The renegotiation question was unfolding, or unraveling, toward the end of 1942. The subject under consideration was whether companies had profited excessively and, if so, whether their contract arrangements with the government were deserving of renegotiation with a corresponding payment back. Four agencies were involved in renegotiation, the Army, the Navy, Lend-Lease, and the Maritime Commission, the responsibility falling to whichever had the most business with the company in question. For Weyerhaeuser, it was the Army. As Phil wrote to Fred K., "If we approach the matter willingly and make a full disclosure, without half-truths or contentions based upon questionable premises, we should expect to be met halfway."

But the biggest news of December 1942 from a Timber Company perspective was the purchase of all the timberland owned by Long-Bell in the Klamath Falls district, amounting to some 87,000 acres at a rate of $6.00 per thousand feet, plus 43,500 acres of cutover lands at $1.25 an acre. Phil had also agreed "verbally" with John Tennant, vice-president of Long-Bell, that the Timber Company would purchase at book value as of December 31, for cash, "the sawmill and the lumber and log inventories (such book values were, as of October 1, 1942, $429,000)." Phil indicated in a memo to Gus Clapp that he and Mr. Tennant "would appreciate your drawing the agreement which will formalize our verbal understanding." Somehow it was all reminiscent of how George S. Long had conducted business. As a matter of fact, Phil passed along to F.E. the copy of his memo to Gus Clapp, observing that it would "demonstrate to you how poor a trader I am," since the final terms represented no change from Long-Bell's original price and terms, except that the retail yards had been excluded. As Phil explained, "Mr. Tennant gleefully quoted Mr. George S. Long when he said: 'This is our price—it is a fair price and we will not deviate from it,' and he said it so emphatically that all of us came to believe him." Phil remained convinced, however, that they had "nothing to regret in this purchase, except that we can take no trading pleasure in it." In F.E.'s response, he noted that while he personally had not heard Mr. Long make any such remark, "I am quite sure that Tennant quoted him correctly." Although Uncle Fred and Horace Irvine were "entirely satisfied with the transaction," Laird Bell continued to worry that they had been "going pretty fast and furious in the purchase of additional timber."

Phil certainly did not hesitate to make timberland purchases that seemed to provide long-term opportunities. He was far less inclined to encourage unrelated or new endeavors, unless there would be some direct application to the task at hand. Thus when F.E.'s son, Frederick, wrote him concerning the possibility of the General Timber Service expanding into a self-insurance program, Phil was anything but en-

thusiastic. He began by admitting that although he had never studied
it, "the question which remains unanswered . . . is whether the game
is worth the candle":

We try to conduct our forest enterprises without getting too far into remanu-
facture or the other fellow's bailiwick: I will grant that in following this policy
we have gone pretty far afield through acquiring steamships, retail yards, fab-
rication plants, and a hundred-and-one by-product enterprises.

Because the management effort required in any venture is so great and represents the difference between success and failure in the long run, I naturally
hesitate to enter a new field, unless the argument for it is pretty strong. Insurance is such a complicated and, to me, dry subject that I personally have no
urge to explore the possibility of self-insurance. That does not mean you
should not; nor does it mean that we should fail to assure ourselves that our
insurance is being well bought.

Young Fred doubtless felt that his uncle Phil sounded a good deal like
father F.E. The fact was that Phil had worries enough without wondering whether the General Timber Service should administer an insurance program to the affiliated companies.

In December Phil informed the directors that the log shortages were
such that they had been forced to drop some shifts and were "pretty
generally going back to five-day weeks." Furthermore, by order of the
War Production Board, the Everett pulp mill had been limited to a
quota of only 4 million feet of logs a month, which was about 50
percent of capacity. The War Labor Board had also recently announced minimum labor rates of 90 cents an hour for both logging
and lumber operations. This amounted to a 7.5-cent advance, retroactive to September 1, and Phil guessed that it would cost the company about $300,000. He was quick to acknowledge a complete lack
of understanding given the wording in the order. As proof he quoted:

Payment to employees no longer employed by the employer by whom they
were employed during the period when retroactive wages were accrued, but
still employed in the lumber industry, and payment to former employees who
for some reason beyond their control were required to leave employment in
said industry and are prevented from returning to employment in said industry, shall be made within 30 days from the date hereof by mailing said payments to their last known address; but, if not so paid, such persons may make
demands for payment at any time within 60 days from the date hereof.

The children all came home for Christmas after a brief stopover in
St. Paul to visit with Fred K. and his family. But this would be a very
different holiday season, much of it given over to serious conversation

about Flip's plans. As Phil would report to Paul Cruikshank, Flip had decided to enlist in the Marine Corps Reserve, which would probably allow some opportunity for college work before being called up to the Officers' Training School. Phil seemed unenthuiastic. He wanted Flip to go to Yale, and the Navy seemed the better route for that objective.

Between Christmas and New Year's came the announcement from Rod Olzendam that MGM would be releasing the movie *Wood Goes to War* sometime during the last two weeks of January. Rod had been on something of a special assignment working on the production of this film, an effort not of the Timber Company but of the industry as expressed through the American Forest Products Industries. Bill Peabody had taken out a full-page advertisement on behalf of the Weyerhaeuser Steamship Company in the program of the 1942 Pro-Bowl Classic between the Washington Redskins and the National Pro League All-Stars. Phil may have paused momentarily at the news of these developments, but his thoughts were more likely with family and timberlands. As to the latter, he acknowledged to Ralph Macartney that "the rumor seems to be pretty well spread that we are in a buying mood."

Gus Clapp was primarily responsible for handling the Timber Company's case in the renegotiation question. Although Phil was much concerned about the decision—after all, it would considerably affect the profits for the period—he was just as concerned that the Timber Company case be well presented. He owed it to the company, to those who had gone before and to those who would follow, that it be recognized as an honorable institution. Phil was proud of its record, and it seemed to him that they had every reason to take a positive approach, apologizing for nothing—certainly not for being good at their work. Thus he insisted that Gus open his presentation before the renegotiation committee with a summary of the history of the Weyerhaeuser Timber Company, a history Phil helped to prepare.

He also wanted the recent record made clear, that "WTC itself shipped in 1942 approximately 978,000,000 feet of lumber, compared with 939,000,000 in 1940 (its greatest previous shipment), an increase of 4%; and it produced approximately 942,000,000 feet, compared with 910,000,000 in 1941 (its greatest previous production) . . . this in spite of all the difficulties, lack of manpower, priorities for equipment, repairs, shipping facilities (loss of boats), etc." In short, it was an impressive performance, one deserving of recognition if not praise.

But renegotiation was simply one distraction, albeit a major one. Another, all too familiar, involved the activities of the Forest Service. The characters had changed with the appointment of Lyle Watts as chief, but as Phil noted in a memo to Clyde Martin, "It seems likely to me that he will be influenced by the palace gang and continue the administration ... very much as it has been under Earle Clapp." (Earle Clapp, no relation of the Timber Company Clapps, served as acting chief of the Forest Service from the death of Silcox in December 1939 until the appointment of Watts in January 1943.) The Forest Service seemed intent on increasing the attacks on the industry, Phil noting recent legislative efforts. Was it not time, he inquired of Martin, for the industry to begin a counteroffensive? He suggested a two-pronged attack, one calling attention "to the good things which the industry has done and is doing," and the other pointing out the short-comings and inefficiencies of the Forest Service itself. He recognized that the second effort would require a serious study, but he thought it would be worthwhile even if it turned out to be expensive. Few things were more exasperating than to have the Forest Service use tax dollars to campaign against the industry that paid plenty of taxes, to be lec-tured about mismanagement of timber when the Forest Service's own timberlands were suffering from an absence of intelligent manage-ment. Phil was convinced that the upper echelons of the Forest Service were far more interested in power than in trees. Clyde Martin agreed that the effort should be made.

One of the statements made by the new chief with which Phil con-curred had to do with the dangers of overstating the accomplishments of the lumber industry. In reference to the education program being put forward by the American Forest Products Industries, Watts had suggested that the materials distributed might "create a false sense of security by making it appear that the forest industries in general have adopted sound forest practices," and that people would therefore be doubly disappointed when they saw "how far short of these ideals present practices fall in the majority of operations." Would it not be well, Watts continued, to show the other side of the picture? "It seems to me you endanger the 'Tree Farm' program by propagating the idea that there is no need for concern about the Nation's timber supply." Phil acknowledged that such criticism seemed "entirely fair and to the point."

Less agreeable was a letter dated February 8, 1943, from an assist-ant secretary of the President's Committee on Fair Employment Prac-tice—War Manpower Commission. The letter noted a report from the U.S. Employment Service that, following a December 14 request for fallers, "you have discriminated against qualified persons referred to you by this agency on account of their race." It was further charged "that efforts of the United States Employment Service officials to ob-tain a change in your employment policy and practice were unsuc-cessful." There followed the inevitable list of instructions, seven in all, the last requiring submission of "monthly reports beginning February

15, indicating the number of Negroes employed, the number in employment at the skill levels (skilled, semi-skilled, and unskilled), the number in employment as Fallers, and similar statistics covering white workers." Phil was angry, more with the arrogance of the bureaucratic approach than with the suggestion of the problem. Indeed, he could well imagine that a black faller would find an unwelcome atmosphere in the logging crews of western Washington.

That situation was clearly recognized in the response by the officers of Local 5–36, IWA-CIO at Longview to the inquiry from Harry Morgan. It was noted that Article I, Section 4, of the International Constitution read: "No worker otherwise eligible to membership in this Union, shall be discriminated against or denied membership by reason of race, color, or religion." But the union leadership immediately admitted that there was likely to be something of a variance between the constitution and the practice: "for the record, we wish to state further that Local 5–36 . . . will in no way be responsible for any action of any individual or individuals as a result of the employment of negroes in the woods operation and particularly as to the said individual or individuals' attitude or conduct toward negroes in the operation because of personal reasons or prejudices." So much for "by reason of race, color, or religion."

In his reply to the letter from the President's Committee, Phil expressed surprise "at the tenor of your letter, as this company has never in all its history discriminated or authorized or permitted discrimination against anyone because of race or color, in the employment of labor or otherwise." He also noted that there had been few instances of employment of blacks in logging operations, "but those who have applied for such employment in our operations have been employed." He then listed the facts of their experiences, which were so few and so recent that he could do so in a single paragraph.

Not only could he discover no instances of company discrimination, he was unwilling to let the matter rest with a simple denial of guilt. He requested that he be furnished "immediately the name and address of each and every official who has attempted to obtain a change in our employment practice, that I may contact them without delay." And he asked, "Will you also please furnish me immediately the name and address of each and every person representing this company who was contacted by the officials you refer to in an attempt to obtain such a change." Two could play at the game of requesting information. In the final paragraph, Phil stated the company position and circumstances: "We are in need of timber fallers who have the requisite skill and experience, and we are not interested in their race or color, and, as above stated, we are and always have been willing to employ qualified negroes to such extent as will not interfere with production."

Exactly two weeks later Phil received his reply. "Under the circumstances," the letter read, "you are relieved of complying with the requests of this Committee that you take all of the specified affirmative steps to implement your obligations under Executive Order 8802, but in order to clear up any misunderstanding concerning your policy, you are requested to advise in writing . . . that you will employ persons solely on the basis of their qualifications and without regard to their race, creed, color, or national origin." Phil was sure that he had already done this, but he did it again. Someone had to have the last word, and he hadn't time to contest merely for that honor.

Concurrent with awaiting notification of the date for the renegotiation hearings in Washington, D.C., was receipt of information that the subject of Red Sea charter profits was to be investigated. Phil was uncertain how to proceed although he had earlier indicated to Bill Peabody that there was "justice in the proposal that some restitution be made voluntarily." That had not been done, Peabody not wishing to act alone. And now, as Phil saw it, "you find yourself a part of the industry which is no doubt about to be castigated in a Congressional hearing." Phil didn't trust the industry, convinced that there was much about it that would not easily withstand public disclosure. "The least we can do," he advised, "is to keep ourselves with absolutely clean skirts and good records." There was no question that profits had been excessive in many instances. Phil later reported to Peabody of an article in a Seattle newspaper in which Mr. John J. Burns, general counsel for the American Merchant Marine Institute, had stated that operators had "no intention of acceding to the suggestion of Admiral Land, war shipping administrator, that some of the profits be returned." As Phil saw it, "I'll be surprised if that is the end of the matter."

For 1943 the profits for log and lumber operations were about equal to those of 1942, but profits for pulp, steamship, and timber sales had declined. Lumber production had dropped by 18 percent and shipments by 15.5 percent, "with continued inventory reductions." Lumber prices were up about 13 percent for fir and down 4 percent for pine. Average hourly earnings of log and lumber workers had increased some 21 percent. Snoqualmie Falls provided a good example. But while the total number of employees had fallen from 838 to 735, the total payroll had increased from the first quarter of 1942 to the first quarter of 1943 from $410,980.82 to $488,752.05.

Although some belittled the tree farm idea as a gimmick to describe what had long been going on, others expressed concern that the publicity given tree farming might tend to increase the prices of some lands to an artificially high level. The West Coast Lumbermen's Association had a booklet ready for publication on the West Coast tree farms, but Colonel Greeley had received a complaint from one of his committee that its publication would encourage speculation in second-growth lands. It was argued that "such a speculative movement would not benefit actual tree growing; its effects would likely be to handicap some of the more stable interests in the region that are seeking to extend and develop their tree farms along solid, permanent business lines." By letter, Colonel Greeley inquired about Phil's "personal judgment." The inquiry brought an interesting but not unexpected response: "It seems to me that the chief virtue in the booklet is that it will create a value in the eye of the reader for such lands. That is our purpose in publishing it. When such a value is created in the eyes of enough people, cutover lands will be respected and protected as a thing of value. As such value changes, of course, we must endure speculation. I have recognized that we were creating competition for ourselves in this matter, but I feel we have much more to gain than to lose."

The forty-third annual meeting of the Timber Company was called to order in the assembly room in the basement of the Tacoma Building on the morning of May 27. A local journalist reported the occasion:

Today a small group of shy, colorful gentlemen gather . . . to conduct the legal routine of one of the world's unique business enterprises. . . .

Camera shy, reporter shy, this group of gentlemen conduct a corporation on standards of ethics and far-seeing vision almost strange to world business as we know it today.

No corporation can boast of a directorate so ingrained and allied with the same business in their private lives as this one. Most large corporations boast of a directorate that knows little about making steel, ships, or running an oil refinery, and, ironically, seem proud of it.

Phil subsequently sent copies of the entire article to the directors, attaching a note which began, "I think you will enjoy the attached effusion. . . ."

At the meeting itself, Phil had been forced to endure a bit of effusion, this provided by Laird Bell. Following Phil's presentation of his report, Laird had stood to move that the report "be received and placed on file," but before doing so, he took the occasion to note the tenth anniversary of Phil's tenure in office. Laird had prepared carefully.

It is ten years ago that Mr. Philip Weyerhaeuser first presented an annual report to this gathering. It is an appropriate time to look back to see what that ten years has meant. We had in the years 1931 and 1932 lost the tidy sum of $3,000,000. Our mills were running three or four days a week or not at all. The camps were down, our ships were tied up in Lake Union, and the industry as a whole seemed flat on its back. It took an optimist to foresee that it would ever improve. At the end of the ten years we have now finished a year with $8,600,000 of profit after contributing practically twice that amount to the war effort in taxes.

But these are mere statistics. Phil has made more remarkable changes in his characteristic quiet and self-effacing way. Most of them we have hardly been conscious of and it is only by looking back that we can see how much progress has been made. I could mention many, but a few will illustrate my point.

Take reforestation first. Ten years ago any talk of better forest practices was a pain in the neck. We thought we simply could not afford to think about it. Quietly and steadily, however, changes have been wrought. Through the creation of the reforestation and land department, through the purchase of immature timber, through enhanced protection of the cutover lands and through improved cutting practices we have approached the total of a sustained operation. Tree farms have been established as a model to the industry and have quite swept the country.

Take the matter of public relations. The annual statements used to be a cold collection of figures. You all know the kind of report that you have been getting recently. The number of stockholders has multiplied about five times and they have been taken into the family. The case for the lumberman has been effectively stated through the movies, through speeches, and through the press. It is now a truism that "timber is a crop."

Another thing which I believe most dear to Phil's heart has been better utilization of our raw material. Development of pres-to-logs, the completion of the second pulp mill, the installation there of a hydraulic barker and giant chipper—an untried experiment on which Phil was willing to bet $750,000 and which has resulted in a 16% greater utilization of hemlock—development of plywood, and many such things have been a real contribution to the industry as well as to our own company. . . .

Of course Phil has not done all these things alone and singlehanded. The able men on his excellent staff have contributed tremendously, but I think those of us who are familiar with many different kinds of businesses are always impressed with the way the personality and purpose of the chief executive in a concern reaches down to the lowest office boy. Credit is due to many men but primarily to Phil.

One who commented on the event was Ed Davis. He wrote Phil for a couple of reasons following his visit with his son Fred to Tacoma. It had been the first chance for sixteen-year-old Fred Davis to meet Phil's children, and Ed expressed the hope that "all the boys in the fourth generation will become actively interested in the business and will get along as well with one another as we have in the third generation." Concerning the tribute to Phil by Laird Bell, Ed observed, "this was ably done and very much deserved."

Phil responded promptly, bringing Ed up to date. Summer studies were increasingly popular, given expected manpower needs, and George had returned to school. Flip was awaiting orders to go into the Marines on July 1, and Wizzie was at camp, so, as Phil predicted, "there will be a great hush around our diggings." Phil soon addressed a letter of thanks to Paul Cruikshank at Taft School, noting that Flip had "had a wonderful experience at Taft, which we all prize very highly." He also reported that Flip had been ordered to the University of Washington to continue his education. As to what Flip's absence from Taft might mean, Phil could only look forward "to a great dearth of news from George, who has not yet learned to correspond." Phil obviously wished that George had not taken after his father in that regard.

By the end of July, Dwight Orr and Gus Clapp had returned from Washington, D.C., with the results of the renegotiation deliberations. Subsequently Phil informed the directors that "the total dollar business of the Company had grown to such a point that . . . we were enjoying 'an accelerated war business'; that this acceleration exceeded the total amount of our business subject to renegotiation; that while we had been of great service in numerous respects, we should not expect more than a fraction of our normal profits on such business; therefore, $2,200,000 (out of our total $4,063,000 profit before taxes on subject business) were, in the opinion of the Panel, excessive." The Executive Committee had approved compliance with the findings, although Phil could express no pleasure in the thing. He noted that the company had spent some $30,000 in providing information to the panel, and "For six months a larger percentage of executive time has been diverted from fruitful pursuits to the same end." He concluded, "Still we sweat to produce what the Government needs; no doubt you'll want us to continue."

The renegotiation decision was disappointing although hardly unexpected. The company might have been treated better, but there was no feeling of unfairness in the deliberations. Phil had far less patience with all the committees and agencies that were studying obvious problems without any real possibility of providing reasonable solutions. His impatience got the best of him in responding to a note from Fred K. telling of the appointment of a Logging, Lumber and Timber and Related Products Industry Committee scheduled to meet in New York on August 30 "to investigate conditions in the industry and to make recommendations for increasing the minimum wage rate that is to be paid employees, subject to the Fair Labor Standards Act." Fred expressed concern that there had been only one representative from the Northwest, and Phil expressed amazement that "anyone with anything substantial to do" could possibly be interested "in a dead duck like consideration of raising the minimum above 40¢ an hour." As he saw the situation, once again manpower was being diverted from actual needs: "24 men required to travel to New York City and talk about such a subject while Rome burns!" He thought they could put those twenty-four on the green chain at Longview and "point with pride to more accomplishment."

In the meantime, Phil was keeping active in the timberlands purchase arena. Large accessions had been made in western Oregon, and at the end of August he reported a verbal agreement to purchase the Coos Bay Logging Company for $700,000. He noted that while there had been talk about keeping the matter secret, he had decided "we have more to gain by telling the community that the purchase makes possible and indicates the probability our timber, or most of it, will be manufactured on Coos Bay."

Back in July an Army procurement officer had visited Phil in his Tacoma office, indicating a need for three hundred or so officers from civilian life, one hundred of whom would be commissioned as lieutenant colonels to serve on renegotiation panels. That may not have interested Phil, but there was surely going to be a need for those familiar with building materials to serve in a world so utterly destroyed. He had obviously been giving the matter considerable thought before writing a personal letter to Uncle Fred on August 21. He began by noting:

Fully three fourths of my college classmates have sharply altered their ways of life during the war to do such jobs as they could find. Many, perhaps most of them, found their businesses disrupted, or had the wanderlust, etc. Still, realization of what they have done provokes me to a little self-analysis. I ask myself if I am hiding behind the knowledge that our family corporate enterprises are doing a war job of large proportions as an excuse for not disturbing my chosen way of life.

He then indicated that he had been approached by Army Procurement regarding the possibility of being commissioned for the purpose of aiding in reconstruction of occupied countries:

Should I do this and be accepted, it would, of course, require resignation from my W.T. Co. job. While, at first blush, it seemed to me that the whole effort would collapse without me, I have since imagined your spending a considerable amount of time in my office in Tacoma with both accomplishment and pleasure. I can see Ingram and Raught and the rest of this splendid group really doing very well without me. . . .

The prospect of leaving family and security for an unknown responsibility for which I may not be fitted, is not alluring. Nevertheless, I can see how the change might benefit all involved. A break in routine and the experience of again being entirely on my own without the backing of power from family and Company organization would be good for me.

He closed by observing that there were many questions to answer, "with Helen especially," but "something urges me to explore this idea, so I have put my thoughts on paper."

F.E. wrote that he was not surprised by Phil's letter and could understand much of what was expressed. At the same time, it seemed to the uncle that his nephew had contributed his share: "you were in the last war, your oldest son, barely 18, is now in the service, and in your capacity as managing executive of the largest organization in the lumber industry you have done everything in your power to supply the government with a critical material." Phil, however, knew that he had only been in uniform in 1918, not in the war, and that his own contributions as lumber executive might well be managed by others. F.E. would have none of the argument that others could manage as well as Phil:

I know none other in the lumber business so well qualified as you are to lead the lumber industry at a time that probably will be more critical than the present.

Also, looking into the future, you haven't a peer in the lumber fraternity, in the field of maintaining the productivity of our forests. You have vision, courage, and determination, and enjoy the full confidence of all your associates. The continuity of your program should not be broken.

Uncle Fred closed assuring Phil that he could produce evidence in support of what he had said, but that would make it an unnecessarily long letter. He did make a final request that Phil not commit himself until he had discussed the matter with him.

Fred K. had received a copy of Phil's letter to F.E. and carried it around in his pocket waiting for an opportunity to respond. He finally did so from the Barclay Hotel in New York. Fred was also uncertain that Phil could be replaced, admitting that "FEW would enjoy going out to Tacoma and getting away from RMW but I cannot help wondering what effect he would have on an organization." Anyway, he knew that F.E. had written a strong letter urging Phil to stay in place, and that "that point of view certainly represents the Family point of view *100% including my own!*"

There is no doubt that Fred K. understood Phil's reasons for being interested in serving, for, as he said, their thoughts were much the same:

You probably feel restless and unhappy being at home in comfort while many men are fighting and dying. So do I.

Then it is sort of trying working for a lot of people like the W. Family, fine as they are! Personal frictions and jealousies seem to be unending. Any attempt to please relatives let alone other stockholders just gets too burdensome. It would be sort of a relief to walk off the job and let the Uncles run it. . . .

And then there is the feeling that you are greatly favored by the opportunity of working for the W companies, and after all could you make a go of it on your own where no favoritism enters in? It would be fun to try! Perhaps you have other ideas or feelings that make you consider the move. Anyway, the above thoughts have certainly occurred to me many times.

Fred K. reminded Phil that he was too old to do any "real fighting," and that if he was truly interested in helping rebuild Europe and Asia, he would probably contribute more in Tacoma than at some clerical job in the Army. Although business hadn't been much fun of late, Fred was confident that conditions would improve, "And nothing would thrill me more than working with you and Ed D. & GFJ in trying to make the most of these opportunities." He too hoped Phil would do nothing until they had talked.

Phil was probably surprised by the unsolicited note he received on an interoffice memo from Nick Genta, his secretary. Nick was hardly one to type letters without paying attention to their contents, and in this instance he was unable to keep his thoughts to himself. Thus he wrote, "Your problem is personal, but having been with you several years may I say this: I believe in you so strongly that, if you wanted, I'd be willing to serve with you anywhere." But Nick's advice was not unlike that of F.E. or Fred K.: "Men like you are needed in the sphere of their greatest possible contribution to the winning of the war." Nick concluded, "If it is the fear of not serving which drives you, it is because of your modesty."

Ed Davis, of course, also heard of Phil's temptations to put on the uniform, and while he expressed his sympathy, he hoped Phil would not "be sold on the idea that you should head up the reconstruction of Sicily or Italy." And Ed was doubtless correct in stating, "From what I have observed I think you would be crazy after about six months of Government red tape."

On September 18, ceremonies were held at Longview on the occasion of the presentation of the Army-Navy "E" Award for production excellence to that branch, the first such award received by a lumber manufacturing plant. There was the usual pomp and circumstance, Phil informing the directors that the affair was "simple and impressive." To one who had written a letter of congratulations, Phil was quick to point out that while "the boys there have done a good job and everything about it is fine, I recognize that there is so much mystery and baloney behind such an award that it takes off much of the edge." Still the ceremony "was inspiring and could not help but benefit all those within reach." The other news of importance had to do with the recent purchase of Northern Pacific timber in the vicinity of Spirit Lake and Mount St. Helens, this in the Longview region. The price was $357,000 or an estimated rate of three dollars a thousand for all species.

Other ceremonies had been held at Klamath Falls, which had been recognized as the first pine tree farm. Phil said a few words, and a portion of his short message had impressed Bob Slaughter, then the president of the Central Lumber Company of Stillwater, Minnesota. Slaughter thought that the next to the last paragraph of Phil's "address" could well be "the slogan for all industrial concerns to adopt. This Company's present and post-Victory policies are entirely predicated upon a belief in a return of endurable taxes and a degree of business freedom commensurate with the responsibilities that we are willing to assume." Phil had thanked his friend for writing "a word of encouragement about a reluctantly delivered speech."

On Christmas Eve day, Phil addressed the last letter of 1943 to the Timber Company directors. The news was varied. The summary for November indicated that lumber shipments were 129 million feet less than the previous year, but the rate of production was greater. There was some hope that legislation under consideration might provide some relief in the excess-profits-tax rates. Disappointment involved the joint cruise of the Long-Bell timber purchase at Klamath Falls, which showed only 235 million board feet instead of the 350 million expected. As Phil observed, "The large refund will not erase our disappointment." They had just received notice that the Willapa Harbor Lumber Mills was to receive the Army-Navy "E" Award; the honor was moving around. And under separate cover Phil sent along a calendar put out by the editor of the Montesano paper for the local Chevrolet dealer. "That community," he said, "is very conscious of the Clemons Tree Farm. Wishing you a Merry Christmas. . . ."

Christmas saw all the children at home, and the occasion was made special by the announcement of Ann's engagement to Private Jack Pascoe, a long-time friend and neighbor from Tacoma and recent graduate of Yale. Phil reported to Uncle Rudolph, "Helen and I are very happy about it."

CHAPTER 12

Postwar Planning

Phil seemed to have regained his enthusiasm for the task at hand. Perhaps the war news had encouraged him to think more about postwar plans and less about not being in uniform. With Russian troops moving doggedly westward, with American troops moving doggedly northward in Italy, with the increasing air offensive over German skies, and with successful landings on New Guinea and other South Pacific islands, it was clear that the winds of war were changing as 1943 gave way to a new year.

Evidence of Phil's reviving spirit was his reference to a letter from Fred K. that contained numerous suggestions for improving procedures in manufacturing by working closely with the General Timber Service Product Development Department. Fred recommended periodic meetings of mill representatives with the Product Development Committee. Phil replied that while that might seem reasonable, it did make for a "lot of meetings." Fred had also suggested that the Timber Company delegate "to one man the responsibility for making all decisions regarding commercializing of developments." To this Phil had a simple question: "What the h—— are we here for? Why have an engineer, a general manager, plant managers, officers, executive committee, directors, etc., if it's as easy as that?" If Fred K. was "insinuating that the reason more developments haven't taken place is because Weyerhaeuser Timber can't make up its mind," Phil wanted it understood, "tain't so!" He suggested that perhaps his brother should make a New Year's resolution: "Write no letters during the holidays."

Despite his apparent disagreement, Phil passed along Fred's concern to Charlie Ingram, and Charlie attempted to put matters right without agreeing to the need for organizational and procedural change. He did acknowledge that the fir mills probably had not shown the interest in the development program that it deserved, but he ascribed this largely to the wartime circumstances. It was now time to look ahead to post-war conditions. Charlie attempted to assure Fred K. that any product that appeared likely to yield a profit would be welcomed, and he offered as examples the recent manufacture of fabricated trusses, pontoon bridges, fence posts, and pallets. Obviously "present circumstances undoubtedly have largely influenced such action," but Charlie said it didn't follow that "the unused suggestions do not have merit and may be taken up under different market conditions."

Ingram repeated Phil's oft-stated maxim: The first requirement is a demonstration that there is a demand for the product. In Charlie's words, we "are not seeking novelties or gadgets" to increase sales. Not only should the Sales Company offer a "studied opinion of the probable volume they can sell . . . but their recommendation should be backed by sufficient study to constitute a conviction." Fred's suggestion that one person assume responsibility for production decisions flew in the face of the Timber Company's organizational practices. Charlie indicated that he would not want to assume such a responsibility, although he would be willing to serve on a committee. The committee could review the suggestions, and "If any mill manager sees merit in a suggestion, it will be pushed, and this office will encourage and assist wherever possible."

But if there was need to think ahead to a postwar world, the war continued to intervene in all manner of ways. Laird Bell was called to Washington and informed that he had been selected to serve as chairman of the Navy Price Adjustment Board for six months beginning February 1. This required that he take a leave of absence from his duties on the executive committees of the Weyerhaeuser Timber Company and Potlatch Forests. Laird was a little apologetic in his letter to Phil announcing this appointment: "I think I have detected a certain lack of enthusiasm on your part for renegotiation," he wrote. "Some time before I disappear into the fog of Washington I should like to write you further in justification of my activities, but I must get the disagreeable jobs done first." There was no need to justify his decision to Phil. As Phil would observe some three months later, "I still admire you for taking it on," admitting that "the general idea of being willing to break your routine and do something for the general good appeals to me tremendously."

The level of earnings continued to encourage investment opportunities. Fred K. favored a wider consideration of opportunities, but generally Phil was reluctant to follow such leads. He explained his reasoning simply: "The thing . . . which always troubles me is how to keep from spreading our management effort so far that we dilute its effectiveness." Anyway there were plenty of opportunities that built on their present strengths:

Many attractive investments from the point of view of earnings can be turned up, but unless they fit into our total picture I try to discount them sharply, in favor of investments which fit in from a geographical point of view, from a sales point of view, or from the point of view of supplementing our line or using more of the raw material we now waste. If you add up investments in money and resultant management effort following these lines, you can see a future so huge that I wonder if we should go outside of those limitations.

That may have seemed too conservative for many who studied the Weyerhaeuser Timber Company and its leadership, but in an industry as competitive as the lumber industry, where keeping costs to a minimum was the essence of successful management, focusing efforts was imperative. Thus Phil countenanced caution, suggesting that they limit their investments, their diversification, to those areas in which they already had skills and experience. Their responsibility seemed clear to him: do even better the job they knew best.

One such area of concern was the management of timberlands and cutover. Clyde Martin had invited Phil to attend the April 7 meeting of the Puget Sound group of the Society of American Foresters, an invitation that Phil was forced to decline. He did, however, ask Clyde to carry a couple of questions along for discussion. First, what recommendations as to a justifiable cut for the Weyerhaeuser Everett mill would the group make, given the Weyerhaeuser holdings, and for the "intermingled timberlands, the production of which we are justified in assuming will be available with ours"? The second question had to do with the costs of fire protection in the cutovers, Phil noting that in the Weyerhaeuser tree farm areas, "where our ownership has been relatively heavy," the company expected to assume the costs of protection. But in other areas, they could not assume the total burden—a burden that would be bearable only if the costs were spread out over all the areas receiving protection. "An answer to this puzzle would result in many scattered areas getting added protection, and ensure the as yet unproven future of existing tree farms."

As interesting and complex as managing timber was, it was no more so than managing people. In viewing the Weyerhaeuser Company and other large corporations of today, it is difficult to imagine the intimacy of the Weyerhaeuser Timber Company of four decades earlier. It was, to a considerable extent, a first-name organization. Phil's total lack of pretension set the tone. Although he was basically shy, in management terms that simply meant that he led more naturally by example than by authority. This did not mean that he was unable to make decisions;

but that his manner—his style—was one of respect and cooperation. He may have been intolerant of sloth or silliness, but he was quite willing to listen to thoughtful opinions with which he disagreed. It was not surprising that his colleagues were intensely loyal to him, and, through him, to the organization. Phil would have been quite uncomfortable analyzing such relationships, but he recognized their importance. A case in point was the birthday celebration of the senior staff employee, J. R. Peetz, on April 4. Mr. Peetz had come to Tacoma in 1902 to become the third member of the office staff of George S. Long. In 1944 Peetz was eighty years old, and it seemed an appropriate occasion to combine recognition of that event with an announcement of plans for a Twenty-Year Club. This was done at a March 31 dinner and George S. Long, Jr., was given the assignment of coming up with a plan by which continuing recognition would be accorded those who had reached their twentieth year of service with the company. The club has functioned ever since.

Phil had been unable to attend the regional Society of American Foresters meeting because he had scheduled a tour of the newly acquired properties in western Oregon in the Coos Bay area. He spent a week there, visiting the facilities, the communities, local officials, and the Timber Company's representative, Robert P. Conklin. After returning to Tacoma, Phil wrote to Conklin, "to thank you and your wife for your hospitality and congratulate you upon achieving an apparent place in the community and knowledge of the district and its problems in such a short time." Then he recalled when he had gone to Lewiston, Idaho, "to get acquainted with the community in advance of building the mill and operating there, and, in a sense, I could step back into those days in your shoes." He also knew that it was not an easy job to represent a large corporation in a small town.

As a possible guide to future dealings, Phil sent along a copy of a letter from a Liverpool law firm written in 1869 to three young partners in San Francisco. The letter amounted to a set of instructions. Included in those instructions was the recognition that those in Liverpool were undoubtedly ignorant of important local circumstances:

In all such circumstances, it is our express request, that you act upon the orders, as you think they would have been framed, had your correspondents obtained all the additional information you possess. While it is thus thought needful to allude to the responsibilities involved to ourselves and others, pecuniarily, in your business acts, we must draw your attention, far more gravely to the importance we attach to your sustaining the name and honor of your firm in every undertaking in which you engage. Every engagement must be uprightly fulfilled by you, and the rights both of neighbors and constituents strictly defined and faithfully guarded by you. In your dealings you will permit no dereliction of right principle to pass unnoticed either in yourselves or others, and carry out fearlessly, under all circumstances, the golden rule: "Do to others, as you would be done by."

As Phil had indicated in noting the inclusion of the old letter, "I think you'll enjoy its simplicity and direction at the points involved."

Phil had found his visit to Oregon interesting and satisfying. In a note to Laird Bell, he remarked on the beauty of Oregon "at this time of year, with the new lambs on the greensward, fruit blossoms, and all that go with them." He expressed the hope that in and around his Navy service, Laird might find time to come west for the annual meeting. The formal affairs had been scheduled to begin on Monday, May 22, with the Sales Company's annual meeting and to end that Friday with a visit by the Timber Company directors and interested shareholders to Willapa Harbor. The following week Phil made plans to take F.E., Horace Irvine, Bill Peabody, and Fred K. on an Oregon trek including a visit to Coos Bay, prior to several days of fishing on the McKenzie River.

Phil and Helen so enjoyed life at their American Lake home that they added on to provide all the comforts and convenience of their house at 417 North E Street, and decided to live "in the country" year round. But there were other important family developments. Ann and Jack Pascoe were married in September. In mid-October, George was inducted into the Navy. This should have passed with no particular notice, but where it was noted, it was also mentioned that this was George Hunt Weyerhaeuser, "famous kidnap victim of nearly a decade ago," none of which made entry into the Navy any easier.

To Phil it must have seemed a little strange to have two boys in the service and be required to think and plan for the postwar world. But plans would not wait. In response to one inquiry, Phil observed that while "our organization is optimistic about the lumber business in the first three postwar years," expecting to resume prewar volumes of business at the fir mills, it seemed likely that the district as a whole would "show some restriction of volume below that of '39 through '41." In part, the reason for such efforts was "to stabilize many units on a sustained-yield basis, which spells the end of operations for those unable now to find adequate sources of timber."

Finding adequate sources of timber continued to occupy Phil's attention. On October 9, he reported to F.E. that he had just received "a hurry up call from Ralph Macartney and Hugh [Campbell] about the Gerhardt timber, which we can now buy for $136,000 or $6.85 a thousand according to our cruise." For years they had been trying to buy it, offering first $75,000 and later $100,000. It was completely surrounded by Weyerhaeuser Klamath Falls ownership, "and since the boys all feel that this is the best we can do, I told them to go ahead and wind up the deal if possible, without my previously having gotten authority from the Executive Committee." Uncle Fred must have found Phil a good deal like his grandfather when it came to buying timber, and he could only hope that he was as good a judge.

Occasionally Phil still worried that they were not getting the sort of commitment or cooperation, one or the other if not both, down the line when it came to logging practices. What should have been the policy too often seemed like so much window-dressing. The wartime demands had, of course, required a good deal of overcutting in certain areas; one simply couldn't balance future plans against present needs in those circumstances, even if the logs went to competing sawmills. There were, however, unnecessary acts. Colonel Greeley had written to Phil on October 18, enclosing a report on the condition of some Weyerhaeuser cutovers. Phil was more than a little disturbed. Seldom did he address Charlie Ingram as he did in the covering note to Greeley's letter: "This repeats the information hurled at us periodically by our own Forestry Department, and I wonder if this office is placing the emphasis which it should upon providing seed sources through the various means at hand?" To emphasize his concern, Phil noted that if the forestry laws that had been proposed in either of the last two legislatures had been passed, the company would have been in violation of the law. "The war has caused many shortcuts—this, I suppose, among them—but I write to inquire if we are pursuing the right policy, all things considered?" Charlie knew when Phil was unhappy, and this was clearly one of those occasions. And when Phil was unhappy, so was he—and so would be those directly involved.

There was some good news. Ed Davis had come west in mid-October, and a week had been spent in discussing the development program. As Phil reported to the directors, this was "always hard work, but interesting and encouraging." Log supply problems continued to frustrate operations of Washington Veneer. It had been hoped that the timber purchased from the Sound Timber Company would keep it supplied with logs, but as Phil described it, thus far that operation had produced "on a very slow bell." Nonetheless, the Veneer Company was showing some handsome profits, and "a new item in the line INDERON [a pheno-impregnated paper-clad plywood]" showed special promise. The Executive Committee approved the construction of a new barker and chipper for the Longview mill at an estimated cost of $800,000, and permission was subsequently secured from the War Production Board.

When the Executive Committee met in Tacoma October 27, they faced a long list of proposals, most involving postwar capital requirements. Phil had based his estimate of needs on the probable end of the war in Europe within the year, and he was viewing the Timber Company in terms of a postwar 1945–49 period. He offered two reasons for considering the list of proposed projects: first, "We should test the adequacy of our reserves"; second, "we should get as clear a picture as possible of how we can discharge our postwar job responsibility to the 1,600 employees now in the military service, to the communities in which we operate, and to those communities in which we own large blocks of timber which are now undeveloped and withheld from development by others." His list included nineteen items and involved a capital commitment of nearly $50 million.

The first item was first for good reason: "We have for years found it expedient to purchase timber intermingled or near our operations to lengthen the life of those operations and to create new ones where our ownership gave promise of so blocking as to make it possible. Timber purchases in the years 1940–44 (with 1944, of course, estimated) have averaged a little over $2,500,000 a year. I assume that the need will continue at the same rate, or $12,500,000 for the period."

The next sixteen items ranged from an estimated $800,000 for renegotiation refunds for the years 1943 and 1944 to $2 million for inventory replacements of war-depleted stocks. But most of the items had to do with new equipment and construction at the various plants, much of which had been delayed because the War Production Board had refused to approve it. An estimated $7 million was indicated for the development of operations at Coos Bay, and Phil also pointed out the need to build new plants for the Willapa Harbor Lumber Mills "to cut hemlock lumber and reduce low-grade and side cut to chips, for marketing to our own pulp plants at Everett or Longview or for sale to other pulp manufacturers." Another special item involved the results of development work. Phil believed that these efforts indicated need for a plywood plant at Longview. He also thought "a hardboard plant somewhere will be a waste-user and justified," and a bark utilization plant and "a paperboard plant to use low-grade fibres may be needed."

Phil concluded his report by noting that the postwar requirements called for nearly $30 million of construction, which "will provide thousands of jobs at the building sites over and above the jobs involved in the machinery and equipment purchases." And, as expected, although there was no doubt in his mind concerning the legitimacy of his statement of needs, he closed by noting that "business conditions" would determine what could be managed.

The committee approved the report on capitalization with the understanding that it would be presented to the shareholders at the next annual meeting. Phil had also proposed that $250,000 be budgeted for the development program for 1945, a proposal to which, as he reported to an absent F.E., "no objection was raised." He also outlined the application recently made to the War Production Board for a defective-log pilot plant, with an estimated cost of $147,000. But even in Uncle Fred's absence, the committee was unable to reach a decision on a pension program, Phil admitting, "It was apparent at this late date that no pension plan could be approved for this year's consummation."

For all the planning ahead, there were occasions that permitted a backward glance or two. F.E. was busily putting together what he called "The Record," a collection of stories, reflections, and letters pertaining to the life and accomplishments of Frederick Weyerhaeuser. A forty-five-year-old Phil was beginning to admit an interest in such things, and in the fall of 1944 he and his uncle corresponded concerning the history of timber ownership of the company. F.E. had indicated that on May 31, 1914, the Timber Company had over 1.5 million acres, comprising an estimated 34.3 billion feet of timber. Phil added the subsequent purchases, which brought the totals as of December 31, 1943, to 2.6 million acres and 99 billion feet. But given timber sales and logging operations, they had liquidated 1.3 million acres of 58.6 billion feet, so that in fact the December 31, 1943, inventory of Timber Company acres and timber amounted to 2.1 million acres of 40 billion feet. As both Phil and F.E. understood, the estimates of the number of feet were very approximate. In the early years the definitions of merchantable timber were far more stringent; hemlock, for example, seldom was included in the totals. Even later estimates were given to large overruns. Indeed, Phil noted, "as I write, I have a latest cruise figure before me, giving the total timber at December 31, 1943, as 44,101,000 M feet," and he noted that "probably the total recovered will exceed the book figures." Still he found it all interesting, particularly the 58 billion liquidation figure, which he determined corresponded to the amount of timber originally purchased from the Northern Pacific in 1900 (original purchase 900,000 acres, plus subsequent purchase of 397,000 acres), estimated "by multiplying 1,300,000 acres by 45M feet an acre." As he pointed out to F.E., "in other words, we have released the freight equivalent of the N.P. purchase in 43 years."

Admitting to an interest in history was perhaps not unrelated to Phil's increasing interest in religion. Both satisfied a need. In the matter of church involvement, Phil and Helen had gradually transferred their allegiance from the Immanuel Presbyterian in Tacoma to the Little Church on the Prairie in suburban Lakewood, the latter much more convenient to their American Lake home. The Little Church was appropriately named, and as it grew, modestly, there were more than enough opportunities to contribute. Phil, in particular, took increasing pleasure in serving in various capacities, from personally designing benches for the sanctuary to membership on the church board.

Less enjoyable for Phil were the renegotiation hearings. These took place in early November and, as he indicated to F.E., had not been particularly successful from a company consideration. Some $31 million worth of business was determined to be subject to renegotiation, and "the margin of profit realized was slightly over 15% and the margin of profit allowed was 10%, which resulted in a net refund, after taxes, of $345,000." Nevertheless, the process had been respectfully managed. The Army's chief negotiator, Lieutenant Colonel Carl M. Sciple, addressed a letter to Phil on November 23, 1944, noting, "It was a pleasure to see you and your associates recently in Seattle, although I am sure that the *occasion* was not, from your viewpoint, the happiest that might have been imagined." Phil responded, thanking the colonel for his consideration, adding, "We have the greatest respect for the way in which you are doing an unpleasant job." Then in a comment that was typically Phil, he observed, "Somehow or other, one of two things must be so—either we are in a politically indefensible position, or we fail properly to portray our needs." But, as was the case with the election, even bad news could clear the air. At least they knew where they stood.

News from the battle fronts was generally good. After three full years of war, American troops were back in the Philippines, and what became known as the Battle of the Bulge had been costly but, as it turned out, more so to the Germans. Soon the advance toward the Rhine resumed. The Weyerhaeuser Steamship Company had its own scoreboard noting losses. A total of three ships had been sunk in 1942 and another damaged. In 1943 no ships were lost, although two were torpedoed. And on December 10, 1944, the SS *William S. Ladd*, one of the Liberty ships assigned to the company for operation, was sunk off Leyte in the Philippines.

In naval news of a decidedly less significant sort, George received orders to proceed from San Diego to Chicago for a month of preliminary training for radio technician's school at Wright Junior College. Since Phil planned to go east later in January, he hoped to visit George along the way. But before he was able to do so, Laird Bell managed to make connections with George in Chicago, reporting the event and the pleasure that it occasioned. He noted, "It is a pity that parents can't more often see their children when they are on their own."

As the figures for the year 1944 were being assembled and digested, plans went forward for the Executive Committee meetings to be held at Everett, Tacoma, and Longview the week of February 26. Previously, in St. Paul, the committee had finally given approval to a retirement plan, and specialists had been retained to develop the specifics and ensure that they would be approved by the Treasury Department. As Phil indicated to the directors in mid-February, he expected that a pension plan would be inaugurated in the course of the year. Two additional questions of significance and sensitivity involved the future of General Timber Service and of Allied Building Credits. Phil believed that the one should be dissolved and the other either sold or liquidated, but since family members were much involved in both, the decisions were neither as clear nor as easily made as they might otherwise have been.

F.E. notified Phil of his intentions to be present at this Executive Committee meeting, although the manner of his arrival would create a good deal of excitement. Indicating that Horace Irvine and perhaps Laird Bell would be accompanying him, Uncle Fred said their "present plan is to get a business car from the Great Northern in order to be very sure that Horace will have the kind of food he needs on this trip." He further thought that they might be able to hold the car over for the night spent in Everett, suspecting that "the Monte Cristo Hotel is no more attractive than it used to be." Within months, F.E. would regret having used a private car.

In addition to the usual reports and discussions, there were a number of personnel matters called to the attention of the Executive Committee. George S. Long, Jr., was recovering from surgery; Minot Davis was taking a rest because of high blood pressure; Rod Olzendam was resigning as of March 1 to accept a position on the editorial staff of *Reader's Digest*; there was dissatisfaction with Ed Westman's performance at Washington Veneer; and there was consideration regarding the possible move of Dave Weyerhaeuser from the Tacoma staff to Eugene. "As I see it," Phil forewarned, "we have rather important changes to make involving six replacements and possibly three new jobs." The meeting seemed to go well, but the fallout would be bothersome.

In mid-February Phil had had an interesting exchange with Rex Black, new vice-president for public relations with the Sales Company. Rex had apparently said something to the effect that the Timber Company forestry results "were perhaps no worse but certainly no better than the average of the fir industry." Phil had to believe that Rex's opinion was uninformed. Thus he wrote to John Wahl, the logging superintendent at Vail, suggesting that they try to get Mr. Black into the woods in the course of his next trip west. "Perhaps we can have a break in the weather and you can work on him," Phil suggested to John. In late March, Rex did come west, did visit the Vail operation, and, with some prodding from Phil, did apologize for his earlier statement. "I learned that John Wahl is very definitely interested in adjusting his logging operations in the future so natural reforestation will

Phil and his associates, shortly after his arrival in Tacoma in 1933. From left to right: Rod Titcomb, general manager of the Weyerhaeuser Timber Company; Bill Peabody, manager of the Everett branch; F. S. Bell, president; Phil Weyerhaeuser, executive vice president; W. L. (Bill) McCormick, secretary; John Philip and F. E. Weyerhaeuser, directors.

(*Above*) Helen Weyerhaeuser enjoying a cruise aboard Ed and Anna Hayes's boat, 1936. One suspects that Phil is the object of her attention and amusement; (*below*) Helen and her "boys," Flip, Phil, and George, at the American Lake home.

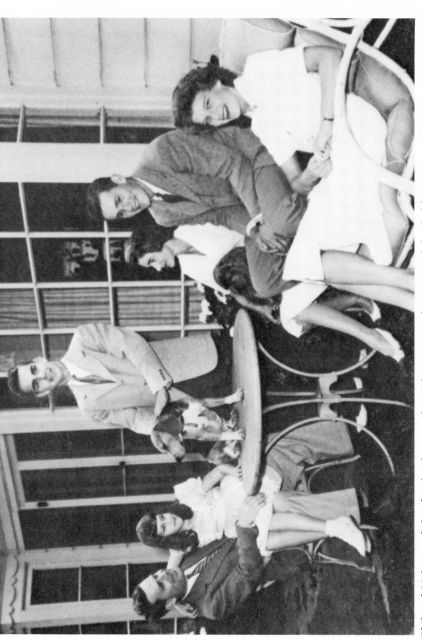

Phil and Helen used this family photo as their Christmas card in 1944. Phil is holding Wizzie, George is standing, and then, left to right, Helen, Flip, and Ann.

Phil and Dave Winton visiting a Swedish mill in the summer of 1939.

In front of the company plane, ca. 1944. From left to right: Phil, pilot Nappy Wildhaber, Elizabeth (Bette) Davis, Frederick W. (Eddie) Davis, and Fred K.

Wells Gilbert has the attention of Minot Davis (seated in truck bed), but Phil has apparently heard that one before.

Dinner gatherings were a regular item, and the occasion and the food were often indifferent. Good company saved many such evenings. In this exchange, Phil, Harry Morgan, Sr., Charlie Ingram, and Al Raught make the most of a pause in the program.

Ray Saberson of the Weyerhaeuser Sales Company was a gifted raconteur. Here he demonstrates his skill, to the obvious pleasure of Laird Bell, Phil, and Charlie Ingram, at a November 14, 1949, dinner.

Time for lunch in the Oregon woods. That's Wells Gilbert watching Phil at a respectful distance.

Phil and Fred K., relaxed and happy together in the woods in the summer of 1946. The photo was snapped by Charlie Ingram and contributed by his daughter, Marion Baldwin.

Phil and Owen R. Cheatham, president of the Georgia Hardwood Lumber Company (soon to be Georgia-Pacific), both looking pleased at the sale of Weyerhaeuser stock in the Washington Veneer Company, in 1948. George S. Long, Jr., looks on in person and Frederick Weyerhaeuser does so in portrait.

All of the legal questions were not amusing, but lawyers Gus Clapp and Laird Bell are pleasantly relaxed in this instance.

Clyde Martin inspects the leader on a young Douglas fir. This tells the story—
the forester and a growing tree.

Coos Bay (Oregon) manager Art Karlen hosting the Weyerhaeuser brass in 1950. First row, from left: John Wahl, Fred K., Phil, Charlie Ingram, John S. Abel; second row: Dave Weyerhaeuser, Joe Nolan, Bob Douglas, Howard Morgan, Ed Hayes, Clark Heritage, Laird Bell, Karlen, and Harry E. Morgan.

Phil speaking at the tenth anniversary ceremony of the dedication of the Clemons Tree Farm in 1951.

Chapin Collins, Mrs. C. H. Clemons, Phil, and Col. William B. Greeley at the Clemons Tree Farm anniversary, 1951.

The platform party at the tenth anniversary ceremony of the Clemons Tree Farm. Phil Weyerhaeuser is almost conspicuous by his absence from the front row. Those chairs belong (left to right) to Col. W. B. Greeley, Governor Langlie, Governor McKay, Mrs. Clemons, and Stanley Horn. Second row: Phil, W. D. Hagenstein, Dr. Wilson Compton, Clyde S. Martin, Ben Allen, Stewart Holbrook, David Graham, Charlie Ingram, Dwight Merrill, and Robert Ramstad.

Weyerhaeuser family meeting, St. Paul, January 1954. The third generation—standing: Fritz Jewett, Carl Weyerhaeuser, Ed Davis, Phil; seated: Fred Weyerhaeuser, Fred K., Dave Weyerhaeuser.

Board of Directors, 1955. Seated clockwise: O. D. Fisher, C. Davis Weyerhaeuser, Norton Clapp, John Musser, F. K. Weyerhaeuser, Laird Bell, George S. Long, Jr., J. P. Weyerhaeuser, Jr., Edmund Cook, Edmund Hayes, Carleton Blunt, Chas. H. Ingram, Henry T. McKnight, F. W. Reimers.

As always, Phil has Helen's attention.

Phil and Helen, together aboard the *Wanigan*.

Phil looking at model of the Everett facility.

occur more rapidly," Rex wrote, adding, "Anything I may have said, indicating that Mr. Wahl was not interested in forestry, was a misstatement." He attributed his earlier impression to a couple of individuals, "outside the company, who told me, in their opinion, Weyerhaeuser was 'just about average.'" After observing operators at Vail and Longview, Rex indicated that "perhaps we should feel rather happy that we are 'average.'" He concluded by noting that the problem had less to do with the operations than with "our volume of talk . . . but perhaps that is the future worry of the *Reader's Digest*, not ours!"

On March 21 Phil reported to the directors that the 1944 net profits for the Timber Company and its wholly owned subsidiaries, before renegotiation, totaled $9.5 million, an increase of $1.1 million or 14 percent over 1943. It represented an all-time high. Other good news involved the effects of recent legislation that permitted "the treatment of the excess of market value over book basis of timber cut as a 'capital gain'" to be taxed at a 25 percent rate. That would mean a major portion of the increase in value from tree to product would be taxed at about half the rate of the usual taxes on profits. It also meant that the operations should make certain that the mills were charged market value for their sawlogs, because any saving or shaving at that end would result in higher taxes at the product end. But in one of the clearest examples of the sawmill mentality, "efficiency" continued to be measured as of old, and the cheaper the logs, the more favorable the figures appeared. Thus despite the saving in real dollars that would result from taxing logs as capital gains rather than lumber as profits, cheap logs continued to be delivered to Timber Company sawmills, producing more costly lumber than was necessary. It was a high price for statistical efficiency. It was a high price for decentralization and intermural competition.

In mid-March Phil attended an Operations Committee meeting of the Sales Company in Lewiston, a trip he always enjoyed. Bill Peabody was in attendance and announced that the War Shipping Administration had requisitioned the *Winona* for sale to Russia. Money from the sale would be placed in their construction reserve fund, it being assumed that if they were to continue the Steamship Company, new vessels would be required after the war. Four of the old fleet remained. Ed Davis was also at Lewiston and after returning to St. Paul, he wrote Phil, telling of his enjoyment in being "with you people in the West." He added, "as usual, am again impressed with the apparently easy way big things are accomplished in the W.T. Co." Cousin Ed then included something of a rare compliment: "I think you are a better executive and have better business judgment than any in your generation." Phil would reply, "can the soft soap."

No doubt of greater interest to Phil was the March 26 issue of the

Chicago Journal of Commerce, which included quotations from Laird Bell's recent commencement address at the University of Chicago. In essence, his remarks attacked the current thinking that spoke of a "matured economy." In Laird's words, "The theory of the matured economy is a defeatist doctrine, an alibi for tired old folks." He also attacked the attitude of "security," the belief that people were entitled to jobs, to job security, to a pension, and all the rest. "Security is the very basis of something static. It is the antithesis of progress," spoke Laird. And his third target was "planning," which he said was fine for the planners: "It may be exciting for the few—but it is deadening for the many." Laird Bell was a liberal but only to a point. Obviously he feared that that point was threatened.

The copy of the *Journal of Commerce* had been sent to Phil by F.E., who was, as Phil reported to Laird, "impressed by what you had to say, and surprised, I take it, to be in such complete agreement." Phil also agreed, observing, "It sounded like very good sense, put in a masterful way." Laird's response was interesting: "I find that altogether the wrong people agree with me, but I suspect the young have been impervious to my eloquence."

Occasionally Phil rebelled at requests for information from governmental agencies. One such instance occurred in the early months of 1945. A questionnaire had been sent to thousands of business firms, including supposedly all the larger companies, concerning "the probable level of capital expenditures in the period immediately after victory in Europe, and the financial requirements associated with them." Phil had ignored the original request, covered by a form letter from Jesse H. Jones, secretary of commerce. He also ignored the second letter from an undersecretary of commerce. A third request, dated March 26, which began "Sometime ago . . ." finally got a response. Phil's answer was an efficient expression:

From your letter of March 26, I suppose you do not realize the pleasure it gives one to ignore government requests for information once in a while.

We would prefer to direct our energies toward completing our postwar plans rather than assembling them (such as they now are) for transmittal to you.

Lacking such a summary, I am giving you some offhand answers, which I am afraid will have to serve your purpose. These will cover the activities of the Weyerhaeuser Timber Company.

This, of course, was a minor and passing irritation. Fires were a constant and considerable concern. In his April 19 report on the St. Helens Tree Farm, Clyde Martin indicated much unhappiness, especially over fire losses. "At this rate," he observed, "we would have to plant a section per year to keep up with our fires." In the previous twelve months, fifteen fires had burned over 2,600 acres, cost the company in damages $23,268.16, killed 13.5 million feet of standing timber, and burned 675,000 feet of logs. Specific problems were noted. For example, it had taken two hours "to get action on the Winston Creek fire which occurred on one of the worst days of the season and might have been disastrous had the weather not changed the first evening." Martin also maintained that although fires, for the most part, had been "attacked rapidly and effectively" during the summer months, "detection and action on early and late fires were deplorable." And he closed by stating, "This is not the sort of protection W.T. Co. should have." Forester Martin knew, as did Phil Weyerhaeuser, that without effective fire protection the experiment called tree farming was doomed.

The General Timber Service and Allied Building Credits questions continued to nag. It was not that there was any hope for either; they simply refused to die quickly and quietly. In a confidential letter to Phil, dated April 21, F.E. indicated that he had received a "long statement" from Fred K. and John Musser arguing for a continuation of A.B.C., but that he had not changed his mind, and neither had Horace Irvine. The final decision was in the hands of the directors of the Timber Company and Potlatch Forests, but F.E. had apparently decided that the question had resolved itself: "Remembering your remarks at our meeting in Chicago approximately two years ago, the last report that I saw indicates that we are using over 16 million dollars in the business of the company and are not making any substantial profit." It seemed simple enough. They were supplying a service for many, employment for a few, but the dollars involved were earning little or nothing. Uncle Fred closed typically: "In view of the uncertainties ahead of us, an investment of 16 million dollars is somewhat disturbing to me, and also to Horace."

Phil wrote to Fred K. from Del Monte where he, Helen, and Ann had gone for a brief vacation, in part to relax and in part to see George, who was on leave before going to Corpus Christi for radar school. Fred K. had sent Phil copies of his letters to F.E. on the A.B.C. and G.T.S. matters, and Phil reported that he had heard recently from their uncle, who was "in a crusading mood." The other news passed along concerned Laird Bell, who had just been appointed counsel to the Allied Control Commission in Europe. As Phil noted: "Curtains for the time being in any efforts in our behalf."

The war came close to home in a curious and tragic manner. The Japanese had attempted on many occasions to strike at American territory directly, through the use of balloon bombs carried eastward by the prevailing winds. Although the concept occasioned much enthusiasm in Japanese military circles and much fear among western Americans, particularly the owners of timberland, the results of the balloon attacks had been trivial. It is perhaps in keeping with the nature of the war that the only casualties proved to be innocent victims. On May 5, 1945, near Bly, Oregon, about forty-five miles east of Klamath Falls, a group of school children were enjoying a picnic in the parklike setting of a pine tree farm of the Weyerhaeuser Timber Company. In the course of their wanderings the youngsters came across an unfamiliar object, picked it up, and an explosion occurred. Killed were Elsie Mitchell, one of the group's leaders, and five students, the only deaths resulting from enemy action in the then forty-eight states. Five years later the tragedy was commemorated with the dedication of the Mitchell Recreational Area in a brief and simple ceremony on August 20, 1950. In that same summer another war was commencing in a place called Korea, perhaps encouraging Conrad Speidel, the editor of Weyerhaeuser employee publications, to observe regarding the Klamath bombsite dedication, "At least 400 Americans had an hour to think about the futility of war—war which kills young women and picnicking children."

The long-awaited news was officially announced on May 8, 1945. The war in Europe was over. War, however, was anything but over for the U.S. Fifth Marine Division on Okinawa, and for millions of others. Phil and Helen, with one son in the Marines and another in the Navy, could only hope that the war in the Pacific would soon end too. Phil assured the Timber Company directors that the surrender of Germany meant changes, although these might not be noticed in the Pacific Northwest for some time, what "with B-29s still needed, naval construction scheduled to proceed, and accelerated Pacific loading." The directors were also advised that they were scheduled to meet on May 29 and 30, and that the annual meeting of the Timber Company would be held on May 31, "with a junket to Everett or elsewhere on Friday, June 1."

Phil sent an agenda for the meetings to F.E., many of the items being the usual. There was, however, to be a report by Fred K. on Allied Building Credits, and also considerable discussion led by Minot Davis on "unfinished timber matters." These included Phil's recommendation for settlement of the Seattle watershed question: "An agreement has been reached with the City Water Department and City Council, providing for orderly timber liquidation in the area and providing for sacrifice on our part of some cutover land with which the City can acquire all of the Federal land in the watershed." While it may have been a compromise that favored the city, it could hardly be opposed, ensuring as it did one of the great municipal water systems. There was also to be a report on sustained-yield endeavors, on the development program, on prospects for replacing the Steamship Company fleet from reserves created for that purpose, and, finally, "for approval of the Board," a recommendation to shareholders that the declared value of the Weyerhaeuser Timber Company stock be fixed at $90 million. Phil also hoped to have a completed proposal to submit on the retirement plan.

As expected, the Timber Company directors instructed Phil "to seek a market for the company's stock in Allied Building Credits, Inc.," and accordingly Phil wrote to Fred K.: "I take this to mean that you will now catch the ball and act for all A.B.C.'s stockholders in seeking a satisfactory buyer." Laird Bell also received a letter reporting on the meetings. Phil was most pleased to pass along the news that the directors had unanimously approved a retirement plan that covered all salaried employees. "I know you would have been happy to be present," he wrote, in recognition of the long effort Laird had led in that connection. He also noted that Laird had been reelected to all his offices and that they were looking forward to his return. In the meantime, Phil could repeat earlier observations: "I know your job must be interesting, and, as I told you, [I] envy you your ability to make the sacrifices which you are making and have made."

One of the items not discussed at the Executive Committee meeting was the suggestion that consideration be given to an increase in the stock of the Timber Company with a view to acquiring the minority stock in the Wood Conversion Company and in Willapa Harbor Lumber Mills. As Phil admitted afterward to F.E., he had not brought the question up for discussion, "partly because I am not personally of a mind now to present the matter." Phil much preferred a discussion of recommendations rather than wasting time "batting balls up in the air." In this instance he just wasn't clear what would be the best course for Willapa. Perhaps they should simply look toward its liquidation. As for Wood Conversion, it was not an immediate problem, but it would remain a concern, complicated by the presence of Ed Davis.

F.E. had some afterthoughts of his own on the recent meetings. He was certain that they had acted wisely regarding A.B.C., and was only sorry that Fred K. had felt compelled to defend so vigorously. "Perhaps it is well that the discussion took place," he wrote to Phil, "but it certainly brought out some curious reasoning," adding, "In his great loyalty to Fred K., dear old Fritz never did get on the beam." He was apparently less certain about the retirement plan, which he figured would add about $100,000 to their already record wage costs. "I am happy in the thought that our employees can earn so much, but I do have some misgivings as to the future," and he predicted that the prosperous times would end. "When the break comes there will be new problems," he continued, "but why worry now—you will be equal to the task of solving them." Phil may have appreciated the expression of confidence, but there was a hint of something unwelcome—that soon those who had so long shared the responsibility would be giving it up.

In mid-June, Phil, Helen, and Wizzie went to the Elkhorn Ranch in Bozeman, Montana, for two to three weeks of vacation, "If my seat doesn't wear out," as Phil wrote to Ann, Flip, and George. He also noted that the annual meetings had passed again "without my losing my job," although "everybody was growing older and crankier." As things turned out, it was a good time to be hidden away on a Montana ranch, and perhaps he should have stayed longer. On July 12, charges began to be published concerning the use of private railway cars by the Weyerhaeusers. "Weyerhaeusers Rail Joy-Riding" read headlines in the *Seattle Times*. Chief protagonist was a Democratic representative from Washington, Hugh De Lacy. The *Minneapolis Morning Tribune* repeated the story on July 13, noting the De Lacy charges that "members of the Weyerhaeuser lumber family, officials of the Great Northern railway and others were using private cars for vacation trips, while returning veterans are crowded into hot day coaches." The congressman was quoted, "If we are to provide luxury, let us provide those who deserve it most—the returning battle-weary GIs." Phil, of course, received a bit of attention. He merely indicated that he had "never ridden in a private car in my life." Responding to Harold Richardson's expression of sympathy over the "current tempest in a teapot," Phil admitted, "we are all too sensitive to the white light of publicity," adding, "I am sure I am, and I suspect that other members of our group also suffer inordinately when publicly attacked."

If F.E. was embarrassed by the unwelcome attention he had brought to himself and the family, Phil could see to it that his uncle had other things to think about. One of the items sent along in early August had to do with a proposal to purchase some 6 billion feet of Canadian timber, with mills capable of producing 150 million feet a year. Phil had indicated to the person who suggested the opportunity that while a possible Canadian investment had often been discussed, they had "always concluded to stay out; also that unless there were strong corollary advantages, we were adverse to expanding." Phil saw certain advantages, such as acquiring "their knowledge of the export business." In this instance, however, there was no hurry. "If we have an interest, it can be pursued at our leisure." A part of the relaxed approach to opportunities was, of course, a result of a well-earned security provided by their timber resource base. The Weyerhaeusers could afford to be casual on occasion, pushing uncertainties momentarily aside. In that sense, Phil had replied to an inquiry in the following manner: "Our timber quantities have never been determined with enough accuracy to allow us to publicize them. We have enough acres and land in our ownership, together with intermingled lands which can be considered controlled by the geography of the situation, to encourage us to feel we are on sustained-yield bases for many of our operations."

On August 17 Phil sent along one of his reports to the Timber Company directors, indicating that profits for the first half of 1945 were off more than 20 percent from the previous year, that dollar sales had declined by 15 percent, and the quantity of lumber shipped by 20 percent. "It looks as though peace means cancellation, strikes, and building up of inventories before we can again serve our customers," he concluded. But those were obstacles that would be managed. It was a cause for great celebration when the news of the Japanese surrender on September 2 was received. Families throughout the country rejoiced and gave thanks. So it was with Phil and Helen and their scattered family.

CHAPTER 13

The Changing of the Guard

As he looked ahead to the end of the war and what it would mean to the lumber industry and the Weyerhaeuser Timber Company, Phil assumed, of course, that there would be large problems in adjusting to a peacetime economy. He also admitted to being puzzled about "what the war's end is going to mean" and concluded that their energies should be directed at relieving "the shortage of lumber and pulp with the object in view of getting controls released and a normal market reestablished."

One of the certainties seemed to be a renewed cycle of labor disruptions. "Certainly we will be under great pressure to allow wage raises to compensate for a return to the 40-hour week whenever that takes place," Phil wrote to F.E. on August 18, 1945. Within a week of V-J Day, he repeated his concerns: "I am afraid that the psychology of the war workers on the West Coast is going to lead to a complete disagreement as to wages and working conditions in the coming negotiations." The government had removed all restrictions except price, but Phil doubted they could do much about prices in any event. But the work force seemed incapable of such reasoning: "No one seems to be willing to work for the moment for less than they have been receiving in war work." The adjustment obviously would not occur without confrontation and difficulty. "We are using our influence to solidify the industry in a strong stand," Phil assured Uncle Fred.

Whatever the problems, they were preferable to war. Among the most pleasing of tasks were those of putting the family back together. Phil addressed a letter to the children in which he informed them collectively of what was going on. He had heard, "by the underground," that Ann and Jack would be home by the end of September and that they would spend a few days relaxing before Jack began "seeking new experiences." He also passed along the rumor that George's school was "about to disgorge him unless he enlists in the Navy for four years." He acknowledged that he hoped George wouldn't enlist, "but my advice hasn't been sought." Flip was still at Pendleton, nursing a damaged car, with "no news as to his overseas chances." As for other news, "The Jewett cruiser at Lake Coeur d'Alene is a wow," and "so's Tom Murray's 100,000 acre ranch at Ellensburg," and Wizzie was starting back to school at a renovated Annie Wright Seminary, with "lots of new paint and faces there." He also noted that business was booming, "but nobody is willing to work," and that a strike was expected soon. He closed, "If any of you are wondering what to do next, take a little time out like me and drop us a line."

Phil tried to explain the labor circumstances to the Timber Company directors in a letter of September 24, but explaining something he didn't understand himself wasn't easy. "It takes a soothsayer to foresee our way out of the current situation," he admitted. The AFL was then involved in an industry-wide strike, partly having to do with the refusal of operators to engage in individual negotiations for fir lumber, pine lumber, plywood, and other separate activities. As a result, Snoqualmie Falls was shut down. "How long it will last, nobody knows."

Klamath Falls had been on strike, but it looked as if that would soon be settled. As to the CIO, Phil thought they continued to be as much actuated by a desire to discredit the AFL as to get wage or other concessions. It seemed that government pressure would be exerted on the side of wage concessions, or so Phil expected; but the lumber industry appeared to be firmer than usual "in the belief that further wage advances cannot be long supported." Through it all, the market remained surprisingly strong.

Phil had been carrying on a long-distance conversation with Uncle Fred for some time regarding a possible history of Grandfather Frederick's life. F.E. had worked tirelessly at assembling information for "The Record," and Phil, while interested in the compilation, wasn't enthusiastic about expanding the effort. He was certain his uncles and others in the family would be difficult to please. It had been suggested that historian Stanley Horn might be employed to write the history, but Phil replied, "I am very doubtful if anyone, Mr. Horn included, can write a history of grandfather's life and enterprises which will satisfy you or the family as a whole." Months earlier he had suggested that they should content themselves with "The Record," satisfied that "somebody will probably see enough in the story to undertake it someday, however, whether we like it or not." Those discussions and all others with F.E. ended on October 18, when Frederick E. Weyerhaeuser, clearly the transitional figure between the first and third generations, died at a St. Paul hospital. The funeral was held at the House of Hope Presbyterian Church in St. Paul on Saturday, October 21, with Phil and his cousins serving as pallbearers.

In so many ways F.E. seemed irreplaceable. It was he who had served at his father's side in the St. Paul office, and better than anyone else it was he who understood his father's ability, philosophy, domain. It was, of course, appropriate that F.E. should attempt to preserve "The Record" at least as far as the family was concerned. But if that effort seemed limited in purpose, such was not the case with his larger interest in the history of the industry. Like others before him, F.E. worried lest *that* record be lost or, worse, misrepresented. Through him that interest was carried forward, largely by nephew Fred K.— an interest that would eventually result in the establishment of the Forest History Society.

Business, of course, went on. The day after his uncle's death, Fred K. announced the sale of Allied Building Credits to the Occidental Life Insurance Company of Los Angeles and its parent organization, the Transamerica Corporation of San Francisco. Labor problems continued. The CIO plants continued to operate during negotiations which resulted in an industry-wide agreement to increase wages 12.5 cents per hour. Salary rates were also adjusted to compensate for the loss of overtime, the forty-hour work week having returned. AFL plants remained on strike through November. Additional timber purchases had been made in the Sutherlin district of Oregon, and Laird Bell returned from his European assignment.

Horace Irvine was elected Timber Company president in place of F.E., and the responsibility for leadership in family matters passed to Fred K. The nephew wasted no time in taking charge. He, and Phil to an even larger extent, had been unhappy with the unstructured approach traditional at the family meetings. Thus it was no surprise when the male members of the family received a post-Christmas detailed outline of an agenda. Phil immediately supported this new approach. "I think you have started something which will endure," he observed.

The year ended with another sort of observation: "A recent survey of material still left on the ground after our current relatively 'close' logging at Longview indicates that there remain 26 cords of sound material of all kinds per acre which we are not recovering." There was obviously more that could be done even without cutting any more merchantable timber.

Given the limited availability of Minot Davis, Dave Weyerhaeuser had assumed more responsibility, and any thoughts of reassigning him elsewhere were forgotten. His first report in 1946 looked back at recent rates of cutting, acquisitions, and total supplies, and endeavored to forecast future needs and whether the company could supply those needs and remain on a perpetual-yield basis. The key prediction assumed an average drain of 245 million feet—from sales, cutting, and fire and insect losses—over acquisitions; and given the inventory of mature timber, that would allow for 170 years of operation, "plenty of time to convert our acres to growing conditions and continuity." There were many other variables and unknowns in such compilations, but little by little the company was in a better position to make decisions leading to desired objectives. As evidence of changing attitudes, Dave Weyerhaeuser recommended the exchange of mature timber in certain sectors for young, growing timber. Minot promised to give the "interesting memorandum" consideration, wanting it understood that "this is quite a large subject, and you will readily see that it has many angles other than the forestry angle."

Given the great demand for lumber, those at the sales end naturally favored increased production. The Timber Company Executive Committee considered the question at length, and as Phil informed Fred K., "We found difficulty justifying a return to overtime weeks in view of its effect upon wage rates when a return becomes necessary to a 40-hour week." They had decided that only those increases possible within the forty-hour week would be attempted. Log supplies continued to be the limiting factor, and until they had passed through the difficulties imposed by the heavy snows, there was not much anyone could do. Once logging resumed and they got all the machinery working again, it was assumed they would soon approach the 1936 to 1939 average cut, "except as that cut is affected by our overall sustained-yield limitations, which require that we reduce Klamath from 173 millions to 150 millions; Snoqualmie from 112 millions to 90; Longview from 320 millions to 300; and Everett from 276 millions to 250." In short, the year's projected production of 785 million feet should be close to what their postwar sustained-yield average would probably be.

The Executive Committee also gave its approval to a program in Oregon of proceeding "in an orderly fashion toward acquiring mill sites, developing plans, and proceeding with logging and mill construction," with an objective of reaching a 200 million feet of annual lumber production capacity. This would return them to a forty-hour week total production of about a billion feet, close to the wartime maximum, and was, "according to our calculations, susceptible of being maintained continuously."

But pressures to increase production immediately were considerable. The National Association of Manufacturers was sponsoring a tour of Washington industries by journalists, and the Weyerhaeuser plant at Longview was on the itinerary. Thus Harry Morgan made specific inquiries of Phil about what his answers to various questions should be, and Phil thought the only possible answer to some was, "I don't know." Phil did advise that he believed they "should get over the thought that sustained-yield deals in averages and this is an emergency year so we will deliberately attempt to overcut our sustained-yield average." Morgan was able to announce Weyerhaeuser's plans to construct a new plywood plant at Longview employing some two hundred, with a production capacity of 40 million feet per year and expected to be in operation by July 1947.

In late January, Phil had gone to St. Paul, primarily to attend the family meeting. He reported to sons Flip and George on happenings there, "an interesting time," he said, "a meeting of all members of my generation of our family . . . as there are lots of matters in which the family acts as a unit and a few corporations are owned entirely by the family, which makes it necessary to get a cross-section of opinion." He further noted that with F.E.'s death "and R.M.'s feebleness, the responsibility for all decisions now rests firmly on our generation, and this is the first time we ever met actually to make decisions."

There were other changes. On February 27, Phil Weyerhaeuser Pascoe arrived, the first of the fifth generation. Grandfather and grandmother were pleased, although Phil pretended to take the event in stride. To George he wrote on March 11, "The young one yells sometimes at night, but not enough to keep us awake." And he had closed by saying, "It is fun speculating on your return to leading a more or less normal life." In early April, Phil indicated to Walter Rosenberry, Jr., that all was well with the grandson and with Ann, also that Jack had been discharged and was at home, "and recently Flip showed up on what he hopes will be a terminal leave." But George was "still in the South Pacific."

Another development was the acquisition of a company airplane, a Beechcraft 18-S, complete with pilot Nappy Wildhaber. Phil may have felt a twinge of guilt at such a purchase, but it was anything but a luxury item. As he explained to Horace Irvine, "to umpire its use by those in the office . . . is one of the major problems," but the important consideration was that "it will afford us all a means to get to Klamath Falls and Coos Bay oftener." If Oregon was to become increasingly important in Timber Company affairs, and it obviously was, then the plane was the logical means for making those properties accessible.

And it *was* important to get around. Like old Frederick Weyerhaeuser, Phil realized that others would care if they knew he cared. A case in point was his visit to a logging operation under contract to the Washington Veneer Company which "revealed, to my mind, a very wasteful attitude on the part of the logger." As he informed Charlie Ingram, too much was being left on the ground. When he had questioned the logger, he had been told that the logs had been left behind "because he could not get back a new dollar for an old" on them. To more specific questions, the logger had been "quite indefinite." Phil suggested that they do one of two things: either pay on a basis that made for a cleaner operation, or "organize a small salvage unit of our own and seek permission to operate it on the cutover areas still unburned." In any event, something was required, "as no one can look the ground over without wondering what kind of outfit is running it."

In mid-April Phil sent along another report to the Timber Company directors. The news was mixed, what with bad weather and the threat of strikes "keeping us short of logs and understaffed." Al Raught was spending "day after day" in Portland, involved in the first industry-wide negotiations with the CIO. The present contract was due to run out April 1. Phil wasn't predicting what would happen. He did know that the annual meeting would once again open with a Sales Company meeting of directors Monday, May 27, and he advised them all to make early hotel reservations. As for himself, he was off for two weeks in California.

Upon his return from Del Monte, Phil encountered the usual accumulation of work. One of the letters was from Fred ("Long" Fred) Weyerhaeuser announcing his resignation as president of General Timber Service, a decision to which Phil could hardly object. Still he hoped that feelings had not been damaged too much in the process. Realizing that he was writing after the fact—the matter had already been settled—Phil nonetheless tried to express an awareness of the situation. "I have the feeling that heading up G.T.S. has become an unpleasant burden," he wrote, "and one which you find it harder to justify because you don't really believe G.T.S. has the function to perform." Phil readily admitted that "running an animal of that description would be no pleasure to me and have, therefore, tried to express to you my gratitude at your continuing to do so." Dave Weyerhaeuser was naturally concerned about his brother and developments with G.T.S., and in a note to Phil he had shared a concern for the estrangement the Tacoma situation gave to St. Paul-based activities. Phil replied, acknowledging an appreciation for Dave's "feeling of detachment about G.T.S." He was quick to point out that the disadvantages of separation worked both ways: "I have the same feeling in regard to matters which come up for discussion and decision in St. Paul. Two thousand miles in itself seems to change our viewpoints." John Musser was elected president of General Timber Service to replace Fred Weyerhaeuser.

There were other actions as a result of recent meetings. Rudolph was replaced as president of Potlatch Forests by Fritz Jewett, this, as Phil wrote to his uncle, "in response to your wish to be relieved, as verified by Aunt Louise and Peggy." Within the Timber Company, Horace Irvine was elected president, with Ed Hayes as a new vice-president, Fred K. as treasurer and a director in the place of F.E., and Norton Clapp as a director in the place of his father, Dr. E. P. Clapp. Rudolph died at his St. Paul home on July 12, 1946. Only Aunt Lonie Davis survived among the second-generation Weyerhaeusers.

Some changes were inevitable given the passage of time and the passing of family members. Other changes would be required by new legal rules and restrictions. Gus Clapp was beginning to worry some about the interrelationships of all the many organizations. In a memorandum to Phil, dated July 3, he attempted to describe the interlocking directorships that existed. In fact, the interlocking of directors was not prohibited except for companies in competition, and that was a very complicated question, one that clearly merited attention. Phil's response was significant. He maintained that until there was "some affirmative happening" that suggested his service on the various directorates was going to be challenged, "it would be my inclination to continue to serve and to induce others similarly situated to do the same." The reasons were clear enough: "Most of the family interests are so thinly populated with males with a knowledge of our business that providing a different director candidate in the various companies would become quite burdensome and the quality of the representation in each company would undoubtedly be reduced." So unless Gus had something else to advise, "I will put your memo sleeping in the file." The problem, however, would not go away.

Phil attended the Sales Company operations committee meeting at Glacier Park in mid-July, in the company of Laird Bell and Bill Peabody. Subsequently they took the plane to look over the Klamath Falls timber from the air, "traveling about 350 miles in a circle to accomplish it." As Phil reported to Horace Irvine, the reproduction looked good. They then proceeded to inspect the new millsite at Coos Bay and the initial efforts at clearing and grading. The convenience of air travel was appreciated, and the acceleration it provided to life continued to amaze them. Phil noted, "Laird is supposed to be back at his office in Chicago this morning, after having had lunch with me in the heart of the Coos Bay timber yesterday!" Horace agreed that such a thing was "certainly remarkable," adding, "Distance doesn't seem to amount to anything nowadays." Phil might have maintained that Tacoma and St. Paul remained far apart, but that distance too seemed to be diminishing. In Laird's first letter from Chicago, he thanked Phil for his "royal entertainment," and noted that he could think of no questions he had failed to ask, and "the only thing wrong is that I see nothing really to worry about."

There were, of course, problems. Rates of production continued to lag at lower levels than had been hoped for and, indeed, planned for. "Instead of getting easier, it seems harder," Phil admitted to the directors on August 5. Great uncertainty also surrounded the question whether to invest in a new fleet of ships for the Steamship Company. Over $3.5 million had been accumulated in the construction reserve fund, and Phil addressed a note to Peabody that was intended to paint a smile on a serious subject. Outlined in the middle of the page was a frame, and within was the "Picture of a man with $3,607,000.00 in the bank and not knowing what to do with it." The text below read, "While I am glad you have the money in the bank, I regret the paucity of ideas with regard to its intelligent use." Phil was reasonably certain that they should reinvolve themselves. But earlier he had suggested that they might be better off chartering ships, that they served themselves "and the industry only if we are able to perform a service cheaper. When we get to the present sorry pass where the Maritime Commission is petitioning for raises in rail rates in order to enable the shipping fraternity to survive, we are doing exactly nothing for ourselves, in my opinion." By late September the decision was reached to purchase four Liberty ships, to make a new westbound charter agreement with Captain Howard's Pacific Coast Direct Line, and to operate eastbound as a contract carrier rather than a common carrier, this for legal purposes. In short, the Steamship Company was back in business, or soon would be.

A major personnel change occurred in mid-August with the news that Howard Morgan, then manager of the Munising Paper Company of Munising, Michigan, had agreed to assume management of the pulp division, beginning the first of the year. Bob Wolf was approaching retirement, and everyone seemed genuinely pleased, and some relieved, by the change. And there were other happenings at Longview. The hydraulic barker was operating to apparent satisfaction. The sulphate mill construction was progressing well. And the bark production plant was scheduled to start up in September. Phil observed that Longview was "going to be a busy place."

The start of the school year found both George and Flip back at Yale, and if that must have seemed something of an anticlimax, Phil had to be understanding. He could remember nearly twenty years earlier when he had faced the same frustration, returning to classes after wearing a uniform. It hadn't been easy then and it probably wasn't much easier now. "Don't forget to write your mother once in awhile," he advised.

An unexpected development occurred on October 5 when Gus Clapp died. Phil and Charlie Ingram were fishing at Cowichan Bay, British Columbia, when news of his death was received. Bill Billings wrote a brief note to Phil after learning of the loss: "I know you will miss him. He was a good and lusty man. I often wished I could have seen more of him before 5:00 P.M." To the directors, Phil acknowledged, "He leaves a great hole here." A replacement would be difficult to find. As Phil would write to Horace, "Gus' death is more of a shock to me than many might suppose. His analytical mind and good business judgment have helped in so many ways that in thinking about a successor all possibilities seem inadequate." The feeling had been mutual. Gus's widow, Gladys Clapp, later wrote to Phil, "His devotion to the Weyerhaeuser organization was the biggest thing in his life and he was so proud and happy in his association with you."

It was indeed a time of great difficulty. Horace Irvine was unable to assume any real responsibility as president of the Timber Company, since he himself was not healthy. Phil reflected on the general situation in a letter to Laird Bell:

It rather seems as though a lot of props were being knocked out from under us—F.E.'s and R.M.'s deaths and Horace's apparent disability, to which now we must add Gus' departure. On looking over the list of directors, it seems to me that our current list of eleven will either shrink to eight or nine, or require replacements, within the next two years. As we discussed some time ago, we may be at the point where directors from within the operating organization are desirable, or, perhaps, from the general public. I am not quite sure that we should keep our Board as big as it now is.

Horace's health did not improve. In late October his secretary wrote an optimistic letter indicating that he was feeling better following an attack of pneumonia, but he could not attend the November 11 meeting of the Executive Committee. Laird too was worried about Horace's condition, having recently tried to see him in St. Paul only to find that "they were not letting anyone except family see him . . . and were keeping all business matters away from him." He admitted that it was all quite disturbing and found it hard to think of holding an Executive Committee meeting without either Horace or Gus Clapp. He assumed that Phil wanted to go ahead on the basis of their own availability and that of Fred K. and Ed Hayes, "but I confess to some dread of passing on the pretty imposing agenda without the balance and judgment of those two men."

The meeting was, of course, held according to plan. In addition to the usual discussions, a program was authorized involving "very substantial purchases" at the state timber sale on December 3, "if we are the successful bidder." The withdrawal of OPA controls was also noted, which Phil assumed would lead to "a return to freedom and prices, no doubt, will be at new highs." Plans for Springfield were approved, "The snowball thrown at the cost of the sawmill and woods construction was ten millions, which was not authorized, but the timing . . . looking to getting a plant there in production during 1949 was not criticized." The Development Department's program was approved and a 1947 operating budget of $270,000 authorized. Finally, Laird agreed to accept "certain matters in fields which Gus Clapp used to cover," and Phil was clearly hopeful that Laird might agree to be the general counsel. To brother Fred, Phil subsequently wrote that it had been the best meeting he had ever attended "because it resulted in an unrestrained forthright expression of opinion by all concerned."

Phil was obviously pleased with many developments. One had to do with John Wahl's work at Vail in salvage logging. He sent some pictures of the effort to Horace Irvine. This involved "prelogging" or bundling of small logs, which were then transported as a unit, strapped on the truck, transferred onto the cars, "dumped, and towed to Everett, and taken out of the water at the pulp mill," still as a unit. They hoped to have four such operations going next summer, "and we will have a very substantial recovery per acre out of prior wastes."

That same morning, word was received that Colonel Long had died in Newark. Many then with the company would not even have heard of the colonel, and Phil reminded the directors that the old gentleman had been active during the whole history of their Atlantic Coast yards: "He gave energetic and wise management to the remotest venture of WTC until Bill Peabody began to take over during the Great Depression." The colonel had continued to keep regular office hours "and died at his desk at the age of eighty-two or three."

The state timber sale December 3 resulted in the "expected fireworks," and Phil informed Horace that the Timber Company had been successful in purchasing about $1.3 million worth of timber, "all the way from the appraised price up to rather fantastic stumpage figures, the exact amount of which I do not know and would not like to write about if I did." They were not universally successful, Phil noting that they had been outbid in the Longview area on several tracts.

All in all it had been quite a year, and Phil and Helen were looking forward to gathering the family together at Christmas. Phil wrote to Flip and George in a post-Thanksgiving letter, telling of a recent duck hunt with Jack Pascoe at the Nisqually Flats Duck Club during which, "and he is still willing to bear witness . . . I shot once and three ducks fell." He also noted a recent letter from George in which it was suggested that he could graduate more quickly "by short-cutting the frills" and could then begin graduate work. "I don't think I understand quite the difference between taking your time at a full undergraduate course as opposed to hurrying through and spending an equal time in post-graduate work," Phil responded, but "perhaps you can explain that to me a little better at Christmas time."

Aside from the expected holiday pleasures, the most welcomed news was the negotiated settlement with both CIO and AFL unions, "a unanimity of action which was unprecedented," with all parties agreeing to a 15-cent hourly wage increase, bringing the minimum hourly rate in the district to $1.25. It all seemed incredible, but even Phil was forced to admit that prices were such that they could readily absorb the additional costs. Still, "I think we would all be much happier had a price recession come to justify a continuance of the old rates, instead of what has happened," or so he told the directors in a New Year's Eve report.

Minot Davis continued to work at a reduced schedule, and in January he left for a three months' stay in Santa Barbara. Phil had responded to an inquiry from Horace Irvine about Minot's condition, noting that when he came across a piece of timber that might be purchased, "he is still as vigorous an advocate as possible." Phil was himself planning a vacation, going to St. Paul for meetings before heading for Florida, where he and Helen would spend a couple of weeks in the company of Dave and Kay Winton. The next Executive Committee meetings were scheduled for February 24 and March 3, "with trips to Vail, Klamath Falls, Coos Bay, and Eugene coming in between, depending upon flying weather."

As usual during Phil's absence, Nick Genta sent along letters full of news. One item that might have caused considerable concern, had things been slightly different, involved Wizzie. She and some Annie Wright Seminary classmates had gone to Mount Rainier on a skiing excursion and, owing to heavy snows and slides, the group had become stranded at Paradise Valley. As things turned out, it was more an occasion for fun than anything else. Dave Weyerhaeuser was planning the annual forestry meeting to be held after Phil's return. He addressed a note jointly to Phil, Charlie Ingram, and Al Raught in hopes that one of them would offer some opening remarks. "It helps our forestry program a great deal to have someone from the Tenth Floor give expression in favor of the broad forestry program of the company," he observed.

Phil, of course, returned for the Executive Committee meetings, but Helen continued her vacation at an Arizona ranch. He wrote to her on the morning of the committee's departure for Klamath Falls, February 26, "a beautiful, sunny morning." It so happened, on that same morning, Horace Irvine died in St. Paul. His death truly marked the end of an era. The son of lumberman Thomas Irvine, Horace was born in Alma, Wisconsin, January 12, 1878. He had been a member of the Weyerhaeuser Timber Company board of directors since June 19, 1902. Expressions of sympathy would arrive from many sources.

C. Sterling Bunnell, vice-president of the National City Bank of New York, wrote to Phil, "The passing of your Uncle Fred and your Uncle Rudolph, and now Mr. Irvine in so short a space of time deprives you of a wealth of senior counsel of the sort on which we all rely in piloting our businesses through these troublous days." Fred K. addressed a lengthy letter to Rudolph's widow, Aunt Louise, noting that since the last annual meeting of the Timber Company, three of the thirteen directors had died, and of the Executive Committee of six, only four remained: Ed Hayes, Laird Bell, Phil, and himself.

On the eve of the annual meeting, Phil heard again from Harold J. Richardson. Harold had written the previous May 13, suggesting that he be retired from the board of directors, but for various reasons it was not an opportune time to accede to that request. He repeated the suggestion, more strongly, in a letter of May 19, 1947. "In these times of stress," he wrote, "the Company needs active representation, which I cannot supply." The resignation was accepted, Phil writing, "I think you must realize from the action a year ago the deep regret which was felt by all that you found it necessary to relinquish your duties in this connection." It was further determined, in accordance with Phil's recommendation, that the board would be reduced from thirteen to eleven members, and Charlie Ingram and Ed Davis were elected to the vacant positions. Phil was elected president, and the old position of executive vice-president was eliminated.

Congratulations were many and effusive. Harry Kendall correctly observed that the new office would not add much in the way of work, "but is more a recognition of that work than anything else." In response to a telegram from Bill Peabody, Phil acknowledged that it really didn't make much difference, "although, of course, I enjoy being considered the top guy." He was a bit more specific in his answer to a letter from Aimee Lyford, noting that previous presidents had acted more "like absentee chairmen of the board," so he was suspecting "that life will go on much as usual."

If Phil's life would go on much as before, it was in part because he refused to let what he considered to be extraneous matters distract him. Evidence of the intensity and, perhaps, narrowness of his interest and attention was revealed in a letter he wrote to Ralph Macartney, manager at Klamath Falls. Many Weyerhaeuser personnel were invited to assume responsibilities of a larger sort, involving community work or industry representation. Macartney had been requested to serve on an Oregon State NAM public relations committee. Phil wasn't arguing against the purposes of the organization, but he wanted it understood that he felt it was time wasted. If Ralph had any doubts about the existence of a company policy, Phil stated his own personal belief: "I do try to make it a practice, however, to act on no committees and to sponsor no efforts with which I cannot be enough associated to share in the responsibility." He was not exaggerating.

Not unrelated was his attitude toward new ventures for the company. It was a time of interest in South American opportunities, encouraged by the leadership of Nelson Rockefeller. Fred K. was enthusiastic about investigating the possibilities of South American lumber, and he favored sending "a couple of promising young men" down there "with no reference to the Rockefeller proposal at all if any of my associates (including yourself) saw merit in the proposal." Phil's answer was somewhat curious, although probably Fred K. was not surprised. Phil didn't want his "conservatism and lack of vision to be the cause for our failure to learn about South America, Russia, or what-have-you." And he followed that observation with another: "Sometimes, I guess, I allow my own laziness to temper my thirst for knowledge." If Fred K. was convinced that they should investigate South America "as a source of lumber for purchase, or timber, or its merits as a harbor for capital in flight," Phil said he would "willingly agree."

Phil found more than enough to do closer to home. On August 5 he announced that a sulphate plant would be constructed at Springfield, Oregon, the unbleached pulp product to be used in container board manufacture. It may have seemed just more evidence of expansion to most, but it was part of the long-range plan for integrated utilization. As was stated in the announcement, the mill would "operate entirely on slabs, edgings and trimmings from the sawmill and undersized trees, chunks and tops from our logging operations." In the press release, Jon (Jonathan Ross) Titcomb, manager of the Springfield branch operation, was quoted as saying the new plant would "provide an economic incentive for practicing good forestry in the woods and in that way will enhance the mill's timber supply."

Questions of organization were omnipresent. Fred K. inquired about the possible advantages of an insurance manager for the affiliated companies. Phil was not enthusiastic, noting that at present the Weyerhaeuser Timber Company did not consider itself ill-served. The comptroller's office administered insurance of all kinds, and other decisions were reached among "Messrs. Ingram, Orr, and myself, pretty largely on the recommendation of Sexton Company." Most important, however, the matter brought into focus differing views as to the nature of management. "Here again is a place where we could centralize authority," Phil responded, "but I have never been convinced that by doing so we had more to gain than we would lose by the red tape and withdrawal of initiative which it involves."

In mid-July, Phil reported another timber purchase. Mason, Bruce,

and Girard, the old, friendly consulting firm from Portland, offered
some timberlands from an estate they were handling, and the Timber
Company was the successful bidder at $355,100. Phil indicated to the
Executive Committee that they had treated it much like a state purchase, "for which we have in the past made a practice of securing no
authority before bidding." In any event, it was too late to object. Phil
did note that Dave Weyerhaeuser, "upon finding us the successful bidder, is now wondering if he bid more than he had to, which is a worry
I for one do not share."

Laird Bell came west for a visit, much appreciated by Phil. One of
the results of recent considerations was the commission of a study of
the organization by the Chicago firm Booz, Allen and Hamilton,
"with the object in view of studying jobs, building up understudies,
and staffing the Company adequately to meet future replacement ne-
cessities, and fill the new jobs created by expanded operations." To
Laird, following his visit, Phil noted that it had been a "wonderful
week for me, as I appreciate more than you probably realize an opportunity to discuss matters with you." None of which meant that
they were in perfect agreement. Indeed, shortly after Laird's departure, Phil received an article written by his recent visitor—an article
with which Phil had basic disagreement. "You tear down those giving
merely lip service to the name 'free enterprise,' without sufficiently
asserting your own allegiance to a purer interpretation," Phil replied.
He further observed, "Whether a proper version of Free Enterprise
under a capitalistic system or socialism endures out of the current
struggle appears to be less important than puncturing the balloon of
monopolists under a false banner." Laird would subsequently admit
that these were among the best criticisms he had received.

As the years passed, Phil continued to increase his involvement in
church activities. The fall of 1947 found him on the building committee for a Church Sunday School for the Little Church on the Prairie.
He did not enjoy soliciting contributions, but he probably did it about
as effectively as anyone. To his friend Ernest Demarest he wrote, "I
think you will find few opportunities as worthy to spend your charitable, religious dollars," and promised to call on him in a few days. It
would be difficult to say no.

That fall, Phil took time to offer a little advice to son George on his
academic plans. Under normal circumstances, George would have
been beginning his junior year, scheduled to graduate in June 1949.
But things weren't quite normal, and George admitted that "academic
interest is not too strong with me at this point," explaining, "The stuff
we get in Mechanical & Civil Engineering is pretty dull so it's hard to
do much for it." He thought he had a solution. He wanted to go to
the Stanford Business School, but not if he had to spend an entire two

years there to obtain a degree, "unless they will accept me without a degree from Yale *next* fall." The next fall George would be a senior, and he would have completed all the requirements for a degree except a term's worth of elective courses. Yale appeared to be firmly against granting a degree without full completion of requirements, elective or otherwise. George closed, "Anyway, I'm sort of dumping my hopes in your lap, pa, thinking that perhaps you know somebody connected with Stanford who could offer some advice."

In response Phil began by thanking George for his "interesting letter of the 20th." And he noted, "a transcript of your grades is a thrilling thing to look at, and I congratulate you on them." Then he gave his advice. It had to do with "putting first things first." Phil advised that George should complete his degree at Yale, "even though the last half year is spent entirely in elective courses aimed at broadening your education." If after graduating, he still thought there were courses offered by the Stanford Business School that seemed to be of interest, "certainly you should take them; but from my point of view, I would not fear failing to get a certificate graduating you from the Business course."

Another holiday season was fast approaching. Minot Davis was now in retirement in Santa Barbara. George and Flip were due to arrive home December 19. Clyde S. Martin was elected president of the Society of American Foresters. And, not as a result of the Christmas spirit, Laird offered "another idea that has been buzzing around in my mind that might go a little way in the direction of decreasing our apparent earnings." He was suggesting the formation of a corporate foundation to manage public and charitable contributions. He called Phil's attention to the experience of the Inland Steel Company, "which, like us, is in a feast and famine business." In their good years they made substantial contributions and "in bad years they make no appropriation from earnings, but continue to take care of the charities out of the Foundation." Laird admitted that contributions to such a foundation would not "make much of a dent in our bloated earnings for this year," but he thought it might help a little.

Phil responded on the day after Christmas, indicating that he was about to play hooky for a week at Sun Valley. As to the foundation suggestion, he had been thinking along similar lines, more from a public relations point of view. He acknowledged that their actual donations, "ranging from $25,000 to $35,000 a year over a period of years, don't make a very impressive reason for a reserve for these purposes." And he closed by wondering if they might not endow a museum "or something spectacular of that kind," admitting, however, that his thinking hadn't yet gone "quite that far."

CHAPTER 14

There's More to This Business Than Boards

In many respects, the Weyerhaeuser Timber Company had grown up rather casually. Its management constituted something of a closed circle, composed either of members of the family or the families of significant shareholders or else of acquaintances of long standing. Tip O'Neil, for example, who had been in charge of the Snoqualmie Falls operations, was the son of William O'Neil, John Philip Weyerhaeuser's logging manager at Lake Nebagamon. For the most part, those who worked in responsible positions had enlisted for life, with little consideration given to looking for other opportunities in other organizations. In terms of the management of responsibilities, the approach was relaxed, or at least it would so appear to outsiders.

Everyone seemed to possess a sufficiently clear idea of his own role, although the assumption of duties may have evolved rather than been assigned. Phil Weyerhaeuser, Charlie Ingram, and Al Raught occupied offices side by side on the tenth floor of the Tacoma Building, and they constituted something of a troika. They went about their business aware of what they had to accomplish in relation to the total effort. Any disagreements were differences of opinion regarding the correctness of a particular decision; they were not disagreements involving prerogatives. In truth, disagreements of any sort were uncommon. They had worked together long enough to be conscious of a consensus, one no doubt reflective of Phil's philosophy, but a consensus nonetheless. To suggest to any of them that they ought to have a detailed job description would have been something of an insult.

But the days of doing business by informal association and assignment had passed, and Phil Weyerhaeuser, no doubt with a good deal of reluctance, was ready to admit the fact. The company was not only growing rapidly in the extent of its operations, but there were ever-increasing demands in other areas such as public relations and those having to do with governmental agencies. This growth made it impossible to continue to satisfy management personnel needs from within. Furthermore, it was assumed that every organization deserved to be studied and that, in the process, all could be made more efficient. The age of the expert was at hand, even for the Weyerhaeuser Timber Company.

The first complaint of 1948 came, however, from within. It was unusual for Fred K. to question his brother's management of the Timber Company, but in early January he did just that. He was unhappy with plans to proceed with the construction of the plant at Springfield, Oregon, given the fact that the Southern Pacific was the only railroad available. He would have delayed a decision to begin construction until they had been assured that the Great Northern and Northern Pacific officials would secure permission to build into Springfield. He wondered "if we have made a sufficient effort to *sell* them on the importance of serving the Springfield plant." It was that suggestion that most bothered Phil. He replied that he was sorry Fred was in disagreement with the decision to proceed with construction at Springfield, but if they had followed Fred's suggestion, there would have been a long wait, and "I can't think the matter is important enough to delay developments which are timely." Regarding the charge that he and Charlie had made insufficient effort to convince the Great Northern and Northern Pacific officials of the wisdom of a Springfield connection, he had to disagree: "We have done, in my opinion, everything possible to stimulate the interest of two railroads, which have, apparently, not the capacity of looking after their own interests." For all intents and purposes, the matter was closed.

In the meantime, important and confidential negotiations were taking place with a view to selling the Weyerhaeuser Timber Company stock in the Washington Veneer Company to the Georgia Hardwood Lumber Company of Augusta, Georgia. Weyerhaeuser had purchased the controlling interest in Washington Veneer in 1940 and had subsequently directed its development and expansion, including the construction of production facilities of its subsidiary, the Springfield Plywood Company. The decision to sell was occasioned by the recent involvement of the Timber Company in plywood manufacture through the construction of the new plant at Longview. As Phil explained the situation, "officers of the Company felt that future embarrassments might arise through the competition which might ensue and, therefore, looked with favor upon a sale to a strong, ably-managed competitor, in whose control it appeared the Company could prosper."

The biggest news from the recent Sun Valley vacation had nothing to do with skiing. As Phil reported to Ed Davis, with obvious pleasure, "George induced Cordy Wagner's daughter to say 'Yes' publicly." It was, he said, a "swell occasion." George and Wendy would be married the following summer. There was considerably less enthusiasm over developments in Washington, D.C., where the Gamble committee of Congress was continuing its investigation of building costs. Laird Bell, Fred K., Ed Hayes, Harry Kendall, Fritz Jewett, and others were going to Washington January 9 to be present at the hearings. Phil saw little opportunity for positive results. "No program for correction of the price rise seems practical except one calling for restraint of the impulse to spend not only today's savings but tomorrow's anticipations," he stated to the Timber Company directors in a January 6 letter.

The meeting in Washington, D.C., before the joint congressional committee, went about as well as could be expected. Phil heard from Ed Hayes, who described the scene and circumstances. It seemed impossible for the Weyerhaeuser representatives to escape without some specific indication of plans for a price reduction. Ed told of a meeting in the hallway involving himself, Laird Bell, Fred K., and Harry Kendall at which they "discussed the statement which Laird finally made, namely that the WTC was in sympathy with the objectives of the Committee and the controls of inflation; that we would go home, consider the matter of adjustments in price and make a statement through our regular sales channels." That, of course, suggested that a price reduction would be forthcoming, but they thought that by announcing the change in the normal manner, it could "not be construed as a violation of the consent decree."

Laird's detailed report of events arrived later. It is interesting to participate through his perspective:

Like all these other hearings, the congressmen came and went and you never knew just who would be present at any given moment. The only ones who were continuously active were Congressman Gamble, Senator McCarthy, and most of the time Senator Cain [of Washington] and Senator Sparkman of Alabama. McCarthy kept shouldering Gamble out of control, interrupted outrageously and talked, at a guess, more than half the time during the hearing. But he is nobody's fool, has really studied the situation pretty carefully and gave the appearance of being both well posted and anxious to do something. Senator Cain came to the rescue of his boys from time to time, and Senator Sparkman smiled benignly most of the time.

From the start it was clear that McCarthy was going to bore in on us. Rustling some papers on his desk, he said repeatedly that he had some statements of some of the companies and wanted to know whether they could not afford to reduce prices. Finally he put the question directly to me. I said of course we could, but that we had so small a part in the market we could not affect the whole. He never really treated me very roughly, although he was a little hard on Charles Hines [Hines Lumber Company] again, and gave very few of us a chance to finish a sentence.

On the industry side, the usual arguments were offered that "high prices brought out production, which would disappear if prices were lowered ... and Judd Greenman made ... a slashing speech to the effect that prices were not only not too high, but not high enough." Laird had telephoned Phil, recommending that they might do well to suggest the possibility of a reduction, and Phil had obviously told Laird to do what he thought best. Thus it was agreed to indicate that Weyerhaeuser thought prices were too high, and would give the matter further consideration, announcing its conclusions through the normal channels.

Laird closed expressing gratitude that Fred K. had come to Washington, "removing the impression that we were sending only the hired men like Harry and me." And as for Ed Hayes, he was "more helpful than I can describe ... calm and sure in his judgments and I imagine has better contact with what our competitors think than any of the rest of us."

Fred K., as president of the Sales Company, issued the resulting statement to the newspapers January 14. It noted that the company intended to do its part in checking the inflationary trends "now threatening our national welfare," and announced a reduction in prices averaging 10 percent, effective immediately. Two days later the Weyerhaeuser Timber Company completed negotiations for the sale of its stock in the Washington Veneer Company to the Georgia Hardwood Lumber Company. The public announcement was made Sunday, January 18, by Phil in behalf of Weyerhaeuser and Owen R. Cheatham, president of Georgia Hardwood.

All the while, representatives of Booz, Allen and Hamilton, the firm specializing in business surveys and management counsel, were wandering about the Tacoma Building offices, interviewing, drawing organizational charts, and thinking of better ways to administer a lumber company. Stuart Campbell was the leader in the Booz-Allen survey, which not only suggested new positions but candidates to fill them. Phil told of the Booz-Allen presence in a report to the directors, also of the completion of the sale of the Washington Veneer stock. He further indicated that the Timber Company had acquired all the stock of the Weyerhaeuser Sales Company, and a new contract was being negotiated with its suppliers "on the basis of charging cost plus 8% for its selling services." In the future, Sales Company earnings would appear in the Timber Company consolidations. Finally, it was announced that an understanding had been reached with Edmond Cook by which he would spend a third of his time working as general coun-sel for the company. In Phil's words, they would "see how it works." Cook was general counsel and a director for Deere and Company of Moline, Illinois, and planned to retain that position while spending part of his time in Tacoma.

It was indeed a busy time, and Phil might have preferred to be with Helen, vacationing at San Ysidro Ranch in Santa Barbara. On Febru-ary 23 he did take a few, very few, moments off to write her the follow-ing: "Dear Helen: Love and kisses. Thanks for the wire. Will be with you if I can. Enclosing mail. Yours, Phil. P.S. Nick made me write this." The "Nick" was, of course, Phil's secretary.

The Booz, Allen and Hamilton summary of recommendations based on the survey of "top organization" was completed on schedule. Several personnel recommendations were made. In addition to deci-sions to create positions of financial vice-president, comptroller, direc-tor of industrial relations, manager of the special products division, and manager of the lumber division, there was that of legal counsel, already filled by Budge Cook; a merchandising vice-president; an as-sistant manager for logging (it being agreed that John Wahl should assume that responsibility); and an assistant manager for lumber and plywood. The report emphasized the need for indoctrination of new executives, including suggestions such as, "Provide counsel and assist-ance as necessary in connection with adequate housing and other per-sonal problems of relocation." It recommended the development of "programs of action for the guidance of both new and present exec-utives," implying that the casualness of former days could no longer be tolerated. "More and more this coordination will need to be ac-complished by means of formal programs and written reports rather than by casual and informal personal contact." It also noted the need for organization manuals, policy manuals, and the like, providing "organization charts, together with specific statements of functions, duties and responsibilities attaching to each key position in each area of the business." There was a call for remodeling the Tacoma Building "to provide for the company's central activities," and prompt initia-tion of a program of regular staff meetings. Finally, it was observed, and correctly so, that there needed to be a sound program of executive compensation established. Phil assumed rather innocently that every-one sort of worked away for the love of it, and it was not easy for him to share attitudes regarding fiscal needs. Booz-Allen let him know that Weyerhaeuser was a good step behind in this regard, a consideration that would be of great importance in the coming days of the profes-sional manager.

As he read through the Booz-Allen report, Phil probably felt a good deal like the old logger receiving a lecture from the young forester: it might be the coming thing, but it didn't sound like much fun. Further-more, did everything have to be so complicated? As with most rec-ommendations, there were doubtless useful items and those that could be ignored. Still the survey was expensive (the Booz-Allen fee and ex-penses from July 1947 through April 1949 came to $262,785.52), and it would have seemed strange indeed to pay for the privilege of being studied and then ignore the results. Certainly much could be done to improve procedures, and Phil had never pretended to be an expert in office management. That he did exceptionally well had little to do with an outlined format. He did what he did naturally, not because it was "according to policy." One thing was clear: things were going to change.

If there was a momentary longing for the world as it had been, Phil was afforded a lesson in perspective with the receipt of a letter from "old C. A. Schenck," as he signed himself, "reaching in March my 80th completed year." Schenck was still active, having been called out of retirement by the occupation forces to aid in the forestry program in the American Zone. He complained of a lack of writing paper "and whatsoever paraphernalia a scribe may need," but he seemed chipper enough, recalling his American experiences with more than nostalgia: "If I ever concoct my memories in writing, that halcyon day spent with you . . . on the Clearwater in March, 1931,—that day will stand out like the moon among stars!" Phil answered, indicating that he was sending along a box of writing materials, and adding, "I wish I could send you a banana split such as the one consumed by your niece in Orofino on that hot day!"

The annual report for 1947 was mailed to the directors March 2, 1948. The figures were impressive, reflecting for the wholly owned group a net income of almost $28 million, compared with the 1946 net profits of $13 million. Profits, before taxes and other adjustments, indicated an increase of 136 percent for log and lumber operations, 93 percent for pulp operations, and 111 percent for all operations. Dollar sales totaled $102.5 million, compared with the previous high of $66.3 million in 1946. From every consideration, 1947 had been an amazingly good year.

There were some reactions to the Georgia Hardwood, now Georgia-Pacific, purchase of the Weyerhaeuser share of Washington Veneer. Owen Cheatham sent a copy of his company's annual report to Phil, and Phil found it a bit surprising. "It was somewhat of a shock to me to find you reporting the exact dollars in view of the fact that I had been telling all and sundry that we were not making those figures public," Phil wrote to Cheatham. "I was under the impression that was by agreement with you, and, in fact, partially at your request." The other statement that surprised him was the implication in the

Georgia-Pacific report that "there was something reprehensible about owning timber." Others were also interested in that assertion. Keve Larson, of pulp sales for Weyerhaeuser in New York City, wrote to Phil, "According to their theory, those of us who hold extremely large timber tracts are assuming an unwarranted risk and stand to sacrifice profits during hard times." Keve closed wondering just "what Phil Weyerhaeuser thinks of it." Phil soon said what he thought. "Georgia's report was amusing to me also," he replied, "but, in fairness, it must be said that if our thesis is that there is sufficient forest growth in this country to support the requirements of industry, then the man who bets upon others to grow it instead of wanting to grow it himself need not be considered a fool." In short, there were two ways of looking at the matter.

The Timber Company directors were scheduled to meet on May 25, and the agenda was full. Included among the items was the introduction of three new key personnel: Roy A. Dingman, director of industrial relations; David Graham, financial vice-president; and Edmond M. Cook, legal counsel. Also scheduled was a discussion of a possible Snoqualmie Falls Lumber Company merger and an increase in Timber Company capital stock to allow for that and other merger possibilities. There were the usual dividend decisions, reports of timber trades and purchases, an updating of the development program, an account of a Securities and Exchange Commission inquiry, and recommendations of additions in the capital budget. The meeting concluded with no surprises.

Laird Bell had continued to give serious thought to the question of corporate foundations, going so far as to publish an article, "If Corporations Will Give," in the May 1949 issue of the *Atlantic Monthly*. For the most part it dealt with the needs of higher education and the advantages to society—and to corporations—of support for higher education. As a result of the article's appearance Laird received related material from many sources, all of which he was happy to pass along to Phil. In a letter of July 8, he noted, "I am playing at odd moments with the idea of proposing a policy for consideration by our Board." Phil was less certain, having given the matter less thought, but he recognized the need to move in the direction Laird was pointing.

Within the week, Phil was reading specific suggestions from Laird on the subject of corporate contributions. "I believe that, in conscience as well as a matter of our relations with the public, Weyerhaeuser Timber Company has some sort of duty to make contributions to charity," Laird began. He was not about to assert that a corporation had any right to give away the shareholders' money, and therefore the contributions should involve some endeavor "which benefits, with reasonable directness, the corporate enterprise." He also recognized the cyclical nature of their industry, and suggested that a method of contribution would need to be devised "which will smooth out these variations." He proposed the creation of a "not-for-profit corporation affiliated with the Company, to which substantial contributions can be made in good years but which will be paid out to the selected charities on a program that will even out the distributions in bad years as well as good." He suggested, for a start, that they call it the Weyerhaeuser Timber Company Charity Fund; that its trustees be the same as the directors of the company; and that its purpose might include such things as contributions to community chests in places where they did business, scholarships to employees and children of employees to attend any college or graduate school approved by the trustees, fellowships for forestry students, contributions to educational institutions for research programs in areas of company interest, and contributions directly to educational institutions in the general areas where the company did business. Laird was uncertain regarding the specific formula for giving, but he thought a percentage of profit a better yardstick than a percentage of sales. One-half a percent of profits before taxes for the previous year would have amounted to $212,487, a figure which, in Laird's opinion, "doesn't look too bad, but neither does it look lavish."

Phil had no objection to the idea; it was the administration of it that bothered him. As he responded to Laird, "I read your article on the subject, and recognize the thought which you've given the matter, but when it comes right down to brass tacks, our difficulty looks big." For example, "I founder . . . because I dread having to find worthy causes which stand out as deserving our support without inviting in a whole flock of other more questionable causes." Phil knew that he didn't want to be the one to make the distinctions and decisions, and he was not yet prepared to think about a separate organization to manage the responsibility.

That same evening, August 3, a spectacular fire swept the one-third-mile-long lumber cargo dock at Longview. Phil described the loss to the directors: "Longview has been dogged by hard luck this year; first, the boom strike; then, the flood; last evening the cargo dock was completely destroyed by fire." The origin appeared to be a defective power connection used to serve docked ships, and "A west wind, creosote construction, plus accumulations of sulphur sifted throughall, contributed to a mean fire." But it could have been worse. No ships were tied up at the time, no one was injured, and damages were limited to the dock. The main plant was operating the next morning.

Phil also reported that a quorum of the board had met on July 29 to approve proceeding with the Snoqualmie Falls merger, and all that was needed was shareholder approval. The Executive Committee had recently elected Robert W. Boyd comptroller, and Frank Walling, the new manager of the sawmill and logging division, was on the job.

And at long last a resolution of the position of general counsel had been managed. Budge Cook's part-time effort had been honest but clearly insufficient. After considerable negotiation, Joe Nolan, a partner in Laird Bell's Chicago law firm of Bell, Boyd and Marshall, agreed to assume the responsibility. Gus Clapp would finally be replaced, although Nolan was about as different from Gus as could be imagined. Gladys, Gus's widow, would hardly have approved of anyone selected, but she had obvious reason to complain of Nolan; and complain she did, inquiring of Phil how he could have chosen a Democrat. Phil reportedly replied by inquiring of Gladys whether one should be selected on the basis of brains or political preference, a reply that was not quite honest. There were, in fact, few Democrats to be found on the tenth floor, and Joe Nolan would later recall, only half in jest, "God, how they hated me; I was a lawyer, I was an easterner, I was a Catholic, and I was a Democrat!" Nolan *was* different, but he wasn't hated; he was hired. Phil liked him, and Nolan liked Phil, and that is how it had come about.

The shareholders held a special meeting on September 9, at which time final approval was given to the merger of Snoqualmie Falls Lumber Company and Grandin-Coast Lumber Company into the Weyerhaeuser Timber Company, to be effective September 30. During the gathering, Phil had failed to raise the question of a foundation, and he waited until Laird had returned to Chicago before writing him on the subject again. Phil was prepared to offer something of a halfway covenant. He did note that "inevitably if you create a charitable trust its existence will subject us to pressures which we do not now have." Still, since they were obviously in agreement that they should be doing more, he suggested that they agree to some policy "and see how close we can come to living up to it without making as public an announcement as the creation of a charitable trust would be." In short, they might be able to make contributions on their own terms without being forced to decide between proposals that wide publicity would encourage.

In the meantime Fred K. had been pondering a different sort of question, a "suggested program of Weyerhaeuser family for sons." On November 3 he sent along an outline of his thoughts, asking those of the third generation to offer comments and criticism. As he looked ahead, Fred saw that some fifteen to twenty men of the fourth and fifth generations would be entering business or professional careers over the next twenty-five years or so. He observed, "We are interested in what happens to them, both from the point of view of personal interest and from the point of view of developing able business men

302 PHIL WEYERHAEUSER: LUMBERMAN

to look after family affairs." The proposed plan did not envision that all would become involved in affiliated companies, and indeed one of the points specifically indicated that "nobody should be urged to go into an affiliated company or business against his wishes or natural inclination." Another paragraph noted that "each young man should understand that the Family owes him nothing that he does not earn by his own efforts, that he stands on his own feet and secures advancement in any business, including an affiliated business, on the basis of merit." But the very existence of such a proposal presupposed that each young man would also receive assistance and guidance to the fullest extent. In other words, it was not simply an individual matter; it was a family affair.

The elections in 1948 proved disappointing, but Phil and his like-minded colleagues had grown accustomed to such disappointments. Life went on, although in this instance there did begin to appear a decline in demand for lumber. Phil informed Budge Cook that the change in "the business cycle hasn't got us too badly worried yet, but there are a lot of long faces around the lumbermen's table these days." Regarding Joe Nolan's work, Phil was pleased, commenting that Joe seemed "to fit in like a glove, and the expanded Tacoma office organization is beginning to work together." There would, of course, be exceptions, and not all of the new appointees would "fit in like a glove."

One of Nolan's current responsibilities, following the decision of the recent Executive Committee, concerned the development of a Weyerhaeuser Timber Company foundation. Phil wrote to Laird December 3 reporting that he had just talked over Nolan's plan, "which sounded fine to me." To the directors he suggested that they ask "W. L. McCormick, Ed Hayes, and Norton Clapp to act as instigators (wrong word) and elect David Graham, Dwight Orr, and George Long officers" of the foundation, noting further that he wasn't aware if news of the plan had "leaked out yet or not, but quite a few matters are ready to refer to them for action."

In a pre-Christmas note, Laird Bell wrote requesting that he be kept slightly better informed on market conditions. Phil replied that he shared the concern, and every third day or so went down and paid Jim Morris, Sales Company representative, a visit "to inquire on the state of the market and find that we are piling up inventory and nobody is buying, we shouldn't expect anybody to buy until after the first of the year, etc." There were the usual mixed opinions on what the response should be, and prices had been reduced by about 5 percent. Looking ahead, Phil informed Laird that he was planning a late January trip to St. Paul and New York, among other things to discuss matters with Bill Peabody. Specifically, "F.K. and I rather feel we should divorce Bill from the sales and yard work and ask him henceforth to concentrate on Steamship Company," Phil acknowledging that "this may be an emotional disturbance for him, but it seems to me we can justify it to him." Business decisions involving friends were almost as difficult as those involving family. Closer to home, Phil noted that they had been spending a lot of time lately in "weekly luncheons and other meetings in an effort to get our Tacoma Office group working together and in complete understanding as to the various problems that face us." Phil and others undoubtedly occasionally yearned for days past, when the noon break involved a hurried lunch followed by some serious dominoes.

Phil transmitted Laird's concern regarding information on market conditions to Fred K.; and Fred indicated that there were several ways to provide such information to both Laird and Phil, but none were very easily managed. As he wrote:

Your impatience in respect to getting our prices on the market is identical to what I have been experiencing myself.

The fact is, however, that people start to buy lumber not when they think the price is cheap but rather when they think the price has reached a low point and then is apt to turn up. In other words, the great bulk of lumber buyers are in a sense speculators. It would be very hard to scare people to the point where they would be afraid to buy lumber and thus delay the next buying wave for an extra 30 or 60 days.

Fred closed by noting that these were considerations facing every sales organization, "but I doubt that you and Laird will want to go through all that mental turmoil."

The response was not entirely satisfactory, at least not to Laird. As he subsequently wrote to Phil, the "main idea in urging that we take over the Sales Company was that you might tell 'em and not have to reason too much." In that connection, Laird reported a recent conversation with Stuart Campbell of Booz-Allen, in which Sales Company problems were discussed at length. Also discussed were problems concerning Bill Peabody. "Campbell wants to move him out of the Newark office as well," Laird noted, "but as I have thought about it I wonder whether it isn't better to run the risk involved in leaving him there rather than give his life another wrench." To those who assumed that Weyerhaeuser made heartless decisions easily, the case of Bill Peabody offered strong evidence to the contrary. Concerning the matter of pricing policies, Laird thanked Fred K. for his "prompt reaction to Phil's letter about keeping posted on the market situation." He acknowledged that "pricing is a delicate art," but he also expressed an interest in arriving at "better coordination between production and distribution . . . and I trust that something can be worked out along these lines." The old complaints regarding the Sales Company would simply not go away.

A special occasion was announced by brief personal notes to a selected group. They read about as follows: "On Tuesday next, January 18, Helen has arranged food and drink for such of my friends as are able to be abroad that night without wives. Might be games of chance later, but no singing. Hope you can make it." The event was celebration of Phil Weyerhaeuser's fiftieth birthday. Most did make it. As Phil reported later to his scattered children: "Your mother gathered 30 stalwarts to do me honor, and a hilarious event resulted. Pop guns, firecrackers, pictures, and engraved objects arrived as offerings. Anyway, out of it all I was all softened up, and thankful for family and friends who successfully conveyed to me a feeling of affection."

He also thanked the children and spouses for remembering his birthday "so dutifully and suitably that I am forced to believe that a world-shaking event occurred." As to other matters, he noted that they had just completed a series of meetings "trying to revive the energy and performance of the salesmen," explaining, "No longer do people clamor for our lumber." And he told of plans for Helen and him to leave on January 23 for St. Paul, "via Milwaukee's new streamliner," for family meetings, and then on to New York for a week. During that time they expected "to make sure that George emerges from Yale and that Flip and Wiz are as hard at work as reported."

Another event of note was the January retirement of Al Raught, after forty-two years of service with Weyerhaeuser and affiliated companies. His contribution at each stage had been significant, and he would truly be missed. There were, of course, plans for his replacement; this had been part of the Booz-Allen survey. But although the chart might have looked quite complete and secure, one hardly replaced the experience and wisdom of an Al Raught. Probably related to that same survey were discussions regarding Phil's own role, many suggesting that there were responsibilities beyond those of the Timber Company routine. Whether these "larger responsibilities" had begun to weigh or not, Phil did do something untypical for him: he accepted election to the board of the Puget Sound National Bank, making no promises about the level of his participation to its president and his friend, Reno Odlin.

Phil and Helen's trip went as planned, and they and their new daughter-in-law Wendy attended George's graduation from Yale. Helen was unable to conceal her delight in the academic honors accorded to George. Phil was also pleased and proud.

He returned home to find the governor and the state legislature "at loggerheads about the passage of a State income tax." As Phil saw the situation, the increased revenues were needed "in order to meet the extraordinary demands of the schools and the socially insecure," adding that "economy arguments go largely unheard." Regarding business, he noted that lumber orders since the first of the year had exceeded production "but are of such mixture as to require more inventory and time in accumulating, so that shipments have not kept up." He further informed the directors that they could expect the annual report in a few days, and the auditors promised their certificate by March 1, representing "a considerable acceleration in our timing." He also mentioned that a regular Monday luncheon had been instituted for senior management at the Tacoma Club.

Within a year Phil would bring even more formality and purpose to these Monday gatherings. No one had to convince him of the importance of communicating the Weyerhaeuser story to others, and it was in recognition of this importance that he reluctantly accepted occasional offers to speak publicly. It never came easily for him, but he could not escape a responsibility merely for reasons of discomfort; there were times when only he was the appropriate spokesman. But there were also many occasions when others could represent the company, and it was partly in recognition of this and partly in recognition of needs for improved communication skills within the organization that Phil arranged a speech class. The "students" were from top management, and they met every Monday for instruction and speechmaking. Participation was supposedly voluntary; but since all volunteered, it is apparent that Phil would not have taken kindly to nonparticipation.

One assignment involved a brief introductory speech, the students being paired off to introduce each other. Phil's partner was George S. Long, Jr., and his introduction recalled their long association. Thus he observed regarding "this old friend of mine": "No research on my part was necessary in looking up the background for an introduction. He and I started out together in his father's school for aspiring young lumbermen, cruised, scaled logs, made maps, layed out railroads, studied the life of the yellow pine bark beetle (*Dendroctonus brevicomis*), and did many other things which have remained in our memories."

One of Phil's subsequent speeches concerned the general subject that had encouraged the idea of a speech class in the first place: the need for communication. He recalled the muckraking days early in the century, specifically the *Cosmopolitan* article of December 1906 on his grandfather Frederick under the headline, "Richer than Rockefeller," and examples of subsequent misinformation concerning the Weyerhaeuser Timber Company. At the time, he recalled, the response had been curious: "Strange it is that industry people, and our people, although they resented these attacks and could have disproved most of the charges if given the opportunity, instead pulled in their necks and adopted the attitude that their good works would speak for themselves." That, of course, had not happened. Even so, Phil recognized that there remained "some among us who would prefer to go back to the days when Weyerhaeuser Timber Company did not send out annual statements or quarterly statements or put out institutional advertisements in the newspapers and give wide distribution to its house organ." Phil clearly thought otherwise. If they did not provide information in their own behalf, no one would, and those who wished to study the subject would find "the weight of evidence to be in favor of the lurid rather than the conservative." Phil's thesis was that they should have learned from past experience.

For some, getting up and speaking even before friends and colleagues was a fearsome experience, but there were a few who enjoyed the opportunity. One was Joe Nolan, who offered the most memorable line. Senator J. Allen Frear, Jr., Democrat from Delaware, had recently introduced a bill that would place all corporations as measured by number of shareholders under the regulations of the Securities and Exchange Commission. Although the Timber Company would not immediately be affected, it surely would be soon. Thus Nolan managed to observe, "The only thing we have to fear is Frear himself." That alone did not make the class a success, but it helped.

During the first week of March 1949, the Executive Committee exhausted itself in studying mill reports, visiting plants, and "acting upon various problems." One of the actions authorized a course aimed at merger negotiations with Willapa and White River. A consideration awaiting resolution had to do with membership on the Timber Company board. Phil addressed a note on the subject to Laird from Tacoma. He indicated that he was still in favor of involving O. D. Fisher, "because he is, after all, the best able to help and the shortest lived of the possible Grandin-Coast nominees." He was also in favor of recommending that Budge Cook be added, bringing the total number of directors back to thirteen. In response, Laird expressed a willingness to "reconcile myself to the idea of taking on O. D. Fisher, who won't live forever, although membership on the Board seems to be a pretty good guarantee of long life." On another matter, Laird was pleased that Phil had accepted a speaking assignment before the U.S. Chamber of Commerce in Washington, D.C., trusting that "you will become reconciled to the lawyers by the time I get out there."

Progress came more slowly than had been hoped, at least by Phil, concerning the Willapa Harbor merger negotiations. For a time it seemed as if things were "going to disintegrate before it ever started," and then there was all "of the abracadabra which Joe [Nolan] insists we must go through in order to inform all of every angle." But things did go through, and on April 18, when Phil wrote to Laird, "both Boards of Directors have unanimously approved both mergers and the matter will come before the Timber Company board on the 23rd." He apologized for sounding "a little surly over the telephone the other day." Laird accepted the apology for the surliness, observing, in behalf of Nolan and himself, "Lawyers are used to it anyway." He complimented Phil on the annual report, calling it a "beautiful job."

The appearance before the thirty-seventh annual meeting of the Chamber of Commerce was a difficult assignment. Phil was one of four participants, and the program, chaired by ex-governor Ralph Carr of Colorado, featured remarks by Fairfield Osborn, president of the New York Zoological Society and author of *Our Plundered Planet*; Charles E. Kellogg, chief of the Division of Soil Survey of the U.S. Department of Agriculture; Louis Bromfield, author, and owner-manager of Malabar Farm; and Phil Weyerhaeuser. The title of the symposium was "Our Renewable Resources Can be Sustained," and following prepared remarks by the participants, there was a round-table discussion. If Phil didn't particularly relish the experience, he endured it, and he made friends for himself and the Weyerhaeuser Timber Company.

Phil observed, to one who commented favorably, that he had been amazed that "such procedures can last so long, and more especially that the patients are willing to sit there that long." He also noted that "the group of persons there were a compliment to all involved," and "the subject is so near to my heart that my ambition to perform far outstrips my ability." Charles Gillette, managing director of American Forest Products Industries, sent along a copy of a letter he had received from W. J. Bailey, vice-president of West Virginia Pulp and Paper Company, thinking that Phil would be interested in these words: "We were especially proud of the statesman-like and skillful manner in which Phil Weyerhaeuser defended the forest-using industries—not only in his direct remarks but even more so in answering questions from the floor."

Phil spoke again at the annual meeting in Tacoma on May 26. In that setting there was little outward disagreement with what he said, but he was undoubtedly no less in earnest than he had been at the Chamber of Commerce gathering. He talked of market conditions and production figures, and introduced the new personnel in management. He spoke about the creation of the Weyerhaeuser Timber Foundation and the fact that the company had contributed $100,000 to the foundation in the last year. He reviewed the mergers that involved Willapa Harbor Lumber Mills and the White River Lumber Company, "aimed at simplification of our corporate structure." He expressed hope that these mergers would receive "your approval at a special meeting of Shareholders to be called on June 29." And then he preached:

There seems to be a movement more concerted than ever to scare people into wanting a more powerful central government. This applies especially to natural resources and the industries involved. Authors like Fairfield Osborn and William Vogt achieve wide interest in books aimed to prove we are destroying the environment in which we are living. Last year *Life*, recently *Collier's* and *New York Times* gave space, either editorial or news, to prove that our forests are being destroyed and that legislation is needed to preserve them. Official backing for all this comes from interpretation of forest inventory information by the United States Forest Service. Many bills have been introduced in Congress, any one of which might empower some federal agency to dictate our rate of cut, methods of cutting, and other procedures.

House Bill 2223, now under consideration, increases Forest Service appropriations $23,500,000 a year to provide three to four thousand additional employees. Future regulators, no doubt! Senator Anderson, former Secretary of Agriculture, has introduced the current version of a federal regulating bill. The Columbia Valley Authority bill would give the Authority the right to do substantially anything deemed necessary to improve watershed protection, including condemnation of private timberland and controlling private operation on forestlands. Moreover, the Columbia watershed would include all areas in Washington and Oregon except a small bit in Southern Oregon in the Klamath Basin (which would mean from Bellingham to Coos Bay).

Phil noted the misuse of statistics, and he argued in favor of a "militant defense of our performance, that of the forest industry, and the over four million owners of forestland who will keep their forests productive if they see a profit in it." Laird Bell knew that nobody could be more sincere than Phil in defending what he was convinced was right. He also knew that in defending his position Phil could occasionally swing a bit wildly.

If few rose to dispute Phil's position on matters of philosophy, the merger questions did bring forth an occasional complaint. One who wrote, wishing to cast his vote against the Willapa Harbor merger, argued that Willapa looked "like a sick kitten to me," and suggested the result of "combining a strong company with a weak for rescue purposes is invariably lower net profits." Phil answered the complaint personally. He acknowledged that the analysis was correct about Willapa being a "sick kitten." Still, the Timber Company owned 70 percent of the Willapa stock, and also owned land and timber "surrounding Willapa's ownership for which it will some day have to provide pulping facilities" and otherwise ensure efficient utilization. In other words, with or without Willapa, the Timber Company "would be a bidder for lands and millsites." His answer was, "therefore . . . I am in favor because I think the merger eases our preparation for and accomplishment of the permanent solution for capturing some income from our prolific acres in that rapid-growing country."

Phil took a few days out for an eastern swing, during which he visited St. Paul, Chicago, and New York, and attended Flip's graduation at Yale. He also visited Bill Peabody, who, as he informed the directors, would "confine his activity from now on pretty largely to the Steamship Company." Upon his return to Tacoma, he gave some attention to a letter received from a Forest Service forester in Virginia who had taken particular exception to the substance of Phil's recent address at the Chamber of Commerce symposium. It was a thoughtful letter.

The Virginia forester began by noting that he was one of many in his profession "who are not in sympathy with the position of Mr. Watts and his close advisors in regard to regulation," but he added, "neither do I like the unfairness of much of the industry rebuttal. I do not condone some of the extravagant statements made by the old timers, except to point out that they were a small group engaged in arousing a large and very complacent public from their lethargy. And when it comes down to brass tacks, who was farthest from the truth: Those few zealots who were preaching 'exhaustion' or those thousands of operators who were shouting 'inexhaustible supplies' while one region after another was cut out?"

The forester had difficulty believing that the president of Weyerhaeuser could argue that his company could be much affected by even "the most fanatic type of regulation," and he concluded that they ought to be working together. Those in the Forest Service "are fighting many of your battles, yet they must defend themselves against attacks from you, from the range livestock men, from the park enthusiasts and from every special interest group whose plans (not always altruistic) are threatened."

In his reply, which was equally thoughtful, Phil attempted to find a common ground. He, of course, did not see the Forest Service as being the abused party. Neither did he see the benefits of extreme statements on either side. "Is it not about time," Phil asked, "that we abandon that tactic for a considered and friendly study of facts and a real cooperative solution of national problems?" He also wanted it understood that he did not regard public foresters, individually, as adversaries.

By late summer the Timber Company had a "press book," which had been developed by its department of public information. To a large extent, the information it contained attempted to explain the company's strategy and long-range operational plans. For example, why had mill construction proceeded at such an intensive rate?

In our industry, whole crop utilization means getting the maximum use and dollar value out of every log processed at the mill, in addition to using every fiber of all sizes and species of trees grown. This means that each log should be made into the product for which it is best suited . . . and which will have the highest market value relative to consumer demand. This also means that marketable products must be made from previously unused sound wood . . . such as bark, slabs, etc. . . .

Diversified production requires diversified processing plants. Grouping mills on one site permits the by-products of one plant to become the raw material for another . . . and provides for economical production through savings in transportation, power distribution, and administration.

Phil considered himself a lumberman, but there was much more involved in the business than making lumber. And he was just as proud of the diversification and integration at the production end as he was of the advances that had been made at the tree-growing beginning.

That same summer Phil announced the establishment of forestry fellowships at the University of Washington and Oregon State University, to be known as the Weyerhaeuser Fellowship in Forest Management. One thousand dollars a year was to be awarded to students selected by the deans of the forestry schools of the two institutions, and those receiving fellowships would also be encouraged to pursue
* their research in the forests and facilities of the Weyerhaeuser Timber Company. Phil was quoted in the press release as saying, "True conservation of our forest resources can only be achieved through improved forest management," and he concluded: "We hope these fellowships will contribute toward that end."

The Springfield sawmill began operations during the last week of March 1949, and aside from the usual start-up difficulties, things had gone well. Certainly the citizens of Springfield and neighboring Eugene were enthusiastic about the economic benefits of such a significant operation. In the summer, however, when the sulphate pulp mill began to emit the inevitable odors as well as pulp, local residents were less certain of their good fortune. Despite the assurances of the secretary of the Springfield Chamber of Commerce that the community "was proud of its million-dollar stink," Phil knew that they had a serious problem in public relations. He went into the odorous atmosphere in an attempt to assuage feelings, knowing he could do absolutely nothing about the smell. Jon Titcomb was manager at Springfield, and he spoke first and briefly before introducing Phil. "I suspect he gives way on this occasion without too great reluctance," Phil began, "on account of the wave of unpopularity which has no doubt swept the community, along with the obnoxious odors which have commenced to descend upon you with the starting of the pulp and paper venture at Springfield." Phil said he wished he could promise that "those odors will become sweeter," but he could not. "We think we have built as odorless a sulphate pulp mill as knowledge of the art permits," and he only hoped that "as time goes on our representatives can stand before you, and not be defensive about it." He then proceeded to explain the importance of the pulp mill in terms of utilization. The odor was, and remains, a problem and part of the price to be paid.

There was much else to worry about in the early fall of 1949. The Russians had successfully tested an atomic bomb. There was increasing concern regarding the invasion of the American market by Canadian pulp and paper and lumber. Prices and profits were on the decline. There had been some flash fires in a period of very dry conditions. And the proposal for the establishment of a Columbia River Valley Administration, CVA, along the general lines of the Tennessee Valley Authority, seemed to portend all manner of tragedy. In his letter of September 30, Phil notified the directors: "we have decided to break precedent and address a letter on the subject to all our employees and shareholders."

That letter, dated October 3, was addressed to "Our Employees and Shareholders." It described the Columbia Valley Administration bill (Senate Bill 1645) as setting up "a huge monopolistic government corporation controlled by three men whose actions would be well protected from interference by the states concerned and practically independent of Congress." One and all were urged to write to their senators and representatives "expressing your views on this important subject." The letter asserted that the purpose of the legislation was "contrary to our basic idea of representative government, and we believe that the purposes to be achieved can far better be accomplished under our present form of government."

There was, of course, every reason for Phil to feel threatened by the Columbia Valley Administration bill; but the manner of his response, at least in the instance of the letter to employees and stockholders, was questionable. One who questioned, on just those terms, was Laird Bell. If Laird was disappointed in Phil, he was downright angry with Joe Nolan. As Nolan later recalled, it was the only time "Laird really put the whip to me." Whether they had been correct or not in opposing the Columbia Valley legislation, Laird said, they had absolutely no business in stating their opinion in such a manner. "You just permitted the grossest error to be perpetrated," he chastised his former junior partner, explaining, "we have all kinds of shareholders and we have no right to instruct them in subjects political." Laird was probably not as direct in conversations with Phil, but there had to have been some serious discussion.

The feistiness, however, remained, and many who received the CVA letter were ready to applaud Phil for his stand. In thanking one who responded favorably, Phil asserted that the trouble with these "fair New Dealers is that they never stay licked!" He said that the demise of the Missouri River Authority had lulled them all to sleep, and they may have awakened too late. He also admitted, "This political business defeats me."

The major announcement of the fall had to do with the progress on the Coos Bay property. A bulkhead of about 1,900 feet was required to protect the plant site from the bay area, and construction of an 800-foot shipping dock was about to begin. Phil and Helen took some much needed time away from Tacoma, vacationing in Mexico and Guatemala with Dave and Kay Winton. As Phil later described the experience to Laird, they had flown practically all the way "and never had an unpleasant moment. . . . Had some good fishing, swimming and sun, and had enough change of scene to keep constantly interested." He had also read the Pope and Talbot story, *Time, Tide and Timber*, by Edwin T. Coman, Jr., and Helen M. Gibbs: "the best history I have seen yet."

CHAPTER 15

The Wanigan

As had become traditional, one of the first concerns of the new year was planning for St. Paul meetings, including those devoted to family matters. Although Phil and Helen participated more out of a sense of responsibility than pure enthusiasm, Phil did encourage the boys to take part. Fred K. had sent along his usual memorandum on matters to be considered, and, as usual, the 1950 list included suggestions for the better management of investments and for opportunities and assistance to the young men beginning their business careers. Phil was sufficiently impressed to write a lengthy letter in response.

Another reflective activity involved the question of how best to recognize the fiftieth anniversary of the Weyerhaeuser Timber Company. The logical answer seemed to be a history of the organization, an undertaking that Phil approached with some reluctance. Laird had obviously complained a bit about a lack of enthusiasm concerning one prospective author. Phil replied defensively, "I surely thought that I was giving an enthusiastic push." On matters of more genuine interest, Phil had been on a schedule of visiting the operations, an activity that always seemed to invigorate him. As he told Laird, "as usual, I am intrigued and recharged by the visualization of what makes us succeed." Of subjects to be considered at the pending Executive Committee meeting, Phil noted the Columbia Valley Administration and the Forest Service, adding, "I'll be glad to talk about both of them, or listen, if you please."

Phil had been studying the address Laird had given at the University of Chicago midyear commencement. While he agreed with many of the particulars, he did think that Laird was too willing to accept the unwelcome changes taking place in the system, and that Laird's em-

phasis on individual responsibility and effort ignored the larger problems, those laws and rules and regulations that seemed to restrict what
individuals would be allowed to accomplish. Thus he wrote, "Isn't my
trouble today that I want to do something affirmative aimed at directing the trend of the times, while you advise against the danger of doing
other than adjusting ourselves to whatever that trend may turn out to
be?" It is significant that Phil and Laird genuinely wished to discuss
their differences in philosophy, which in the course of any such discussion would appear to be small and insignificant. But finding time for
such talk was not easily managed. As Phil acknowledged, "I suspect
the time for clarification, argument, discussion, debate—whatever it
might be—will always be just around the corner."

In this instance, Laird decided not to wait for a future possibility of
discussing nonbusiness matters. He began by indicating that he was
"not quite prepared to accept your diagnosis," although his defense
against Phil's "diagnosis" was unspecific:

I want to do something about the trend of the times, too, but I think we have
to recognize that a whole lot of changes have come to stay—all over the world
and not solely the work of That Man. That is at the bottom of my feeling that
the role of mere opposition to the changes that have taken place and the
changes that are likely to take place is futile. I am not prepared to announce
an affirmative program aimed at a sane carrying out of valid social objectives,
but I think one has got to be framed somehow. I refuse to be intimidated by
the charge of "me-tooism." Sometimes I fatalistically feel that there is no answer except to let the current play itself out and smash—which I suppose
makes me a complete Tory.

In the next breath, Laird noted that he had kept silent about the
recent budgeting of a "handsome amount" to the National Association of Manufacturers. He considered such expenditures a waste, or
worse, but he presumed that "pressure on you men who are active is
very strong, quite independent of your inclinations, and I see no use
in my constituting a noisy minority so long as you know how I feel
about it."

Laird agreed that they should discuss the CVA and Forest Service
questions. As to the former, he might concede inequities in the bill as
proposed, but also thought that he and Phil probably would not agree
on the response that should be made. "On our relations with the Forest Service, I am pretty clear that officially we are in bad and that
affirmative steps should be taken to get into a more cooperative relationship."

The meetings in St. Paul went according to schedule, although for
Phil they were somewhat special because Flip and George attended for
the first time and, as he later reported to Ed Davis, "showed a great

deal of interest." But the real reason for communicating with cousin Ed had to do with the relationship of the Timber Company to the Wood Conversion Company. It was clear to some, most notably Joe Nolan, that the interlocking nature of so many of the affiliated organizations provided a legal headache with the likelihood of difficulties down the road. The manner of growth and company ownership and administration had not been intentionally guileful. It just seemed to make sense at the time. But trying to correct what had evolved was, in Nolan's words, "like trying to unscramble eggs." Inevitably such efforts at reorganization would involve family members and hurt feelings. Such was to be the case with Ed Davis and the Wood Conversion Company, Ed unwilling to oppose frontally what appeared to be a legal requirement but nonetheless throwing every conceivable obstacle in the path of early resolution of the problem. In short, it would be a long and frustrating process.

Another reorganizational effort involved the Weyerhaeuser Steamship Company, particularly as concerned Bill Peabody's role. This too would result in personal hurts that Phil would have greatly preferred to avoid. The relationship between the Weyerhaeuser Steamship Company and the Pacific Coast Direct Line had never been very clear or clean, and it was largely to the credit of Bill Peabody, Captain L. C. Howard, and Phil that things were managed as well as they were. In early March 1950, with a view to Peabody's retirement the following year, agreements were reached whereby the Pacific Coast Direct Line would be purchased by the Steamship Company. Previously the Steamship Company had been responsible only for the eastbound voyages of its six vessels, the lumber-carrying half of the operation. Captain Howard's Pacific Coast Direct Line assumed responsibility for the westbound voyages under a charter arrangement. As the March 9 announcement noted, the "effect of the consolidation will be to streamline the operation of both lines by placing them under a single management."

The new single management would bring Captain Howard's former Pacific Coast manager, Don Watson, into the Weyerhaeuser Steamship Company as general manager. Peabody would continue, for the time being, to work out of his Newark office, serving as executive vice-president and treasurer for the company, but Phil expected that he would begin to relinquish the details of management responsibility to Watson. As Phil described the situation to an elderly C. R. Musser, Captain Howard and Don Watson would head up the company after Peabody retired and it would be "a well-rounded freight carrier operating in both directions under the name of Weyerhaeuser Steamship Company." Phil added, "Every one connected with it, I think, feels it is a move toward simplification and better direction." He might have said "everyone except Bill Peabody." An indication of trouble to come was Peabody's decision to cancel plans for a trip to Panama. Phil wrote his old friend that he was sorry of hear of it, "as I can't believe this reorganization is going to require that you keep your nose to the grindstone every minute."

Business was moving at a fast pace. Phil reported to the Timber Company directors in mid-February that the order files were so big that they were "virtually off the market as to lumber and plywood." It was a good situation in which to have an Executive Committee meeting, but a review of income and capital budgets was just one part of an agenda that included thirteen items. Among these was a report from Ed Hayes, who was chairing a committee to recommend a solution to the Wood Conversion Company relationship; a report from Laird Bell on the company history project; and "consideration of matters politic, such as relations with the Forest Service, C.V.A., etc." Laird was concerned about politics generally, and not just in ways that touched on Timber Company interests. Indeed, on his Pacific Northwest visit, he took time on February 24 to address the Portland City Club, whose bulletin announced his title as "We Must Not Submit." He warned the overflow audience that they should be concerned about the methods of those who were hunting so-called subversives: "Political tempers can shift with great suddenness and all of us could find that these abusive tactics might strike very close to home. Freedom and personal integrity and respect for individual rights are all of one piece. We cannot protect them for people we happen to like at the moment."

There seems no doubt that Laird talked to Phil as well, probably in reference to the position on CVA that Phil had assumed in behalf of the company. In any event, following his return to Chicago, Laird addressed a brief note to Phil, suggesting that one of the advantages of flying home was that there was less time for "any afterthoughts." He did want to make certain that Phil knew of his appreciation of "the way you took criticisms which I had finally screwed my courage up to make," adding, "I hated to do it, but you made it as pleasant as it could be." The relative ease of such exchanges, of course, was the result of their own security and their respect for each other. It was not in Phil's nature to overreact, as he had obviously done in addressing the CVA letter to shareholders and employees; but the idea of a CVA had seemed threatening to the future of the Timber Company, with no regard for the efforts and vision of those who had preceded him and for the opportunities of those to follow. In short, he had reacted with anger.

That was not Phil's style. There were almost as few opportunities to compliment him as there were to criticize, primarily because everyone knew that he was simply doing his job as he saw fit, and to compliment someone for doing his job seemed silly. Still, Ray Saberson, long-time manager of the Trade Promotion Department for the Sales Company, took the occasion of his own retirement to throw some bouquets in Phil's direction. "You have made many important contributions to my happiness during my thirty-five years and two days with Weyerhaeuser," he wrote. "As I leave your house, I carry with me the firm conviction that you can make more important decisions without tearing yourself to pieces than any executive I have ever seen in action."

Phil wasn't tearing himself to pieces over the matter of labor negotiations, but he was willing to admit "it's a difficult path we walk" trying to deal fairly with two unions "and have some regard for our competitors." The IWA had turned down the pension offer while the AFL locals had accepted it. A strike vote was being taken, and in Phil's words, "a flexing of muscles is evident." Better news was the approval by the Maritime Commission of the purchase of the Pacific Coast Direct Line by the Weyerhaeuser Steamship Company, and Phil wrote immediately to Bill Peabody expressing his hope that they could now "consummate the purchase and get to a definition of jobs," adding, "If I can help in this, I'll be glad to come East for the purpose."

Phil, of course, hoped that help would not be required. He assumed that each of the parties had understood what was expected in the matter of reorganization, but he assumed too much in this instance, at least concerning Peabody. Don Watson indicated that Peabody had requested that he come to Newark on April 25, and two days later Watson wrote to Phil, "Would like very much to talk to you regarding my meeting with Bill and Capt. in Newark." As matters developed, Peabody was inflexible in refusing to accept certain aspects of the new arrangements, specifically the appointment as officers in the Steamship Company of those who had formerly been serving their own interests "in our stevedoring and westbound solicitation." But Captain Howard and Don Watson could hardly be expected to involve themselves in the reorganization in a lesser capacity than previously. It was an impasse. And it could only be settled by Phil.

He called the three to Tacoma in late April. It was difficult for all, but especially Phil. He was forced to tell his old friend Bill Peabody that the decision had been made, regardless of Peabody's position. Upon his return to Newark, Peabody wrote on May 2, "Under the above circumstances, I think the interests of the Company will best be served by asking you to accept my resignation as a Director and Officer of the Weyerhaeuser Steamship Company . . . effective immediately or at your convenience." Phil would announce the retirement on May 15, having previously written to Peabody: "I found it pretty hard in our discussions to stay completely factual and unemotional. How entirely appropriate it would have been to try to review some of the great things you have done for us and the deep and enduring friendship which you have created with almost everyone in the organization with whom you had contact. A time will come, I hope, when we can have a suitable event in your honor when we all feel up to it."

Phil was sincere. Peabody had served the company since 1914, literally starting at the bottom as a compassman for a timber cruiser. His career had been successful, but it had ended regretfully. Phil hoped that time would heal wounds and that Peabody would once again be counted as a friend.

Business continued good. The annual report for 1949 was well received, including as it did a story of "Fifty Years of Progress in the Forest Industry." Among those reacting to the report was Richard C. Lilly, chairman of the board of the First National Bank of St. Paul. Lilly noted that he had been so impressed that "I immediately bought 500 shares of your stock at 71, and you can readily see the effect of good advertising, even on a hard-boiled banker." There was another item that had impressed the "hard-boiled banker": "I note that you have increased your net assets $87,000,000 in ten years, or $26 a share, in addition to paying a reasonable dividend and spending over a hundred million dollars for addition to plants, equipment and roads. I assume that your working capital position in the ten-year period also shows a substantial increase. All in all, I am happy to have my name appear as a stockholder."

But any assumption that all was right with the world of Weyerhaeuser was soon to be altered. By mid-May most of the Timber Company operations were closed by strikes, the major point of contention the question of a union shop, which, Charlie Ingram observed, "the company has not seen fit to give." It was hardly an opportune time for a shutdown, with business good and getting better—the market receiving an added impetus from the loss of Weyerhaeuser production. Ingram was hoping for a quick settlement, "but I am making no predictions."

Phil was distressed by the strike and was also disappointed with his handling of the May board meeting. He shared his feelings with Laird Bell:

I felt depressed about the meeting, what with bad news of the strike and lack of reaching decisions on any of the difficult subjects. I feel I should alter my procedure with the board with the purpose of confining discussions in formal board meetings to matters on which I have a definite recommendation. I don't quite see how the other matters of a more general nature can be put out for consideration, but something has to be done because the strain of just sitting around is just too great.

It used to be when we operated largely as a committee, I got a good deal of help out of a general conference discussion-type of thing, but when it gets to a board meeting, I guess the crowd is just too big. I am disappointed myself because I don't think the Board can be nearly so helpful as the Committee used to be, unless I learn a technique.

He closed by thanking Laird for compliments on his recent speaking efforts: "I know they'll never be very good, but I can suffer through that if I can avoid disagreement on attitudes which the Company should take." That final observation undoubtedly referred to the CVA controversy. Nearly a month later the debate continued, Phil forwarding what he thought was evidence of a similar involvement by another corporation. Laird saw it differently. "There the company itself, and the interests of all its stockholders, were directly involved . . . but our case was more general, and verged on the political," he explained. "In retrospect, however, I think I was more irritated by the cheapness of the propaganda material than the substance."

Suffering through the strike was another matter. Negotiations continued, but there was no noticeable progress. Federal Conciliator Leo Kotin met with representatives of the company and the Northwest regional negotiation committee in Tacoma on June 1, but the positions had not changed since the meeting a week earlier. The union had then proposed a 7.5-cent-per-hour wage increase, a deduction of up to 7.5 cents per hour from an employee's pay for a health and welfare program, three paid holidays, and a union shop. The company's position was that it had "no right to deduct money from an employee's paycheck for a benefit plan unless the employee voluntarily authorizes the Company to do so." Instead, it offered its own pension plan and a 10.5-cent-per-hour wage increase.

Following the June 1 meeting, the Timber Company's report stated: "The Company is unchanged in its belief that the Union's health and welfare program is neither legal nor practical and that a union shop—even though it is in effect in the pulp operations—is not in the best interests of employees or the company. Furthermore, we consider that either of the proposals made by this Company is of greater benefit to you." The union leadership obviously took a different view of the matter.

Although the company could have put together a more effective negotiation team, the nature of organization and procedure left the mill managers in the responsible positions. There must have been occasions when they felt at a disadvantage as they faced union representatives whose main skill was on display at the negotiating table. Perhaps simply to get away, Phil decided to accept an invitation from Harry Kendall of the Sales Company to visit timberlands and lumber operations in Mexico. It proved to be more a vacation "than a business accomplishment, but the impressions I got will remain vivid, and it was a complete change," Phil subsequently wrote to Kendall.

In Phil's absence, Charlie Ingram coordinated the company effort. It is revealing to read his assessment of the situation as of June 7. It was apparent to him that the union had simply determined to raise an issue and the one "selected by them was union shop": "We find it difficult to insist that our old employees not now members of a union be forced to join. It seems to me that there won't be many freedoms left in this country if a stand is not made for that principle of freedom of choice. The many letters we have received from union and non-union employees commending our stand have greatly strengthened my convictions in this matter."

The fact was, however, that in a previous settlement as a member of an industry negotiation group, Weyerhaeuser had been forced to accept a union shop. In the summer of 1950, they maintained their opposition alone, watching their competitors working away at peak levels. As Charlie reported to Laird Bell, "Great activity in the industry has absorbed quite a few of our employees which makes it more difficult for our other unemployed men to act."

Phil did cancel plans to attend his thirtieth reunion at Yale. As he explained to Peavey Heffelfinger, there seemed to be some change regarding the strike positions, "and in view of its importance to many individuals, and on the chance that I can help, I am foregoing our 30th reunion." He closed his note to his old roommate with "just a word of advice: Take it easy." But despite Phil's presence in Tacoma, the deadlock continued, and the negotiations that took place June 26 were the first in three weeks. As he reported to the directors, "Signs of brewing interest in returning to work encourage us to feel something will break soon." Laird generally agreed with the letters that had gone out to employees during the strike, although he wondered whether the company's position on the union shop question had been made sufficiently clear, and there is evidence that his own feelings were not those held by Phil and his management team. Laird indicated in a letter of July 5 to Phil that although "we are unwilling to force present employees to join any union," he saw no great difficulty in imposing a union shop on new employees, adding, "lots of corporations seem to live comfortably under that arrangement."

July was nearly three weeks old when the strike was settled, and more than two months had passed since the walkouts began. The losses would be hard to measure, but they were certainly considerable and especially so when the details of the final agreement became known. These included a 5-cent hourly wage increase, three paid holidays, a company-paid health and welfare program, a checkoff arrangement (automatic deduction) for union dues, and the "wording in the Maintenance of Membership clause which tends to strengthen company support of the union." The principle of freedom of choice may have been maintained, but barely so, and it must have seemed to both sides that the compromise had been delayed to no real purpose. Lessons had been learned, but they were the lessons of trial and error. Phil sent along his own thoughts in an end-of-the-month report to the directors:

A great sense of relief is felt throughout the organization by reason of the strike's end. Appraisal of the cost versus the benefits, though difficult so close to the event, leaves me few regrets. We are all hopeful that a clearer understanding of the things which influence our employees will result.

In view of the price advances, it should not be difficult to make up the current budget deficit during the last half. We are completely in the dark, though, as to the effect of the imposition of threatened war controls.

American troops were fighting in South Korea and, from all reports, fighting for their lives.

On the more pleasant side of foreign affairs were the occasional invitations for possible ventures by the Timber Company in exotic opportunities. One of these involved Ethiopia, and although Phil was pleased with the expression of distant interest, he indicated that the company was not in a position to give serious consideration:

It would be a great departure from our past practices for this company to engage in any foreign venture. Its activities have thus far been confined to the United States, and its manufacturing efforts have been confined to the states of Washington and Oregon, though, of course, it seeks wide markets for its products.

Until the company achieves much better integration than has yet been possible, its available capital funds will be required in adapting its manufacturing plants to complete use of the product from its tree farms. There seems little probability that its directors can divert from this course.

Capital expenditures were being made at the Coos Bay branch with the start of mill construction at North Bend, Oregon, and logging also began in the company's Millicoma Forest. In the meantime, there were increasing concerns about the effects of the Korean War on the economy. In less than two months, lumber prices had advanced some 20 percent. Harry Kendall participated in a high-level discussion of the inflationary problem with Department of Defense representatives, and subsequently an official statement was issued detailing the likely needs of the government and emphasizing the absence of any stockpiling requirements. It was hoped that assurance that the military foresaw no enormous needs would, in Harry's words, "prick the inflationary boom," his feeling being that "in the long run the industry will be far better off with prices back where they were the early part of the year." The problem, however, was complicated by a lack of railway cars to move the West Coast inventories to eastern markets. In a moment of despair, Phil wrote to Fred K., "If it isn't a strike, it's the war and controls or a vicious car shortage." It certainly seemed so in the summer of 1950.

Phil had managed to take a couple of days off to escort a party that included Fairfield Osborn, president of the Conservation Foundation, through various Timber Company operations. Phil realized the importance of Osborn and his friends, although it may have largely been in recognizing the damage they were capable of doing. In any event, he was convinced that once others were shown what Weyerhaeuser was accomplishing in managing its forest responsibility, these others would become supporters. In that conviction he was occasionally disappointed, and following the visit of the Osborn party, he addressed a note to Fred K., who had agreed to serve in Phil's stead on the board of the Conservation Foundation. "You've really got a job on your hands if you associate with these blokes," Phil wrote, enclosing a recent article by Fairfield Osborn. To Osborn, Phil expressed thanks for putting up with three days of "our salesmanship," but then explained the reasons for his unhappiness with the approach the writer so often seemed to take, specifically the use of statements for excitement rather than education. Phil referred to the tactic as "shock treatment": "Use of the 'shock treatment' in arousing people to a cause is unnatural to me, smacking as it does of over-statement. In the long run, reactions are likely to be the reverse. Moreover, creating fear in those uninformed breasts may lead to a solution that is wrong."

If the summer of 1950 had more than its share of worries, demand for lumber and lack of rain were not among them. Most plants were working on Saturdays in an effort to keep up with the demand, although the shortage of railway cars continued to be troublesome. And fires had been at a minimum as a result of well-spaced showers. By the end of August, the Timber Company's profits were equal to those of 1949, in spite of the strike, and business continued to boom through September. In early October, however, the market began to decline, and Phil told Laird they would probably have to "take some hitches in our belts before things start rolling again." Business or no, there were plenty of "extracurricular activities," including efforts aimed at designing "an effective plan for management and executive development within the company and its subsidiaries." It was recognized that the management requirements were increasing rapidly, "both for replacements and to man the new jobs which come with our diversifying activities."

The fall meeting of the directors was scheduled for November 13, and there were a number of agenda items that were out of the ordinary. Ed Hayes's Wood Conversion Committee had recommended at the April meeting that the Weyerhaeuser Timber Company undertake to purchase the minority stock of Wood Conversion. That of course required a recommendation by the management to the stockholders—a recommendation Ed Davis had so far declined to make. Thus on September 1 Phil admitted to Laird, "As far as I can judge, the matter rests exactly where it did before the committee's recommendation." Phil hoped for some action at the November meeting. In the agenda he simply indicated, "It may be that Wood Conversion Company will have some response to the suggestions of the Committee of Untouchables." There were also proposals to expand pulp production at Longview to provide a closer balance between wood supplies and consumption. Finally, there would be considerations relating to the impact of the war on Pacific area development, a possible delay in the integration program and the effects it would have on dividend policies, as well as other likely wartime adjustments.

Laird Bell was continuing to look for an author for the planned Weyerhaeuser Timber Company history and had offered the suggestion of Allan Nevins. Phil replied that he thought Nevins was "the kind of man I'd like to do the job," but he was less certain about the nature of the effort: "when it comes to stressing personalities I wonder if the enterprise is now old enough to do so?" He also inquired who would own the manuscript. "Can we veto it, or, at least, not publish it if there are those among us who feel violently about it?" he asked Laird.

In conjunction with the gathering of the directors in Tacoma, Phil planned a dinner for those he considered the upper-level management of the Tacoma office. The suggestion had been made in the course of the speech class that it would be beneficial if they had "occasional informal dinner meetings four to six times a year to get better acquainted and learn more about the Company, its policies, etc.," and Phil looked upon the November 14 affair as perhaps the start of that plan. Accordingly, he invited Laird Bell, Fred K., and Charlie Ingram to make presentations of ten to fifteen minutes each, with Laird talking about "a director's place in the overall Company picture . . . or whatever he'd like." Fred K.'s assignment was a discussion of prices, "how they are made; our price philosophy; our influence on prices; what he expects of business in 1951, or whatever he likes." Charlie wasn't given quite the latitude of the other two, Phil directing him to discuss "the peculiar position of the management people (the hundred present) in the Tacoma Office in relation to the decentralized line operating management, etc."

In the first week of November, the Timber Company published a booklet entitled *Men, Mills and Timber in the Nation's Service*, which attempted to summarize the progress made by Weyerhaeuser in recent years in increasing its productive capacity, just one indication of its "readiness and willingness to serve our nation." In the covering letter that accompanied distribution, Phil was quoted, "I hope it will aid you in understanding what this company is doing and can do." The effort, of course, was inspired by the hope that it would not be necessary to return to an era of government regulations, wage and price controls, and the like. As events would prove, controls and regulations never reached World War II levels, but business affairs were considerably scrambled.

Immediately after the directors' meeting, Phil and Helen headed east for business and pleasure. Phil attended a retirement dinner for Bill Peabody in Newark. They went to the Yale-Harvard game. They helped celebrate the fiftieth anniversary of the Yale School of Forestry. In that regard, a couple of concerns bothered Phil. First, it seemed that the school was in need of a library building and an endowment fund, in order to give it "an income more comparable to the schools with which it now competes." Second, Phil wondered why the Forestry School at Yale seemed so isolated from the West, noting that the Weyerhaeuser foresters came not from Yale, "but rather from the forest schools which Yale spawned." The financial needs of the school interested Phil, thinking that perhaps that sort of contribution might appeal to the Weyerhaeuser family. He expressed the possibility to Fred K., observing that such a gift might be something "around which even the Harvard members of the family could rally with some equanimity, but it doesn't seem to me that it answers what I had in mind, that is, some public recognition of our family's plowing something back into the communities whence sprang its prosperity."

Phil and Fred K. also met General Dwight D. Eisenhower, then serving as president of Columbia University, and heard him discuss what was called the American Assembly program. In general terms, this envisioned the organization of conferences on major issues of concern, utilizing the support and participation of the best that was available in experience and theory. Phil was sufficiently impressed to recommend to the Timber Company directors that a contribution of $25,000 be made. To General Eisenhower he indicated his personal willingness to participate, offering to "propose to our group that they undertake to finance a conference on conservation, although it is clear our name should not be directly associated with it."

Christmas of 1950 saw the family together in Tacoma. Flip was working in Dallas, "trying to sell lumber," as Phil indicated to a friend. George was working as a shift foreman in the Longview pulp mill. Wiz was still attending the Ethel Walker School and would be graduating in June. Ann was the mother of three boys.

An object of attention and occasional comment early in 1951 was the organization book of the Weyerhaeuser Timber Company, which, as Phil explained to Laird, undertook "to indicate lines of authority with charts and specific job descriptions." It was a somewhat painful admission of bigness, but at least the thing was done, and the continual updating would not be as difficult as the initial effort. The reactions were interesting. Tip O'Neil observed from his Snoqualmie Falls desk that the book seemed "to have grown almost as fast as the Company." Harry Kendall simply commented, "As your operation becomes more complex, things like this are necessary, and I want to compliment you on the clear graph of organization and job analysis."

Harry Kendall and Phil Weyerhaeuser both knew that charts and job descriptions told only a small part of the story. Still it would have been a relief if some progress had been made in rearranging the relationship of the Wood Conversion Company to the Weyerhaeuser Timber Company. It was apparent that Ed Davis was doing more than dragging his feet; he was in a state of siege. Laird Bell finally got disgusted with Davis's resistance and wrote him a lengthy letter in an effort to answer all possible objections. To begin with, it was a matter of Wood Conversion and the Timber Company having common ownership and at the same time dealing in business that was increasingly competitive. That much should have been obvious. Nonetheless, Laird had been upset when Ed Davis had stated at the November directors' meeting that the subject of the relations between the two organizations simply was a "lawyer's question." As Laird noted, "It *is* a lawyer's question, but not only a lawyer's question. . . . Realistically and whether we like it or not, lawyers' questions are compelling a great many changes in business these days which might not otherwise be made and the lawyers' reasons for getting out of the present relations between the two companies seem to be pretty compelling."

Then Laird proceeded to recall the events that had led to the formation of the Wood Conversion Company, listing himself as "one of the few survivors" who had been present at that meeting held in F.E.'s old office:

Mr. F.E.'s idea was that as there were a great many common concerns it was absurd to have each of the companies going off on its own in sales, legal matters, insurance, tax matters, etc., and that it was only good sense to create some central agency which would serve all the companies in which the men present were in varying degrees interested. . . . The question of utilizing by-products was a major one under discussion, and as I recall it there was a By-Products Committee headed by Uncle Bill Carson. I remember being present at a meeting at which Howard Weiss described something which I think turned out eventually to be Nu-Wood, and I think this was the beginning of the activities which eventuated in the Wood Conversion Company.

In short, what Laird was trying to tell Ed Davis was that Wood Conversion had not been organized as a separate enterprise but as one whose purpose was simply to find uses for the by-products of those plants making up the affiliated group, "And the major interest of that same group is now the Timber Company." Laird concluded his lecture by asserting that others in the group could legitimately ask that "the interests of the group as a whole should be considered predominant—and this without regard to the lawyers."

Ed Hayes's "committee of untouchables," as Phil referred to it, made specific recommendations in late January 1951. These involved a tax-free statutory merger of the Wood Conversion Company into the Weyerhaeuser Timber Company based on an exchange of the minority stock of Wood Conversion for Timber Company stock on the basis of four for seven, Timber Company for Wood Conversion. This report was given consideration at the February 26 meeting of the directors, and at the Executive Committee meetings that followed. The immediate result was no result. The report of the special committee was "accepted and filed," and thanks extended for its efforts, but the Executive Committee decided that the time was not right for the merger to proceed. As Phil later explained, that "action puts everybody on notice that the antagonism expressed in some circles toward the Timber Company's acquisitive attitude was recognized and that the company itself would not be put into the position of advocating a course which could not be put across without broken bones." The problem that had occasioned the discussion in the first place remained unresolved.

Phil was fifty-two years old, and although he had certainly indulged in his share of foolishness along the way, for the most part such moments came in the course of normal activities. Even vacations for Phil and Helen had usually included company responsibilities. It wasn't that he felt overworked or anything of the sort. Indeed, it is hard to imagine that Phil ever went through an entire day without some cause for unalloyed happiness, whether at work or at home, but the fact was that he seldom indulged himself by specifically reserving time for pleasure or spending money. Now he decided, with Helen's encouragement, that it was time to invest in a cruiser. Easy access to Puget Sound and the waters beyond made such interests rather commonplace among Phil's friends, one of whom, Ernest G. Swigert, had come across just the boat. But the *Snuffy* was sold before Phil could make arrangements for its purchase, and Swigert then suggested that Phil consult with a boat builder in Jacksonville, Florida, this in the course of a March vacation with Dave and Kay Winton.

Before his mid-March departure, Phil received the news that a certificate of necessity had been granted the Timber Company, permitting construction of a $19 million pulp plant at Everett, provided of course that the materials could be procured. Phil was leaving to his managers and Roy Dingman the decision on how to conduct the pending labor negotiations, some arguing in favor of a company-wide approach while others talked against anything that "smacked of unanimity." In the absence of Charlie Ingram, the compromise was reached whereby a company approach was agreed on provided that "local operations would all be represented and that all local problems had to be settled at the time of the general settlement if any."

The Florida vacation was delightful in every respect, and Phil and Helen got their boat. Ernie Swigert met Phil and Helen in Jacksonville and introduced them to Frank Huckins of the Huckins Yacht Corporation. As Phil later reported to Dave Winton, "When we got down to the Hotel in Miami after leaving you, Helen pushed me over the cliff and I wired Mr. Huckins in acceptance of his proposal and sent in his contract."

Phil described his vacation in glowing terms in a letter to Laird Bell, without once mentioning the boat purchase: "Our vacation in Florida was all we could have asked—good weather and a lot of fun with Dave and Kay in their boat, fishing on the Keys, including a trip to Havana, and, on the way home, we saw Flip for two days in Dallas, and Don Watson in San Francisco." Furthermore, he noted that "all the knotty problems, including the wage negotiation and the legislature, were settled in my absence, and Helen and I returned feeling like a million." It was, however, the boat about which he was most excited. After brief uncertainty, and the suggestion that they call her the *Breather*, it was decided to name the cruiser the *Wanigan*, a reminder of the log drives of yesteryear.

The Timber Company annual report for 1950 provided some revealing statistics. Aside from the usual references to profits and taxes, wages and salaries, it was noted that over the past five years Weyerhaeuser had invested more than $100 million in new plants, equipment, and road construction. In his accompanying statement, Phil observed that "emphasis in forestry research is shifting toward the problems of reproducing, protecting, growing and improving new timber crops as the virgin forests are harvested and replaced by young trees." It was true that the old-growth timber was rapidly disappearing, but what had long constituted a concern now seemed merely to involve a different approach. For some it continued to be difficult to accept an end to the old ways, but to most, the permanence of operation afforded by the growing forests more than compensated. It was a very different Timber Company from the one Frederick Weyerhaeuser and his associates had envisioned in 1900, but it was a company now even more secure in its future.

There were a number of opportunities to take note of change and developments. One was the publication of Colonel Greeley's book, *Forests and Men*. Phil wrote to the author on May 15 telling that he had sat up the previous night reading, "and enjoyed it immensely." He continued, "I suppose, more than anybody else, you have watched the progress of the conservation movement from its beginnings to the present situation of most encouraging progress," and concluded that the book had been generous in crediting others, "but I suspect that nobody has played as big a part in the successful application of forestry as you have yourself." It is interesting that Phil used the word conservation in this instance, usually maintaining that it implied something static; he preferred to talk in terms of reforestation. But he had not succeeded in altering definitions or usage, and others continued to speak of conservation.

Another occasion for pause was the celebration of the tenth anniversary of the Clemons Tree Farm dedication, Phil noting that "it seemed a worthwhile plug for tree farmers nationally, as well as locally." At the June 23 ceremony, broadcast nationwide on the NBC radio program "The Farm and Home Hour," there was a nice mix of the local and the well known. The Montesano High School Band provided the music and Chapin Collins, editor of the Montesano paper, was honored as "Chairman of the Day." "Keep Washington Green" balloons were given to all children in attendance. Stanley F. Horn, editor of the *Southern Lumberman*, served as master of ceremonies, and among those recognized were Colonel Greeley and Governors Arthur B. Langlie of Washington and Douglas McKay of Oregon. A plaque commemorating the beginning of the American Tree Farm Movement was unveiled by Mrs. C. H. Clemons, after which Phil made a few brief remarks. He noted that more than three thousand owners of private timberlands in twenty-nine states had become involved in the effort, observing that voluntary participation had taken place "because it is good business to treat timber as a crop," and while much had been accomplished in the course of the ten years, "a bigger job lies ahead":

There are still other thousands of landowners controlling both large and small forest tracts, who must be convinced that tree farming is a paying business—

that timber is indeed a profitable crop. In the years ahead, let all of us remember that tree farming has been made possible because of economic incentives. The program will continue to grow insofar as we are able to offer landowners this inducement to take the risks involved in growing trees. Working together, we can prevent forest fires; we can maintain a permanent timber supply for our peacetime and wartime needs. We need your continuing support.

At the same time, plans were going forward for the dedication of the Millicoma Forest Tree Farm at Coos Bay, to be held July 7. Clyde Martin had suggested that they invite Dr. C. A. Schenck to attend, and Phil wrote to Art Karlen, manager at Coos Bay, that they should name a tree or a lookout for the old German forester, certain that he would be "an appreciative and distinguished receiver."

Following the June meetings, which included a reunion of sorts involving both the Denkmann and the Weyerhaeuser families, Phil wrote a lengthy and revealing letter to Laird, apologizing that there had been so "many Weyerhaeusers evident." For the most part, however, that had been simply a pleasant distraction. The lack of progress on the Wood Conversion problem was a major disappointment, Phil admitting he felt "a little chagrined" that it seemed impossible for him to deal effectively with cousin Ed Davis. "I can't discuss anything with him with any feeling that we understand each other," Phil complained. "I guess it's just his defense mechanism trying to protect himself against the octopus which evidently controls his company, but which is unable to exercise that control in any perceptible way." It was doubly frustrating to be perceived as powerful while at the same time being unable to effect needed change.

Among the problems more recently considered were those having to do with General Timber Service and the relationship of Thompson Yards to the Sales Company. The Weyerhaeuser Timber Company directors had given Fred K. the authority to sell Thompson Yards, an authorization that was to have been confidential, but the management of Thompson Yards somehow learned of it even before Fred K. had returned to St. Paul. As Phil observed, the news "destroyed the morale of the organization to some extent and seems so unnecessary that it makes me mad." Regarding General Timber Service, since John Musser was its current director, any rearrangement there seemed likely to involve personal-family relationships on the order of those encountered in Wood Conversion. Thus it was that Phil noted, "A matter which has been glossed over and which seems to me to be pretty important is the activity of General Timber Service; that one is difficult for John to meet, but I think it must be met promptly." There was plenty to do, and not all of it pleasant.

Laird had also been disappointed at the lack of progress, but he wanted it understood that he was not holding Phil responsible. "Don't under any circumstances blame yourself," he wrote after receiving Phil's letter. Laird was willing to admit that the problems were complex, and to agree that "the suppressive atmosphere of a large group" was not conducive to resolving them. On the more positive side, he was enthusiastic about the publicity surrounding the Clemons Tree Farm ceremonies. "You seem characteristically to have stayed in the background all you could," Laird wrote to Phil, "but I hope you take a real personal satisfaction out of it." Then he offered his own assessment, questioning "whether anything has been done which better dramatizes the forestry activities of the industry."

Also satisfying was the Millicoma Forest Tree Farm dedication July 7. Phil wished that Laird could have attended, for they had listened to some "real good speeches made about tree farming, capped by old Dr. Schenck's glowing personality." They had honored the German forester by designating the growing forest area lying between the Millicoma and South Coos rivers as the Carl Alvin Schenck Working Circle. It was an unusually dry summer and the threat of fires hung over the forests, but the importance of being aware of fire dangers had been driven home as a result of the tree farm publicity.

Aside from a lack of rain and the organizational frustrations, the summer of 1951 was one of large pleasures, and in the process Phil became something of an advocate of rest and relaxation. Happily received was a letter from Aimee Lyford, written in response to the announcement of Flip's marriage to Clara Dracoulis. Phil apologized for dictating his reply, admitting that perhaps Helen was correct in saying that "I have forgotten how to spell." He also said it had been a real pleasure to see Miss Aimee's "fine handwriting" again, "which takes me back to my youth." He then described the family circumstances: Flip was "very much in love"; Wiz was in Europe with a classmate, having graduated from the Ethel Walker School with plans to enroll in Mills College in the fall; George and Wendy were living in Springfield; and Jack and Ann's three boys "are a great joy to us." In general, life was good.

In general, business was good too. The Coos Bay plant had started up with no more than the usual difficulties, and carloads of chips had begun to arrive at the enlarged Springfield pulp mill from Coos Bay. Plans were nearing completion for the construction of a plywood plant at Springfield, and although problems remained, the commitment to proceed with the construction of a sulphate pulp mill at Everett had been made. The *W. L. McCormick* was christened at Olympia on August 1 following the completion of its first round-trip voyage under the flag of the Weyerhaeuser Steamship Company. The decision to purchase this ex-Liberty ship had not been an easy one. Indeed, the

Steamship Company directors had hesitated in their deliberations, apparently awaiting some signal that would indicate the proper course to follow, at which time Phil had nudged a dozing McCormick and whispered, "Come, Bill, make a motion to purchase another ship and we'll name it for you." Bill made the motion, and the *W. L. McCormick* was the result. In the course of its christening ceremonies, its captain promised "the biggest eastbound load of lumber yet achieved." In recent months the steamship business had witnessed substantial rate increases, but, as Phil noted, "wage costs rise faster." In an August 23 letter to the directors, Phil reported, "all records for dryness are broken and we are praying for rain."

But market reports, fire fighting, and steamship christening did not totally occupy Phil's thoughts. He was eager for the work on the *Wanigan* to be completed and was not above sharing his feelings. As he made plans to organize the crew for the maiden voyage, he addressed a late August communication to Captain L. C. Howard, Norton Clapp, Ralph Boyd, Don Watson, and Fred K., admitting that it may have seemed "like inviting you to the races in Timbuktu, but this is a new kind of venture for me and I'm all excited about it." It was determined that they would sail the *Wanigan* from its Jacksonville launching site up the coast to Norfolk, Virginia, where it would be loaded on a Weyerhaeuser Steamship Company vessel for shipment to Tacoma. All the invited crew with the exception of Fred K. were able to serve, and the *Wanigan* somehow arrived safely at Norfolk on October 19, after a voyage of five days. It had been a wonderful time, and now Phil couldn't wait until the *Wanigan* was off-loaded from the *F. S. Bell.* The forty-five foot cruiser was indeed bringing great pleasure to Phil and Helen. Ironically, it would be the cause of much suffering as well.

CHAPTER 16

The Changing Scene

In mid-November 1951, the Timber Company board of directors gathered in Tacoma. Among the more unusual agenda items was attendance at a buffet luncheon at the College of Puget Sound fieldhouse at which General Douglas MacArthur was the honored guest. Also unusual but more directly related to business was the request to proceed with what was termed a "national advertising campaign," at an approximate cost of $500,000. A so-called Crystal Ball Committee had been organized at the management level, and the work of this group was summarized for the directors in the form of a report of sales, investments, and profits as projected ahead five years. In part a result of the increasing concern for planning, the new top-level position of economist was created. It was presumed that he would report directly to the president and would be the company's expert, particularly in forecasting "business conditions in the forest industry and general industry useful in preparing the company for impending changes." Although there was nothing unusual in recognizing the need for economic expertise, the job description did contain a paragraph that specifically detailed Phil's concerns and hopes: "Appraises the economic consequences of the company's sustained yield and forest management policies for use by management (1) in decisions as to major expenditures for further capital investments and (2) interpreting its sustained yield and management policies and operations thereunder to taxing and other governmental authorities, shareholders, labor, and the public."

The November deliberations of the directors were apparently more productive than had recently been the case, Phil subsequently commenting to Laird that he felt they had "removed a few cobwebs without producing the normal amount of headaches." One of the matters under consideration involved compensation practices for key executives in the company, it being apparent to most that Weyerhaeuser's policy was exceedingly conservative and would prove detrimental in attracting and keeping able executives. Phil was partly responsible for the problem, since he tended to discourage any increase in his own salary, not seeming to appreciate fully that his salary served as the standard for the overall schedule. In any event, the directors approved in principal a stock option plan for upper-level management employees and encouraged a review of the salary program, armed with data from other corporations. A Compensation Committee was appointed, with instructions to make a full recommendation to the directors at the May 1952 meeting.

Following the Friday adjournment, Phil and Fred K. rushed off for a little duck hunting, and on the next day, November 18, Phil and Helen boarded the Great Northern to begin an eastern trip of about three weeks with an itinerary that mixed about equal measures of business and pleasure. Phil had interviews with candidates for the positions of economist and financial vice-president, a brief meeting with General Eisenhower on American Assembly matters, a party honoring Bill Peabody, a visit with Carl and Edith Weyerhaeuser at Cambridge, and attendance at the Yale-Harvard game. In addition he met with representatives of the Harvard Business School and with Dean George Garratt of the Yale Forestry School. He also attended the National Association of Manufacturers meetings in New York, primarily because Clyde Martin was a featured speaker, and took Helen to see *South Pacific* on Broadway. For all the excitement, the two were probably happiest when they arrived back home in the early morning of December 13.

The *Wanigan* continued to provide much pleasure and a few surprises. Ernie Swigert had warned Phil about some things: "Believe me, your worries about what to do with your spare funds are at an end." He had not warned him of the dangers of shipboard life; Phil discovered some of these for himself. In a December 20 note to Lieutenant Charles Pascoe, son-in-law Jack's brother, Phil felt "at rather a low ebb with three busted ribs, having stepped into a hole in the boat for no good reason." It would not be the last accident he would experience on the *Wanigan*. While seldom serious, broken ribs are not easily ignored, and so it was with Phil. In the course of one sleepless night, at three o'clock in the morning, he finally picked up the annual report of the College of Puget Sound and read it from cover to cover. As a result, he wrote a brief letter to the school's president, R. Franklin Thompson. He congratulated Dr. Thompson on the report and on the excellence of his administration generally, adding, "It is probable that

spending your life as you do complimenting others on their performance right and left too seldom you receive a deserved pat in return."
Phil was taking more time along the way, and taking less for granted.
There is no doubt that Dr. Thompson appreciated the kind words and
was properly solicitous of the giver of those words and other gifts.

Fred K. was, of course, also sympathetic "about your busted ribs,"
but he remained the brother. "It seems to me that you are getting more
awkward as you get fatter and no doubt you don't see where you are
placing your feet," he wrote. "It sounds like the end of the athletic
contests between us which must be goading to you when you reflect
on how well I have kept my figure and my agility." Fred K. was making plans for the January family meetings, and on January 3 he addressed letters to the family with a suggested agenda and invitations
for socializing. The agenda began with "reports of corporate performance during 1951 similar to those which have been prepared for past
meetings," and the next item involved individual reports by family
members "on those activities with which they have been principally
connected." There was always time set apart for questions deserving
family consideration. In this instance, "Have we need for an investment service other than that now available here?" and "What should
we do to make our estates more liquid?"

Fred K.'s feelings may have been stronger than those of many in the
family, but they were undoubtedly representative. He had "inherited"
the responsibility for leadership, and he took it seriously. In some pen-
ciled notes he had prepared for his own use, it is apparent what he
considered important to share. He intended to call on Dave Weyerhaeuser for an opening prayer, "in appreciation of blessings Family
has received during year." Fred, aware that there were always new
members present, obviously felt a need to remind them what the family meant, or should mean. He divided his outlined remarks into two
sections, the first having to do with the purpose of the meetings, and
the second made up of his own "suggestions." The purpose was "to
inform everyone of business progress, to encourage interest in group
activities, to develop unity, and to develop continuity of planning and
thinking." His suggestions were both reminders to himself and comments to be made to the family. He listed, "Family interest comes first,
express views frankly—discussion of differences leads to unity," and
"Please return papers . . ." In two separate notations, Fred had written: "If stock is not too easy to get at, it is more apt to remain intact"
and "Power is valuable to our Family in many ways. Individually we
have *little* power, together we can have much."

The St. Paul interlude was pleasant, at least for the most part. Phil
inevitably complained that it took too much time to accomplish too
little, and that his backside suffered in the process. It was nothing

serious, however, as he was quite willing to sit for hours in other situations, at the thick end of a fly rod for example. A good deal of accumulated work awaited him when he returned to Tacoma. Much of February was given to visits at the various plants and operations in the company of Charlie Ingram, Howard Morgan, Dave Weyerhaeuser, John Wahl, Bob Douglas, Clark Heritage, and Joe Nolan, or as many of them as he could corral. In a sense, these amounted to annual meetings for each branch or division. Art Karlan, for example, was expected to give a report on the 1951 operation at Coos Bay and to present a budget covering 1952 earnings and capital expenditures, "and any other pertinent matters." Phil suggested that luncheons with "your supervisory people are in order," and added, "If you wish to include local friends, do so." The method was clearly in keeping with the autonomous nature of the Timber Company organization.

Nick Genta was of increasing help to Phil, relieving him of the burden of much correspondence and other routine responsibilities. But it was Nick, ever worshipful, who marveled at his boss's ability. In one of his own communications, he took note of the sort of man Phil Weyerhaeuser was, observing that the latter had been "snowed under since his return from St. Paul, what with meetings, appointments, mail. But he takes it nicely in a steady stride. He sure does a lot of work in a quiet way. He reminds me of the power that generates quietly in the depths of a dam—not the wasted spectacularism of the water that spills over the dam. That looks powerful, but the real power comes through the quietly running turbines." Nick doubtless liked that and blew a thick cloud of cigar smoke toward the ceiling.

One of those with whom Nick had been corresponding was Charles E. Young, who had accepted appointment to the newly created post of economist. A graduate of Northwestern, Young had previously worked for the Westinghouse Corporation and the Ford Motor Company. He was already "Chuck" to Nick, who wrote glowingly of the good life in the Northwest. "It's a great country and a grand company," he observed. The official announcement indicated that Young would report to President J. P. Weyerhaeuser, Jr., and "will prepare economic data to assist in planning company policies, forecast business conditions and trends, and advise company officials on economic matters." Sometime later, answering an inquiry about just what the economist really did, Phil replied typically. In effect, he said, our foresters tell us how much we can cut, the salesmen work hard or not as the circumstances require, and the economist peers as far into the future as he can, then tells anyone who will listen what he sees.

There was finally some progress in the matter of the Weyerhaeuser Timber Foundation, a general policy having been drafted. It prescribed that gifts would be limited to persons living in the United

336 PHIL WEYERHAEUSER: LUMBERMAN

States or its possessions; that the recipients must be from the area in which the gift was to be used; that gifts could be made for religious, charitable, scientific, literary, and educational purposes, but could not involve health and welfare benefits or be made to organizations "a substantial portion of whose activities is propaganda or influence of legislation." One "guiding principle" was preference for "fewer and more substantial contributions, rather than a large number of small ones," it being suggested that such an approach would encourage a better understanding of the particular organizations or causes, to greater benefit all around. As had been the case previously, it was noted that a large percentage of the total contributions should be made to causes that pertained to the localities in which the Timber Company had its operations, and that "contributions made outside of these areas should emphasize support of programs which in some direct or indirect manner will contribute to the welfare of the timber industry, its employees and customers."

One of the relatively new areas of foundation interest was a scholarship program for children of company employees. Because this necessitated a method of selection and award, a scholarship board was appointed consisting of Al Raught, Mrs. F. R. (Liz) Titcomb, and Aubrey R. Watzek, whose only previous involvement with Weyerhaeuser had been as a competitor. In his letter of appreciation for Watzek's willingness to help, Phil noted that "by selecting the candidates and following their careers in college, you will be in close touch with one of the most interesting and vital processes I know—the development of mature, educated individuals."

The annual report for 1951 received much comment, most of it commendatory. The Timber Company Foundation was featured prominently, leading one stockholder to ask for "some additional particulars." Phil's response was typically low-key: "There is not anything of interest that I can send you on it. It is merely a charitable nonprofit corporation to which the Timber Company has made contributions as it felt able. Its contributions to date have been more of a long-range nature than those which the company still assumes, such as Community Chest and Red Cross, etc. However, the time may come when we will rely on the Foundation for even such donations."

The same writer inquired about disease in the forest, obviously assuming that Weyerhaeuser had "quite a problem on your hands in this connection." Phil admitted that the annual report had skimmed over some problems, but there was a reason for it: "I don't suppose we have much about forestry troubles and how we are going to treat them, because we probably don't know. I spent two days last week at a meeting of our company foresters; absorbed about all the gloom I could stand. After all, though, the antidote seems to be that we do have forests and they got here naturally in spite of bugs, disease, and fire." The final sentence said more than it seemed. It summed up the fundamental philosophy, or faith, of the forester: "After all . . . we do have forests." When picking partners, one could do worse than selecting nature.

Laird Bell's reaction to the annual report was unreserved. It "looks lovely in substance and in form," he wrote. There did seem little to complain about. The income per share for 1951 stood at $6.39, an increase from the $5.27 in 1950. Sales for 1951 also set a record, amounting to $213,175,000. Two and one-half million acres of forests were now owned by the Timber Company, amounting to nearly half an acre per share of stock. Put in dollar terms, the estimated 40 billion board feet was charged at a book value of less than $2 per thousand feet, when the current market price of standing timber was somewhere between $25 and $30 per thousand feet—a difference of $1 billion. If Weyerhaeuser was conservative in its approach, there seemed little reason to be otherwise. At the same time, large changes had been effected: the forests were growing, being managed with the future foremost in mind, and the production efforts had become increasingly diversified, resulting in increased utilization. There were more than enough problems, but in view of the accomplishments, there were reasons for an occasional fishing excursion aboard the *Wanigan*, even in the rain.

Plans for the annual meeting were somewhat different in 1952, for it was determined that the shareholders would gather in Longview, marking the first time that the meeting had been held outside Tacoma. By the end of April, the Timber Company and the CIO representatives had reached a settlement, and in this they were unusual. The rest of the industry was on strike. As Phil noted in his agenda letter to directors, dated April 29, "Weather is already beautiful," adding, "Pleasant feeling it is this morning to be on the other side of the situation prevailing two years ago."

In May Phil took time to prepare, carefully as always, an address to be delivered at the Golden Anniversary Meeting of the National Lumber Manufacturers Association in St. Louis. The talk, entitled "Fifty Years of Progress in Forestry," was given on May 8. Phil recounted the development of forestry in the West, what had happened since the great Yacolt burn of 1902. He took note of those individuals who had contributed so much to the progress, from George S. Long to Colonel Greeley, E. T. Allen, Dave Mason, C. S. Cowan, and many more. But despite the very best efforts of these and others, Phil reminded his audience, "forestry is essentially a development which must be based upon a sound economic background." The progress had occurred as a result of five factors: "The gradual development of forest protection; the recognition of principles of taxation which would permit the long-time ownership of forestlands for the purpose of growing timber crops; the development of road-making machinery and logging methods compatible with good forest management; the development of markets for forest products, aided by the wider use of cellulose products and the expansion of the paper and pulp industry; and the growing recognition by the public that forestry was largely a matter of creating a sound economic background for growing wood and being able to utilize more completely all forest growth." He concluded by looking to the future of the industry, a future which in large measure depended on "what the general public believes is the forest situation, and what it is being told is the proper solution to it."

Although these appearances never got to be easy for Phil, they were of value. Certainly no one else was in quite his position to speak in behalf of the West Coast industry. Also it was good for him to be forced to think in larger perspectives of time and territory and to meet others and learn of other opportunities. There was nothing wrong in being western, but there was little advantage in being only western.

Werner P. "Gully" Gullander, who had become the new financial vice-president (replacing David Graham), and Charles Young, economist, were about to experience their first directors' meeting and annual meeting. It was a good time to be introduced, what with problems and conflicts seemingly at a minimum. The directors adopted the foundation's statement of policy and the incentive stock option plan for key management employees. They also authorized a special payment to the foundation for an initial gift of $100,000 "as a memorial to Mr. C. S. Chapman," in support of an endowment campaign for Yale's forestry program. Colonel Greeley was the solicitor in chief, and Phil sent word of the decision to him, "pleased to express in this manner our respect for Yale University's contribution to the forest industry," adding: "We assume that the operation of the Forest School will be improved not only as a result of the beneficial effects of the endowment you are raising, but by more adequate provision in the University's regular budget in the future."

There was one large surprise at the directors' meeting. Phil subsequently wrote to Laird Bell, "I can't tell you what a jerk it gave me to have you calmly announce your retirement next year. It will be a different sort of place for me to work, I can assure you." The announcement would prove a bit premature, but the intention was clear.

Aside from the political conventions and the Korean War, the big news of the summer of 1952 concerned strikes. Although the steel strike was more important nationally, to Weyerhaeuser and other West Coast shippers, the strike that had kept their vessels tied up seemed interminable. There also seemed little chance that the settlement would be at all agreeable. Phil wrote as much to Don Watson in a letter of July 16, the day before he left on the *Wanigan* for a ten-day fishing cruise to Stewart Island waters. In a word of encouragement, he told Watson that he expected to learn of the settlement of the strike over the *Wanigan*'s radio. Fred K. had invited Phil and Helen to come to California for a visit, but they declined, Phil explaining, "this matter of fishing is also important." The trip was satisfying in every respect. Most satisfying, however, was that they had managed by themselves. As Phil subsequently told Norton Clapp, the trip "built up my confidence in the ship and its master's accomplishments."

The shipping strike was indeed settled by the time Phil returned to work, and he announced the fact in a July 29 report to the directors. He also admitted that the terms of settlement left the Weyerhaeuser Steamship Company "in a precarious position as to profit margins. By and large, we were licked." If the steel strike negotiations proved something of a management victory, that was not the case in the shipping contracts. Phil also included the figures for the first six months of 1952. These were somewhat unusual. Sales were down from the previous year by some $7 million, but net operating income before federal taxes had decreased by only $8 million. This reasonably agreeable situation was partly the result of a favorable decision regarding excess profits taxes. As Laird advised, "We shall have to be careful not to have too good a last six months." Laird also inquired about the availability of the *Wanigan* in the latter part of September. "I must make the most of my remaining time in the brass," he wrote, "and would like to contemplate a short trip out there some time in the last half of September." Phil assured him that all would be in readiness, complete "with crew now very adept at its management and navigation." Nothing would please him more than to entertain his valued friend and colleague aboard the *Wanigan*.

A sure indication that the Timber Company had nearly completed its westward shift was the fact that a quorum of the Executive Committee was possible among western members only. Charlie Ingram was now a member, and when he, Phil, and Ed Hayes got together, they could conduct business. They did get together on Monday, August 25, at which time they declared the third-quarter dividend of 50 cents a share, authorized the expenditure of up to $15 million of company funds in commercial paper, and elected some assistant comptrollers, the last two items in accordance with recommendations of the new financial vice-president, W. P. Gullander. In this and so many other matters, it was increasingly apparent that the nature of Phil's responsibility was changing. One supposes that he noticed he was less concerned with details and spent more of his time responding to plans and proposals than initiating projects. Perhaps for the first time he was able to sit back and watch the organization at work, reasonably confident that it was working well. This did not mean that he was inactive, but only that his activities were changing. He was, for example, making more public appearances in behalf of his company and industry, reluctantly agreeing with Laird's assertion, "these appearances may be painful, but I am sure that they are good for business."

His involvement with the Little Church on the Prairie continued. He accepted appointment to the board of directors of the Boeing Airplane Company at the insistence of its president, his good friend Bill Allen. He had previously served on the board of the Puget Sound National Bank, again largely because a friend, Reno Odlin, was the president; but following his return to Tacoma, Phil asked to be relieved of that responsibility. "Pleasant as is the association," he wrote to Reno, "I have the conviction that I am contributing nothing but a poor attendance record." Phil was also taking greater interest in the affairs of the College of Puget Sound.

Finally, Phil was becoming increasingly receptive to new opportunities for investment and expansion. The reasons for this were clear enough. Without saying as much, Phil could congratulate himself that the Timber Company had nearly accomplished its work of meshing resources with production facilities, tree farms with plants, the process of diversification and integration. Now it seemed appropriate to consider the forest products subject from the perspective of the national market. Even without the growing problems with the maritime unions, any national industry dealing in bulk materials whose production operations were restricted to a geographic corner had to have distribution problems. Furthermore, despite traditional prejudice, it was no longer feasible to maintain that the South was anything less than the new frontier for forest products industries. In the 1950s, even a Weyerhaeuser was willing to look in that direction.

Phil was willing to look in a good many directions, and not all had to do with business. One of the directions was backwards. As the years passed, the old college friendships were retained, and the memories embellished. Art Vorys, Peavey Heffelfinger, Walter Hochschild, Spider Reinhardt, and Phil were planning a Sun Valley reunion of their own, spouses included. The exchanges that preceded the event were filled with the usual banter. Heffelfinger apparently "recalled" that Phil and he had once shared a date, Phil being unable to secure his own. In his response, Phil allowed that "Heffelfinger has the most distorted memory," and assured Spider that "taking her to the Prom in tandem is a figment of his fertile imagination." In conclusion he expressed the hope that "she *has* enjoyed better things in life than came her way from big Heff." Regarding his own circumstances, with

some exaggeration Phil reported that he was "keeping so many en-
gagements on our new cabin cruiser that I can't tend to business."

Another direction for Phil's attention was family matters of both an
immediate and an extended nature. Fred K. had addressed a midsummer letter to the male members of the family Weyerhaeuser on the
subject of a "training program" for the young men in the family interested in beginning careers in the lumber business. As Fred explained, "I am trying to cut a pattern for Fritz Jewett, Jr." The program included a bibliography and a timetable for on-the-job
experience. He recommended that the "trainee" initially spend four
months in forestry and logging activities, perhaps a month cruising, a
month as a camp timekeeper, and two months working in a logging
operation. There were six additional areas of training, from sawmilling to auditing, involving a total of twenty-two months. He also suggested that the trainee prepare a report at the conclusion of each
phase, "describing the operation in which he has worked, the part he
played therein, and his appraisal of the efficiency of the operation,"
adding that "comments regarding the management, morale, personnel
relations, and any other pertinent factors are invited."

Such a proposal might have been well received by the previous generation, but Phil was having none of it. As he stated in the second
sentence of his response, "I don't like the tone of it, starting on page
4." Since the first three pages were bibliography, Phil's disapproval
was general. More specifically, he objected to the timetable: "Seems
to me that we create the impression, by giving out such a document,
that the managers of the various available enterprises are both able
and willing to subordinate their regular operation organizations to the
needs of our family in training young men. The boys should realize
that when they latch on somewhere they are expected to give more
than they get, and that if the people they work for can be induced to
move them around enough to give them all-around training, they are
lucky."

Phil also complained of the implication that "the candidates are
expected to carry tales." He agreed that they wanted them "to be
thinking about people and the problem of the business they're studying, but not to be busybodies." Being a Weyerhaeuser assured some
advantages, but not at the expense of the Weyerhaeuser Timber Company, at least not if Phil had anything to do with it.

Laird Bell was able to spend the last week of September in Tacoma
as planned, and he was joined by a contingent from the St. Paul office
who came west to attend the Washington-Minnesota football game on
September 27. Phil was hoping for rain, not to influence the game but
to put out fires that were burning in several places. The late summer
of 1952 had been unusually hot and dry, and the logging crews were

devoting more time to fire fighting than to logging. Laird held to his intention to resign from his chairmanship of the Timber Company's board of directors, and although Phil was not looking forward to the day, he certainly did not wish it to pass unnoticed. In connection with the directors' meeting in mid-November, the new annual dinner for supervisory employees of the Tacoma office had been scheduled. Phil told Laird that he planned to be master of ceremonies and hoped to "call on Clark Heritage for a talk on wood uses of the future and on you for a final word on any subject you wish (except complimentary remarks about me)." Phil continued: "It must be about 20 years since you took an active part in Weyerhaeuser Timber Company affairs, including your efforts with Carl Stevens on various mergers. The depression times and efforts to help ourselves through NRA contrast so sharply with the present that it seems to me an interesting and worthwhile subject could be generated. Maybe you'd rather Monday morning quarterback the election? But this is, according to your plans, one of the last chances to talk from on high."

Another bit of looking back had to do with the long-discussed Timber Company history. Fred K. was now carrying the burden of negotiations, and his report to the directors of his arrangements with Columbia University would indicate an agreement at hand, the result of which would be *Timber and Men* by Ralph Hidy, Frank Hill, and Allan Nevins. And on November 4, Dwight D. Eisenhower, Republican, was elected president. It must have been a cause for some satisfaction, but Phil seemed to take no special note of it. In the meantime Laird Bell was, predictably, taking his assignment for his "talk from on high" seriously. He wrote to Tacoma, requesting some additional financial records. He assured Phil that he was not going to be "very statistical" in his presentation, "but I would like to be sure of what facts I do offer." Then he made an interesting observation: "I have been going through the files and the diary I kept at the time and I will swear that most of the things mentioned did not happen. It is a very enlightening experience." In reply, Phil admitted to having had the same feelings when looking through old files.

The board authorized Fred K. to complete his arrangements with Columbia University and accepted Phil's recommendation on most other matters. The directors did not encourage an expressed intention to study the world timber situation "from the point of view of possible investments in other areas than the Pacific Northwest." Phil had specifically wished to investigate an "offer of timber in Mexico from the Vancouver Plywood Company." Laird subsequently worried that Phil might have been disappointed at the rejection of this consideration and wrote in behalf of the directors, "We have to flatter ourselves once in a while by a show of independence." Phil assured him that he had not been disappointed and that he had looked on the question as "a pretty good case to air for an expression." Laird had been very pleased with the meetings in general. Gully Gullander had made a good impression, and, as Laird wrote, "I am very happy about the progress of the Company, and I hope you are." There was, however, one major area of continuing concern. "My only complaint," Laird indicated, "is the paucity of number two men up and down the line," although he assured Phil that the problem was one they shared with many other corporations. From Phil's perspective, the more immediate problem was to find a replacement for Laird. He still hoped for a reconsideration, admitting, "there's nothing new in that." His December 5 note closed, "It won't be the same around here."

As always, years ended and years began, encouraging reflections and resolutions but without interrupting the continuum. One problem that had endured the passage of time—too much time in Phil's estimation—was that involving the Wood Conversion Company. In a letter of December 30, Laird Bell had raised the question once more, in effect asking Phil what he now planned to do. Phil's response was one of frustration. "Reviewing the Wood Conversion file," he observed, "reveals years of lack of accomplishment," and he admitted that it was unlikely that anything would ever be done, "except in line with the wishes of E. W. D." The reference was, of course, to cousin Ed Davis, and Phil assumed that Ed would insist on "an independent company with no parent, whether control was exercised or not." Phil didn't want to play the villain in the matter and wished the thing would go away. To Laird he quoted that comic strip philosopher, Li'l Abner: "What cannot be cured must be endured." Concerning Laird's announced intention to resign from the Wood Conversion board, Phil could see relatively little harm in that, especially compared with Laird's Timber Company resignation. Phil admitted that he had considered doing the same "in order graphically to portray my desire to have a subsidiary without *exercising* control," but Fred K. had convinced him that the time for such a resignation was not right.

Phil had a suggestion of his own for brother Fred. They were looking for a person who would assume the public relations responsibility that had been performed by Rex Black and Leo Bodine within the Sales Company. Phil recommended B. L. Orell, Washington State forester. Phil told Fred K. of Bernie Orell's reputation in Washington, that he had reorganized the State Forestry Department into a well-functioning agency, and that he had "a quiet, forceful manner in conversation, and speaks well in public." Fred K. would likewise be impressed, and Orell soon began what would prove to be a long career with Weyerhaeuser.

It was once again time for Fred K. and others to look forward to the family meetings. His letter of reminder, dated January 7, expressed the hope that all had enjoyed "a Merry Christmas and a Happy New Year and that you are now mentally, morally, and spiritually equipped to face and endure the Family Meeting." Then he added an interesting postscript detailing just who was properly included in the family meeting group. As Fred K. explained the "rules," all direct descendants were welcome, and "female members of the fourth generation are also cordially invited to bring their husbands," but "male members of any generation are not allowed to bring their wives because most of them are so beautiful that attention might be diverted from the business of the meetings." In other words, Helen was not "welcome," but daughter Ann was encouraged to bring Jack Pascoe. Apparently no one complained.

A new administration was assuming responsibility in Washington, and it was naturally assumed by most in the business world that life would be happier under the leadership of President Eisenhower and the Republicans. Charles Briggs, of the St. Paul firm Briggs, Gilbert, Morton, Kyle and Macartney, continued to watch Washington developments with Timber Company interests in mind, and he viewed the future optimistically, although warning that "the perplexing task that Congress faces is to reduce government expenditures substantially." Briggs had written largely for the purpose of addressing political questions, but he took the occasion to comment on a statement that had appeared in "Notable Quotes" as published by the National Lumber Manufacturers Association: "It requires work and understanding and faith in the future to keep our political institutions free and unfettered. We must compete; we must produce. We must increase the benefits which accrue from our system. Free men can operate free enterprise with free minds and extend our system—a working symbol for those people elsewhere who have traded their freedom for security."

Phil Weyerhaeuser was indicated as being the source of the quote, and Briggs observed, "With such sentiments issuing from the top of Weyerhaeuser Timber Company the perpetuity of its strength and influence in the economy of our country is assured." In his reply Phil wrote, "I didn't know I was a notable," but added, "it must be [true] if you noted."

One of the subjects long discussed was the need for an industry response to what was considered erroneous information put forward by the Forest Service. The problem in responding, however, was a complex one. The counterargument had to be credible. Nothing would be accomplished in a shouting match between two diverse interests, each compiling statistics in its own behalf. The industry could never hope to succeed in that sort of contest. Better that the industry support an independent survey by an agency of sufficient integrity to be able to withstand charges of bias. Such a project was simpler in concept than in its formulation. The general question to be considered was easily described: Phil desired the best possible prediction on the ability of the forest products industry to meet the nation's future needs. The Forest Service had habitually contended, first, that the industry's practices were needlessly wasteful; second, that as a result the timber resource would be insufficient for future requirements; and third, that because of these circumstances there should be greater public involvement—that is, the Forest Service should assume a larger management responsibility. Phil viewed this as self-serving propaganda. The Forest Service's earlier predictions of a timber famine had been about as accurate as the predictions of doomsday. Furthermore, and this was most galling, Phil and others failed to see any evidence of a record of management excellence in the Forest Service. But the question remained: how to respond?

On December 30, 1952, Phil had written to Dean Garratt of the Yale School of Forestry introducing the subject and asking for suggestions. Already, however, Phil had some doubts about the desirability of involving Yale and perhaps other schools of forestry, and he suggested as a possible alternative agency the Stanford Research Institute. Although the Research Institute had no "long association with forest problems," this could be remedied through some sort of advisory committee. Anyway, it might not be a disadvantage to begin such an inquiry from strictly an economic outlook, unburdened by much of what had gone before in public-private contentions. Ed Hayes suggested that the survey might be financed by the National Lumber Manufacturers Association; if this was not possible, then a number of individual companies could assume the costs. Clyde Martin warned, however, that the greater the number of contributors, the slower the progress: "Each will take a different viewpoint on what is needed and how it should be produced."

By mid-April the decision to undertake the study had been made, the Timber Company approving a proposal received from the Stanford Research Institute. All earlier concerns seemed to have vanished. The Timber Company footed the bill and the institute conducted the survey without benefit of advisers.

The news was mixed that spring of 1953. Although Phil noted a "continuing market weakness," in his May 1 letter to the directors, he also reported that earnings for the first quarter were about equal to the previous year's. As always, it seemed to Phil that labor leaders were not sufficiently impressed with the difficulties threatening, with the result that negotiations on a new contract had reached a stalemate. As Phil described the situation, "The issue is drawn and no one knows what will result." More certain was the fact of forthcoming meetings of the directors in mid-May at which Phil planned to present a report on the company's growth potential with special attention to the availability of new funds for reinvestment. Laird Bell was scheduled to discuss the Wood Conversion question, perhaps recommending "a method of disposing of our stock as an alternate to the proposal some years ago of acquiring the minority." There were other matters to be considered, such as whether efforts should be encouraged to broaden the market for Timber Company stock, a report on the Stanford Research Institute project by economist Charles Young, and the designation of a replacement board member for the late Bill McCormick, Phil recommending Henry T. McKnight, "son of Summer McKnight, representing a substantial stock interest in the Company." An interesting aspect to Henry McKnight's credentials was an active role in conservation matters.

The highlight of the May meeting was a visit to the Snoqualmie Falls branch, some two hundred making the short trip from Tacoma. Phil gave a brief preliminary presentation on "our oldest integrated plant," in continuous operation for thirty-seven years. He noted that Snoqualmie Falls had been largely "the creation of George S. Long, first manager of Weyerhaeuser Timber Company," and that its subsequent success was evidence that "Mr. Long built a monument." It was indeed an impressive plant, but Phil and some others were undoubtedly as pleased with the 160,000-acre tree farm that provided the basis for Snoqualmie's continuing production. He was equally pleased and proud to have the directors and shareholders meet some of those directly responsible. As he wrote in his letter of appreciation to Snoqualmie manager Tip O'Neil, "It added up to a very friendly occasion, and it seems to me we need to show the human side of business as often as possible."

The fact was, however, as the visit to Snoqualmie demonstrated, there simply were no similar opportunities for such development in the Pacific Northwest. George Long and then Phil Weyerhaeuser had built well, but the growth had been largely limited to the original context of Timber Company involvement. Phil realized if further expansion was to occur, it would most likely be in the South, although he was not yet ready to make the jump. To Fred Reimers he admitted, "I am interested and enthusiastic about the timber-growing possibilities in the South," but "when I try to project the W.T. Co. into that activity, I have trouble picturing how to administer it unless it is a pretty sizable property." There were also financial uncertainties, not so much about the ability of the Timber Company to manage such an investment but about its wisdom, its timeliness: "I have trouble with the idea that we are at a time, after 12 years or more of unprecedented prosperity, when the buyer had better wait until the climate changes and a few clouds appear to encourage present owners to sell reasonably." As always, it seemed Weyerhaeuser could wait.

Phil was far less patient regarding the future of the Wood Conversion Company, or more specifically the relationship between Wood Conversion and the Timber Company. As much as Ed Davis might wish it so, the problem would not go away, and the late spring announcement that the Department of Commerce planned to undertake economic studies of the steel, chemical, capital goods, and pulp and paper industries "in connection with House Judiciary Committee surveys of antitrust legislation" did little to ease the pressures. Still, progress was slow and painful. On the last day of July, Joe Nolan wrote to Davis indicating that Phil had inquired "as to the status of our discussions with respect to merger and spin-off," reminding that the Timber Company board expected a recommendation at its November meeting. Nolan offered his services to facilitate the matter, but neither he nor Phil could provide the necessary leadership.

Nolan wrote again on August 20, indicating once more that it had recently been made clear at an Executive Committee meeting that "I should have a complete program of spin-off ready for presentation to the Board" in November. Davis finally wrote to Phil August 27, and he raised eleven specific questions regarding the discussions, but the essence of his position was contained in a single sentence: "Spin-off or merger, to my mind, is a choice between two evils." He later observed that it was "not too important today" which decision they reached, but added, "It is difficult to evaluate the future in making [the] decision." Phil answered immediately, initially commenting on the questions that had been raised. He continued to favor a merger but he realized that cousin Ed was unwilling to take that route.

Phil left no doubt about his frustration. "The matter will probably be decided by default," he wrote, "because, as you know, Weyerhaeuser Timber Company directors have made up their minds and will spin unless there is something negative uncovered taxwise or a satisfactory substitute." He further observed, "If you can't make up your mind as to what is in the best interest of Wood Conversion, I wouldn't expect the so-called minority stockholding group to make up its mind." After noting that merger had originally seemed preferable "because nothing need be changed once an exchange ratio was agreed to," Phil outlined the results of a spin-off settlement. First, it would end a discussion "which has borne no fruit during the years it has continued." Second, it would give to those in Wood Conversion "who dread becoming part of something bigger a feeling of independence evidently not to be anticipated in case of merger." Third, it would reduce the sales diversification currently required in the Timber Company's public statements. And the most important reasons were already well known.

In early September Joe Nolan once again patiently explained the spin-off procedure to Ed Davis, and he also included what would be necessary if the decision was made to effect a merger. The essence of the spin-off was the creation of a dummy corporation comprising former Timber Company stockholders in the Wood Conversion Company, and it was in the Corporation X phase that the decision could be made by the individual stockholders whether to retain or dispose of their stock in Wood Conversion. With the new distribution of stock, the Timber Company would no longer have any relationship with either Wood Conversion or Corporation X, and the effect would be, as Nolan explained, "much the same as though 4,000 additional shareholders were added to WCCo. and thereby to change it from a closely-owned to a publicly-owned company." And perhaps most important, the interlocking directors between the Timber Company and Wood Conversion would be eliminated.

Still no action was forthcoming. Laird Bell shared with Phil a conversation he had had with Ed Davis on the matter. As Laird recalled the discussion, it had less to do with the relative merits of spin-off as opposed to merger than how any decision of the sort was reached: "Should we call the Board of Directors and put it to them; should we call the stockholders and ask their advice? Finally, more or less in exasperation, I said, 'Ed, you just must face the fact that you are the fellow that will have to make the final decision. The directors and stockholders will do what you say and regardless of what they indicate they want you will have to decide in the last analysis.' . . . I can't remember that Ed said anything, but he certainly looked unhappy."

There followed a brief discussion regarding the basis for a merger, and Laird indicated that it seemed an advantageous time to follow that route, "in view of Wood Conversion's highly prosperous year and the weakness of the market price of WTC stock lately." He admitted to Phil that such "probably wasn't good trading, but I hoped it would make him want to trade."

But time forced even Ed Davis's hand, and a meeting of the board of directors of the Wood Conversion Company was called for Friday, October 2, to consider a number of questions, most importantly "a merger with Weyerhaeuser Timber Company or a 'spin-off.'" Phil went to St. Paul for the long-awaited occasion and returned immediately to Tacoma for a weekend on the *Wanigan*. On Monday he took time to address a note to Ed Davis on the most recent developments. After observing that he was "in accord with the decision to spin," Phil also apologized—almost—for his inability to "keep my mouth shut." Apparently he had made one last plea in favor of merger. "Merging offered an opportunity to say 'You take this one; I'll take that one' with no one to suffer," he maintained. Now it seemed inevitable that the competition between the Timber Company and Wood Conversion would be intense in some product areas. "I guess it's healthful," Phil wrote, "but I'd rather compete with outsiders." Without doubt, the fact that a decision had been made was most welcomed. Laird was also relieved, admitting "a merger would have been tidier, but I think perhaps the result of the spin-off will be good." He concluded by noting the obvious: there had been "personnel and psychological considerations that are hard to weigh."

Business did not boom as 1953 moved through the summer months, and the Timber Company budget figures required a slight adjustment downward. Some also complained that the weather was depressing, "not designed for sunburns," as Phil described it, but he also noted that the threat of fire would be minimal. Professors Nevins, Hidy, and Hill paid an August visit to Tacoma, and Phil was pleased that they seemed genuinely interested in the Weyerhaeuser history project. Being a realist, he also forewarned the directors that "the five years will run before the job is done."

In the late summer of 1953 there was more to worry about than the Weyerhaeuser history. On August 20 the Russians announced that they had successfully tested a hydrogen bomb. The American economy seemed hesitant at best, and not a few wondered if the Republican leadership was as able as had been assumed. Charles Wilson's observation that what was good for General Motors was good for the country prompted Joe Nolan to comment that the secretary of defense "could not keep a civil foot in his mouth." Nolan did so in a memo to Fred K., written in an effort to justify support for increased government funding for the Forest Products Laboratory in Madison, Wisconsin. Congress appeared determined to reduce such expenditures, a determination that Phil and his brother supported enthusiastically. But they also recognized the need for the work being done at the Madison research facility for an industry so sadly deficient in that respect. Fred K. had posed the dilemma: "Having taken the position repeatedly in favor of reducing the cost of government, it seems a little illogical for us to turn around and support increased appropriations for this particular institution, beneficial though it be to the lumber industry." Nolan reasoned that it was not illogical to support expenditures for functions that "are essential, do the country good, are performed efficiently, and do not preclude fields which private enterprise might occupy." Bernie Orell also saw the matter as something other than a pork barrel issue, with "each activity assessed on the basis of its own merit in the light of public service rendered."

Phil's letter to the directors, accompanying the report of August performance, noted that "the downward trend of earnings continues." On the brighter side, the American Paper and Pulp Association had met in Seattle, resulting in "our stealing the show—a good day, well

organized, and a group impressed by the forestry story." The paper
and pulp representatives got to visit the Everett sulphate mill in its
first week of operation. It had been a most successful start-up, with
production moving along at such a pace that they ran out of chips;
"temporary, we hope," Phil noted. But the high point of the day had
been the visit to the Mount St. Helens Tree Farm. James L. Madeen,
president of the Boston firm of Hollingsworth and Whitney, subsequently wrote a note of appreciation to Phil, and he paid particular
attention to the visit to the woods: "The day at the St. Helens Tree
Farm was a thrilling one for us Easterners, some of whom had never
before seen such timber and those who had seen it, had forgotten how
big it really was. It was an inspiring trip, and I was particularly impressed by the high morale of your young forestry group and their
enthusiasm for the work they were doing. They certainly gave us an
enjoyable and inspirational trip through your Tree Farm."

There were some special items on the agenda for the directors'
meeting of November 18, including what was hoped to be the final
resolution of the Wood Conversion problem. There was to be considerable discussion of the level of company support to the Weyerhaeuser
Timber Foundation. During the previous year, $300,000 had been
contributed by the company to the foundation, and Phil was recommending that the directors approve that $100,000 of that amount be
carried over with an additional $100,000 contribution from the com-
pany. He worried some about "lean years in the future" for the foundation and wanted it to be able to have flexibility of a sort in the
management of its funds. He also wanted the directors to be informed
in detail about the program of scholarships for the children of employees, a program that was being directed by Sam Brown, son-in-law
of Laird Bell.

Finally, Phil questioned whether they should continue to support the
Conservation Foundation, Fairfield Osborn's organization, at the rate
of $5,000 a year, although, since Fred K. had been active on its board,
Phil was willing to leave the final recommendation to Fred. Charles
Young, the economist, was scheduled to give a progress report on the
timberland survey then under way, a most important study in that for
the first time the company was accumulating data on the sustained-
yield capacities of various blocks of timber. Theories were being tested
on the ground and revised every five years to note the actual growth
in different sites. In the process, better ideas on the allowable cut for
each year were formulated in keeping with the principle of sustained
yield. Not unrelated was Young's report on the status of the Stanford
Research Institute project.

One of the invitations to serve that Phil reluctantly accepted came
from Leonard E. Read, president of the Foundation for Economic

Education, with headquarters at Irvington-on-Hudson. Phil had tried to decline, pleading distance from the scene of major activity and his already full schedule, but Read assured him that it was their policy to keep distant and busy directors informed through a system of regular reports. Phil's acceptance was typically phrased: "You make it very hard to turn you down on being a trustee. I am lazy enough to think I have no time for anything new. I don't see how I can be helpful to you, because meetings will be few and far between. I am no good raising money. I do have great interest and faith in what you are trying to do. If with such a bill of particulars you still want me to be a trustee, I am willing to run."

One of the less welcome benefits of the company's very successful national advertising campaign was the loss of individual privacy. It was good for the public to learn that Weyerhaeuser was the tree-growing company, but a little information is likely to encourage further inquiry or at least inquisitiveness. Just who were these Weyerhaeusers? Anonymity was no longer possible, but it didn't mean that Phil and other Weyerhaeusers had to enjoy the results of change.

Back in midsummer Phil had accepted an invitation to attend a conference of the American Assembly, that "non-partisan organization" General Eisenhower had initiated at Columbia University when he was president there. The subject of the November meeting to which Phil was invited was "Economic Security for Americans," and as Edwin T. Gibson's letter indicated, "We intend to discuss (1) what a person can and should do for himself, (2) what his company or union can do for him in the way of a pension or retirement program, and (3) what his government can and should do for him via Social Security and other programs." Phil was genuinely interested in the subject and perhaps a little curious about the other participants. It was a distinguished list, including Arthur F. Burns, Oveta Culp Hobby, and Nelson A. Rockefeller.

Following the conference Phil sent a note of appreciation to Frank Patton of the Guaranty Trust Company of New York, chairman of the panel in which Phil had participated. He admitted that "it was too damned exhausting for a country boy." And to the conference director, Phil noted that "enforced close association with people of a different stripe develops many worthwhile by-products, which must be considered in any appraisal of the Assembly's accomplishments." That assessment provides a hint of Phil's lack of ease with the unfamiliar, his basic shyness. It was drawn more honestly and graphically in his postconference note to Paul Cruikshank, headmaster of the Taft School. "I can't say that I enjoyed the experience," he began, speaking of the conference, "inasmuch as the group was pretty largely intellectuals—either university people, social workers, people in government, or talkative union economists. . . ." He further observed that he was the only one in attendance who lived west of Pittsburgh and that "no industrialist that I could locate was in the process of manufacturing something." In short, Phil felt out of place and "the upshot of the matter was that I listened and had little to contribute." What he failed to understand was that it was possible to talk casually about matters of great importance. Phil allowed himself no such luxury, at least not in public. There was little theoretical in the life of Phil Weyerhaeuser. There were other hurts, one of which he described to friend Cruikshank. It involved what seemed to him to be the rewriting of history by "union people," to the effect that "anything good in the way of pensions or anything else which industry had given was the result of union pressure and was, therefore, a union accomplishment, not an industry accomplishment." Needless to say, Phil felt aggrieved by that sort of assessment.

After the American Assembly, the meeting of directors in Tacoma might have seemed like pretty tame stuff. In any event, here Phil walked on familiar turf and he walked with confidence. The meetings went well. Laird Bell had continued as chairman of the board, reluctantly but nonetheless with no lessening of interest and commitment. He continued because there seemed no appropriate replacement, although, in fact, he worried more about who would replace Phil when that time came. The decision had been reached to promote Jon Titcomb to assistant to General Manager Charlie Ingram, with young George Weyerhaeuser replacing Titcomb as Springfield manager. It seems that Laird may have read more into Titcomb's future role than Phil. For one thing, Laird thought that while at Springfield, Titcomb had been successful in working with those in both the pulp division and the lumber division:

. . . it seems to me that the wall should be broken down if we are not going really to run two companies indefinitely in the future. I suppose the autonomy of the Pulp Division is an inheritance from the days of Bob Wolf, but I can't see that Charlie has done much to break it down (I don't know even whether he wants to), and certainly a man of Howard Morgan's vigor is likely to insist upon the integrity of his empire. You yourself have practically grown up with the two branches, but your successor almost necessarily must come up through one branch or the other, unless he has had training in the field in a certain amount of cooperation.

A related concern was that Titcomb would be placed in a Tacoma responsibility and get "immersed in the details of his new job," without opportunity for broadening experiences. Laird recommended that he be sent to a top-flight business school, and he added, "perhaps for once . . . my connection with Harvard may be useful to the Timber

Company and productive of a place for him." He closed warning Phil, "Please don't let Charlie save dollars by sending him to a cut-rate school."

In his answer Phil noted that he didn't think Jon Titcomb's presence in Tacoma would have much effect on the schism between the pulp and lumber divisions of Weyerhaeuser. As a matter of fact, they now had a third division, special products, "which, though an infant, will grow to produce three-way management divisions at most of the operations." Laird was right, however, about there being a problem. Phil had worked hard to build plant units that were integrated, that made maximum use of the timber resource. But what had been designed so carefully in a productive sense had been less perfectly managed, and what was needed was to integrate management. "I think we can have the sort of management division that we want," Phil contended: "How to get from where we are now to a situation where we have a man in charge of a forest and all of its liquidating agencies with the Tacoma office charged with overall responsibility and special advisory staff in pulp, sawmilling, logging, special products, personnel, etc., I am frank to say I don't know. Largely, I would guess, it is a matter of training men broad enough to be administrators, to whom technically trained saw mill, pulp, special products persons must report locally."

The scattered Weyerhaeusers gathered as best they could to celebrate Thanksgiving. Phil and Helen drove to Eugene to spend the day with George and Wendy in their new home, and to see for the first time "another swell grandson!" In a newsy letter to Flip, grandfather Phil reported that Wendy, barely a week out of the hospital, was already doing the shopping "and lots of things, which seemed amazing to me." He also noted that George was "chewing his nails a little bit about the responsibility he is going to undertake next year as Plant Manager, but I'd bet that he'll carry it off in good style." And according to Phil, there was considerable room for improvement in the Springfield situation. Wiz, who had transferred to Northwestern University, was spending Thanksgiving with Flip and Clara at their St. Paul home.

Phil obviously had confidence in George's ability to be successful in the Springfield responsibility, but the pressures on both of them must have been significant. Being a Weyerhaeuser did not automatically ensure opportunities, but others could hardly think otherwise when such opportunities befell someone like George. He had to prove himself twice, and every error was likely to be magnified. Things had changed considerably since Phil's father had arranged for his appointment as manager of the Clearwater operation. Phil tried to explain the new circumstances to a young aspirant, Carson Fleming, who just happened to be a descendant of one of the Timber Company's founders, William Carson. Thus Phil wrote: "It will be an asset in this matter that your name is Carson. However, I have done everything in my power to dispel the notion, which lurks in some corners, that this is still a family company. It has outgrown such status and has a fine esprit, due somewhat, no doubt, to the fact that ownership representatives have been willing to pitch in and take their turn." In other words, it may not have been family in the privileged sense, but at the same time it wasn't just another investment for many.

In that same letter Phil outlined what he had intended to be the policy, that of hiring the "new blood in the bottom echelons, so that promotion within the organization is recognized as the practice, and promising beginners can feel sure that plums in the way of advancement are coming along regularly." He noted that what might have seemed like violations of this policy had involved "specialists clearly not existing inside," such as economists, engineers, and various other technical experts. He also pointed out that they had "bent every effort to decentralize," thereby leaving to the branch managers and department heads most of the personnel decisions. His advice to the young man was clear enough: if interested, he was welcome to give it a try, starting on some bottom rung.

The end of the year saw no improvement in the market, a very brief strike at the White River branch, and the retirement of Ralph Macartney, long-time manager of the Klamath Falls operation. Macartney was one of the extended family of Weyerhaeuser, having begun work with Uncle Rudolph's Cloquet organization in 1910, then coming west in 1927 to assume responsibility at Klamath Falls, even before construction had begun on the sawmill there. He was to be succeeded by Hugh Campbell, and Phil invited them both to attend the meetings in Tacoma later in February. Phil's note to Macartney simply expressed his thanks "for the years of successful effort you've put in for our enterprises." Nothing more was required. Ralph knew Phil and knew he meant what he said.

Thus one by one the characters changed, and little by little the stage enlarged. But to many it seemed that the director had always been Phil Weyerhaeuser. And some presumed that he always would be. They were wrong, of course.

CHAPTER 17

The Green and Growing Forest

The advent of a new year usually encourages a pause for a mirror and window look at the world, with glances backward and views ahead. For a number of reasons, the advent of 1954 seemed especially encouraging in this regard for Phil and the Weyerhaeuser Timber Company. He had completed two decades as the operating director, and in the process much had been accomplished. Most significant, what had been a traditional approach of liquidating old-growth timber had evolved into a managed system of sustained yield, although not all the procedures were proven and much remained to be learned. Nonetheless, a fundamental change had occurred, a change that would not have occurred without vision and leadership.

The Stanford Research Institute study was nearing completion. Its objective was to forecast the extent of the nation's requirements for forest products twenty years hence. As Phil indicated to his senior executives, a "natural concomitant of such a prognostication would be a forecast of the size and nature of Weyerhaeuser Timber Company, 1975 model." Accordingly he requested that they take some time to give serious thought to "where we would like to be in 1975." He included some statistics that indicated how the company had "changed its spots" over the past twenty years, using figures from 1932 to 1952. It was noted, for example, that no dividends had been paid in 1932 and an actual loss had been recorded, whereas in 1952 dividend payments totaled $15.6 million and net income $36.7 million. Net working capital had increased from $6.5 million to nearly $58 million; net real estate, plant, and equipment from $36.3 million to $150 million; and net sales from $12 million to $260 million.

But figures, as always, told only a small part of the story. Even Phil had difficulty disguising his pride in summing up the years of his involvement:

During that period, our growth and change have been adjusted to the concept of rounding out our land ownership into operating tree farms, building facilities to serve those areas as primary production units, intensifying the utilization by building conversion units capable of converting to useful products a greater and greater percentage of the annual crop, and finally making sure that the relationship between allowable cut and the rate of plant operations was consistent with our desire for perpetual operation.

We have now achieved, or can foresee, the point at which our forests are being picked clean by any past comparisons and no manufacturing waste occurs other than the consumption of great quantities of bark, and sawdust, and shavings, and unchippable material to manufacture process power and steam.

Phil suggested a number of specific questions for consideration as his associates looked into their crystal balls. For example, should they become more active in the export business and should diversification encourage them to seek "a portion of our sales outside the forest industry?" He also asked them to think about the possibility of greater involvement in more highly manufactured products: "Now that we approach our capacity in basic raw products, should we seek to make paper instead of pulp? Containers instead of container board? Trusses instead of timber? Panels instead of sheathing?" Needless to say, the questions were more easily asked than answered.

The responses were sufficiently varied to indicate that little or no preliminary discussion had taken place on the subject. Fred K. held small hope that any such forecast would be immediately helpful, "any more than I believe that Stanford Research Institute is going to be very accurate in its prognostication of wood use, but I do believe the effort leads to a lot of thinking and planning with the resultant improvement in policies and programs." Not surprisingly, he made special reference to matters of advertising and marketing, in the process evidencing the eternal sensitivity that troubled and divided those in production from those in sales: "I don't know whether you and others fully appreciate what a high degree of acceptance our trade marked lumber receives in the market today. I can remember vividly the argument that went on over the years to the effect 'you can't advertise lumber,' that lumber is a raw material like coal, and that it is not susceptible to the same kind of merchandising as finished consumer products."

Over the years Fred's most difficult selling job was to sell the Sales Company to such as his brother. If lumber moved, the market was responsible. If lumber failed to move, the salesmen were responsible. As to the other questions that Phil had raised, Fred K. gave conservative agreement to continued growth and development. As an example, he acknowledged that they should "get into more highly manufactured products, but I think the progress in this direction will have to take place slowly."

Regardless of differing views of the future, the mere fact that Weyerhaeuser was attempting a long-range planning effort bespoke a basic optimism. When the moment is all-consuming, long-range plans can hardly merit much attention. This is not to say there was no reason for worry on the 1954 horizon. Laird Bell, for one, continued to fear the results of the excesses of Joe McCarthy and others who rode the anticommunist wave of hysteria to popularity and power. Laird had taken the opportunity of an all-college convocation at Carleton College to deliver one of his most direct attacks on the fearmongers. No doubt because of his long and close association with higher education through Harvard, the University of Chicago, and Carleton, he saw the threat to education in stark terms. He observed:

In the academic world, the creeping fear created by this hysteria is unqualifiedly bad. It is not that there are or ever have been in the colleges more than a handful of subversives—of professing Communists or of persons who had any idea of overthrowing this government. But the academic folk are apt to be liberal or nonconformist and they have a weakness for sponsoring good causes and joining those organizations to help mankind that always seem to disturb the more conservative minded. While of late the search has been confined to actual Communists, there is reason to fear that the inquisitors are likely to confuse liberalism and independent thought with their professed objections to subversion. Note that what is being investigated is un-American activities. Un-American can be interpreted to mean almost anything that the inquisitor doesn't like. . . .

Many, of course, were quick to take exception to the public position of the chairman of the Weyerhaeuser board of directors. Phil inevitably heard from some of those who happened also to be shareholders in the Timber Company. Peter H. McCarthy, descendant of a Dubuque lumberman, composed a three-page, single-spaced tirade attacking Bell's position and expressing wonderment that the chairman "of such a vast organization" could justify the expenditure of time to present "the anti-corporation, the anti-business, and the anti-investor side" of the story. The writer further held that "anyone who opposes any one of our congressional investigators should be locked up as a menace to the peace and security of these United States." Phil responded: "Your recent letter complains that our Chairman is not publicly defending the system under which we became a great nation. I suspect that he would disagree with you." After noting the importance of Bell's contributions to the organization, he observed, "In matters which are or verge on the political, business associates, like other members of the body politic, often go separate ways." Acceptance of such a policy would permit Mr. McCarthy to retain his Weyerhaeuser stock and still sleep at night. One suspects that it wasn't that easy.

In the course of January, Phil paid a visit to the Virginia Mason Clinic in Seattle for a routine physical examination. There had been no reason to suspect that anything unusual would be found or that he would receive anything but the standard advice that he lose a few pounds and take some additional rest. The report was unexpected and disturbing. Phil had leukemia, test results indicating the presence of chronic myelocytic (granulocytic) leukemia. Given his overall condition, no specific treatment was immediately called for, although it was recommended that he begin to see Dr. Ralph Huff of Tacoma on a regular basis. Initially only Helen and Fred K. were informed of the fact. Phil may have offered a brief "damn" at the development, and he undoubtedly felt considerably more mortal on January 18, the date of his fifty-fifth birthday. But outwardly, life went on as before.

For most of the Weyerhaeuser shareholders these were pleasing times. The Executive Committee declared a dividend of 62.5 cents as of March 1. The annual report for 1953 was distributed on schedule, and for the most part the response was favorable. Fellow lumberman H. R. MacMillan took the occasion to offer congratulations to Phil for "the leadership you are giving the forest industry in the fields of accomplishment for your shareholders and for the public at large in bringing about a great improvement in the public attitude toward the industry." Different but equally positive was the reaction of Dean Witter, who commented on his good fortune in owning 2,000 shares of Weyerhaeuser, indicating "the high regard I have for you and your company and my confidence in your future."

But not all shareholders were happy. The dividends could have been larger, and there were those who complained of the tendency to think only of the future, seemingly forever exchanging security for return on investment. From the beginning it had been necessary to defend the Timber Company's commitments to some of those who found themselves partners in the venture. In that spring of 1954, Laird Bell sent along one such complaint for Phil to answer. Over the past few years, the company had generally paid about 40 percent of its earnings in dividends. It was true that those had been years of relative prosperity, but it was also true that Phil and some of the other directors could recall all too well the early 1930s, when no dividends had been paid. Whether or not they said as much, they did adopt a conservative approach that sought to maintain liquid reserves to the extent that hard times or not, dividends would continue.

More important, however, in the policy of returning only a moderate percentage of earnings as dividend payments, as Phil explained, had been "the constant opportunity to invest for the purpose of diversifying products and reducing waste and improving our ability to withstand depressions by having low-cost operating plants." Such opportunities continued, and since their policy called "for treatment of its timber as a crop," this "justified long-term investment in timber, land, and plants." To Phil's way of thinking, "squeezing out the highest possible current dividend at the expense of such a program is parallel to refusing to maintain enough mature timber in our ownership to insure a sustained yield from our lands." He concluded his response by suggesting that the shareholder come west to see things for himself: "Surely a much better understanding of our hopes, aspirations, and performance can be had if you visit some of the properties."

Phil must have occasionally tired of telling the Weyerhaeuser story, but he never seemed to doubt the need to make the effort. One of the opportunities to speak publicly that seemed to have been more welcomed than most was an invitation to address the annual meeting of the Forest Products Research Society in Grand Rapids, Michigan, in early May. Phil's willingness undoubtedly reflected the fact that Robert D. Pauley, manager of the Timber Company's special products division, was the current president of FPRS. In addition, the timing was such that Phil could present the first commentary on the forthcoming study by the Stanford Research Institute.

Dean Garratt of Yale introduced Phil, and the "wood leader" proceeded to summarize the predictions of future needs of the nation and the ability of the forest products industry to meet those requirements. "Scarcity has been preached so long in the interest of promoting better forestry," he noted, "that the shoe is on the industry foot to prove the adequacy of the supply." Phil spoke with conviction, as always, but also with confidence. He told of the progress to achieve greater utilization, "whole-log use," and of his belief that true conservation had to be defined as the "wise use" of resources: "In whole-log use, together with tree farming, lies the forest industry's practical answer to its critics and to the skeptics who have cried 'Waste' and 'Timber Famine' in bygone days."

To a large extent it was through the auspices of the Stanford report that Phil, his company, and the industry were able to take the offensive. In his Grand Rapids address Phil expressed his belief that the industry could perform even more efficiently than the Stanford researchers had predicted:

These projections take only general account of the possibilities for cleaner logging, salvage of dead and down timber and more intensive forestry practices, including a greatly expanded volume of thinnings from second-growth forests without reducing the final crop. Knowing as we do that these things, too, are on the way, it is clear that we are closer than many of us dared hope, and far closer than our critics have admitted, to the day when all the forest products that our dynamic, growing economy demands can be met from current forest growth.

At no time did he call attention to the fact that Weyerhaeuser had sponsored the Stanford study. Rather he emphasized that the effort had been "a joint one in which many of you cooperated." Weyerhaeuser's interests and successes could not be separated from those of the industry.

In the meantime, plans for another significant gathering were proceeding. For the first time, the American Forestry Association had scheduled a meeting in the West—indeed, west of Wisconsin—in Portland on Labor Day, September 6. Dave Mason and Paul M. Dunn, dean of the Oregon State College School of Forestry, were co-chairmen for program arrangements. It had been determined that they should instruct "our eastern visitors and the western public in general how some of the most progressive companies have moved toward more or less complete integration of forest resources and the use of those resources so that the many products of the forest go to their most suitable use."

In the area of industrial integration, Mason observed, "the timber company is the outstanding example," and thus it followed that Phil was the logical one to accept that program assignment. But Mason knew Phil well and knew that he would be tempted to pass the responsibility along. He urged that in this instance Phil do the job himself: "You have personally done so much beginning before the organization of Potlatch Forests in the fields of better forest management, better utilization, and in more recent years 'integrated forest industry' that we feel it highly important to the success of the meeting that you yourself handle this subject."

Phil answered along the expected lines. After noting the difficulty of turning down a request from Mason or Paul Dunn, he added, "I hate to talk so much that surely you can get someone to do a better job," and closed by asking that "you consider the quality of your program carefully." Dunn replied that they interpreted Phil's response "to mean that you will accept the invitation." For the moment, however, Labor Day seemed far away.

The annual meeting was another matter. It was close at hand. In order to provide more complete information to shareholders in a timely manner, Phil requested that the annual report be published before the annual meeting. This required an advance in the customary dates for receipt of information from the various divisions and branches. Most complied with the new schedule, but not all. One of the tardy ones was Robert S. Douglas, responsible for certain whole-sale operations. Douglas was not recalcitrant by nature and Phil's admonishment was appropriate. "I don't suppose it is of very special import," he began his letter to Bob, "but, as you know, this year on February 22 we went over annual reports of everything in regard to WTC, and it occurred to me that receiving reports on the Eastern and Twin City yards on April 28 was rather an anticlimax." And he closed, "Certainly it represents a leisurely approach." Douglas had no real excuse and could only promise, "since this is to be a continuing proposition we will gear up accordingly." The point had been made, in good humor but effectively.

The 1954 annual meeting included visits to Longview and Everett. The board meeting held in conjunction featured a summary presentation of the Stanford study. There were no particularly worrisome matters to consider, although Phil did endeavor to provide information that would serve as a basis for recognition of the changing nature of company involvement. Long experience indicated that Weyerhaeuser directors seldom moved into new territories without careful study and cautious probes. Phil was making his preparations.

In late June, labor problems again closed down many operations. The pulp and paper unions had negotiated a 2 percent increase in wages, and in the wake of this announcement, both the AFL and CIO unions representing lumber, plywood, and logging employees called an industry-wide strike. Even though the Weyerhaeuser fir mills were paying wages somewhat in excess of the industry average, all were closed by the strikers. The pulp mills continued operations, but the lack of sawmill waste shortly took its toll. No one seemed troubled by the problems. As Phil observed in a July 2 letter to the directors, "what with vacations and the Fourth of July, everyone seems to be thinking of something else."

Seemingly good news was an announcement by the National Institute of Management that the Weyerhaeuser Timber Company had been selected as "the best managed firm in its industry in the country." Phil, of course, heard of the selection from a number of sources. His response was anything but gloating. To one friend he noted that as far as he knew, no one representing the National Institute of Management had "ever been out in these parts," so "in spite of the claims to the contrary, the study must be rather perfunctory." He would have been far more pleased about a break in the strike situation, but that was slow in coming. It was not until late August that operations began to resume production. For the most part, the summer of 1954 had been lost.

Still there had been plenty to think about. Within the management circle, much attention continued to be given to the Stanford report. In light of its predictions and all the other changing circumstances, Phil found himself thinking increasingly of new and sometimes distant opportunities. Matters of international trade had always been of interest, but often in a narrow sense—a sense of protecting home markets. Phil's own views of the world had evolved considerably. He would not likely have written in his early years what he wrote in an August 13 letter to Don Watson of the Steamship Company: "My own hunch is that as far as Canada is concerned we had better learn to get along with her on a pretty close to a free-trade basis. Occasionally the Swedes and Finns will dump and there will be currency manipulations of various kinds, but it does not seem to me that as an industry we should be seeking protection, except in situations which can justify themselves at the time."

Of greater immediate interest were southern opportunities, especially those having timberland and production facilities as well as marketing experience. In this connection, Phil made plans for a St. Louis meeting September 20 for a discussion of possible purchase of stock in the Gaylord Container Corporation. Since there was a meeting of the Boeing board scheduled in Wichita, Phil could make such arrangements without seeming overly eager. That Howard Morgan, Gully Gullander, and Joe Nolan accompanied him, however, indicated a seriousness that appeared unmatched by the officers of Gaylord. In fact, Phil was unaccustomed to the sort of bargaining that took place. His memo of the meeting suggests that they were not dealt with fairly, or at least directly. The president of the Gaylord board apparently said something to the effect that he and his fellow directors were "secure in the knowledge that it controlled 50% of the stock, and (pounding the table) 'nobody was going to disturb that comfortable situation.'" The point made was that it would require a "fantastic" offer to interest them in selling. Phil and his colleagues had expected to discuss facts and figures. They were uncomfortable in a situation that seemed to require haggling, and Phil's instinct in such situations was simply to end them. This he did, noting, "we opined that he had given us nothing to put our teeth into, and we departed." Fred Reimers, who had encouraged the discussions, was subsequently apologetic for leading Phil on a "wild goose chase." In his answer Phil assured Fred that he didn't consider it "a wild goose chase, and I think it was, all told, an interesting experience, though fruitless." But Gaylord was not the only possibility for association and expansion.

More satisfying had been the involvement in the American Forestry Association meetings September 6 in Portland. Phil had entitled his address "Integration—A Modern Approach to Conservation." He began by noting the variety of products made from trees, including the wooden cross ties on which the delegates' train had traveled west-ward, during which trip "the braver of you continued to rip off cello-phane wrappers from cigarette packages—in spite of medical re-searchers' warnings." The point was that at every turn there was a demand for forest products, and Phil assured the representatives that "tree farming, combined with whole-crop utilization in efficient for-est-product plants, is providing the products you need and use today and will continue to provide them for your children and their chil-dren."

After noting that lumber continued to be the major product of the Weyerhaeuser Timber Company and many other firms and that it had "paved and paid the way for integration," Phil turned specifically to that subject. "In this age of greater utilization," he observed, "a log is considered a bundle of fibers delivered in an overcoat of bark," and he further noted that they were now able to make economic use of practically all of every log. The old days of waste resulting from turn-ing round logs into square lumber were indeed old days. Phil paid particular tribute to the activities of some of the smaller firms, unable themselves to incorporate all the installations necessary for utilization but nonetheless adapting their operations to be part of the process. He mentioned a firm for which he had the highest respect, the Long-view Fiber Company, which collected chips from so many plants in the region that its president referred to himself as "the garbage man of the Pacific Northwest."

Phil closed by returning to the subject that had most concerned him through the years. "All too long, we in the industry had listened to the cries of the prophets of gloom," Phil reminded his audience. "They have said that we are running out of timber, and many sincere people have listened in alarm." But no longer, he proclaimed. "The turning point has been reached."

The conferees not only had the opportunity to listen to the views of the president of Weyerhaeuser but also to visit the Longview plant and woods operation. No doubt for many the latter was the more notable experience, but in any case Phil was pleased to be involved and proud to have his organization and its personnel on display. Thus he ob-served to one of the organizers of the program, "I can't help thinking how different the party would have been ten years ago," concluding with obvious satisfaction, "We are making some progress." In his brief comment on the meeting to the Weyerhaeuser directors, Phil men-tioned in passing that the field trips had been "interesting" and "quite convincing as to tree farms and utilization."

He also informed the directors that all the plants were again in op-eration, although a fact-finding panel was attempting an industry-wide approach to labor questions and it seemed likely, in Phil's estimation, that Weyerhaeuser would be "as unpopular as ever in this matter, and probably always will be." Business continued to be good. There was again uncertainty whether the fleet of the Steamship Company should be increased. And finally, the Crystal Ball session had "produced some interesting future possibilities." Other events of the early autumn included the retirement of two valued employees. Harry Morgan, manager at Longview, was honored at what Phil described as "just about the swellest party I ever attended." Morgan was pleased with the occasion but felt more honored by his association with Phil and Weyerhaeuser over the years. To Phil he sent a personal note. "You have the faculty of making people feel at home and making them like you," he said and added, with some nostalgia, "This is seldom found in top executives nowadays."

Clyde Martin's retirement ended a career with Weyerhaeuser that had begun in the first decade of the century, while Clyde was still a forestry student at Yale. Because his duties had become so varied, replacing him would not be easy, and Phil called attention to the problem in an October 8 memo to Gully Gullander. The position of forestry counsel was, of course, vacant "and the duties to which we have looked to Clyde are divided up pretty generally among others in the organization as, for instance, Dave's department is taking over a lot of the fire association activities, and Bernie Orell is, as Vice-President of the Weyerhaeuser Sales Company, in charge of Resource Relations, undertaking to do nationally a lot of the jobs that formerly Clyde undertook." Just how the new arrangements would be reflected on the organizational chart was only an indication of the problem. Phil suggested that they simply add a box for Bernie Orell, "reporting to me in the same place that Clyde Martin used to," rather than waiting for any suggestions from the Sales Company. In passing, Phil observed that the Sales Company had been working on its job descriptions for the past six years, "and I would like to express this new relationship in some way before another six years run out."

The distribution of the Stanford report began to bring responses from far and wide. A Canadian lumberman took the occasion to compliment Weyerhaeuser for its leadership in the industry, observing that the Timber Company had "again done something important that will accrue to the advantage of everyone in the timber industry." He concluded his letter by noting his "high regard" for Weyerhaeuser, "and this research job, so generously made available to everybody, simply confirms my high opinion of the company and its management." Pierre Prentice, the editor and publisher of House and Home, wrote a careful analysis of the report, disagreeing with some of the findings. In his reply Phil indicated that he didn't expect great accuracy in the predictions but felt that the effort was "worthwhile, as it focuses attention on the problem areas in the forest industry." Phil typically played down the Weyerhaeuser role. It should not be considered "our effort," he wrote, "because all we did was pay for it, and we deserve neither applause nor criticism."

The Timber Company directors gathered as scheduled in Tacoma for their mid-November meetings, and the agenda was completed without unusual difficulty. There were some frustrations, particularly concerning the ability or willingness of the board to consider the long-term investment program. Although there seemed to be a consensus that the Timber Company should continue to be just that, a producer of forest products, the matter of where new investments should be made geographically was unresolved. John Musser, a relative new-comer to the board, was imbued with a healthy idealism on the role and responsibility of board members. He was troubled on the one hand by the reluctance of the directors to engage in give-and-take discussions, and on the other by a general lack of information on which to base determinations. As a possible answer to the second concern, it had been agreed that the entire board would meet with the management group for a week in February. Although Phil could understand Musser's frustration, he could also remember all too well the board of uncles and the difficulties of those days. In any event, his response is of interest. "It seems to me," he began, "that such directors . . . not actively engaged in some part of the business, view their activities more in the nature of a group interested in broad generalities wishing to exercise vetoes but in general being more interested in convincing themselves that the active persons in the company are performing satisfactorily than in ruling upon particular matters put before them." Regarding the failure of the board "to come up with constructive criticism or suggestions," Phil indicated that this didn't bother him much, "but I, too, feel it will be helpful to all concerned to have the company expose its guts in some detail after the fashion planned in February."

Somewhat more difficult was the response to a thoughtful letter from old friend Chapin Collins, once again the editor of the *Montesano Vidette*. Chapin had been trying to look into his own crystal ball concerning the Grays Harbor area, but the fact was, as he wrote to Phil, "The future of this important area of our state is inescapably linked with your decisions . . . for nature has made this a tree land." The future of Aberdeen and Raymond and other such communities did indeed depend on the management of the area timberlands:

I feel certain that you have this question in mind. I know that community considerations of this sort loom large in your mind. I was impressed by your remark that the company could not make up its mind to pull out of Raymond.

That was certainly a decision in which a strong sense of community responsibility played an important part.

I was about to say "aside from business considerations." But I don't mean just that, for in my opinion, and I am sure in your opinion too, a sense of community responsibility is good business, perhaps the best business in the long haul.

In his reply, Phil could hardly make any specific promises, but there was no question of his sincerity: Chapin was "absolutely right about Grays Harbor's dependence upon us for the benefits which will come from operation of our timber." The same had been true of the earlier cutting, of the old-growth timber. Indeed, Phil now acknowledged that "the current hiatus arises out of the fact that we were a little too vigorous in the original liquidation program." But a new forest was returning and new operations would develop, "and I hope we will do nothing to violate your confidence in our feeling of community responsibility."

Almost no timber seemed too distant at the moment in terms of seeking information. Phil expressed little interest in some 300,000 acres of forest in northern Michigan on the basis that it was "mostly cutover land and is probably the slowest growing area of anywhere we could pick, consequently the most difficult to make something of." Laird Bell agreed, with the added consideration that since it was probably adjacent to his Huron Mountain Club, "everybody would get after me for everything that went wrong in our relations." At the same time, however, inquiries went forward in places as far removed as Peru and the Philippines.

January 1955 brought with it accustomed activities and some new and important developments. The problems associated with timberland investment were temporarily superseded by a potentially sensitive alteration in the advertising approach. For several years the Weyerhaeuser Timber Company had been telling its story of tree farming and full-log utilization in a format that featured illustrations of wildlife by such artists as Fred Ludekens and Stan Galli. So successful had this become that the decision to begin a new series honoring persons who had made significant contributions to the art of forestry seemed fraught with dangers. Phil admitted as much in a January 20 letter: "As we switch from animals to men as interest arresters in our national advertising, we become susceptible to jealousy of those not included and criticism of those chosen from many unanticipated angles." No doubt some would have preferred to stay with the animals, but in fact the new series proved exceedingly popular and the few negative reactions were hardly noticed.

There were other changes. One of the first involved the long-expected, and much-delayed, retirement of Laird Bell as chairman of the board. The principal reason for the delay, other than Phil's reluctance to have it occur at all, had to do with a suitable replacement. But the nominee had been there all along—Fred K.—and it may simply have been a matter of the Laird-Norton representatives reaching agreement that there would be no objection to Weyerhaeusers serving as both president and chairman. In any event, Laird Bell indicated in a February 4 letter to Phil that "Norton [Clapp] and Carleton [Blunt] and I are in hearty agreement that it would be fine to make Fred chairman in my place," adding, "It makes much more sense than my holding the office, much as I have enjoyed both the job and the distinction." Fred K. acknowledged the decision and accepted with enthusiasm and appreciation, noting that even if the title didn't mean much, it was "a mark of confidence, good will or something," and he paid particular note to Phil's part in the election.

What with the new schedule of reporting, the figures for 1954 were available in early February. They were better than expected, and Laird sent his congratulations to Phil on the results. Phil was more than willing to share the credit. "Maybe I can just turn around and congratulate you on it also," he wrote in reply, "as, frankly, I can't take too much credit for anything that is accomplished in the name of W. T. Company." He did express the hope that all would maintain their complimentary attitude during the February gathering of directors. Phil referred to the occasion as "hell week," although that was a bit of an exaggeration. In truth, he looked forward to such opportunities, forever convinced that the better the understanding, the fewer the problems.

"Hell week" ran from February 28 to March 4, the directors being provided with more information than most of them wanted, or could absorb, regarding Timber Company affairs. Fred K. was officially elected chairman of the board and Norton Clapp was named a vice-president and a member of the Executive Committee. But most paid less attention to these changes than to the handsome annual statement for 1954, whose cover featured a pair of band-tailed pigeons in the midst of the branches of a mature Douglas-fir. As had become customary, the figures inside were equally satisfying.

Following the meetings, John Musser once again passed along his concerns to Phil. He worried, for example, that the Timber Company was not sufficiently prepared to deal with union relations, and suggested the creation of a special group with negotiating responsibility. Musser also wondered whether there could be greater coordination between the lumber and pulp divisions. To many it seemed that the two divisions still went separate ways, united only by the name of Weyerhaeuser.

In his thoughtful response, Phil assured John that "the matter of union and employee relations probably receives more attention from our management group than any other subject," but, "in the end, brother Ingram calls the turns." Phil saw little purpose in having a special group, since the questions were "under almost constant study" and the situations varied so greatly from place to place and time to time. "It would take a Solomon to sort out the ideas for improvement and determine just the right degree of firmness in negotiations on various matters," he wrote. In short, he thought they were doing about as well as could be done in an area of such large and complex concerns. There were no easy answers. What he refused to acknowledge was the possibility that being knowledgeable in production matters did not necessarily make one an effective negotiator. To Phil, anyone ought to be able to negotiate. After all, it was primarily a matter of sharing hard facts and figures.

Regarding the competing pulp and lumber divisions, Phil was all too aware of the problem, admitting that pulp had always been something of an "off ox" in the Timber Company. But placing the blame was not so easy. Phil believed "the crux of the matter lies in Howard Morgan, who, though he loudly proclaims to the contrary, really wants the pulp division to be something separate and apart which can protect itself from the older and better intrenched lumber and timber men." Basic to the problem, however, were the differences in accounting practices, specifically as to how timber was charged to sawmill and pulp mill. The pulp managers were assessed at the market rate, while the sawmill managers—well, they also managed the tree farms. Revision in the accounting procedure was being proposed by Gullander and comptroller Robert W. Boyd, but progress was slow. In the meantime, as Phil noted, "Rivalry we will always have and should have probably, and it is a little hard to know when a competitive influence goes too far within an organization."

Generally there seemed reason for optimism. The first quarter earnings report showed sales of nearly $73 million, up more than $11 million from the previous year. Net income for the period was $11.5 million, an increase of nearly $3 million from the first three months of 1954. One could point to the increasing efficiency of Timber Company operations as an important factor in the results, but as Phil acknowledged in his April 22 letter to shareholders, "The improved results are attributable principally to the record breaking level of activity in the construction industry and the high level of business generally." In any event, there was little reason for celebration, much less complacency. Conditions could change in a hurry.

It was, however, a favorable time to consider new investments, and

Phil continued to press his directors about southern opportunities. Laird Bell had responded to one such shove, agreeing that "an ownership of growing timberland and conversion facilities in the South is a proper place for us to be investing, and I would answer your question that there *is* interest in it." Translating interest into action was the problem confronting Phil. More easily managed was an open house May 19 at the White River branch of the Timber Company near Enumclaw. In his invitation to shareholders Phil expressed the hope that they would "take advantage of this opportunity to visit the White River Tree Farm and inspect the recently modernized sawmill operations." Nearly three hundred accepted the invitation and, as Phil reported to Laird, "it turned out to be a very pleasant occasion."

These were busy days, and apparently Phil continued to feel quite well, although it sometimes seemed that he was testing his strength and, by doing so, reassuring others. In late May he addressed a note to Flip in St. Paul, opening with the complaint, "our news from you somehow seems to be second hand." As to his own activities, Phil noted: "Last week Helen and I flew to Springfield for the night with the youngsters; went on to Klamath for a meeting of the supervisory training group; wound up in Spokane on Saturday night for a dinner of the Historical Society; I went on to Boise for a meeting of the shareholders, at which they presented a very carefully worked out program for the entertainment and instruction of all present; joined Lynn and Fred in a quick trip around the Potlatch plant."

The Springfield youngsters were George and Wendy and family; it was brother Fred K. and niece Lynn at Potlatch; and attendance at the Washington State Historical Society function fell within Phil's tenure as president of that organization. By any measurement it had been a full week, beginning with the White River celebration and ending at Potlatch, and Phil returned home feeling "fresh as a daisy."

For some reason, Ed Davis was collecting lists of titles and positions held by the four cousins. The list Phil submitted was undoubtedly the shortest. As of June 15, in addition to the Timber Company and related involvements, he was a director of the Boeing Airplane Company, the Stanford Research Institute, the Association of Washington Industries, the American Council to Improve Our Neighborhoods, and the United Good Neighbor Fund of Pierce County; he was a trustee of the American Forest Products Industries, the Foundation for Economic Education, and the College of Puget Sound; and he was president of the Little Church on the Prairie, and a curator of the Washington State Historical Society. Probably to indicate his opinion of this list-making exercise, Phil also noted that he was captain of the *Wanigan*. It may not have been an impressive list, but it was in keeping with his philosophy that one should not be involved for superficial reasons. Fred K. took special notice of the inclusion of the *Wanigan* responsibility. "I am glad," he wrote, "it is not yet sunk."

The month of June saw several significant developments. Weyerhaeuser announced the exercise of its option on the Ultican mill site at Cosmopolis, indicating an intention to construct a 400-ton sulphite plant. The Executive Committee also authorized negotiation with the Simpson Logging Company regarding an exchange of lands. Public announcement of the exchange was made jointly by Phil and Bill Reed of Simpson on June 16. The announcement reported, "Simpson is exchanging approximately 45,000 acres of forest lands owned by it, principally in the tree farm of Schafer Bros. Logging Company . . . for approximately the same number of acres of forest lands owned by Weyerhaeuser Timber Company in the South Olympic Tree Farm situated within the Shelton Cooperative sustained yield unit in Mason County." The Weyerhaeuser cash payment in this exchange amounted to nearly $8 million, but, as Phil indicated to the directors, the block of growing land "just north of Aberdeen will be a great asset." Indeed, things hadn't looked so promising in that region for many years. What with the Raymond sawmill development and the plans for Aberdeen/ Cosmopolis, Phil acknowledged that the two communities were full of "rumors and excitement," and he hoped to convince them that "something beneficial is happening."

But not all the developments concerned Weyerhaeuser. Particular notice was taken of a merger of two of the largest producers in the pulp and paper field, Crown Zellerbach Corporation and the Gaylord Container Corporation. Some, even including Fred K., wondered if they were being aggressive enough in seeking southern opportunities by whatever means. "Mergers seem to be in the air," he wrote, although he admitted that he was not yet sure what direction Weyerhaeuser ought to take. Laird Bell, for one, was quite satisfied that Phil's conservative approach was the proper one. "I have a comfortable feeling that these things won't panic you into doing anything brash," he wrote. "I know of nothing more dangerous than having a lot of cash around." In Laird's opinion, the deal with Simpson was "much more in our line." In truth, timberlands and mergers were probably not first in Laird's thoughts. He had just been appointed as an alternate representative to the tenth session of the United Nations. Phil made appropriate and typical recognition: "So many honors come your way these days that I don't know exactly what to congratulate you on, but I am proud to know you."

It was not as if Phil had no "extracurricular" opportunities of his own. On July 22 he addressed the Los Angeles Rotary Club, talking once again on his comfortable topic of growing trees and fully using logs. He did include one variation, observing that so much of contemporary life on the Pacific Coast had to do with two words, "growth and speed." Such, however, was not the case when it came to forests. "Regardless of today's emphasis on pace," he observed, "it still takes from 80 to 100 years to grow a Douglas fir to useful maturity." He did note that the foresters were "working with Mother Nature to hasten this unseemly slow process—and who knows—they may be successful." But the message was clear. Growing trees was a singular commitment, one that would continue to be based on faith—faith in the world of nature and the world of economics and politics.

Phil declined an invitation to serve on the President's Committee on Government Contracts, an invitation proffered over the signature of Vice-President Richard Nixon. Part of his reason for refusing to accept this responsibility was his acceptance of another. At the request of the Department of State, he agreed to serve as a delegate to the United Nations Economic Commission for Europe Timber Committee, meeting in Geneva in mid-September. As he indicated to the Timber Company directors, "it sounded so interesting that I accepted and will fly to Geneva the 10th and return from Rome the 30th," explaining that the "added interval is my wife's."

On September 7 Phil and Helen departed Tacoma for Washington, D.C., and then Geneva, in his words, "full of excitement but woefully ignorant of what is expected." Elizabeth Titcomb accompanied them on the trip, and as a vacation it was highly successful. As Phil later described the tour to Fred K., "Helen and Elizabeth just jumped up and down they were so excited about Switzerland and some of the things in Italy." Phil also enjoyed the opportunity, but he was less sanguine about the importance of his contributions. "I came home with the idea it didn't make much difference whether anybody went or not," he admitted to brother Fred. And to Laird Bell, he observed, "Couldn't get much satisfaction out of it so far as accomplishment is concerned, but in every other way it was rewarding." No doubt part of his discomfort with the proceedings had to do with the unfamiliar manner of the diplomats and his own uncertainty concerning the nature of his involvement. Phil never had much patience with the simple discussion mode of operation. He had adjourned meetings summarily when it seemed that the sole purpose was discussion. To sit around a table, whether in Geneva or Tacoma, and listen to conversations slowly leading nowhere tired him quickly. He subsequently wrote to Bernie Orell that he had been "impressed by the one world mindedness of the secretariat and their shrewdness in conduct of their affairs." But he immediately observed, "Evidently the UN jobs are rather highly prized because of their tax-free status and the smart boys are all in there." In any event, he had tried to help and it had probably aided his education, even if he was relieved to be back home in Tacoma.

Back home he found that the lumber market had slowed a bit, although the figures for September showed it to have been "quite a month." He immediately set about planning the agenda for the November 16 meeting of the directors, and the lead item was determination of the fourth quarter dividend. Phil recommended $1.25, making a total for the year of $3.75, or 75 cents larger than that for 1954, and $1.25 more than had been paid from 1951 through 1953. The $3.75 dividend would result in a total distribution for 1955 of $23,437,500, approximately 44 percent of the estimated earnings. This and other factors prompted Phil to request consideration of another stock split. He reminded the directors that a year earlier there had been considerable discussion of stock splits and listing. "No action was taken," he noted, "but I would like to consider again the pros and cons of a stock split." Other items on the agenda included a recommendation that a gift of $300,000 be made to the Weyerhaeuser Timber Foundation. Then there were numerous reports, one concerning possibilities for outside acquisitions and another dealing with plans to enlarge the Tacoma Building headquarters.

Laird Bell was unable to attend the meeting of the directors. Phil missed him and while noting that "what you are doing is more important," expressed the hope that it wouldn't happen again. Concerning the meeting, Phil reported, "We may have done some things which you would have been against, such as a big dividend and a big split, but there was lots of discussion, and I gather that as the average age of the group is going down we will have more arguments and debates." It wasn't just the youngsters who held forth, however, Phil noting that O. D. Fisher had "put on the usual show," and that Laird would have been amused to see how Fred had suffered as chairman, "trying to get him back on the rails." Laird replied that he had "hated more than I can say to miss a meeting," but added that it seemed "only fair to let F.K. struggle with certain problems on his own without surveillance." As to the results of the meeting, Laird had no complaints.

Not everyone was enthusiastic about the four-for-one stock split proposal. To one shareholder who questioned the wisdom of such a move, Phil explained his belief that "it will minimize the reported earnings and dividends per share, will tend to encourage employee and customer purchases of stock, and tend to make a wider market for the stock, e.g., more liquidity for the shareholders and a surer reflection of the intrinsic value in the price of the stock." Those arguments, of course, carried the day, and the decision was announced on December 22. Labor negotiations had resulted in long-term contracts with both the CIO and the AFL, Phil noting in a December 1 memo to directors that there had been "pretty general agreement among our management people that extension of the contract" would be "worth what we had to pay for it." He added, "We hope you will agree that we have bet right." Nature was not a party to the settlement, and late December storms brought an end to most logging operations. Some worried about a possible log shortage developing at the mills. Phil was not among them.

Neither was Fred K., whose younger daughter Lynn was about to be married to Stanley Ray Day of Detroit. Fred sent his agenda for the family meetings out on January 4, in his words the "hush before the storm" of the January 6 wedding. Phil and Helen attended the happy event, also enjoying an opportunity to visit with Flip and Clara, and plans were in the making for a family vacation in Hawaii the last two weeks of March.

It had been two years since Phil's visit to the Virginia Mason Clinic and the diagnosis of leukemia. For the most part, life had gone on as before. It was, however, impossible not to worry, to avoid anticipating symptoms of changing conditions. In mid-January Phil and Helen made a swing through Oregon with Ed and Anna Hayes, but they were forced to cancel a portion of the trip because Phil wasn't feeling well. He subsequently wrote to Ed, thanking him for his hospitality and reporting, "Helen got me home and mothered me until she has practically pronounced me cured." As evidence of his return to good health, he announced plans for a southern tour after the St. Paul family meetings, to visit the Southern Lumber Company and generally become better acquainted with the area. He invited Ed and Norton Clapp to accompany him.

Phil enjoyed this trip, especially the chance to visit with Dave Fisher of the Southern Lumber Company at Warren, Arkansas. Dave was looking for a partner with means and experience whom he might interest in a joint pulp venture. Phil couldn't imagine anyone becoming involved on the terms offered. He wrote to Fisher in February: "It is hard for me to see how someone who has enough know-how to be a desirable partner will wish to dilute his interest to the point suggested or forego any land ownership in view of the fact that success and growth of the enterprise will, of course, reflect itself in the value of the annual crop of adjacent land owners." At the same time, however, Phil acknowledged, "there seems to be rather universal optimism throughout the South that such deals can be made, and we wish you success in your search." Ironically it would be Potlatch with whom the Southern Lumber Company would shortly merge.

The interest in mergers continued to be the order of the day. On his return to Tacoma, Phil took time to write to Jack Leland, president of

Long-Bell, primarily to offer his sympathy at the news of the death of T. E. Hoppenstall, who had served for so many years with the Long-Bell Company. But Phil also took note of the news of a pending merger between Long-Bell and International Paper Company. Rumors had been about, but still it was something of a surprise. Phil admitted "the possibility of your merging the whole operation with somebody like International never occurred to me, and perhaps never has to you. It is astonishing how many of these sorts of things are going on around the circuit, though, isn't it?" It wasn't all that astonishing, of course, and all the while Phil was casting about for just such an opportunity for Weyerhaeuser.

The March vacation to Hawaii with the children came off as planned. All but Flip and Clara were able to participate, although their reason for absence could not be questioned. Clara gave birth to Elizabeth, their third child, in St. Paul on March 31. For the rest it was a delightful reunion. As Phil wrote to Dave Winton following his return to Tacoma, "I came back from Hawaii very much rejuvenated after cavorting in the waves with children and grandchildren and doing practically nothing for two weeks." He invited friend Winton to visit the Northwest "on a shareholder inspection trip." He even suggested that Winton might learn something about the lumber business. "So please take some advice," he closed, "which I am very seldom offering you, and snap out of that Middlewestern provinciality." Family and old friends were becoming of larger importance.

One of the first post-Hawaii responsibilities was a matter of great personal interest. Phil was invited to attend the annual forestry meeting to be held at Coos Bay on April 5 and 6, and in his invitation Dave Weyerhaeuser asked if Phil would offer some comments "about intensive forest management as you have seen it down South," and perhaps say a few words about the establishment of "a forest management tour which would be a credit to the company." Most important, however, was the opportunity for Phil to indicate once more the interest he had in the program. He readily accepted, and among those loggers and foresters he joined in the discussions with enthusiasm. As Dave subsequently noted, "It means so much to all of the foresters to hear directly from you an expression of deep and concerned interest in the progress of our forestry program."

Phil was also eager to discuss with Dave and Ed Heacox a possible fact-finding tour of southern opportunities. Early May found Dave and Ed in the midst of that tour, Dave reporting back to Phil that they were having "the time of our lives!" They had visited three potential areas, "South East Texas, Central Louisiana & the Chapman area in Alabama," and were about to head into southern Arkansas. Dave wrote, "these four areas seem to offer the only chance of setting up any new & sizeable development." Although they had no offers in hand, he seemed confident they had "picked up some additional information that will be helpful," and he looked forward to giving Phil a complete report on his return.

Phil wanted to move Weyerhaeuser off what seemed to be dead center, but expansion by any means was no easy proposition. So many factors had to be considered; but there must have been times when Phil wished that he were capable of dealing with greater abandon. In early April he and others agonized over an offer from the Reed interests which would have Weyerhaeuser "take over the Oregon part of their contemplated purchase of Malarkey." As he indicated to Fred K., "it just seemed too much for our blood to fit into a sustained yield pattern." Perhaps it would have been all right to liquidate the timber, but, as he noted, "we don't become popular by liquidating plants in Oregon and trying to ship the timber to Longview, or some of it."

Perhaps it was with relief that Phil turned to subjects having to do with logging practices. Given the national advertising campaign, many suggestions crossed his desk from those who wished to help the company in its conservation efforts. One suggested that Weyerhaeuser could utilize much more of the tree if it experimented with the machine that reduced branch trimmings to chips—a machine being introduced in connection with electric and telephone line and roadway maintenance. Phil appreciated the thought but noted that the problem with the "branch chewer-upper" was that the chips and bark "are inexorably mixed," and while each could be used separately, together they were not very useful. He did note that there was a good deal of experimentation going on in this area:

. . . no doubt the answer will some day be found which will permit the use of the smaller material now left in the woods.

This makes me express to you our great appreciation for your writing about this subject. If you are west sometime we would be delighted to show you how much of the material we are able to use even from decadent Old Growth forests. Your impression will be, I am sure, that we are leaving a good deal still, and that will be the truth; although we are proud of how much more we are taking now than we did fifteen years ago.

Phil's monthly note to the directors at the end of May included a number of items, beginning with the report that "we seem to be ahead of last year in most categories." Business was good. He also mentioned the continuing rumors of acquisitions and mergers, that the National Lumber Manufacturers Association's spring session delegates were to be the guests of the Snoqualmie and Everett branches, that the pulp and paper negotiators had reached a settlement, and that *Saturday*

Review had once again awarded the Timber Company second place in the category of public interest advertising campaigns. Finally he noted that "Dave Weyerhaeuser and Ed Heacox made a quick tour of the South and came back enthusiastic about southern forestry." That same day Phil informed Fred K., "I have a confession to make." That confession involved the purchase of 10,000 shares of Longview Fiber Company stock in behalf of the Timber Company. But, as Phil indicated, he had no authorization to do so. "What do you think I should do?" he asked brother Fred. The fact was that Phil would have been quite satisfied to take it personally. That would, of course, be unnecessary, Fred immediately returning his "vote in favor thereof!"

Phil returned to the South in early June with Dave Weyerhaeuser, the two reviewing some of the opportunities that Dave and Ed Heacox had come across. Fred K. subsequently came out to Tacoma, and there was much discussion about the most appropriate course to take in the South. In the Pacific Northwest, the Weyerhaeuser Timber Company had almost always dealt from strength in negotiating for properties. In the South that was not the case, and new standards were required; new definitions of what was advantageous had to be accepted. In short, a good opportunity did not have to be perfect in all respects. "Maybe we make the southern venture unnecessarily complicated in our own minds," Phil admitted to Fred K., "but whatever we do other than spend money has to have the approval of lots of people." And so the investigations continued.

That others seemed to be improving their positions through mergers while Weyerhaeuser stood idly by was a source of some concern, but it was by no means the only thing troubling Phil from a business consideration. Indeed, he had little doubt that an opportunity to become involved in the South would eventually be realized. If the search was tiresome, so be it. Sooner or later it would be successfully concluded. Less certain of happy resolution was the more basic question of overall leadership. Who was thinking imaginatively of the future for Weyerhaeuser? A great many capable people were working away, for the most part efficiently, but the truth was that they had been working too long. Where were the new leaders? Phil wasn't convinced he saw them in the organization; or if he saw them, they were not yet ready to provide the sort of help needed. This wasn't a question he could discuss much with others, in a sense because it was a personal one. He was recognizing that he needed help in his responsibilities as head of the Timber Company, particularly as he tried to look beyond the midfifties. The Stanford report had been useful, but specific direction was going to have to be determined, and that determination should be made by the president. Phil needed someone to talk to, on a regular basis, about such matters.

Phil had been watching John Aram, president of the Boise Payette Lumber Company, for several years. This able and energetic individual had directed his organization in a manner that greatly impressed Phil, no doubt in part because he was in basic agreement with Aram's approach. Boise Payette had altered its policy from one of liquidation to one of sustained yield, but large problems remained and Aram was searching for new operations that the company might undertake profitably. It was ostensibly in response to this search that Phil invited Aram to inspect the Timber Company's particle board plants at Longview and Coos Bay. It seems doubtful that Phil shared his intentions even with Fred K., although in a letter of June 25 he did mention that Aram was coming over later in the week to "see what we can do to help him in particle board and have a visit with him."

Initially their talk was of a general sort. Aram would recall being impressed once again with Phil's commitment to forestry and timber management, particularly in the course of their flight from Longview to Coos Bay. As they looked down on thousands of acres of beautiful second-growth timber, the two were able to share a feeling of accomplishment. Whatever the problems, those green trees seemed to make it all worthwhile. It was in Phil's hotel room in Coos Bay that he asked John Aram to join him. Given Phil's tendencies to be less than serious, Aram at first assumed he was joking. Assured otherwise, John refused to give an immediate reply. He did agree to come back for another discussion in July. In the July visit, the talk was open and honest. When Aram inquired about Timber Company plans, asking what Phil was trying to do, Phil's answer illustrated his concerns. "I'm sorry, John," he replied, "I can't answer your question. I wish I could, and that is one of the things we have to work on." It was hard to say no to Phil in situations such as that; and after due deliberation with family and Boise Payette directors, Aram agreed to come to the Timber Company as assistant to the president beginning the first of the year. Phil was elated. "Boy, I sure pulled one on Fritz Jewett," he reportedly exclaimed gleefully, referring of course to his cousin's considerable involvement and interest in Boise Payette.

In any event, Phil felt like celebrating his capture of Aram when he and Helen headed out into the Sound aboard the *Wanigan*. It was mid-July, and they were looking forward to two weeks of going nowhere in particular, alone. The weather cooperated and so did the boat. It was not until nearly the end of their vacation that an accident occurred that marred an otherwise perfect cruise. Even so, it didn't seem very serious at the time. Phil slipped on the boat ladder when climbing up after a swim, in the process chipping a tooth and wrenching a shoulder. Initially he probably worried more about the tooth, but it would be the shoulder and associated complications that merited real concern. Upon their return home, he was in considerable pain and his shoulder was terribly discolored. He was immediately hospitalized, where he would remain for two weeks. As he wrote to son Flip, all this had been something of a surprise "because I hadn't realized anything was wrong especially." He then explained that he was weak from so much internal bleeding, that it had been necessary to drain the damaged area of a quart and a half of blood. Still he tried to be reassuring: "Now I am feeling like a million, and will be back on the job next week." But he closed on a somewhat somber note. "This is my first hospital experience and it is hard to rise above it mentally."

Phil did return to the office as planned, but to those who looked closely it was clear that he wasn't himself. In an August 14 letter to Laird Bell, he said, "I expect to be 100% before long and fully expect to get back to have a visit with Walter." The Walter referred to was Walter P. Paepcke, chairman of the board of the Container Corporation of America, and the visit, of course, had to do with a possible merger. The visit did take place the following month, but no merger between Weyerhaeuser and the Container Corporation would result. More important, Phil would never be 100 percent again.

The interest in Paepcke's company resulted from the belief that Weyerhaeuser would reap benefits from entering the container field. But a merger with such a giant as the Container Corporation would involve great changes in the nature and management of the company. Perhaps that was too large a leap. Ed Hayes, with whom Phil had been spending increasing amounts of time, counseled a more conservative involvement, suggesting "a merger with a smaller company such as Kieckhefer Container Corporation." In early October Phil addressed a note to John W. Kieckhefer, inviting him to a duck shoot in the course of a pending visit to Tacoma. Phil suggested November 7 as their day for ducks, indicating that the following week the Timber Company directors would be in town, "so that it would be hard for me to get away." Both Phil and his guest had a good deal more on their minds than ducks.

Phil tried his best to work to good purpose, but he was tired. He sent an agenda for the November board meeting to Fred K., then vacationing in Europe. From Madrid Fred K. acknowledged its receipt, expressing the hope that "*any* agenda will *help* hold O.D. [Fisher] in check," referring to their loquacious senior member. Phil personally arranged with the staff of the Hotel Winthrop for the annual group dinner, typically selecting the least expensive choice from the menus. "The $4.75 dinner sounds just about as good to me as any of the others," he wrote. "Maybe that's because I like roast beef as well as steak." In late October he called the Executive Committee together to approve a proposal "to acquire some Mississippi timberland without disclosing our identity," and he reported to the directors on October 29, "we have taken the first steps in such a program." These properties, nearly 55,000 acres, were actually in Alabama and Mississippi and involved the Mississippi Pulp and Paper Company and five other organizations. The southern invasion had begun in earnest.

There was other good news to share, of a personal sort. On election day, November 6, Phil wrote to a vacationing Dr. Charles Pascoe, clearly delighted with what he had to report: "We've had a round of excitement around here since you've gone, because all of a sudden Wizzie has got herself engaged to Howie Meadowcroft. Everybody's happy and the goose hangs high." It may have seemed sudden to Phil, but Howie Meadowcroft was anything but a stranger, and indeed was at the time a promising employee in the Timber Company's special products division. Phil was also looking forward to a mid-November trip down to Klamath Falls with Jack Pascoe and Flip and George, "in the hope of capturing some geese." The national election results were as expected and, for the Weyerhaeusers, as hoped. Much was right with the world.

The directors met as scheduled, and Phil managed as best he could. The questions concerning southern opportunities were many, and even had he been feeling fit, he might have tired of trying to explain matters so complex. Naturally the directors wished to understand as much as they could, but with so many possibilities considered—with no great results as yet—it proved a frustrating session. As always, Laird Bell was sensitive to such matters. He wrote a note by hand after returning to his Winnetka, Illinois, home. "I hope you're not bothered by the occasional critical questionings of directors," he began. "That's what they're for." Once again he reassured his friend, "You have done a great job with the Company & there's no reason to think you are not going to continue doing it." There was a reason, of course, but Laird had not been told. Or maybe he had been.

The directors had been home scarcely a week when they received a November 27 memorandum from Fred K.: ". . . Phil is seriously ill in Tacoma General Hospital. He has been under the doctor's care for some time for treatment of chronic leukemia and has been optimistic that the disease could be successfully controlled for a long time to come. During the past week it has flared up in very serious form. The doctor is trying another type of treatment, which he hopes will be effective."

The news of Phil's illness brought responses from family and friends, endeavoring to be of help to Helen while holding out hope for him. On December 6, Chapin Collins published an editorial in his *Montesano Vidette*, "Remarks About a Man Named Phil." He said that he had been inspired by a recent conversation with a friend to the effect that "it's too bad newspapers usually wait until a man is gone before they say the nice things they have in mind about him." He decided not to wait. He recalled the circumstances of his long acquaintance with Phil Weyerhaeuser and the important decisions Phil had made which had meant everything to Washington communities. "I hope that nothing we do in Grays Harbor will make you think ill of us," Phil had once said to him. In recent years, of course, the Timber Company had increased its operations enormously, investing in plants at Cosmopolis and Raymond. "Don't you agree with me," Collins wrote, "that a great part of this decision was made by a man who, in 1941, told us that tree farming would help our own communities? Phil made a promise in 1941, a vague, hopeful promise. In 1956, he remembered that promise, and kept it."

Collins concluded his piece by paying tribute to the manner of the man who was Phil Weyerhaeuser:

Often, you can judge men by the offices they keep. Phil's is only slightly larger than mine. He has a desk and a few chairs. But I think his real office is what he sees outside the window. He looks across industrial Tacoma with Mt. Rainier rising clean above the factory smoke. . . .

Some men could boast such a view, as they would expound their imported wallpaper. I suspect that this view has been a different sort of inspiration to Phil Weyerhaeuser. It has contributed to what I would term an almost religious attitude towards his enterprise. His efforts to be "practical" don't conceal this attitude. After all, what IS practical, when your mind sweeps ahead 100 years or more, and you make up your mind with the Mountain that was God looking down on you?

Sentimental? Sure it is. A man like Phil proves there's sentiment in business. That's one of the reasons why his illness distresses so many. Another reason is that people just like a guy named Phil.

Phil died in the late afternoon of December 8. Helen knew her own loss, but even she must have been amazed at the extent to which Phil had been treasured by others. Aunt Maud, Charlie's widow and now Maud Sanborn, recalled the first time she had seen Phil. It had been at his mother's funeral in Rock Island, "a small baby in arms," and also she remembered that Charlie had "always said, it is Philip we will rely on." From his colleagues in the company, heartfelt condolences came. Joe Nolan cried for the first time as an adult. Charlie Ingram promised to try to pass along Phil's philosophy to his successor. And George S. Long, Jr., admitted that he was "completely unable to express the admiration, love and affection I had for Phil and my only consolation now is that I think he knew it." The "Woods Gang" at the White River Branch forwarded a contribution to the Sloan-Kettering Institute for Cancer Research in accordance with Helen's request. Up and down the line those associated with the Timber Company mourned the loss of the only leader most of them had known, and one they regarded as a friend.

The funeral was held at the Little Church on the Prairie on the afternoon of December 10. Reverend William P. McCormick conducted the services, assisted by Harold Long, Phil's former pastor. To the overflowing crowd, Reverend McCormick observed that Phil would not have liked any recitation of accomplishments or contributions. "One of the things which has endeared him to our hearts is his simplicity, his lack of show, his deep and utter humility," McCormick noted. "So today, we will bear tribute silently in our hearts and make no attempt to voice it with our lips." It seemed appropriate that the remembrances be personal.

There was no graveside ceremony. Phil was cremated, and on a bright day in early spring, Helen and the children went out on the *Wanigan* to scatter his ashes on the waters he had so enjoyed. Some may have questioned this, thinking that such a man ought to have been honored with a monument of sorts. But those who knew him best understood. There was no need for a stone monument or even a marker. The green and growing forest marked the spot.

The 1956 annual report of the Weyerhaeuser Timber Company was dedicated to Phil, with the following words offered in commemoration:

He was a man of exceptional vision, kindliness and executive talents. It was he who activated the philosophy of managing forest lands for perpetual growth and harvest. Under his leadership also emerged this Company's long-range operating policy toward maximum utilization of timber through diversification, plant integration and development of new practices and products. His influence in the industry and the American community will be felt for generations to come.

Fred K. had succeeded Phil as president, and in an insert to the report he announced that a merger of the Kieckhefer Container Company and the Eddy Paper Corporation with the Timber Company had been "approved in principle." Things did, of course, go on. It would not be business as usual, however—not yet, and not for some time to come.

Four Generations of Weyerhaeusers, 1857–1957

John Philip Weyerhaeuser
Nellie Lincoln Anderson
Anna Mary Holbrook

- Elizabeth Weyerhaeuser
  Francis Rodman Titcomb
  - Edward Rodman Titcomb
    Julie Crommelin
  - John Weyerhaeuser Titcomb
    Diana Corse
- Frederick King Weyerhaeuser
  Vivian O'Gara
  - Vivian O'Gara Weyerhaeuser
    Frank Nicholas Piasecki
  - Elizabeth Lynn O'Gara Weyerhaeuser
    Stanley Ray Day
  - Ann Weyerhaeuser
    John James Pascoe
  - John Philip Weyerhaeuser III
    Clara Dracoulis
- John Philip Weyerhaeuser Jr.
  Helen Hunt Walker
  - George Hunt Weyerhaeuser
    Wendy Wagner
  - Frederick Weyerhaeuser
  - Elizabeth Hunt Weyerhaeuser
    William Howarth Meadowcroft

Elise Weyerhaeuser
William Bancroft Hill

Margaret Weyerhaeuser
James Richard Jewett

- George Frederick Jewett
  Mary Pelton Cooper
  - George Frederick Jewett Jr.
    Lucille Winifred McIntyre
  - Margaret Weyerhaeuser Jewett
    William Hershey Greer Jr.

Frederick Weyerhaeuser
Sarah Elizabeth Bloedel

A sister of
Anna Catherine Bloedel
F.C.A. Denkmann

Apollonia Weyerhaeuser
Samuel Sharpe Davis
- Edwin Weyerhaeuser Davis
  Catherine Lyman Mills
  - Elizabeth Mills Davis
    Albert J. Moorman Jr.
  - Frederick Weyerhaeuser Davis
    Mary Ellen O'Connor

Charles Augustus Weyerhaeuser
Frances Maud Moon
- Carl Augustus Weyerhaeuser
  Edith Greenleaf
  - Charles Augustus Weyerhaeuser
  - Henry Greenleaf Weyerhaeuser
  - Robert McClelland Weyerhaeuser
  - Elizabeth Maud Weyerhaeuser
  - Carrie Ann Weyerhaeuser
- Sarah Maud Weyerhaeuser
  Walter Samuel Rosenberry Jr.
  Robert J. Sivertsen
  - Walter Samuel Rosenberry III
  - Margaret Jane Ross
  - Charles Weyerhaeuser Rosenberry
  - Elise Bancroft Rosenberry
  - Robert Moore Phares
  - Lucy Rosenberry

Rudolph Michael Weyerhaeuser
Louise Bertha Lindeke
- Margaret Louise Weyerhaeuser
  Walter Bridges Driscoll
  - Walter John Driscoll
  - Elizabeth Maud Slade
  - Rudolph Weyerhaeuser Driscoll

Frederick Edward Weyerhaeuser
Harriette Louise Davis
- Frederick Weyerhaeuser
  Margaret Ludwig
  - Frederick Theodore Weyerhaeuser
    Nancy Lane Neimeyer
  - Charles Ludwig Weyerhaeuser
    Muriel Anne Hamm
  - Virginia Weyerhaeuser
    William Richard Rasmussen
- Charles Davis Weyerhaeuser
  Annette Thayer Black
  - Jane Clark Weyerhaeuser
  - William Bancroft Weyerhaeuser
  - Harriette Davis Weyerhaeuser

Bibliographic Essay

The decision to forgo footnotes was, of course, somewhat disappointing. But the reasons for that decision were clear enough: the book was already long, and, more importantly, the majority of citations referred to one source—the papers of John Philip Weyerhaeuser, Jr., which are at the Weyerhaeuser Company Archives in Federal Way, Washington, home of the company's corporate headquarters. Assuming that serious students of the subject will be likely to work at that archives, a footnoted copy of an earlier draft of this manuscript, somewhat lengthier than this published form, will be kept available there.

From a consideration of business and economics, I have tried to benefit from some excellent recent studies. Among these are the works of such scholars as Alfred D. Chandler, Jr., Thomas C. Cochran, and Louis Galambos. Perhaps most helpful were Chandler's books *The Visible Hand: The Managerial Revolution in American Business* (Cambridge, MA: Harvard University Press, 1977) and, with Stephen Salsbury, *Pierre S. du Pont and the Making of the Modern Corporation* (New York: Harper and Row, 1971).

Historians have long noted the importance of the so-called immigrant letters, an importance clearly evident in the Weyerhaeuser experience. Much of the information regarding the early life of Frederick Weyerhaeuser has as its source a brief essay that he composed, "Some Recollections of My Early Days." This is available at the Weyerhaeuser Company Archives. But the most valuable source is the material that was included in Frederick Edward Weyerhaeuser's biographical collection, *The Record.* Truly a labor of love and devotion, *The Record* endeavored to document the accomplishments of Frederick, largely by the means of reprinting letters of both a contemporary and reflective nature. FEW mailed copies to his brothers and sisters on November 21, 1934, the hundredth anniversary of their father's birth. The covering letter included this admonition: "Kindly remember, first, this is a record for our family and no one else." Copies of *The Record* have been passed down to subsequent generations who, obviously, feel much less protective in this regard. This is of interest in itself. In any event, one need not depend solely upon accounts such as that which appeared in the *Lumber World Review* of April 10, 1914, following Frederick's death.

I would like to mention a few of those who have helped me reach some understanding and appreciation of the Pacific Northwest and its lumber industry. Among these are Norman Clark and Gordon Dodds, the former for his study of Everett (*Mill Town* [Seattle and London: University of Washington Press, 1970]), and both for their bicentennial state histories of Washington and Oregon. I also wish to note the forest history publications of Robert Ficken (*Lumber and Politics: The Career of Mark E. Reed* [copublished by the Forest History Society, Santa Cruz, and the University of Washington Press, Seattle and London, 1979]) and Tom Cox (*Mills and Markets: A History of the Pacific Coast Lumber Industry to 1900* [Seattle and London: University of Washington Press, 1974]), and to thank Murray Morgan for providing an outsider with something of a "feel" for the Puget Sound area (*Puget's Sound: A Narrative of Early Tacoma and the Southern Sound* [Seattle and London: University of Washington Press, 1979]). Still in a general sense, I must acknowledge that although I have consciously avoided any direct dependence—I hope successfully—upon *Timber and Men: The Weyerhaeuser Story*, by Ralph W. Hidy, Frank Ernest Hill, and Allan Nevins (1963), it has admittedly been very helpful along the way. Recognizing that *Timber and Men* has been treated rather carefully through the years by many critics, I would suggest that it may best be managed as a series of essays rather than a single narrative. In addition, it has the ultimate virtue of being extremely accurate throughout. Also helpful, time and again, has been the *Encyclopedia of American Forest and Conservation History* (1983), edited by Richard C. Davis, under the auspices of the Forest History Society.

A few other published sources should be mentioned. Perhaps the best discussion of Idaho forest history is Ralph W. Hidy, "Lumbermen in Idaho: A Study in Adaptation to Change in Environment," *Idaho Yesterdays* 6, no. 4 (Winter: 1962): 2–17. An interesting biography of Laird Bell is provided by Erling Larsen, *Something about Some of the Educations of Laird Bell*, published by Carleton College of Northfield, Minnesota, in 1967. Most helpful in providing a background for

Longview, Washington, home of the Weyerhaeuser Timber Company's largest plant, was *R. A. Long's Planned City: The Story of Longview*, by John M. McClelland, Jr.

Major collections other than those directly involving Phil Weyerhaeuser that have contributed to an understanding of the subject include the Weyerhaeuser Business and Family Papers at the Research Center of the Minnesota Historical Society in St. Paul and the George Frederick Jewett Papers at the University of Idaho. The University of Washington Library houses a great many collections in its archives which pertain to Pacific Northwest forest history. Although I have only begun to sample these, some such as the Merrill & Ring Lumber Company Records have proved of interest and help. I should also note those collections at the Idaho State Historical Society in Boise, including the papers of Harry C. Shellworth and C. L. Billings. Newspapers, of course, have also been important sources.

The primary source for the section on the kidnapping of George Weyerhaeuser was the report of the special agent in charge for the FBI, E. J. Connelly, dated July 18, 1935. This and much more material relating to that event has been provided readily by the Department of Justice under the terms of the Freedom of Information Act.

The use of interviews has been noted in the Preface. For the most part, those that I conducted were for quite specific purposes and have not been made generally available. But the interviews done by Elwood Maunder with this project in mind have been transcribed and are available both at the Weyerhaeuser Company Archives and at the Forest History Society headquarters in Durham, North Carolina. In addition, it should be noted that Weyerhaeuser has a continuing program of oral interviews so that its collections in this regard are forever increasing.

Index

Abe Lincoln in Illinois, 200
Allen, E. T., 337
Allen, William, 340
Allied Building Credits, Inc., 224, 270, 273, 275, 280
Allied Control Commission in Europe, 273
Allied Weyerhaeuser Logging and Engineering Bureau, 28
American Assembly, 324, 333, 351–52
American Council to Improve Our Neighborhoods, 369
American Federation of Labor (AFL), 106, 119, 120, 138–39, 150, 183, 186, 223, 244, 279, 280, 288, 317, 361, 373
American Forest Congress (1905), 133–34
American Forest Products Industries, Inc., 232, 250, 251, 307, 369
American Forestry Association, 360, 362–63
American Merchant Marine Institute, 253
American Paper and Pulp Association, 349–50
American Red Cross, 19–20, 25, 336
Anderson, Sen. C. P., 308
Anderson, Lucy, 47
Annie Wright Seminary (Tacoma), 279, 288
Aram, John, 377
Architectural Forum, 179
Association of Washington Industries, 369
Atlantic Monthly, 299
Atwood, George, 12

Atwood Lumber and Manufacturing Company (Park Falls, Wis.), 12

Bailey, W. J., 307
Baltimore yard (Weyerhaeuser Timber Company), 38
Barton, C. A., 82
Barton, Walter A., 28
Beach, R. C., 58
Bell, Frederick Somers, 39, 65, 68, 80, 85, 106–7, 110, 119, 123, 150–51
Bell, Laird: Potlatch (Idaho) merger negotiations, 79, 80, 82, 85, 87; early life and education, 80–82; relations with Phil Weyerhaeuser, 81–82, 96–98, 109–13 passim, 129, 147, 151, 156, 161, 162–63, 173–74, 180–89 passim, 199, 214–18 passim, 239–40, 241, 262, 269, 272, 273, 275, 284, 291, 292, 299–300, 306, 308, 311–19 passim, 330, 337, 338, 348, 357–58, 370, 379; politics, 81, 102, 125, 189, 218, 220, 272, 291, 308, 313–14, 357; western Washington and Oregon merger negotiations, 96–98, 101–4 passim, 169; National Recovery Administration and the Lumber Code Authority, 105, 107–8, 109, 113, 129, 130; Tillamook merger negotiations, 110–13 passim; attitudes toward labor, 146–47, 150, 161, 180–81, 186–87, 191, 241; views on tariff policy, 162–63; management concerns, 173–74, 180, 186, 204–5, 210, 214–17 passim, 220, 225, 235, 239–43 passim, 302, 303,

311–12, 343, 352–53, 358, 369, 370; government relations, U.S. Forest Service, 199, 206–7, other, 218, 220, 295–96, 308, 311–12; family, 203, 225; relations with Peabody, 203–4, 216; views on timberland purchase, 239–40, 248, 369; tribute to Phil Weyerhaeuser (1943), 254–55; service on Navy Price Adjustment Board, 262, 265; service on Allied Control Commission in Europe, 273, 280; views on corporate contributions (Weyerhaeuser Timber Foundation), 292, 299–300, 350; Wood Conversion Company–Weyerhaeuser Timber Company merger negotiations, 325–26, 329–30, 343, 346; mentioned, 115, 121, 123, 159, 167, 182, 193, 195, 207, 209, 211, 231, 247, 270, 286, 287, 289, 301, 307, 323, 327, 332, 339, 341, 342, 366, 367, 371, 372, 378

Billings, Charles L. "Bill," 50–51, 56, 58, 61, 64, 65, 68, 69, 80, 145, 181, 185, 191, 285

Biltmore Forestry School, 165

Black, Rex, 270–71, 343

Blodgett, John, 104

Bloedel-Donovan Mills, 109, 125, 127, 139

Blunt, Carleton, 367

Bodine, Leo, 343

Boeing Airplane Company, 340, 369

Boettiger, John, 196, 220

Bohemian Club, 179–80

Boise Payette Lumber Company, 56, 62, 65, 79, 82, 83, 90, 219, 246, 377

Bolling, W. K., 142

Boner, William H., 36

Bonners Ferry (Idaho) Lumber Company, 62

Booz, Allen and Hamilton, 291, 296, 297–98, 303, 304

Booz, Fry, Allen and Hamilton, 174

Boyd, Ralph, 331

Boyd, Robert W., 301, 368

Braddock, C. G., 57

Briggs, Charles, 344

Briggs, Gilbert, Morton, Kyle and Macartney, 344

Brigham, Earnest J., 28–29, 88–89

British Ministry of Supply, 215

Bromfield, Louis, 307

Brown, Sam, 350

Bruce, Arthur, 109

Brundage, F. H., 243

Buck, C. J., 197

Bunnell, C. Sterling, 289

Burgess Laboratories (Madison, Wis.), 32

Burns, Arthur F., 351

Burns, John J., 253

Cain, Senator Harry P., 295

Campbell, Hugh, 227, 265, 354

Campbell, Stuart, 296, 303

Camp Jackson (S.C.), 23, 24, 25

Camp (Fort) Lewis (Wash.), 19, 29

Camp Zachary Taylor (Ky.), 25, 26

Carr, Governor Ralph, 307

Carson, William, 39, 90, 326, 354

Case, Louis S., 36, 52

Central Lumber Company (Stillwater, Minn.), 260

Chaney, Henry F., 135

Chapman, Charles S., 95, 117, 121, 215, 220, 225, 338

Chapman, Herman Haupt, 137

Charles W. Sexton Company, 201, 290

Cheatham, Owen R., 296, 298–99

Chicago Journal of Commerce, 271–72

C. Lamb and Company (Clinton, Iowa), 40

Clapp, A. W. "Gus," 82, 83, 95, 96, 108–9, 111, 119, 129, 131, 146, 150, 170, 191, 193, 205–6, 210, 211, 216, 217, 222, 234, 246, 248, 250, 284, 285–86

Clapp, Earle, 251

Clapp, Dr. E. P., 85, 89, 90, 246, 284

Clapp, Gladys, 286, 301

Clapp, Norton, 246, 284, 302, 331, 339, 367, 373

Clark and Wilson Lumber Company, 138, 139

Clearwater Timber Company (Lewiston, Idaho), 3–4, 24, 28, 37, 38, 42, 48–84 passim, 86, 198

Clemons, Mrs. C. H., 328

Clemons Logging Company, 97, 106, 155, 158, 171, 175, 179, 222

Clemons Tree Farm (Weyerhaeuser Timber Company), 228–32, 328–29, 330

Cloquet (Minn.) Lumber Company, 32, 62

Coeur d'Alene, Idaho, 43, 185

College of Puget Sound, 332, 333, 340

Collier's (magazine), 308

Collins, Chapin, 232, 328, 365–66, 379–80

Collins, Truman, 243

Columbia University, 324, 342, 351

Columbia Valley Authority bill, 308, 311–14 passim, 319

Coman, Edwin T., Jr., 312

Committee for Industrial Organization (CIO), 154, 183, 186, 209, 210, 223, 244, 252, 279, 280, 283, 288, 337, 361, 373

Committee on Fair Employment Practice (War Manpower Commission), 251–53
Community Chest, 197, 336
Compton, Dr. Wilson, 156–58
Conklin, Robert P., 264–65
Conrad, Fred W., 232
Conservation Foundation, 322, 350
Constans, Will, 48
Container Corporation of America, 378
Cook, Edmund M. "Budge," 296–97, 299, 301, 302, 306
Coos Bay, Oreg., 109, 264–65
Coos Bay branch (Weyerhaeuser Timber Company), 264, 282, 284, 288, 321, 330, 335, 363, 374
Copeland Report (Senator Stuart Copeland), 136
Cosmopolitan (magazine), 305
Cowan, Charles S., 337
Cowlitz County (Wash.), 231
Coy, Sherman, 54
Cronemiller, Lynn, 110
Crossett Western Lumber Company, 109, 127
Crown-Willamette Corporation, 236
Crown-Zellerbach Corporation, 370
Cruikshank, Paul, 216, 245, 246, 351–52

Dainard, William (alias William Mahan), 141, 167
Davis, Apollonia Weyerhaeuser (daughter of Frederick Weyerhaeuser), 4, 7, 34, 284
Davis, Edwin Weyerhaeuser: birth, 7; early life and family, 12, 13; World War I, 21, 26; Wood Conversion Company, 34, 38, 91, 208–9, 233–34, 236; engagement to Kay Mills, 38; family relations, 90–91, 145, 177, 201, 255–56, 259, 271, 314, 329, 369; relations with Phil Weyerhaeuser, 91, 233–34, 325, 343, 347–49; management concerns, 164, 171; Wood Conversion Company–Weyerhaeuser Timber Company merger negotiations, 275, 315, 323, 325–26, 329, 347–49; mentioned, 32, 85, 247, 266, 289, 295
Davis, Frederick, 255
Davis, Kay Mills, 38
Davis, Minot, 31, 32, 57, 89, 95, 98, 118, 124, 168, 169, 175, 185, 193, 207, 209, 240, 247, 270, 280, 281, 288, 292
Davis, Samuel Sharpe, 7, 225
Davis, T. B., Jr., 85
Day, Lynn Weyerhaeuser (daughter of Frederick King Weyerhaeuser), 369, 373
Day, Stanley Ray, 373

De Lacy, Congressman Hugh, 276
DeLong, E. W., 95
Demarest, E. W., 127, 240, 291
Denkmann, Ed, 68
Denkmann, Frederick, 66
Denkmann, Frederick Carl August, 4, 5, 59
Denkmann family, 42, 49, 51, 59, 82, 329
Department of Justice, 217. See also Federal Bureau of Investigation (FBI)
Dingman, Roy A., 299, 323
Division of Emergency Shipping, 226
Donnelly, Charles P., 49–50
Douglas, Robert S., 335, 361
Driscoll, Egbert, 29, 216
Driscoll, Margaret Louise Weyerhaeuser (daughter of Rudolph M. Weyerhaeuser), 31, 284
Dunn, Paul M., 360

Eddy Paper Corporation, 381
Edward Hines Lumber Company, 137
Edward Rutledge Timber Company (Coeur d'Alene, Idaho), 34, 35, 40, 41, 42, 46, 48, 50, 51, 52, 54, 55, 62, 70, 71–72, 78, 82, 84, 86
Eisenhower, Dwight D., 324, 333, 342, 344, 351
Elma, Wash., 230
Elma Chamber of Commerce, 230
Ethel Walker School, 325, 330
Everett (Wash.) branch (Weyerhaeuser Timber Company): pulp production, 93, 129, 132, 133, 161, 165, 179, 181, 249, 327; relationship to Weyerhaeuser Steamship Company, 115–16; labor relations, 122, 140, 150, 152, 153, 158, 163, 193–94, 217, 222, 231, 242; selective logging–sustained yield (Everett-Vail), 123, 263, 281; lumber price-wage statistics, 163; lumber production, 181, 188, 189, 231, 242, 281; mentioned, 42, 177, 375
Everett (Wash.) News, 133
Eyman, Lewis E., 35

Fair Labor Standards Act, 195, 256
"Farm and Home Hour" (NBC), 328
Farnham, W. H., 56, 58, 66, 74
Federal Bureau of Investigation (FBI), 142, 147
Federal Housing Authority, 224
Fifty Years of Progress in the Forest Industry (Weyerhaeuser Timber Company publication), 318
Fires, 28, 40, 109–11, 195, 209, 217, 243, 272–73, 300, 341–42
Firmin, A. F. "Fred," 168

First Congregational Church (Tacoma), 145, 202
First National Bank of St. Paul, 318
First National Bank of Seattle, 142
Fisher, David, 373
Fisher, O. D., 164, 225, 306, 372, 378
Fleishel, M. L., 218
Fleming, Carson, 353–54
Fohl, Theodore, 56
Ford Motor Company, 335
Forest History Society, 280
Forest Products Laboratory (Madison, Wis.), 349
Forest Products Research Society, 359–60
Forestry: views of George S. Long, 3, 61; Bill Billings and Phil Weyerhaeuser, 50–51; Clearwater Timber Company policies and practice, 61–62, 69, 72–74, 75, 85; Mason and Stevens report, 72–73; Weyerhaeuser Timber Company acceptance, 88–90, 94–95, 106, 114, 116, 123–24, 151; Article X of the Lumber Code (NRA), 117–18, 125, 130, 137, 157; Weyerhaeuser public relations, 130, 137–38, 156–57, 183, 187, 211–12, 226, 231–36 passim, 245–46, 251, 253–54, 328–30, 337–38; timber management policies, public (Forest Service) and private, 134–37, 157–58, 197, 199, 201, 206–7, 220, 226, 251, 309, 314; Weyerhaeuser plans and procedures, 156–57, 168–70, 206, 208, 210, 226–28, 255, 263, 266, 270–73 passim, 276–77, 280–81, 282, 299, 327–28, 332, 336–38 passim, 356; Logged Off Land Company, 168; Reforestation and Land Department, 178, 228; Clemons Tree Farm, 228–32, 328–29; forestry fellowships, 310
Forests and Men, 328
Foundation for Economic Education, 350–51, 369
4-Square (special train), 174–76
Frear, Senator J. Allen, 306
F. S. Bell (steamship), 331
F. Weyerhaeuser Company, 177

Galli, Stan, 366
Gamble, Congressman Ralph A., 295
Garratt, Dean George, 333, 345, 359
Gaylord Container Corporation, 362, 370
Geddes, Captain Edward D., 243, 244
General Timber Service, Inc., 115, 148–49, 172, 173, 179, 192, 224, 233, 234, 236, 249–50, 261, 270, 273, 283, 329
Genta, Nick, 195, 259, 288, 297, 335

Georgia Hardwood Lumber Company, 294, 296, 298
Georgia-Pacific Lumber Company, 298–99
Gibbs, Helen M., 312
Gibson, Edward T., 351
Gillette, Charles, 307
Graham, David, 299, 302, 338
Grandin-Coast Lumber Company, 301, 306
Graue, C. O., 38, 191
Graves, Paul, 216
Great Northern Railway, 133, 156, 276, 294, 333
Greeley, Colonel William B., 97, 108–9, 120–21, 128, 131, 162, 175–76, 186, 236, 244, 266, 328, 337, 338
Greenman, Judd, 296
Grogan, Mike, 228
Guaranty Trust Company, 351
Gullander, Werner P. "Gully," 338, 339, 343, 362, 364, 368

Hamilton, Carl, 174
Hanley (steamship), 115, 238
Hanson, A. G., 118
Hanzlik, Ed, 227
Harvard Business School, 333, 353
Harvard University, 17, 18, 81, 324, 333
Hatch, R. W., 166, 175, 176
Hayes, Anna, 373
Hayes, Edmund, 33, 193, 227, 243, 244, 245, 284, 286, 289, 295, 296, 302, 316, 323, 326, 339, 345, 373, 378
Heacox, E. F. "Ed," 168, 227, 374, 375, 376
Heffelfinger, Peavey, 22, 29, 31, 216, 320, 340
Heffelfinger, Walter "Pudge," 22, 216
Heffron (steamship), 238, 243
Hegira (steamship), 238
Henderson, Leon, 217, 246
Heritage, Clark C., 233, 234, 236, 335, 342
Hidy, Ralph W., 342, 349
Hill, Elise Weyerhaeuser Bancroft (daughter of Frederick Weyerhaeuser), 4, 7, 34
Hill, Frank Ernest, 342, 349
Hill, Rev. William Bancroft, 7, 34, 50
Hill School (Pottstown, Pa.), 12, 13, 16, 17, 217
Hines, Charles, 296
Hines, Ralph J., 137–38, 199
Hines Lumber Company, 296
Hitler, Adolf, 165, 190
Hobby, Oveta Culp, 351
Hochschild, Walter, 340
Hollingsworth and Whitney, 350

Hoover, Herbert C., 101
Hope, Charles W., 118–19
Hoppenstall, T. E., 374
Horn, Stanley, 279, 328
Hornby, H. C., 32, 39
Hotchkiss School (Lakeville, Conn.), 17
House and Home, 364
House of Hope Presbyterian Church (St. Paul), 280
Howard, Capt. L. C., 178, 182, 196, 200, 204, 216, 285, 315, 331
Huckins, Frank, 327
Huckins Yacht Corporation, 327
Huff, Dr. Ralph H., 358
Hull, Cordell, 162
Humbird, Thomas J., 36, 37, 39, 51, 58, 61, 66, 74, 79, 80, 83, 84, 85, 87, 192
Humbird family, 49, 51, 59, 82
Humbird Lumber Company (Sandpoint, Idaho), 37, 39, 82, 84, 87
Huron Mountain Club (Mich.), 366
Hutchins, Robert Maynard, 102, 147
Hutchinson, Ernest N., 121

Ickes, Harold, 80, 81
Industrial Materials Division (National Defense Advisory Committee), 217–18
Industrial Workers of the World (IWW), 29, 40, 106, 118
Ingram, Charles H.: appointed assistant general manager (Weyerhaeuser Timber Company), 95; labor policies and negotiations, 139, 177, 180, 181, 187, 196, 223, 318, 320, 368; George Weyerhaeuser kidnapping, 142; appointed general manager (WTC), 173; family background, 173; relations with Phil Weyerhaeuser, 173, 178, 181, 183, 200, 261, 266, 285, 293, 380; public relations, 174, 178; industry relations, 219–20; views on forestry, 228; World War II, 244; product development, 261–62; mentioned, 169, 176, 186, 193, 195, 209, 230, 243, 282, 288, 289, 290, 294, 323–24, 327, 335, 339, 352
Ingram, Erskine, 181
Ingram, Orrin H., 173, 193
Inland Power and Light Company, 57, 58
Inland Steel Corporation, 292
International Paper Company, 374
International Woodworkers of America (CIO), 252, 317
Iowa State University, 168
Irvine, Horace H., 115, 116, 123, 126, 180, 187, 210, 212, 245, 248, 265, 270, 280, 282, 284–89 passim
Irwin, Jack, 87

Jallapa (steamship), 215, 216
Jewett, George Frederick "Fritz": birth, 7; World War I, 18, 21, 26; Clearwater Timber Company, 58, 59, 61; appointed general manager (Edward Rutledge Timber Company), 70; relations with Phil Weyerhaeuser, 78, 91, 136, 377; role in Potlatch merger effort, 78–79, 80, 82, 84, 85; depression shutdown of Rutledge, 90–91; views on public/private forestry, 135–36; family relations, 145, 166, 275, 279, 377; appointed president, Potlatch Forests, 283; mentioned, 28, 101, 187, 234, 259, 295
Jewett, James Richard, 7
Jewett, Margaret Weyerhaeuser (daughter of Frederick Weyerhaeuser), 4, 7, 12, 61
Jewett, Mary Felton Cooper, 166
J. F. Rafailovitch and Company, 215
J. I. Case Company, 177
John Deere Company, 297
John Philip (Weyerhaeuser) Company, 172
Johnson, Gen. Hugh, 105, 120
Joint Northwest Council (AFL), 138, 139
Jones, Jesse H., 272
Journal of Forestry, 137

Karlen, Art, 329, 335
Kellogg, Charles E., 307
Kempe, Stig, 213
Kendall, John, 33
Kendall, Harry T., 105, 178, 186, 188–89, 191, 217, 289, 295, 319–22 passim, 325
Kerstetter, K. C., 232
Kieckhefer, John W., 378
Kieckhefer Container Corporation, 378, 381
King, Stoddard, 19
Klamath (steamship), 238
Klamath Falls (Oreg.) branch (Weyerhaeuser Timber Company): early plans, 48; labor policies, 96, 99–100, 107, 166, 188, 194, 279; lumber production, 112, 181; merger efforts, 112, 133, 156; forestry, 157, 206–7, 281; fires, 209; timberland purchases, 248, 265–66; World War II, 260, 274; management, 354; mentioned, 72, 178, 282, 284, 288, 369
Korean War, 274, 321–22, 338
Kotin, Leo, 319

Labor conditions and relations: class unrest, 19; IWW, 29, 40, 106, 118; Potlatch and Weyerhaeuser Timber Company coordination, 88; Loyal Legion of Loggers and Lumbermen, 88, 96, 119, 138, 151; views and statements of Phil Weyerhaeuser, 88, 95–96, 99–100, 106–7, 119, 122, 138, 146–47, 151–52, 160–61, 181, 194, 201–2, 203, 225, 231, 252–53, 317–21 passim, 368, 372; efforts at wage stabilization, 95–96, 99–100; strikes, 106, 122, 124–25, 138, 139, 140, 149, 152–54, 165, 175, 182–83, 196, 225, 279, 280, 318, 319, 320, 338–39, 361; NRA, 106–7, 118–21, 126; AFL organization efforts, 119–20, 138, 147, 186–87; attempts at industry cooperation, 138, 161, 180, 191, 201–2, 203, 220–22, 320; Weyerhaeuser Timber Company negotiations, 138–41, 152, 153, 166, 180, 209, 220–22, 223, 288, 317–21 passim, 337, 361, 372–73; Weyerhaeuser Timber Company policies, 146–47, 150, 152, 174–81 passim, 186–87, 191, 193–94, 196, 217, 231, 281, 318, 319, 320, 367–68; CIO organization efforts, 154, 183, 186–87, 210; radicalism, 160–61; wages, 177, 223, 280, 288; National Labor Relations Board, 217; charges of employment discrimination, 251–53

Laird, Allison W., 71, 82, 87

Laird, William H., 80

Laird Norton Company, 150

Lake Nebagamon Lumber Company (Wis.), 6, 7, 8, 12, 214, 293

Land, Adm. Emory S., 253

Langlie, Gov. Arthur B., 228, 328

Lapoint, Capt. John J., 244

Larson, Keve, 200, 299

Leland, Jack, 373–74

Lewis, John L., 154, 187

Lewis, Sidney, 203

Lewiston, Idaho, 57, 58, 59, 64–65, 67, 264, 271

Lewiston (Idaho) *Morning Tribune*, 57, 75, 93

Life (magazine), 308

Lilly, Richard C., 318

Little, George R., 85, 90, 193

Little Church on the Prairie (Tacoma), 268–69, 291, 340, 369, 381

Logged Off Land Company (Weyerhaeuser Timber Company), 168, 170, 178

Loggers Timber and Sawmill Workers Union, 119

Logging: research, 61, 233; history, 63–64; importance of scaling, 64; selective logging, 69, 71, 73–74, 75, 89–90, 123–24; relation to marketing, 71–72,

198–99; sustained yield, 73–74, 94, 95, 117–18, 124, 151, 157, 199, 280–81; methods, 118, 157, 232–33, 266, 270–71, 282–83

Logging, Lumber and Timber and Related Products Industry Committee, 256–57

Log of the Edward Sewall, 1911–1912, 182

Long, George S.: forestry attitudes, 3, 61, 183, 337; tribute to Frederick Weyerhaeuser, 15; management of Weyerhaeuser Timber Company, 24, 31, 52, 60, 64, 66, 75, 81, 91, 95, 151, 154–55, 225, 240, 248, 264, 346; relations with Phil Weyerhaeuser, 32, 36, 46, 48, 62, 75, 76; instructor in timber and lumber subjects, 33, 81; Weyerhaeuser Sales Company policies, 39, 63, 65; timberlands sales and purchase policies, 240, 248

Long, George S., Jr., 33, 75–76, 184, 193, 264, 270, 302, 305, 380

Long, Rev. Harold, 200, 202, 381

Long, Col. James, 115, 116, 287

Long-Bell Lumber Company, 57, 65, 105, 109, 119, 120, 125, 127, 128, 138–41 passim, 180, 248, 374

Longview branch (Weyerhaeuser Timber Company): purchase Longview property from Long-Bell, 65; selective logging, 89–90; plant construction, 93, 282, 285, 294; pulp operations, 93–94, 166, 285, 375; labor relations, 119, 122, 138–41, 146–47, 150, 158, 161, 163, 180, 193–94, 209, 231, 251–52; relations with Long-Bell, 138–41 passim, 180; logging operations, 157, 169, 170, 196, 280; research activities, 166, 179, 233, 241, 247; Weyerhaeuser Sales Company, 167; forestry, 170, 227, 282; lumber production, 188, 189, 231, 282; sustained yield cooperative unit, 199–200; management, 203; Army-Navy "E" Award, 259–60; fire, 300; mentioned, 178, 181, 243, 266

Longview Fiber Company, 363, 376

Los Angeles Rotary Club, 370–71

Loyal Legion of Loggers and Lumbermen (4L), 88, 96, 118, 119, 120, 138, 151–52

Ludekens, Fred, 366

Lumber Advisory Committee, 241

Lumber and Forest Products Division (Defense Commission), 218

Lumber and Sawmill Workers Union, 231

Lumber and Timber Products Defense Committee, 218–19

Lumber Code Authority (NRA), 108,

109, 114, 117–21 passim, 125–31 passim, 136, 137
Lumbermen's Finance Company, 101
Lumber Production Control Committee, 127
Lyford, Aimee E., 9, 12, 13, 214, 289, 330

McArdle, Richard E., 337
MacArthur, Gen. Douglas, 332
Macartney, Ralph, 54, 207, 227, 250, 265, 289, 354
McCarthy, Sen. Joseph R., 295, 357
McCarthy, Peter H., 357–58
McCormick, William L., 99, 129, 193, 246, 302, 331, 346
McCormick, Rev. William P., 381
McGough, Charles, 177
McIntyre, Eddie, 211–12, 239
McIntyre, Will, 211
McCoy, H. J., 82, 227
McCoy, Lawrence, 34
McKay, Gov. Douglas, 328
McKnight, Henry T., 346
McKnight, Sumner T., 396
Madeen, James L., 350
Mahan, John W., 70, 74
Maritime Commission, 317
Markham, John, 18, 27
Marsh, E. P., 138, 140, 141, 153–54, 160
Martin, Clyde S., 222, 227, 230, 250–51, 263, 272–73, 292, 329, 333, 345, 364
Mason, Bruce and Girard, 290–91
Mason, David T., 337, 360
Mason, Jack, 90
Mason and Stevens, 69, 73, 75, 84
Massey, Raymond, 22, 200
Masters School (Dobbs Ferry, N.Y.), 195, 224
Meadowcroft, Elizabeth Hunt Weyerhaeuser (daughter of John Philip Weyerhaeuser, Jr.), 103, 256, 276, 279, 288, 304, 325, 330, 379
Meadowcroft, W. Howarth, 379
Men, Mills and Timber in the National Service (Weyerhaeuser Timber Company publication), 324
Merrill, R. D., 92
Merrill and Ring Lumber Company, 92
Meyer, Paul, 228, 230
Millicoma Forest Tree Farm (Oreg.), 321, 329, 330
Millis, Walter, 25
Mills, Russell, 125
Mills College, 330
Minneapolis Morning Tribune, 276
Mississippi Pulp and Paper Company, 379
Mitchell, Elsie, 274

Mitchell Recreational Area (Klamath Bomb Site), 274
Montesano, Wash., 232, 328
Montesano Chamber of Commerce, 232
Montesano Vidette, 260, 328, 365, 379–80
Moore, Annie B., 145
Morgan, Harry, 139, 167, 203, 247, 252, 281–82, 364
Morgan, Howard, 285, 335, 352, 362, 368
Morley, A. J., 97
Morris, James E., 302
Morse, Roy, 119, 139
Mount St. Helens Tree Farm, 272–73, 350
Muir, A. W. "Abe," 139, 140, 153
Muller-Clem, Dr. Hellmuth, 165
Munising Paper Company (Munising, Mich.), 285
Murray, Tom, 175, 279
Musser, C. R., 80, 85, 315
Musser, John M., 179, 273, 283, 329, 365, 367–68
Musser, R. Drew, 85
Myers, Paul, 51, 74

Narcissus (steamship), 215, 216
National Association of Manufacturers, 281, 289, 314, 333
National City Bank of New York, 289
National Defense Advisory Committee, 217, 219
National Home Finance Corporation, 101
National Industrial Recovery Act, 104, 119, 126
National Institute of Management, 361
National Labor Relations Board, 194, 217
National Lumber Manufacturers Association, 101, 104, 135–36, 156, 218, 234, 337, 344, 345, 375
National Lumber Workers, 160
National Mediation Board, 231
National Recovery Administration: Regional Labor Board, 118–19; National Labor Board, 119, 120; mentioned, 105, 114, 117, 125, 157, 342
Navy Price Adjustment Board, 262. See also Renegotiation
Nelson, Donald, 243
Nevins, Allan, 323, 342, 349
New York Times, 15, 308
New York Zoological Society, 307
Nisqually Flats Duck Club, 287
Nisqually Nursery (West Coast Lumbermen's Association), 235–36

Nixon, Richard M., 371
Nolan, J. E. "Joe," 301, 302, 306, 307, 311–12, 315, 335, 347–49, 362, 380
Northern Lumber Company (Cloquet, Minn.), 7, 62
Northern Pacific Railroad, 8, 42, 44, 49, 52, 53, 57, 58, 215, 260, 294
Northwestern University, 335
Northwest Paper Company (Cloquet, Minn.), 37, 62
Nothing Sighted Today (Weyerhaeuser Timber Company publication), 247

O'Brien, William, 64
Occidental Life Insurance Company, 280
Odlin, Reno, 304, 340
Office of Price Administration, 246, 286
O'Gara, Thomas J., 44
Olzendam, Roderic, 178, 180, 183, 186–87, 191, 192, 203, 205, 220, 222, 225, 228, 245–46, 250, 270
O'Neil, E. H. "Tip," 166, 167, 191, 198–99, 212, 225, 293, 325, 346
O'Neil, William, 293
Onstad, Albert H., 95, 224–25
Oregon State College of Forestry, 360
Oregon State University, 310
Orell, B. L. "Bernie," 343, 349, 364, 371
Orr, A. Dwight, 193, 256, 290, 302
Osborn, Fairfield, 307, 308, 322, 350
Ottinger, Lawrence, 149
Our Plundered Planet, 307

Pacific Coast Direct Line, 182, 285, 315
Pacific Coast Lumber Manufacturers' Association, 183
Pacific Logging Congress: (1937), 187; (1938), 196–97
Pacific National Lumber Company, 127
Paepcke, Walter P., 378
Panay (USS), 190
Pascoe, Ann Weyerhaeuser (daughter of John Philip Weyerhaeuser, Jr.), 42, 47, 50, 62, 195–96, 200, 222–24 passim, 260, 265, 273, 278–79, 282, 325, 330, 344
Pascoe, Dr. Charles, 379
Pascoe, John J. "Jack," 260, 265, 278–79, 282, 287, 330, 333, 344, 379
Pascoe, Philip Weyerhaeuser, 282
Patton, Frank, 351
Paul, Judge C. H., 119
Pauley, Robert D., 247, 359
Peabody, W. H. "Bill": manager at Everett branch, 115; appointed manager of Eastern Yards and Weyerhaeuser Steamship Company, 115–16, 287;

education and character, 115; relations with Laird Bell, 115, 204; relations with Phil Weyerhaeuser, 116, 122–23, 200, 234, 265, 284, 289, 303, 315–16, 324, 333; management, 178, 182, 302–3, 315–16; Pacific Coast Direct Line, 182, 200, 204, 285; World War II, 209–10, 238, 243, 244, 271; steamship purchases, 215–16, 285; public relations, 250; renegotiation hearings (Red Sea voyages), 253; retirement, 324, 333
Peabody, William, Jr., 200, 204
Peetz, J. R., 264
Pennsylvania (steamship), 215, 238
Perkins, Francis, 138, 140, 160
Pierrepont, R. Stuyvesant, 239
Pinchot, Gifford, 133–34
Pine Tree Lumber Company (Little Falls, Minn.), 7
Pomona (steamship), 115
Portland (Oreg.) City Club, 316
Potlatch (steamship), 238, 244, 247
Potlatch Forests, Inc., 87, 88, 90, 92, 181, 185, 198, 219, 247, 273, 283, 360, 369, 373
Potlatch Lumber Company, 10, 27, 62, 71, 73, 81, 82, 84, 86, 87, 88
Prentice, Pierre, 364
President's Committee on Government Contracts, 371
Price, W. H. "Bill," 228, 230
Price Adjustment Board (War Department), 246
Puget Sound National Bank, 304, 340
Pulp Workers' Union, 125

Queen Mary, 208
Quickstep, 216

Raught, A. L. "Al," 102, 123, 139, 150, 166, 194–95, 203, 205, 207, 218, 223, 225, 283, 288, 293, 304, 336
Read, Leonard E., 350–51
Reader's Digest, 270, 271
"Record of the Life and Business Activities of Frederick Weyerhaeuser," by Frederick E. Weyerhaeuser, 268, 279
Reed, William G., 98, 102, 125, 370
Reed Mill Company, 125, 127
Reforestation and Land Department (Weyerhaeuser Timber Company), 178, 226, 266
Reichmann, Lyndon N. "Lyn," 150
Reimers, Fred W., 85, 346, 362
Reinhardt, Spider, 216, 340
Renegotiation hearings: Red Sea voyages, 248, 250, 253; Army, 269

Research, 88, 165–66, 176, 179, 208–9, 233–37 passim, 247, 266, 327–28
Reserve Officers Training Corps (ROTC), 21, 22, 23, 24
Rettig, F. E. "Ed," 56, 73
Richardson, Harold J., 59, 66, 85, 276, 289
Rockefeller, Nelson A., 290, 351
Rock Island (Ill.) Lumber and Manufacturing Company, 5–7
Rock Island (Ill.) Plow Company, 172, 177
Rogers, L. J. "Roy," 178
Roosevelt, Franklin D., 80, 81, 98, 102, 104, 120, 123, 125, 149, 151, 314
Roosevelt, Theodore, 133, 134
Rosenberry, Walter S., Jr., 145, 177, 282
Russell, A. J. "Gus," 179–80
Rutledge, Edward, 6–7, 37

Saberson, Ray, 317
Saginaw Logging Company, 97
St. Paul and Tacoma Lumber Company, 109, 219, 236
Santa Fe Lumber Company (Stockton, Calif.), 179
Sassoon, Siegfried, 19
Saturday Evening Post, 135
Saturday Review, 375–76
Schafer Brothers Logging Company, 370
Schechter Corporation v. the United States, 105
Schenck, Dr. Carl Alwin, 165, 190, 202–3, 214, 298, 329, 330
Sciple, Lt. Col. Carl M., 269
Scott Paper Company, 200
Seattle City Water Department, 274
Seattle Post-Intelligencer, 141, 145, 159–60, 183–84, 196–97, 220
Seattle Times, 276
Securities and Exchange Commission, 192, 217, 299, 306
Shellworth, Harry, 56
Shelton Cooperative Sustained Yield Unit, 370
Sherman Antitrust Law, 101, 104
Shevlin, Carpenter and Clarke Company, 92
Shevlin-Carpenter interests, 42, 96
Silcox, Ferdinand A., 134–38, 187, 196, 197, 199–201, 206–7, 208, 251
Silliman, Frank, Jr., 57
Simons, H. A., 75
Simpson Logging Company, 98, 236, 370
Slaughter, Robert, 260
Sloan-Kettering Institute for Cancer Research, 380

Smith, Lawrence, 208
Smith College, 14, 22
Snoqualmie Falls (Wash.) branch (Weyerhaeuser Timber Company), 346, 375
Snoqualmie Falls Lumber Company: management, 62, 166, 167, 173, 198–99; Naches Pass controversy, 121; labor relations, 140, 152, 153, 158, 163, 177, 193–94, 207, 222, 223, 225, 226, 231; subsidiary taxation problems, 155; research, 166; lumber production, 188, 189, 242, 281; merger with Weyerhaeuser Timber Company, 185–86, 299, 300, 301; strikes, 207, 222, 225, 242, 279; nursery, 212; World War II, 219, 253; wages, 253
Society of American Foresters, 134, 137, 190, 263, 264, 292
Sound Timber Company, 266
Southern Lumber Company (Warren, Ark.), 36, 62, 373
Southern Lumberman, 328
Southern Pacific Railroad, 42, 133, 294
South Olympic Tree Farm, 370
South Pacific, 333
Speidel, Conrad, 274
Springfield (Oreg.) Chamber of Commerce, 310–11
Springfield-Eugene branch (Weyerhaeuser Timber Company): plans and plant construction, 286–87, 288, 330; railroad connections, 294; pulp mill, 310–11; management, 310–11, 352, 353; public relations, 310–11
Springfield Plywood Company, 294
Stamm, Ed, 243–44
Stanford (University) Research Institute, 345, 346, 350, 356, 359, 360, 364–65, 369, 376
Stanford University Business School, 291, 292
Stassen, Harold, 200
State Federation of Women's Clubs (Washington), 121
Steamships, 115, 175, 181, 215, 216, 238, 243, 244, 247, 269, 271, 330, 331
Stettinius, Edward R., 217–18
Stevens, Carl, 61, 84, 85–87, 97–99, 102–3, 114–15, 122, 123–24, 137, 342
Swigert, Ernest G., 327, 333

Tacoma Chamber of Commerce, 130
Tacoma Club, 195, 198, 305
Tacoma Daily Ledger, 93
Tacoma General Hospital, 379
Tacoma News Tribune, 141
Tacoma Smelting Company, 19

Taft School (Watertown, Conn.), 216–17, 242, 245, 246, 256, 351
Tariff policies, 161–63, 362
Tate, I. N., 74, 156–57
Taylor, Huntington, 33, 51, 52, 54, 55, 70
Temporary National Economic Committee, 217
Tennant, John, 105, 128, 139, 248
Thatcher, F. H., 150–51
Thompson, Dr. R. Franklin, 333–34
Thompson Yards, Inc., 36, 41, 44, 62, 329
Tillamook burn (Oreg.), 109–11
Timber and Men, 342
Timber Is a Crop (Weyerhaeuser Timber Company publication), 187, 191
Timber Securities Company, 37, 38, 54, 59, 70, 172
Time, Tide and Timber, 312
Tinker, Earl, 200, 206–7
Titcomb, Edward Rodman, 27–28, 167
Titcomb, Elizabeth Weyerhaeuser (daughter of John Philip Weyerhaeuser), 6, 9–13 passim, 16–21 passim, 33, 43, 146, 148, 166, 172–73, 336, 371
Titcomb, Francis Rodman, 17, 19, 20, 25, 88, 91, 92, 93, 95, 99, 109, 117, 129, 131, 142–46 passim, 166, 169, 173
Titcomb, John Weyerhaeuser, 33–34
Titcomb, Jonathan Ross "Jon," 290, 310, 352–53
Transamerica Corporation, 280
Trees and Homes, 220, 225
Trees and Men, 189–90, 191, 208, 220, 224
Turner, William H., 207
Twenty-Year Club (Weyerhaeuser Timber Company), 264

Union Pacific Railway Company, 42, 49, 50, 52, 53, 57, 58
United Brotherhood of Carpenters and Joiners, 138–39
United Good Neighbor Fund of Pierce County (Wash.), 369
United Nations, 370, 371
United Nations Economic Commission for Europe Timber Committee, 371
U.S. Chamber of Commerce, 306, 307, 309
U.S. Forest Service, 101, 133, 134, 135, 138, 157, 168, 187, 196–97, 199–201, 206–7, 217, 244, 250–51, 308, 309, 313, 314, 316, 344–45
United States Plywood Corporation, 149
University of Chicago, 80, 115, 147, 272, 313–14, 357
University of Washington, 310

Vail operation (Weyerhaeuser Timber Company), 123–24, 169, 177, 270, 287, 288
Vancouver Plywood Company, 342
Vassar College, 13, 14
Vessey, Burton F., 201
Virginia Mason Clinic (Seattle), 358
Vogt, William, 308
Vorys, Art, 216, 340

Wagner, George Corydon, Jr., 202, 219
Wagner Act, 120
Wahl, John, 270–71, 287, 335
Waldhof Paper Company, 165
Waley, Harmon Metz, 141, 144–45, 147
Waley, Margaret, 141, 144–45, 147
Walker, Clara (Mrs. George H.), 34, 46–48
Walker, George H., 34, 35
Wallace, Henry A., 220
Walling, Frank, 301
Walnut Hill School (Natick, Mass.), 12
Wanigan, 327, 331, 333, 339, 348, 369–70, 377
War Labor Board, 249
War Production Board, 241, 243, 268
War Shipping Administration, 271
Washington Forest Fire Association, 170
Washington State Forestry Department, 343
Washington State Historical Society, 369
Washington Veneer Company, 210, 212, 214, 234, 266, 270, 282, 294, 296
Watson, Donald, 315, 317, 327, 339, 362
Watts, Lyle, 206, 243, 250–51, 309
Watzek, Aubrey R., 336
Watzek, Harlan, 127–28
Watzek, John, Jr., 218
Weiss, Dr. Howard F., 32
Wendell, James, 217
West Coast Code Administration, 125
West Coast Lumberman, 208
West Coast Lumbermen's Association, 97, 108, 126, 128, 131, 157, 162, 219, 220, 235–36, 253–54
Western Forestry and Conservation Association, 36
Western Pine Association, 112, 272
West Fork Logging Company, 175
Westinghouse Corporation, 335
West Virginia Pulp and Paper Company, 307
Westman, Ed, 210–11, 212, 270
Wetmore, R. W., 92
Weyerhaeuser, Anna Holbrook (wife of John Philip): friendship with Nellie Anderson Weyerhaeuser, 8; marriage to John Philip Weyerhaeuser, 9; life at

Lake Nebagamon, 9, 12; illness, 10; raising children "simply," 10–11; concern for her sons, 13, 18–23 passim; relations with son Phil, 14, 18, 20, 30, 59–60; move to Spokane, 14; move to Tacoma, 16; worries concerning John, 19, 28, 36, 59–60; Red Cross involvement, 19, 20, 25; YWCA involvement, 29; Haddaway Hall, 31–32, 43–44; business advice to Phil, 44; family, 47, 57; death, 103

Weyerhaeuser, Carl Augustus (son of Charles Augustus), 17, 333

Weyerhaeuser, Charles Augustus (son of Frederick): birth, 4; assisting brother John at Lake Nebagamon, 9; assessment of father Frederick, 10, 62; relations with Phil Weyerhaeuser, 16–17, 34, 41, 52, 54–55, 61, 63, 67, 380; Clearwater Timber Company matters, 24, 37, 49–55 passim, 58–59, 61, 65; family, 26–27, 40–41, 51–52, 54, 67, 74; relations with brother John, 36, 37, 49–50, 53, 54–55, 58–59, 63, 65, 68; Boise Payette Company, 65; death, 74–75; brother Frederick Edward's tribute, 74–75; mentioned, 32, 40, 42, 62

Weyerhaeuser, Charles Davis "Dave" (son of Frederick Edward): training and early career, 167–68; survey of Weyerhaeuser Timber Company lands (1936), 168–69; World War II, 237; perpetual yield report (1946), 280–81; family, 283, 334; forestry, 288, 364; timberland purchase, 291; southern timber tours (1956), 374–75, 376; mentioned, 176, 209, 270, 335

Weyerhaeuser, Clara Dracoulis (wife of John Philip III), 330, 353, 374

Weyerhaeuser, Edith Greenleaf (wife of Carl Augustus), 333

Weyerhaeuser, Frances Maud Moon (wife of Charles Augustus), 67, 74, 200, 380

Weyerhaeuser, Frederick: early life, 4; marriage and family, 4–7, 9–14 passim; association with F. C. A. Denkmann, 5; methods of operation, 5, 10; Lake Nebagamon Lumber Company investment, 6; purchase of 900,000 acres from Northern Pacific, 8; and grandson Phil, 9–16 passim; Atwood Lumber and Manufacturing Company, 12; death, 15–16; tribute by George S. Long, 15; Niedersaulheim, Germany, birthplace, 88; American Forest Congress (1905), 133–34; "The Record . . . ," 279; mentioned, 74, 80, 84, 141, 173

Weyerhaeuser, Frederick "Long Fred" (son of Frederick Edward), 176, 233, 234, 236, 248–49, 283

Weyerhaeuser, Frederick Edward: birth, 4–5; family leader, 22, 38, 70, 117, 145, 148, 177, 282; relations with Phil Weyerhaeuser, 22, 55, 61, 63–64, 66, 69, 70–72, 75, 85, 88–90, 117, 125–26, 130, 145–51 passim, 164, 192–93, 198–202 passim, 206, 210–11, 212, 216, 224, 257–58, 266, 268, 273, 275–76, 279–80; relations with brothers, 38, 41, 52, 53, 61, 74–75, 141; Clearwater Timber Company, 38, 42, 51, 52–53, 55, 63–64, 65–66, 69, 70–72; Weyerhaeuser Sales Company responsibilities, 39–40, 62, 65, 79, 115; views on forestry, 61, 70, 72–73, 85, 88–90; Weyerhaeuser Timber Company management, 68, 88–90, 123, 146, 150–51, 198–99, 205–6, 210–11, 212, 247; Potlatch merger effort, 79, 82–83, 87; Potlatch Forests, Inc., 85; Emergency National Committee (1933), 105–6; political attitudes, 123, 126, 129, 134, 147, 149, 151, 272; NRA, 125–26, 129, 130, 146; American Forest Congress (1905), 133–34; views on labor, 146–47, 149–50, 193, 209; industry relations, 182, 201–2; public relations, 192–93, 239; corporate contributions, 197; pension plans, 197–98, 268; World War II, 231, 237, 245, 257–58; research, 233, 234, 325–26; timberland purchases, 247, 248, 266; "The Record . . . ," 268, 279–80; private railway car controversy, 270, 276; death, 280; mentioned, 115, 124, 140, 159, 160, 165, 167, 176, 180, 181, 207, 218, 222, 223, 236, 259, 265, 278, 284, 286

Weyerhaeuser, Frederick King (son of John Philip): birth, 6; Lake Nebagamon childhood, 9, 12; relationship with brother Phil, 9, 11, 14–18 passim, 22–23, 31, 41, 46, 102, 117, 148–49, 171–72, 188–89, 191, 195, 204, 211, 223, 242–43, 256–61 passim, 273, 280, 290, 294, 303, 313, 331, 333–34, 341, 342, 344, 356–57, 358; Hill School, 12–13; Grandfather Frederick, 13–14; Yale, 14, 17, 18–19; introduction to western timber, 14, 18; World War I, 19–20; enlistment in the air service, 21; duty with bomber squadron (Italy), 22–23, 25–26; relations with cousins, 26–27; retailing lumber, 27; career with Weyerhaeuser Sales Company, 31, 53, 62, (assistant sales manager) 63, (elected president) 74, 88, 104, 116, (4-Square Special) 175, 176, 188–89, 219, 303–4, 323, 356–57; George S. Long's practical school for lumbermen, 33; Thompson Yards employment, 36–37, 41; Weyerhaeuser family, 41, 117, 145–46, 172–73, 177, (leadership) 280, 301–2, 313, 341, 343–44; Clearwater Timber Company, 42, 44, 51, 52; marriage, 44; Potlatch interlude, 46; declines Clearwater general managership, 53; views on timber management, 116–17, 204; Weyerhaeuser Timber Company management, 171, 294; corporate contributions, 197; Forest Service relations, 199–200; price stabilization (National Defense Advisory Commission), 219; research program, 234, 236; Lumber Advisory Committee (War Production Board), 241; World War II, 258–59; product development, 261–62; General Timber Service and Allied Building Credits controversies, 273, 275, 280; South American timber investment opportunities, 290; Gamble Committee, 295–96; Bill Peabody, 302–3; Conservation Foundation, 322, 350; sale of Thompson Yards, 329; public relations, 343; politics, 349; chairman of Weyerhaeuser Timber Company board, 367, 372, 378, 379; southern timber investment opportunities, 370, 376; elected president of the Weyerhaeuser Timber Company, 381; mentioned, 36, 40, 59, 66, 67, 85, 105, 157, 216, 222, 230, 233, 245, 248, 265, 281, 284, 286, 289, 324, 369, 371, 373

Weyerhaeuser, George Hunt (son of John Philip, Jr.): birth, 62; kidnapping, 141–47, 153, 159, 265; Taft School, 242, 246, 255–56; Navy duty, World War II, 265, 269, 273, 279, 282; Yale, 285, 291–92, 304; family, 276, 287, 314–15, 379; father's advice on education, 291–92; engagement and marriage, 295; Longview pulp mill employment, 325; Springfield branch manager, 330, 352, 353, 369

Weyerhaeuser, Helen Hunt Walker (wife of John Philip, Jr.): Smith College and Phil Weyerhaeuser, 22, 23, 29; break in relationship, 31; engagement and marriage, 34–35; life in Coeur d'Alene, Idaho, 36, 43, 53–54; family, 38, 46–48, 50, 59, 62, 67, 103, 182, 195–96, 222–23, 242, 260, 265, 276, 277, 287, 288, 304, 369; move to Lewiston,

Idaho, 64–65; relationship with Phil, 65, 67, 102, 178, 180, 297, 326, 331, 371; kidnapping of son George, 142, 144, 145, 146; Weyerhaeuser family, 146, 166, 313, 344; trip to Sweden, 207–8; church membership, 268; the Wanigan, 327, 331; Phil's illness, 358, 373, 377, 379; Phil's death, 380, 381; mentioned, 41, 119, 137, 203, 224, 225, 247, 258, 285, 324, 333

Weyerhaeuser, John Philip: birth, 4; early life and education, 5; marriage to Nellie Anderson, 5; Rock Island Lumber and Manufacturing Company, 5; relations with father Frederick, 5–6, 7, 14; family, 6, 7, 10–11, 13, 14, 16, 18, 28, 31–32, 42, 43–44, 47, 50, 59; Lake Nebagamon Lumber Company, 7–8, 12, 293; death of wife Nellie, 8; marriage to Anna Holbrook, 9; health problems, 9, 13, 32; relations with brother Charles, 9, 27, 36, 37, 49–50, 52, 54–55, 58–59, 61, 63, 65; Atwood Lumber and Manufacturing Company, 12; relations with son Fred, 14, 18, 20–21, 24, 26, 27, 32; relations with son Phil, 14, 16, 17, 18, 20–21, 24, 26–31 passim, 34, 40, 42, 43, 46, 47, 53, 59–60, 68; president of Weyerhaeuser Timber Company, 16, 28, 30, 68; World War I, 19–20, 26; Clearwater Timber Company involvement, 24, 30–31, 37, 42, 44, 48–60 passim, 63, 65, 66, 68, 70; relations with brother Fred, 37–38, 52–53; Weyerhaeuser Sales Company, 38–40, 65–66; death, 141; estate, 172–73; mentioned, 25, 82, 145, 148, 211

Weyerhaeuser, John Philip, Jr.: birth, 7; childhood, 8–9, 10–11; public school, 13; Hill School, 13, 16, 17; early lumber experiences, 14, 18, 28–29, 32; World War I, 17, 18–19, 20, 25; Yale, 18, 21–22, 27, 29; ROTC, 21–22, 23–24; courtship of Helen Walker, 23, 27, 29, 31, 34; commissioned, 25; George S. Long's practical school for lumbermen, 33; Rutledge Timber Company sales responsibilities, 33, 34–35, 38, 40, 41, 43, 46, 48; marriage, 35; life in Coeur d'Alene, Idaho, 43, 53–54; friendships, 43, 53, 65, 191, 195, 202, 216, 304, 312, 327, 331, 339, 340–41, see also individual names; Clearwater Timber Company management, 3–4, 55, 56–75 passim, 82–83; forestry (timber management), 50–51, 61, 69, 72, 73–74, 75, 85, 89–90, 95, 116,

Weyerhaeuser, John Philip, Jr. (cont.)
117–18, 123–24, 130, 137–38, 156–
57, 167–70, 215, 226–38, 234–35,
253–54, 263, 265, 266, 270–71, 280–
81, 282–83, 287, 288, 299, 310, 322,
327–28, 336–37, 337–38, 350, 359,
361, 366, 371; life in Lewiston, Idaho,
64–65; leadership qualities, 60–62, 67,
88, 90, 91, 92, 94, 102, 115, 124, 149,
151, 167, 263–64, 271, 282, 289–90,
316–17, 335, 358, 361, 364; Potlatch
merger efforts, 77, 78, 79, 80, 84–85,
87; Potlatch Forests management, 85,
87–88, 91; Weyerhaeuser Sales Company concerns, 79, 149, 171, 188–89,
296, 329, 356–57; interest in research,
88, 116, 166, 176, 179, 208–9, 233–
34, 236–37, 247, 327; labor attitudes
and policies, 88, 119–20, 122, 138,
140, 146–47, 151–52, 160–61, 176–
77, 180–81, 186–87, 191, 194, 231,
251–53, 278, 317, 318, 319–21, 367–
68; elected Executive Vice President,
Weyerhaeuser Timber Company, 92;
Weyerhaeuser Timber Company management, 93–94, 113, 132–33, 148,
154–55, 164–65, 193, 205, 210–11,
247, 263–65, 271, 286, 358–59, 361,
368, 372, 376–77; public responsibilities, 94–95, 121–22, 137–38, 225–26,
340, 365, 366; organizational philosophy, 95, 124, 148, 164–65, 171, 179,
205, 227, 264–65, 271, 290, 298, 335,
339–40, 354; wage policies, 95–96,
99–100, 106–7, 193–94, 201–2; industry relations, 96, 97, 98–99, 103,
109, 125–28, 131, 138, 181, 191, 194,
201–2, 219–20, 235–36, 253–54, 358,
363–64; Pacific Northwest merger efforts, 96–97, 103, 112–13; Weyerhaeuser Timber Company board, 99,
100, 106, 107, 132, 164, 168–69,
177–78, 210–11, 247, 274, 306, 318–
19, 332–33, 365, 367; production
quota controversy (NRA), 105, 108–9,
111–12, 120–21, 125–28, 131; Article
X (NRA) Lumber Code, 114–15, 117–
18, 125, 137–38; Weyerhaeuser Steamship Company, 115–16, 122–23, 182,
200, 204, 215–16, 285, 302–3, 315–
16, 317–18; conservative business
views, 116–17, 132–33, 204, 248–49,
262, 263, 276–77, 290, 337, 346–47,
358–59; pulp and paper, 116, 129,
158, 179, 200, 352; plywood, 116–17,
149, 204, 210–11, 212; public relations, 121–22, 130–31, 135, 154, 159,
174, 183–84, 187–93 passim, 196–97,
211–12, 220, 232, 235, 242, 245–46,
305–11 passim, 328–29, 337–38, 340,
351, 359–60, 362–63, 365–66, 369,
370–71; politics, 128–29, 130–31,
173, 218, 272, 291, 308, 311, 313–14,
316, 349, 357–58; relations with U.S.
Forest Service, 134–35, 137, 138, 157–
58, 187, 196–97, 199–201, 206–7,
250–51, 309, 313–14, 344–45; kidnapping of son George, 141–47, 159;
General Timber Service, 148–49, 171,
179, 249, 261, 270, 273, 329; subsidiary problems, 155, 171, 204–5; views
on tariff, 162–63, 362; pension plans,
193, 197–98, 201, 239, 268, 270; corporate contributions, 197, 292, 299–
302 passim; church involvements, 202,
268–69, 291, 369; tour of Sweden,
207–8; World War II, 209, 213, 218–
19, 222, 237, 239, 242, 244, 247, 273–
77 passim; timberland purchases, 215,
240, 245–47, 248, 257, 260, 265–66,
291; government requirements and relations, 217–18, 243–44, 246, 249,
251–53, 272, 321–22, 324; Clemons
Tree Farm, 228–32, 260, 328–29, 330;
concerns with personal war-time contribution, 240, 244–45, 257–59; renegotiation (WW II) hearings, 248, 250,
253, 256, 269; tribute to Phil by Laird
Bell (1943), 254–55; postwar planning,
266–67; Allied Building Credits, 270,
273; interlocking directorships, 284,
315; elected president, Weyerhaeuser
Timber Company, 289; management
reorganization, 291, 293–94, 296, 299,
301, 325, 338; sale to Georgia Hardwood Lumber Company, 294, 296,
298–99; Gamble Committee, 295–96;
subsidiary mergers, 308–9, 329; forestry fellowships, 310; opposition to
Columbia Valley Authority bill, 311–16
passim, 319; Wood Conversion Company merger effort, 323, 325–26, 329,
343, 346, 347–49; support of Yale Forestry School, 324, 338; involvement
with Dwight D. Eisenhower (American
Assembly), 324, 351–52; the Wanigan,
327, 331, 333, 339, 377; Millicoma
Forest Tree Farm, 330; five-year planning (1951), 332; College of Puget
Sound, 333–34, 340; health, 333, 358,
373, 377–78, 379; Weyerhaeuser Timber Foundation, 335–36, 350; Korean
War, 338–39; southern timber investment opportunities, 340, 346–47, 362,
368, 373, 374–79 passim; Stanford Research Institute Report, 345, 356–57,

359–60, 376; service on Europe Timber Committee (UN Economic Commission for Europe), 371–72; Chapin Collins' tribute to Phil, 379–80; death, 380; tributes, 380–81; funeral, 381. *On relations with family, friends, and associates, see individual names; see also* Weyerhaeuser family activities and concerns

Weyerhaeuser, John Philip III "Flip": birth, 57; family, 181, 222, 223, 327, 330, 353, 369, 374, 379; Taft School, 216–17, 242, 246; Yale, 285, 304, 309; World War II, Marine Corps enlistment, 250, 255–56, 258, 279; Weyerhaeuser family, 314–15; Weyerhaeuser sales responsibility, 325; mentioned, 62, 147, 276, 282, 292, 378

Weyerhaeuser, Louise Lindeke (wife of Rudolph M.), 31, 284, 289

Weyerhaeuser, Nellie Anderson (wife of John Philip), 5, 6–7, 8

Weyerhaeuser, Rudolph Michael (son of Frederick), 4, 33, 37, 40, 41, 42, 57, 61, 67, 68, 88, 145, 185, 198, 201, 233, 247, 258, 260, 282–86 passim, 354

Weyerhaeuser, Sarah Elizabeth Bloedel (wife of Frederick), 4, 12

Weyerhaeuser, Sarah Maud (daughter of Charles Augustus), 145

Weyerhaeuser, Vivian O'Gara (wife of Frederick King), 44, 46, 52, 146, 194

Weyerhaeuser, Wendy Wagner (wife of George H.), 295, 304, 330, 353, 369

Weyerhaeuser Development Committee, 236–37

Weyerhaeuser family activities and concerns: Clearwater Timber Company board membership, 59; Clearwater financing, 61, 70, 82–83; investment policies and philosophy, 61–62, 84; St. Paul office, 74; Niedersaulheim, Germany (Frederick's birthplace), 88; kidnapping of George Weyerhaeuser, 145–48; shared ownership, 149–50; meetings and reunions, 166, 282, 329, 334–35, 344; Phil and his uncles, 200, 201; Phil and family responsibilities, 223–24, 282, 284, 324, 334–35, 341; "The Record . . . ," 268, 279–80; Fred K., chairman, 280, 301–2, 334, 341, 344; leadership, 280, 301; business opportunity and family membership, 301–2, 341, 353–54; contributions, 324

Weyerhaeuser Fellowship in Forest Management, 310

Weyerhaeuser News (journal), 244

Weyerhaeuser Sales Company: Eastern Yards, 38, 115, 116, 122, 209, 287, 303; organizational controversies, 38–40, 65, 74, 79, 148–49, 167, 171, 188, 261–62, 303–4, 356, 364; Fred K. responsibilities, 51–52, 53, (elected president) 74, 101, 104, 149, 171, 176, 296, 303, 356; debate over location of headquarters, 62, 79, 88; performance and policies, 70, 71–72, 104, 167, 173, 186, 188–89, 219–20, 296, 302–4; public relations, 156, 343; 4-Square Special (1937), 174–76; mentioned 31, 33, 48, 54, 105, 204, 211, 270, 283, 284, 317, 329

Weyerhaeuser Steamship Company: organizational history, 115; Bill Peabody, 115–16, 122, 200, 215–16, 253, 302–3, 309, 315–16, 317–18; strikes, 122, 175, 178, 338–39; ship purchases, 175, 215–16, 275, 285, 330–31, 364; Captain L. C. Howard (Pacific Coast Direct Line), 178, 182, 200, 205, 315; World War II, 209, 226, 238, 241, 244, 247; sinking of SS *Hefron*, 243; sinking of SS *Potlatch*, 244; sinking of SS *William S. Ladd*, 269; renegotiation hearing (Red Sea charters), 248, 250, 253; management reorganization, 315–16, 317; Don Watson, 315, 317, 339, 362; mentioned, 181, 185, 250

Weyerhaeuser Timber Company. *See specific branch or subject*

Weyerhaeuser Timber Foundation, 292, 299–302 passim, 307–8, 335–36, 338, 372

White River branch (Weyerhaeuser Timber Company), 354, 369, 380

White River Lumber Company, 112, 118, 119, 153, 155, 185, 189, 191, 193, 210, 212, 231, 306, 308

White River Tree Farm, 369

Wildhaber, Nappy, 282

Wilhelmi, Fritz, 54

Willapa Harbor Lumber Mills, 112, 138, 140, 153, 155, 160, 165, 182–83, 189, 191, 196, 204–5, 207, 231, 260, 275, 306–9 passim

Williams College, 115

William S. Ladd (steamship), 269

Willkie, Wendell, 218

Wilson, Charles, 349

Wilson River Lumber Company, 110

Winona (steamship), 175, 181, 238, 247, 271

Winthrop Hotel (Tacoma), 175, 378

Winton, David, 43, 53, 54, 137, 159, 196, 203, 206, 207, 288, 327, 374

Winton, Kay, 43, 137, 203, 288, 327

Winton interests, 42, 151
Winton Lumber Company (Minneapolis), 43
W. L. McCormick (steamship), 330, 331
Wolf, Robert B., 93, 165, 175, 176, 179, 190, 214, 285, 352
Wood Conversion Company (Cloquet, Minn.), 32, 38, 91, 166, 224, 233–37 passim, 275, 315, 316, 323, 325–26, 329, 343, 347–49
Wood Goes to War, 250
World War I, 18, 19, 20, 21–26 passim, 209
World War II, 207, 209–10, 215, 217–19, 237–77 passim, 324

Wright Junior College (Chicago), 269

Yacolt Burn, 337
Yale School of Forestry, 324, 333, 338, 345, 359, 364
Yale University, 14, 17–29 passim, 137, 215, 216, 250, 260, 285, 292, 304, 309, 324, 333, 338
Yards Securities Company, 155, 175, 179
Yield of Douglas Fir in the Pacific Northwest (Forest Service Technical Bulletin No. 201), 227
Young, Charles E., 335, 338, 346, 350